Changing Subjects, Moving Objects

Balkan Studies Library

VOLUME 31

Changing Subjects, Moving Objects

Status, Mobility, and Social Transformation in Southeastern Europe, 1700–1850

by

Constanţa Vintilă

BRILL
SCHÖNINGH

The open access of this volume is possible thanks to funding from the European Research Council for the project *Luxury, Fashion and Social Status in Early Modern South-Eastern Europe*, ERC-2014-CoG no. 646489, hosted by New Europe College, Bucharest.

DOI: https://doi.org/10.30965/9783657704873

Bibliographic information published by the Deutsche Nationalbibliothek

The Deutsche Nationalbibliothek lists this publication in the Deutsche Nationalbibliografie; detailed bibliographic data available online: http://dnb.d-nb.de

www.schoeningh.de

Cover image: Miklós Barabás (1810–1898) – View of Bucharest (detail: a great boyar and a Russian officer), 1832, Private Collection. Cited with the permission.
Cover design: Celine van Hoek, Leiden
Production: Brill Deutschland GmbH, Paderborn

ISSN 1877-6272
ISBN 978-3-506-70487-0 (hardback)
ISBN 978-3-657-70487-3 (e-book)

To Ilinca

Contents

PART II
Loyalty and Subjecthood in the Eighteenth Century

PART III
Seeking a Home: People and Destinies in Southeastern Europe

List of Illustrations

List of Maps

Acknowledgements

This is a book about foreigners and the intelligence by means of which they survived on the roads of empires. In following them, I too have, in a way, been on the road, moving among the European archives and libraries where their traces are gathered. Such a venture would not have been possible without the financial support of a research grant obtained in 2015. The book thus appears under the auspices of the European Research Council Grant *Luxury, Fashion and Social Status in Early Modern South-Eastern Europe* (*LuxFaSS*), ERC-2014-CoG no. 646489, hosted by New Europe College, Bucharest, which provided me with the opportunity to carry out research in various archives and libraries. I would like to thank the staff of the Archives Nationales, Paris; the Archives des Affaires Etrangères, Paris; the Bibliothèque Nationale de France, Paris; the Österreichisches Staatsarchiv, Vienna; the Benaki Museum, Athens; the Gennadius Library, Athens; the Kunstbibliothek of the Staatliche Museen zu Berlin; and the Romanian National Archives in Bucharest and Iaşi. At the same time, in 2015–2016, I enjoyed a scholarship at the Wissenschaftkolleg zu Berlin, and it was there that I began to sketch out many of the trajectories in this book. I am grateful to all my colleagues in the 2015–2016 cohort there for an unparalleled intellectual and human experience.

Over the years, I have benefitted from the ideas and the valuable feedback, both criticisms and suggestions, of many friends, colleagues, and teachers. I take this opportunity to express my gratitude to them for their patience, friendship, and tact. I am enormously indebted to Andrei Pippidi, teacher, friend, and mentor. As on every occasion, he has accompanied me in the adventure of my research, reading, criticizing, and offering suggestions, always a valuable partner in discussion with whom I could validate my ideas. My colleagues and collaborators in the ERC project have made up the best possible research team. Michał Wasiucionek, colleague, collaborator, and friend, has been an enthusiastic reader of this book, guiding me in my investigations, correcting Ottoman spelling, completing the names of unknown diplomats, and gently drawing my attention to interpretations of mine that he could not fully agree with. My dear friend and colleague Mària Pakucs provided the moral and intellectual support without which I could not have succeeded in a somewhat difficult period. Giulia Calvi, through her elegance, intelligence, and friendship, was a pillar of inspiration for the whole team. Nicoleta Roman provided unfailing assistance with all the necessary administrative procedures every time my attempts to gain access to a document or an image came up against bureaucratic impediments. Silvia Marton was always by my side, encouraging me with warmth and sensitivity, and proving an admirable partner in theoretical and conceptual debates.

My warm thanks to my colleagues and friends Lidia Cotovanu, Marian Coman, Ovidiu Cristea and Simeon Câlția, who offered to help me when I needed guidance, transliteration of certain documents, suggestions, information, or feedback. Ina Chirilă, Petronel Zahariuc, Mihai Mîrza, and Sorin Grigoruța willingly helped me by checking my uncertain readings of documents, photographing or seeking in the archives in Iaşi the documents that I needed, and without which I sometimes thought my story could go no further. Barbara Stollberg-Rilinger, Daniel Schönpflug, and Peter Mackridge read parts of the book or offered me advice and information.

I am grateful also to James Christian Brown, without whom I could not have made this book. Our collaboration has gone beyond mere translation, as he has been an attentive and interested reader, always proposing the appropriate words to make clear the meaning of my text, and drawing my attention at times to errors made in haste.

New Europe College has not only been the host institution of the European project, but also my own academic home for a time. Marina Hasnaş, Anca Oroveanu, Alina Hera, Lelia Ciobotariu, and Valentina Sandu-Dediu have been there at my side, with friendship and dedication, both the European project progressed, in excellent conditions, and in the finalization of the manuscript.

The advice and suggestions of the two anonymous readers at Brill who read the book with enthusiasm and attention to detail has helped me enormously in restructuring and improving it. I am grateful also to the series editor, Alex Drace-Francis, with whom I have had countless meetings and discussions regarding the manuscript. His insightful comments and suggestions greatly helped me during the editing processes. I take this opportunity also to express my appreciation of his constant support, offered with generosity and patience, throughout the duration of the European project.

I would also like to thank Diethard Sawicki, who first accepted my book proposal and offered me a contract, and who has been efficient and prompt in handling all matters concerning the book.

I dedicate the book to my daughter, Ilinca, a great lover of stories that carry meaning, who, with humour and sarcasm, teaches me every day not to be 'a boring mum'.

Introduction

During the Russian–Turkish War of 1768–1774, many Wallachian boyars, greater and lesser, chose to leave their homeland (*patrie*), their belongings, and their estates in order to save their lives. Leaving ephemeral goods behind, the boyars took with them their families and close relatives and such objects that could be fitted into trunks, chests, and carriages. Their destination was Braşov (Kronstadt), over the mountains in Habsburg Transylvania. For these boyars, Ottoman subjects, Braşov was a convenient place of refuge, given its spatial proximity, but the 'German city' offered a totally different experience from the Ottoman-Balkan world in which they normally led their lives. Among the refugees were members of the great families of Wallachia: Brâncoveanu, Văcărescu, Bălăceanu, etc.—in fact, the entire political elite of the principality. Exile in Brașov marked many of them with the imprint of a 'different' way of life, but it also left the bitter taste of foreignness, of otherness, of the insecurity resulting from unstable times. Here in Braşov, Maria Bălăceanu, a member of an important boyar family, decided to adopt a 'German' child, who was 'poor' but of 'known' and properly wedded parents. We do not know what name this 'German' child had gone by in Braşov, but to be integrated into the Bălăceanu clan in Wallachia he needed a new identity. Maria, his adoptive mother, proceeded to remake this new member so that he could be accepted into the lineage. In a letter of 10 April 1797, she writes:

> [A]nd when we were coming again to our homeland [*patria noastră*], here in this country, I brought him with me too. And raising him as an adoptive son, I had him christened in our Orthodox faith, in the days of His Holiness the late Metropolitan Grigorie, and after his christening, having made him my adoptive son, I also gave him in marriage, and have myself baptized [i.e. been godmother to] his five children up until now.

To cross political and social borders, the 'German' child put on the garb of the Orthodox Petre, his baptismal name. Three decades later, when Maria Bălăceanu recalled her Brașov experience, Petre Bălăceanu was a grown man with a wife and children, a house and outbuildings in the heart of Bucharest. And yet he still carried with him the memory of 'his homeland' (*patria sa*) and 'his kindred' (*neamul său*). For their part, the Bălăceanu kin did not yet consider him one of their own, despite all the efforts of his adoptive mother, who had tried to 'bribe' them, by way of her testament, with various gifts of money or portions of her estate.[1]

For more than a century, the Principalities of Wallachia and Moldavia were integrated into the Ottoman Empire through the intermediary of the so-called 'Phanariot regime'. Lying at the margins of three empires (Ottoman, Russian, and Habsburg), the Principalities often became the theatre of military operations, diplomatic negotiations, and topographic incursions with a view to possible annexation.[2] Traversed back and forth by diplomats, merchants, scholars, artisans, soldiers, and missionaries, these lands were the crossroads of diplomatic, commercial, and cultural knowledge and information. The Phanariot period, essential for an understanding of later developments in southeastern Europe, was long marginalized in the historiography of the region, and catalogued as a 'dark age'.[3] However, a closer examination of the eighteenth century and the first part of the nineteenth century can help us to understand the role of the Phanariots in the spread of Enlightenment ideas, in the education and reforming of local elites, and in the forging of the modern states of the following century. They reshaped the meaning of the word '*patrie*' used by Maria Bălăceanu, which changed from a homeland to a national identity.[4]

For a long time it was supposed that the political elites of the period were immobile, conservative, and reticent towards the Enlightenment. I propose to demonstrate that these elites in fact constituted part of a broader picture, having connections both in the Ottoman world and in the worlds of Vienna, Venice or Saint Petersburg. For example, there were other boyars and dignitaries in exile in Brașov, whom we shall meet in the pages of this book, whose experiences are very useful for an understanding of the way in which people circulated through the empires, changing their identity and allegiance, adapting

1 BAR, Fond Manuscrise, MS 611, ff. 17v–21r. I shall return to this very interesting episode in Part IV chapter 1.

2 Vlad Georgescu, *Istoria ideilor politice românești* (Munich: 1987).

3 See Ștefan Lemny, 'La critique du régime phanariote: clichés mentaux et perspectives historiographiques', in Alexandru Zub (ed.), *Culture and Society: Structures, Interferences, Analogies in the Modern Romanian History* (Iași: 1985), 17–30; Nicolae Bănescu, 'Entre Roumains et Grecs: Ce Que Nous Apprend le Passé', *Νέα Πολιτικά*, 2, 9 (1937), 1049–55; Anca Dobre, 'Points de vue de l'histoire nationale grecque et roumaine sur la question des Phanariotes', in Paschalis Kitromilides and Anna Tabaki (eds.), *Relations gréco-romaines. Interculturalité et identité nationale* (Athenes: 2004, 189–94); Christina Ion, 'The Present Creates the Past: The "Phanariots" in the Romanian Text Books during the Second Half of the 19th Century', *Revue d'Etudes sud-est européennes*, 33, 1–2 (1995), 41–7; Edhem Eldem, 'Greece and the Greeks in Ottoman History and Turkish Historiography', *Historical Review*, 6 (2009), 27–40.

4 Konstantina Zanou, *Transnational Patriotism in the Mediterranean, 1800–1850: Stammering the Nation* (Oxford: 2018), 2.

to different places, and trying to finding a secure home, even if only a temporary one.

Maria Bălăceanu travelled between Vienna and Bucharest for more than half a century (1740–1797), in search of belonging and social recognition, struggling to recover her family wealth, which had been confiscated, first by Constantin Brâncoveanu (1688–1714), and thereafter by various Phanariot rulers, and facing the contempt and hostility of princes and officials because of her family's pro-Austrian orientation. Boyaress, countess, lady-in-waiting to Empress Maria Theresa, Maria Bălăceanu felt acutely the lack of a homeland and the ambiguity of a sense of belonging that bound her neither to one environment nor to the other.

In this book I shall explore how people in the past tried to find a home in which to develop their potential, to feel in safety, to have a family, a career, to be accepted by others. How permeable were social and political borders? How did they define and interpret such concepts as 'home' and 'abroad'? Are they stable concepts or do they incorporate a significant doze of vagueness and malleability? Studying the senses of 'home' and 'away', through the biographies of three nineteenth-century activists, Dominique Reill observes that 'place' is not to be treated as a 'stable category', but 'should be read against the modern geographical grain.'[5] The individuals who feature in this book experience mobility, exile, journeys between empires: if for some, 'abroad' means displacement and precarity, for others, 'away' is another place to live, where they may acquire riches or simply knowledge. People circulate with ease between empires, making use of the fluidity of geographical, confessional, and linguistic frontiers, highlighting the slipperiness and the suppleness of these concepts in the days before nation state-building.

In the course of a century and a half, the dynamics of geopolitics evolved, and with them, the people and ideas that modelled the region changed. This book seeks to interrogate the manner in which mobility and social, political, and cultural transformations determined people to position themselves, to conceive where they belonged and how they would be seen, to map their loyalties and to construct social, political, and cultural bridges for living and surviving together. What sort of belonging did these people construct for themselves? Where did their loyalties lie? What was the status of Ottoman subjects in the Principalities? Where did the boundaries of loyalty and subjecthood begin and end?

---

5 Dominique Kirchner Reill, 'Away or Homeward Bound? The Slippery Case of Mediterranean Place in the Era before Nation-States', in Maurizio Isabella and Konstantina Zanou (eds.), *Mediterranean Diasporas: Politics and Ideas in the Long 19th Century* (London: 2015), 136.

I shall try to address these questions by way of a series of microhistories whose characters illustrate experiences, multiple possibilities, and opportunities arising in the course of a lifetime. In my explorations, I have made use of the *name* as a guiding thread—as defined by Carlo Ginzburg and Carlo Poni in their analysis of microhistory—, reconstructing the web of social relations in which each individual was caught.[6] Microhistory has, however, undergone a re-reappraisal in recent decades as an important tool of global history, generating a series of valuable studies.[7] Starting from the information offered by the primary sources about an individual, an object, or a place, historians have proceeded to reconstruct cross-border connections and cultural and confessional processes, connecting regions, people, and contexts.[8]

Among all the microhistories in this book, four figures for the spectacular quality of their individual trajectories, eluding borders and mixing multiple strategies of integration in different contexts: François-Thomas Linchou, Ianache Văcărescu, Dimitrie Foti Merişescu, and Elena Hartulari. They will be, in fact, the pretext for an analysis of the various facets of being an office-holder (and the wife of an office-holder) in the Ottoman Empire, caught in the Phanariot network. All four were part of a world that was constantly reinventing itself politically, socially, and materially, establishing their social status and identity according to their belonging to spaces, to empires. Studying the lives, networks, and trajectories of these individuals helps us to understand the existence of a cultural and geopolitical space that extended beyond borders, offering people a variety of options and political loyalties.[9] Moreover, these figures generated a rich documentation, providing us with the necessary sources for such an exploration. Linchou left a vast diplomatic correspondence; Văcărescu

6 Carlo Ginzburg, Carlo Poni, 'La micro-histoire', *Le Débat*, 10, 17 (1981), 135.

7 Francesca Trivellato, 'Is There a Future for Italian Microhistory in the Age of Global History?', California Italian Studies, II, 1 (2011), https://escholarship.org/uc/item/0z94n9hq [accessed 11.08.2021]; Francesca Trivellato, 'Microstoria/Microhistoire/Microhistory', *French Politics, Culture&Society*, 33, 1 (2015), 122–134; John-Paul A. Ghobrial, 'The Secret Life of Elias of Babylon and the Use of Global Microhistory', *Past and Present*, 222 (2014), 51–93; Maxine Berg, 'Sea Otters and Iron: A Global Microhistory of Value and Exchange at Nootka Sound, 1774–1792', *Past and Present*, 242 (2019), 50–82; Guillaume Calafat, 'Jurisdictional Pluralism in a Litigios Sea (1590–1630): Hard Cases, Multi-Sited Trials and Legal Enforcement between North Africa and Italy', *Past and Present*, 242 (2019), 142–178; John-Paul A. Ghobrial, 'Moving Stories and What They Tell Us: Early Modern Mobility Between Microhistory and Global History', *Past and Present*, 242 (2019), 243–280.

8 John-Paul A. Ghobrial, 'Introduction: Seeing the World like a Microhistorian', *Past and Present*, 242 (2019), 15–16.

9 See also the trans-imperial figures analysed by Zanou, *Stammering the Nation*. Or Călin Cotoi, *Inventing the Social in Romania, 1848–1914. Networks and Laboratories of Knowledge* (Leiden: 2020).

wrote a *History of the Ottoman Empire*, which contains much autobiographical information; Merişescu kept a journal for the years 1814–1818; and Hartulari set down her memoirs for the period 1810–1856. Another common factor that links them concerns their connections to the Phanariot environment in which they were formed and in which they experienced both success and failure: Linchou was secretary to Prince Constantin Racoviță; Văcărescu held important offices under various princes, while also serving as a high Ottoman official in the period 1765–1797; Merişescu occupied minor posts at the Phanariot court; and Iorgu Hartulari was the prototype of the 'new man' who managed, through his wife Elena (née Plitos), to enjoy all the advantages of a network that he owed to his father-in-law and brothers-in-law, all of them holders of administrative posts and high offices in post-Phanariot Moldavia. They also have in common their mobility, the journeys that they made through the empires in the search of some sort of stability, prosperity, and security. Elena Hartulari herself never went further than Czernowitz (Romanian Cernăuţi, today Chernivtsi in Ukraine, at the time the capital of Habsburg Bukovina), though she 'travelled' assiduously through Moldavia in search of a home. Her husband Iorgu, however, went as far as Istanbul,[10] and his journey is recounted in detail and with much emotional involvement in Elena's journal. And these four figures share something else: their obsession with social recognition. All four repeatedly engage in self-definition, expressing their ideas about who they are, what sort of people they are, what place they occupy in their society, and how they should be received by others.

In the middle ground, the various secondary figures and their trajectories back and forward across borders amount to a panoply of microhistories. Thus the book tracks various destinies that contribute to our knowledge of southeastern Europe over the course of a century. Even if its apparent focus is on Moldavia and Wallachia, where the protagonists tried to find a home for themselves, it transgresses the borders of the Principalities as it follows their individual trajectories across empires, passing through Bucharest, Iași, Sibiu, Braşov, Giurgiu (Yergöğü), Ruse (Rusçuk), Arbanaşi, Nikopol, Edirne, Czernowitz, Vienna, Venice, Trieste, Istanbul, Saint Petersburg, and Paris. Most of my characters speak and write more than two languages: Romanian, Greek, Turkish, Hungarian, Bulgarian, Serbian, French, German, Polish, Yiddish, or Italian. Their multilingualism is reflected in their writings and also in their constant adaptation to the linguistic spaces in which they live and pursue their activity

10 In the sources, the Ottoman city is variously named 'Constantinople', 'Istanbul', or 'Tsarigrad'. I have used 'Constantinople' or 'Tsarigrad' only when citing or referring to these sources.

for a time. Moreover, their linguistic dynamism can be seen in their constant refashioning of their names according to space, time, and interlocutor. The book is full of characters with such names as Dimitri (Dimitrie, Dimitrios, Dumitrache, Tache, Matache), Iane, (Ianis, Ianache, Ienache, Ienăchiţă), Elena (Eleni, Elencu, Elenicu, Ilina, Ilincu, Ilinca), or Manolache (Manolaki, Manuil, Emanoil, Emanuil), often Hellenized under the pressure of the times. Their identification and their introduction into the narrative of the book raise problems that have been observed by Dominique Reill for the Adriatic region.[11] The names of the Phanariots, for example, are rendered in various spellings according to the sources in which they appear, the languages used, and the education of the author: Ipsilanti/Ypsilanti/Hypsilanti; Suţu/Soutzo/Souzzo/Soutso; Caragea/Caradge/Karaca. Collective affiliations sometimes give rise to confusion. For example, the Serbs and Bulgarians of Rumelia are often brought together under the same label, given that both spoke Slavic languages. It is thus quite difficult to tell whether Iana from Rumelia is a Bulgarian or a Serbian or whether Iorgu (Iorgache, Iordache, Gheorgache) of Pindus is Greek or Vlach in the absence of factual criteria. Many of the 'Epirot Greeks' speak Greek or Turkish, but some also speak Romanian. Where possible, I have tried to use the identifying information offered by the actors themselves in the historical sources. In the case of names of places and institutions, I have chosen to use the forms by which they are referred to in the sources, providing where necessary an explanation or a contemporary localization.

The approach adopted in this book has not previously been considered in southeastern Europe historiography.[12] Since the fall of the Berlin Wall, research in social and political history has flourished. However, themes remain fragmentary and are rarely integrated in and circumscribed by the regional context. National borders have often proved impassable barriers, and figures that are important for an understanding of the social and patronage networks woven between empires have been treated only in terms of their 'national' role.[13] It is this danger that Suraiya Faroqhi draws attention to when she points out that Romanian scholars have studied the work of Dimitrie Cantemir 'as a part of

---

11 Dominique Kirchner Reill, *Nationalists Who Feared the Nation: Adriatic Multi-Nationalism in Habsburg Dalmatia, Trieste, and Venice* (Stanford, CA: 2012), xv.

12 On mobility and migration see Stefan Rohdewald, Stephan Conermann, Albrecht Fuess (eds.), *Transottomanica – Osteuropäisch-osmanisch-persische Mobilitätsdynamiken. Perspektiven und Forschungsstand* (Göttingen: 2019).

13 Diana Mishkova, *Beyond Balkanism: The Scholarly Politics of Region Making* (London: 2018).

their national cultural inheritance,'[14] while neglecting, sometimes quite deliberately, the context in which he lived and pursued his career. For this reason, she emphasizes that: 'research which is limited by national borders has been unhelpful to our understanding of many non-Muslim Ottomans with intellectual interests.'[15] In the meantime, Dimitrie Cantemir has been re-evaluated in a new study that follows 'his European adventure' step by step,[16] but he still awaits the researcher who will examine him from the perspective of a global history. The same cannot be said of Văcărescu, another intellectual, not of the stature of Dimitrie Cantemir but nevertheless of some importance for Ottoman and southeast European historiography. Romanian historiography has dedicated studies, monographs, and articles to Văcărescu, and critical editions of his works have been published. Yet for all that, the author of *Istoria prea puternicilor împăraţi otomani* (The history of the most puissant Ottoman emperors) remains an 'illustrious' unknown to international research. As in the case of Dimitrie Cantemir, Romanian historians have not strayed beyond national borders, barely (if at all) following his tracks in his Ottoman adventure.

Recent studies have shown the importance of patronage networks for an understanding of the political history of the Ottoman Empire and southeastern Europe.[17] For example, Michał Wasiucionek has shown how 'Moldavian-Wallachian boyars, Ottoman grandees and Polish-Lithuanian magnates increasingly accumulated power and privatized state resources, becoming the effective masters of their political environment.'[18] Meanwhile, David Do Paço and Florian Kühnel have introduced women and the part they played in the construction and promotion of diplomatic networks, in studies that can help us to understand the active role of women's political networks and

---

14 Suraiya Faroqhi, *Subjects of the Sultan. Culture and Daily Life in the Ottoman Empire* (London–NewYork: 2011), 85.

15 Faroqhi, *Subjects of the Sultan*, 85.

16 Ştefan Lemny, *Cantemireştii. Aventura europeană a unei familii princiare din secolul al XVIII-lea* (Iaşi: 2013).

17 Carter V. Findley, 'Political culture and the great households' in Suraiya Faroqhi (ed.), *The Cambridge History of Turkey*, vol. 3 (Cambridge, 2006), 65–80; Jane Hathaway, *The Political of Households in Ottoman Egypt: The Rise of the Qazdağlis* (Cambridge: 1997); Sanjay Subrahmanyam, *Three Ways to Be Alien: Travails and Encounters in the Early Modern World* (Waltham: 2011); Marie-Carmen Smyrnelis, *Une société hors de soi: Identités et relations sociales à Smyrne aux XVIII*ᵉ *et XIX*ᵉ *siècles* (Paris: 2006); Molly Greene, *A Shared World: Christian and Muslims in the Early Modern Mediterranean* (Princeton, NJ: 2000); Radu Păun, *Pouvoirs, offices et patronage dans la Principauté de Moldavie au XVII*ᵉ *siècle: l'aristocratie roumaine et la pénétration gréco-levantine*, PhD diss., EHESS (Paris: 2003).

18 Michał Wasiucionek, *The Ottomans and Eastern Europe. Borders and Political Patronage in the Early Modern World* (London–New York: 2019), 9.

trans-imperial circulation.[19] Biography has been put to new uses in innovative studies by Konstantina Zanou, Dominique Reill, and Francesca Trivelatto, connecting "humble lives" to the broader picture of global history.[20] To reconstitute the trajectories of the actors and their travels through the empires, I have resorted to the outlining of multiple microbiographies, gathering together the threads scattered in various places in different empires, following the trails of the actors in the attempt to assemble as many pieces of a puzzle as possible.

Home or Away: Foreigners and Their Paths Into the Sources

Foreigners, subjects, and protégés are conceptual categories with the help of which I shall attempt to trace the process by which the people of the past defined themselves. Belonging to one category or another determined the place someone occupied in society, their social status, and the manner in which they were seen and judged by others. Such administrative instruments as censuses, fiscal records, and parish registers were relatively late to appear in southeastern Europe. In the case of Moldavia and Wallachia, for example, parish registers were introduced only with the adoption of the Organic Regulations, the organic laws drawn up during the Russian occupation of 1828–1834. Fiscal records were certainly kept, as they were the basis for imposing taxes, but they are preserved only in relatively small numbers and for the later part of the period.[21] They appeared when the princes felt a pressing need for resources to cover the tribute owed to the Ottoman Empire and the financing of the administrative apparatus. At these moments, the political authorities engaged both

---

19 David Do Paço, 'Women in Diplomacy in Late Eighteenth-Century Istanbul', *The Historical Journal* (2021), 1–23; Florian Kühnel, '"Minister-like cleverness, understanding and influence in affairs": ambassadresses in everyday business and courtly ceremonies at the turn of the eighteenth century', in Tracey A. Sowerby and Jan Hennings (eds.), *Practices of Diplomacy in the Early Modern World, c. 1410–1800*) (London and New York: 2018), 130–146.

20 Zanou, *Transnational Patriotism*; Reill, *Nationalists Who Feared the Nation*; Francesca Trivellato, *The Familiarity of Strangers: the Sephardic Diaspora, Livorno, and Cross-Culture Trade in the Early Modern Period* (New Haven, CT: 2009).

21 For fiscal conscriptions in the Ottoman Empire, see Bruce Masters, *Christians in a changing world*, in Suraiya N. Faroqhi (ed.), *The Cambridge History of Turkey*, vol. 3. *The Later Ottoman Empire, 1603–1839* (Cambridge: 2006), 272–279; Andreas Tietze, 'The Balkans and Ottoman Sources – Ottoman Sources and the Balkans', in Henrik Birnbaum, Speros Vryonis jr. (eds.), *Aspects of the Balkans. Continuity and Change* (The Hague–Paris: 1972), 285–297. For the documents kept by courts of justice, see Cahit Baltacı, 'The Importance of the Kadı Register for the Islamic World', *Studies on Turkish Arab Relations*, 2, 1987, 165–170; Yvonne J. Seng, 'The Şer'iye Sicilleri of the Istanbul Müftülüğü as a Source for the Study of Everyday Life', *Turkish Studies Association Bulletin*, 15/2 (1991), 305–325.

in the reform of the fiscal system and in taking as accurate as possible a census of the population in order to know the value of the resources on which they could rely.[22] In view of this, I shall focus my attention on the sources that are preserved in considerable numbers, in order to get a picture of the social, confessional, and cultural make-up of the region. Beyond the process by which each person constructed their identity as an individual, what interests me is the routes they followed in order to rise above their social condition. In this connection, narrative sources complement the fiscal records. They are not as numerous as we might wish, but those that have been preserved prove essential in reconstructing the process of identity-construction. Family archives, testaments, dowry lists, post-mortem inventories (*catagrafii*), and other property inventories have survived in considerable numbers and have been relatively little used in recent research.

The judicial archives offer valuable clues as to the presence of foreigners in a community and the way in which they were received. When they came before the judicial authorities, they provided identification details: name, parents' names, place of origin, occupation, marital status, permanent or temporary residence, and sometimes the reason for their presence in the Principalities. Most of the foreigners recorded in the judicial sources were of Orthodox faith. Others—Armenians, Jews, and Catholics, for example—tended to resort to their own communities to resolve problems.[23] However, this did not prevent them from appealing to the prince, invoking their status as subjects if they had permanent residence, or referring to their right to be protected if they were merely in transit. The process of identification had a significant oral component for that segment of the poor population who passed from one region to another without having in their possession what is generally known today as an identity card.[24] Among the Moldavians and Wallachians, a whole

22 Mention should be made here of the attempt at a fiscal census under Prince Ioan Caragea (1812–1818), at a time when the Russian–Ottoman war (1806–1812) followed by plague (1812–1814) contributed to a considerable reduction in the number of taxpayers.

23 As Alexandr Osipian has shown, Armenians who settled in Moldavian urban centres received the right to form 'autonomous communities', with their own laws and law-courts. See Alexandr Osipian, *Trans-Cultural Trade in the Black Sea Region, 1250–1700: Integration of the Armenian Trading Diaspora in the Moldavian Principality*, in *New Europe College. Black Sea Link Program Yearbook 2012–2013* (Bucharest: 2013), 120; See also Judit Pál, 'Armenian Society in 18th Century Transylvania', in Gyöngy Kovács Kiss (ed.), *Studies in the History of Early Modern Transylvania* (Highland Lakes, NJ: 2011), 151–178.

24 John Torpey, *The Invention of the Passport. Surveillance, Citizenship, and the State* (Cambridge: 2000); Valentin Groebner, *Who Are You? Identification, Deception, and Surveillance in Early Modern Europe* (New York: 2007); Martin Lloyd, *The Passport: The history of Man's Most Travelled Document* (Canterbury: 2008).

panoply of foreigners thus wound their way, variously defining themselves as Greeks, Serbs, Levantines, Turks, Jews, Armenians, Germans, French, Italians, Muscovites, or Prussians.

Who Were the Foreigners?

Who were the foreigners who moved around the empires in the eighteenth and early nineteenth centuries? How were they characterized and classified in the social hierarchy? How were they received and how did they manage to put down roots? The definition of the term 'foreigner' (*străin* in Romanian) is somewhat difficult to contextualise. Simona Cerutti, Roberto Zaugg or Peter Sahlins offer valuble insights into the subject, helping us to sketch an analytical framework.[25]

The first essential criterion in the definition of the 'foreigner' concerns geographical belonging to a given territory.[26] Might this be sufficient to define the status of a person? The historical sources speak of 'natives' (*pământeni* from the word *pământ*, meaning 'land') and 'foreigners', those 'from here' and those come 'from other lands'. But the documents operate with great ambiguity when they speak of the others, the foreigners, who may originate from beyond the imaginary frontiers of various sorts of community, whether delimited in confessional, linguistic, social or geographical terms. Thus, at a certain moment someone may be considered foreign in relation to someone else. But in relation to whom can a foreigner be defined? Such identities were very fluid and malleable categories in the days before national state-building. In defining the condition of the foreigner, Simona Cerutti includes four variables: succession, mobility, work, and justice; variables that establish belonging and connect the foreigner to local resources.[27] 'A deficit of belonging' is attributed to those who 'come from elsewhere'.[28] To make good this 'deficit of belonging', the foreigner must enrol himself in a line of succession and 'tame' his mobility

25 Simona Cerutti, *Étrangers. Étude d'une condition d'incertitude dans une société d'Ancien Régime* (Paris: 2012); Roberto Zaugg, *Stranieri di antico regime. Mercanti, giudici e consoli nella Napoli del Settecento* (Rome: 2011); Peter Sahlins, *Unnaturally French: Foreign Citizens in the Old Regime and After* (Ithaca, NY: 2004).

26 See Edhem Eldem, 'Foreigners on the Threshold of Felicity: The Reception of Foreigners in Ottoman Istanbul', in Donatella Calabi and Stephan Christensen (eds.), *Cultural Exchange in Early Modern Europe, II. Cities and Cultural Exchange in Europe, 1400–1700* (Cambridge: 2007), 114–131; Rossitsa Gradeva, 'Turks and Bulgarians, Fourteenth to Eighteenth Centuries', *Journal of Mediterranean Studies*, 5, 2 (1995): 173–187.

27 Cerutti, *Étrangers*, 18.

28 Cerutti, *Étrangers*, 18.

by way of integration in the rules of the local community and by practising a trade that ensures access to local rights and justice. Hanna Sonkajärvi similarly emphasizes the importance of local institutions and practices in her attempt to establish 'what a foreigner was' in ancient-régime Strasbourg[29]; while Peter Sahlins links the status of foreigner to citizenship and 'le droit d'aubaine', thus underlining the importance of a normative discourse and of a political authority in the construction of foreignness.[30] Local belonging seems to be the most 'operative' category for the inclusion of the foreigner in the social fabric. My research is thus directed at the paths towards integration and social recognition. 'Le droit d'aubaine' cannot be a criterion as it did not exist; letters of naturalization were very late to appear in the Principalities; they were unknown until the 1830s, and even then they were very seldom used.

One clarification is essential: I shall steer clear of the nationalist discourse that imposes 'ethnic and national identities' onto certain political or cultural figures, forcing them into the mould of national cultural heritages.[31]

But first let us try to see who the foreigners were and how they managed to acquire the status of 'princely subject'. I shall make use of Dimitrie Cantemir's description, because he goes beyond enumerating peoples who have settled in Moldavia, and provides information about their status in relation to the public authorities.[32] In his *Descriptio Moldaviae*, Cantemir remarks that foreigners are everywhere:

---

29 Hanna Sonkajärvi, *Qu'est-ce qu'un étranger? Frontières et identifications à Strasbourg, 1681–1789* (Strasbourg: 2008).

30 Peter Sahlins, 'Sur la citoyenneté et le droit d'aubaine à l'époque moderne. Réponse à Simona Cerruti', *Annales HSS*, 63. 2 (2008), 385–398. See also Simona Cerutti, 'A qui appartiennent les biens qui n'appartiennet à personnes? Citoyenneté et droit d'aubaine à l'époque moderne', *Annales HSS*, 62, 2 (2007), 355–383.

31 See in this connection the interesting study of the multiple identities attributed to Hristofor Žefarović (1690–1753) under 'the influence of nationalist ideologies' and the sterility of such analyses: Vančo Gjorgjiev, Vojislav Sarakinski, 'The Many Nationalities of Hristofor Žefarović', *Analele Universităţii «Ovidius» Constanţa, Seria Istorie*, 16 (2019), 5–17. On Anton Pann disputed by Romanian and Bulgarian history, see Luminiţa Munteanu, 'Being Homo Balkanicus without Knowing It: The Case of Anton Pann', *Turkey and Romania. A History of Partnership and Collaboration in The Balkans* (Istanbul: 2016), 123–138; See also Wladimir Fischer, 'Creating a National Hero. The Changing Symbolics of Dositej Obradović (1811–1911)', in Susan Ingram, Markus Reisenleitner and Cornelia Szabo-Knotik (eds.), *Cultural Practices and the Formation of Imagined Communities around 1900* (Vienna: 2001), 101–121.

32 The ethnic, religious, and linguistic diversity of the region is a frequently occurring topos in the travel literature of the eighteenth and nineteenth centuries. See Rossitsa Gradeva, 'The Ottoman Balkans – a Zone of Fractures or a Zone of Contacts?' in Almut Bues (ed.), *Zones of Fracture in Modern Europe: the Baltic Countries, the Balkans, and Northern Italy* (Wiesbaden: 2005), 61–75.

> I do not believe there is any other country the size of Moldavia in which one meets so many and such diverse peoples. Apart from Moldavians, whose ancestors came originally from Maramureș, there also live in Moldavia Greeks, Albanians, Serbs, Bulgarians, Poles, Cossacks, Russians, Hungarians, Germans, Armenians, Jews, and those Gypsies with many children.[33]

Further on, he describes the way in which they are received by the political community: 'The Greeks, Albanians, Serbs, and Bulgarians live freely in Moldavia, and a part busy themselves with commerce, [while] a part serve with a princely salary.'[34] These foreigners, of Orthodox faith and originating in the Ottoman Empire, came to practise their occupations in Moldavia for a time. The merchants used the Principalities as a zone of transit towards Sibiu and Brașov, and beyond them to Venice, Vienna, Trieste, and Leipzig. They enjoyed the privileges offered by the prince and paid customs duty on the wholesale goods they brought into the country in transit. Others came in the retinue of the Phanariot princes and swelled the ranks of servants at the court, guarding and defending the princely family, providing domestic service, or enrolling in the city guard. Indeed their presence left its traces in the enrichment of Romanian vocabulary with terms specific to the positions they occupied in the military hierarchy, borrowed from Ottoman Turkish or Greek. A series of figures appear in the records who in the process of identification invoke the activities they have carried out, whether military or domestic.[35] In the judicial archives, these 'mercenaries' are a permanent source of disorder: their abuses and violent acts are a frequent motive for complaints from communities to the local and central authorities.[36]

Far more numerous were the Armenians. They were categorized as subjects, and paid the prince 'the same tax as the townsfolk and merchants in other cities and market towns of Moldavia.' They were free to practise their faith and to erect 'great churches.'[37] Also included among subjects were the Jews, who

---

33 Dimitrie Cantemir, *Descrierea Moldovei* (Bucharest: 1973), 217.

34 Cantemir, *Descrierea Moldovei*, 217.

35 Fort all these offices, see Dionisie Fotino, *Istoria Generală a Daciei sau a Transilvaniei și a Moldovei* ed. & trans. George Sion (Bucharest: 1859), 308–313. (Originally published as *Historia tes palai Dakias ta nyn Transylvanyas, Wallachias, kai Moldavias ek diaphoron palaion kai neon syngrapheon syneranistheisa para Dionysios Photeinou* (Vienna: 1818–1819),

36 See Constanţa Vintilă-Ghiţulescu, 'Legal Process and the Meanings of Justice (dreptate) in Eighteenth Century Romania', in *Crime, Histoire & Sociétés/ Crime, History & Societies*, 23, 2 (2019), 5–27; Constanța Vintilă-Ghițulescu, 'Marié à un étranger, marié à l'étranger. Mobilité et statut social dans l'Europe du Sud-Est (1780–1830)', in *Bulletin de correspondance hellénique moderne et contemporaine*, 1 (2019).

37 Cantemir, *Descrierea Moldovei*, 218.

paid 'a special tax each year, higher than the usual one.' They also had the right to practise their faith and could erect synagogues of wood, but not of stone.[38] The only group who did not have the right to practise their faith openly or to build places of worship were the Turks. Although, according to Cantemir, they were to be found in great numbers in Iași and in almost all the market towns of Moldavia, they were not allowed to buy houses or estates.[39] Also mentioned are Russians and Hungarians, who were also visible in large numbers due to the proximity of their countries.[40] In the documentary sources, all these foreigners are put into certain practical categories to make them easy to situate in the process of identification. The documents operated with indicators reflecting geographical origin, religious confession, socio-economic condition, language spoken, and sometimes descent, marital status, and occupation. Jews, Armenians, Greeks, Turks, Hungarians, and Bulgarians formed their own communities, settling on the edge of local communities and building places of worship (except in the case of the Turks), schools, and other institutions to represent themselves. In the towns, they settled in particular districts; in the countryside they formed distinct settlements, due to the policy of colonization practised by the Phanariot princes.[41] As Mathieu Grenet observes, collective identities are much easier to trace both in the documentary sources and in the discourse of political power.[42] Consequently, we find Greeks, Armenians, Jews, Turks, Serbs, and Bulgarians gathered in communities according to their confessional, linguistic, or geographical characteristics. However, within these collective communities, which are easy to trace in the urban environment, there lived individuals who deployed their various belongings and allegiances in diverse and much more nuanced ways.

What sort of mobility can we trace in the South-East of Europe? Lidia Cotovanu speaks of a 'little migration' that went on between the two sides of the Danube, and makes up a detailed map of the localities involved and of the individuals who set out in search of another 'homeland'.[43] Olga Katsardi-Hering,

---

38 Cantemir, *Descrierea Moldovei*, 218.

39 Cantemir, *Descrierea Moldovei*, 218.

40 Cantemir, *Descrierea Moldovei*, 218.

41 See also Andrew Robarts, 'Imperial confrontation or regional cooperation? Bulgarian migration and Ottoman–Russian relations in the Black Sea region, 1768–1830s', *Turkish Historical Review*, 3/2 (2012): 149–167; Constantin N. Velichi, *La contribution de l'émigration bulgare de la Valachie à la renaissance politique et culturelle du people bulgare (1762–1850)* (Bucharest: 1970).

42 Mathieu Grenet, *La fabrique communautaire. Les Grecs à Venise, Livourne et Marseille, 1770–1840* (Rome, Athènes: 2016), 294–297.

43 Lidia Cotovanu, 'L'émigration sud-danubienne vers la Valachie et la Moldavie et sa géographie (XVe–XVIIe siècles): La potentialité heuristique d'un sujet peu connu', *Cahiers*

on the other hand, proposes a schema that reflects the mobility of the Greeks along long commercial routes and speaks of 'a peripheral economic community' with reference to the Greeks settled in Moldavia and Wallachia. These 'Greeks' were, in fact, intermediaries between local communities and large-scale commerce, with an active involvement in agriculture, craft trades, and small-scale commerce.[44] Brașov and Sibiu in Transylvania, important commercial centres of the region, provided luxury products for the Moldavian and Wallachian boyar class, but also functioned as hubs for the collection and redistribution of goods from all over the region.[45] However, the Greeks travelled far, building a large diaspora along the Mediterranean and Adriatic coasts.[46] Venice, Livorno, and Marseilles were home to a considerable Greek diaspora, connected by way of cross-cultural trade with other Greek communities settled along the trade routes of the Balkans. With reference to the changing of routes according to the circumstances of international politics, Grenet introduces the notion of 'space in motion', showing how the 'Greeks' reoriented themselves towards Vienna or Trieste, cities that played a significant role in the cultural preparation of the Greek revolution.[47]

The impressive development of commercial networks between the Ottoman Empire and the lands of the Austrian crown, between Istanbul and Vienna, was a result of the policy of tolerance and the privileges granted by Empress Maria Theresa and later by her son Joseph II to 'Greek' merchants. The conquest of the Balkans by these 'Greek' merchants had begun well before the eighteenth century, as is shown in Traian Stoianovich's study on this theme.[48] However, the eighteenth century brought a much greater intensity of economic migration, especially after the 1718 Treaty of Passarowitz, followed by the Habsburg Monarchy's active policy of developing trade with the Balkan regions of the Ottoman Empire.[49] The founding of the Companies of Greek merchants in

---

balkaniques 42 (2014), 2–19; Lidia Cotovanu, *Migrations et mutations identitaires dans l'Europe du Sud-Est (vue de Valachie et de Moldavie, XIVe–XVIIe siècles)*, thèse de doctorat, EHESS, (Paris: 2014).

44 Olga Katsiardi-Hering, 'Central and Peripheral Communities in the Greek Diaspora: Interlocal and Local Economic, Political, and Cultural Networks in the Eighteenth and Nineteenth Centuries', in Minna Rozen (ed.), *Homelands and Diasporas. Greeks, Jews and Their Migrations* (London: 2008), 173–174.

45 Gheorghe Lazăr, *Les marchands en Valachie, XVII*[e]*–XVIII*[e] *siècles* (Bucharest: 2006).

46 Grenet, *La fabrique communautaire.*

47 Grenet, *La fabrique communautaire*, 111.

48 Traian Stoianovich, 'The Conquering Balkan Orthodox Merchant', *Journal of Economic History*, 20 (1960), 234–313.

49 David Do Paço, 'Extranéité et lien social: l'intégration des marchands ottomans à Vienne au XVIIIe siècle', *Revue d'histoire moderne et contemporaine*, 61, 1 (2014), 123–146.

Brașov and Sibiu encouraged the circulation of people and goods from the Ottoman to the Habsburg territories.[50] An analysis of the body of documents preserved in the archives of Sibiu and Brașov brings to light the importance of the Greek language in commercial communication and the role of these merchants in the circulation of (luxury) goods and the mobility of knowledge. The Greek Companies in the two cities wove commercial networks that linked Istanbul, Bucharest, Iași, Sibiu, Brașov, Trieste, Venice, and Vienna. In each of these cities there were members of the network, defending and administering company interests. Foreign merchants circulated across Moldavia, Wallachia and Transylvania, bringing with them goods that they were only allowed to sell wholesale or to carry further on to their places of residence.[51] By the agreement of the neighbouring states, they paid a single customs duty and, as individuals or as a group, they enjoyed privileges granted by the princes.[52]

I have insisted here on the merchants because they are the most visible category in the documentary sources. They were the bearers not only of a material culture that they succeeded in propagating through their merchandise, but also of a certain type of knowledge that they spread along with the books, maps, 'scientific' instruments, albums, and calendars that they sold. Together with the merchants, a series of tradesmen came and established small family businesses: slipper-makers (*condoragii*), shalwar-makers (*şalvaragii*), hatmakers (*işlicari*), coat-makers (*zăbunari*), dealers in fine fabrics (*bogasieri*), beadmakers (*mărgelari*), shoemakers (*cavafi*), coffee-makers (*cafegii*), sherbetmakers (*şerbegii*), tobacconists (*tutungii*), pastry-makers (*simigii*), butchers (*casapi*), *bragă*-sellers (*bragagii*), money-changers (*zarafi*), and others settled

50 On the Greek Companies see: Cornelia Papacostea-Danielopolu, 'L'organisation de la Compagnie grecque de Braşov (1777–1850)', *Balkan Studies*, 14 (1973), 312–323; eadem, 'La Companie grecque de Braşov. La lutte pour la conservation des privilèges (1777–1850)', *Revue des études sud-est européennes*, 12 (1974), 59–78; Mária Pakucs-Willcocks, *Sibiu-Hermannstadt. Oriental Trade in Sixteenth Century Transylvania*, (Köln-Weimar-Vienna: 2007); Mária Pakucs-Willcocks, 'Between "Faithful Subjects" and "Pernicious Nation": Greek Merchants in the Principality of Transylvania in the Seventeenth Century', *Hungarian Historical Review* 6, 1, 2017, 111–137.

51 See the *ferman* of Sultan Abdülhamid I specifying the rules to be respected by non-Muslim Ottoman merchants in Wallachia and Moldavia. They had to present their documents (Tk. *tezkere*: travel permit) to the princes, to buy merchandise (in this case honey and flour), and to bring it to sell in Istanbul. *Documente turceşti privind la istoria României*, vol. II (Bucharest: 1983), vol. II, 4–8, 7/16 September 1775.

52 On the commercial relations between the Ottoman and Habsburg Monarchy, with the involvement of the Danubian Principalities, see Bogdan C. Murgescu, 'Balances of Trade and Payments between the Ottoman Empire and Central Europe (16th–18th centuries)', in Simonetta Cavaciocchi (ed.), *Relazioni economiche tra Europa e mondo islamico secc. XIII–XVIII* (Florence: 2007), 961–980.

in urban centres. The very names of these occupations testify to migration from the area of the Ottoman Empire. The activity of the Princely Academies of Iași and Bucharest encouraged the presence of Orthodox 'students' sent to complete their education.[53] Some of them chose to stay and to integrate themselves in the administrative systems of the Principalities, putting themselves at the service of the princes.[54] These 'expatriates', as Peter Burke calls them,[55] were invited to contribute not only to the spread of knowledge but also to the setting up of educational and cultural initiatives necessary to their country of adoption. Greek was the language of this cultural elite and the principal language of teaching in the Princely Academies, where many of the teachers were Greeks.[56] Michał Wasiucionek has shown very clearly how the Moldavian and Wallachian elite were quick to adopt the Greek language, which enabled them 'to partake in Ottoman imperial culture as an Orthodox "Ottoman-local elite".'[57]

Princely Subjects and Ottoman Subjects

In the eighteenth century, Moldavia and Wallachia were two political communities made up of subjects governed by a prince (*domn* or *voievod*) appointed by the Porte.[58] The payment of tribute to the sultan assured protection for the two countries, and implicitly for their subjects.[59] As Viorel Panaite has observed, the two tributary provinces had autonomy, but this was an autonomy exercised within the Ottoman Empire.[60] As they 'enjoyed' the protection of the Empire and paid tribute, the people of Moldavia and Wallachia are referred to in the

53 Ariadna Camariano-Cioran, *Academiile Domneşti din Bucureşti şi Iaşi* (Bucharest: 1971).

54 Ştefania Costache, 'Loyalty and Polical Legitimacy in the Phanariots' Historical Writing in the Eighteenth Century', *Südost-Forschungen*, 69/70 (2010/2011), 25–50.

55 Peter Burke, *Exiles and Expatriates in the History of Knowledge, 1500–2000* (Waltham: 2017), 82.

56 Paschalis M. Kitromilides, *The Enlightenment as Social Criticism: Iosipos Moisiodax and Greek Culture in the Eighteenth Century* (Princeton: 2014).

57 Michał Wasiucionek, 'Greek as Ottoman? Language, Identity and Mediation of Ottoman Culture in the Early Modern Period', *Cromohs: Cyber Review of Modern Historiography*, 21 (2017–2018), 70–89.

58 Marian Coman, *Putere şi teritoriu. Ţara Românească medievală (sec. XIV–XVI)* (Iaşi: 2016).

59 Viorel Panaite, 'Power Relationship in the Ottoman Empire. Sultans and the Tribute Paying Princes of Wallachia and Moldavia (16th–18th Centuries)', *Revue des Etudes sud-est européennes*, 33, 1–2 (1999–2000), 51.

60 Viorel Panaite, 'Wallachia and Moldavia according to the Ottoman Juridical and Political View, 1774–1829', in Antonis Anastasopoulos and Elias Kolovos (eds.), *Ottoman Rule and The Balkans, 1760–1858. Conflict, Transformation, Adaptation* (Rethymno: 2007), 24.

sources as *Ottoman subjects*, designated with the terms *re'aya* and *zimmi*.[61] As such, they had the same rights as the other non-Muslim Ottoman subjects in the Empire: the right to practice their religion freely, the right to property, and the right to life.[62] In addition, they made use of their status as Ottoman subjects to resolve disputes, applying to the Porte for assistance and thus recognizing it as a supreme authority and forum of appeal in judicial matters. In the seventeenth century, some Moldavian boyars had invoked the right of the prince to judge lawsuits between Moldavian subjects, while cases between a Moldavian and a Muslim were taken before a kadı (an official judge), but in the eighteenth this old custom almost disappeared.[63] As I shall show, non-Muslim Ottoman subjects in the Principalities sometimes approached the sultan directly, asking him to judge their lawsuits. In other cases, displeased at the judgements delivered by the princely divan, they appealed to the local Ottoman authorities, especially the kadı, or even to the imperial divan.[64] Some cases were judged by the imperial divan, while others were sent to the prince with the request that he resolve them, adding that if the parties did not accept his judgement, they should be sent to the local Ottoman officials, namely the kadıs of Giurgiu or Brăila.[65]

Wallachian and Moldavian Christians who travelled in the Ottoman Empire were subject to the general rules regarding foreigners: they could remain for a short period of up to a year and acquired the status of *müste'min*, if they held a temporary residence permit (*aman*).[66] As Juliette Dumas has shown,

---

61 For an analysis of the use of the term *re'aya*, see Aleksander Fotić, 'Tracing the Origin of a New Meaning of the Term Re'āyā in the Eighteenth-Century Ottoman Balkans', *Balcanica*, XLVIII (2017), 55–66.

62 Viorel Panaite, 'The Re'ayas of the Tributary Protected Principalities: The Sixteenth Through the Eighteenth Centuries', in *International Journal of Turkish Studies*, 9, 1, (2003), 85–86.

63 Nándor Erik Kovács, 'The Legal Status of the Danubian Principalities in the 17th Century as Reflected in the Şikayet Defteris', *Güney-Doğu Avrupa Araştırmaları Dergisi*, 1 (2014), 11.

64 Rossitsa Gradeva, 'Orthodox Christians in the Kadı Courts: The Practice of the Sofia Sheriat Court, Seventeenth Century', *Islamic Law and Society*, 4/1 (1997), 37–69; Sophia Laiou, 'Christian Women in an Ottoman World: Interpersonal and Family Cases Brought Before the Shari'a Courts During the Seventeenth and Eighteenth Centuries. (Cases Involving the Greek Community)', in Amila Buturović and Irvin C. Schick (ed.), *Women in the Ottoman Balkans. Gender, Culture and History* (London: 2007), 243–271; Fariba Zarinebaf, *Crime and Punishment in Istanbul 1700–1800* (Berkeley: 2010).

65 Rossitsa Gradeva, 'On Zimmis and their Church Buildings: Four Cases from Rumeli', in Eugenia Kermeli and Oktay Özel (eds.), *The Ottoman Empire: Myths, Realities and 'Black Holes'. Contributions in Honour of Colin Imber* (Istanbul: 2006), 203–237.

66 Regarding foreigners' period of residence in the Ottoman Empire, see Maurits H. van den Boogert, *The Capitulations and the Ottoman Legal System: Qadis, Consuls and Beratlis in the 18th Century* (Leiden: 2005), 30–31.

'a *müste'min* is not a foreigner like others'; the status involved rights, but also obligations.[67] Analysing the lawsuits opened by *müste'min* and judged by the Ottoman courts of justice, Dumas notes the importance of embassies and treaties (capitulations) in regulating the status of foreigners in the Ottoman Empire.[68] Among the rights of the *müste'min*, the most important concerned exemption from the tax known as *cizye*. After this period, foreigners in the Empire could theoretically be assimilated to the category of *zimmi*, and paid *cizye*, in addition to the taxes paid by Muslims. On the other hand, they were exempt from military service, and they had the right to appeal to Muslim courts of justice and the right to practise their own religion freely.[69] The status of foreigners was much more complex, and included, on the one hand, 'a remarkable, and maybe unique, degree of openness and permeability to aliens,' and on the other, 'a policy of degrading hospitality.'[70] Furthermore, starting in the second half of the eighteenth century, the Ottoman Empire underwent a series of social and political transformations that enabled the rise of local elites among its non-Muslim subjects. Recent research has shown that southeast European elites profited from the changes in the Empire, collaborating with the Ottoman elites, with whom, indeed, they had much in common: as Antonis Anastasopoulos puts it, they 'shared certain basic common experience and values.'[71]

As I shall show in this study, the elites of Moldavia and Wallachia also adapted to the institutional and political changes, preferring to interact with the imperial structures in order not to be left outside the political and (most importantly) economic game.

The transition from foreign subject to princely subject involved fiscal, juridical, and social stages. The Phanariots encouraged the settlement of foreign merchants and skilled craftsmen, especially in urban centres, for their contribution to the prosperity of their host country, but made their status conditional on residence and payment of taxes. A decree issued by Prince Alexandru

67 Juliette Dumas, '*Müste'min* Dealing with the Ottoman Justice: Role and Strategy of the Ambassador', *Oriente Moderno*, 93 (2013), 480.

68 Dumas, '*Müste'min* Dealing with the Ottoman Justice', 477–494.

69 Viorel Panaite, 'Being a Western Merchant in the Ottoman Mediterranean', in Deyfi Kenan (ed.), *Isam Papers. Ottoman Thought, Ethics, Law, Philosophy-Kalam* (Istanbul: 2013), 91–136.

70 Edhem Eldem, 'Foreigners on the Threshold of Felicity: The Reception of Foreigners in Ottoman Istanbul' in Donatella Calabi and Stephan Christensen (eds.), *Cultural Exchange in Early Modern Europe, II. Cities and Cultural Exchange in Europe, 1400–1700* (Cambridge: 2007), 119.

71 Antonis Anastasopoulos, 'Introduction', in Antonis Anastasopoulos (ed.), *Provincial Elites in the Ottoman Empire* (Rethymno: 2005), xvi.

Ipsilanti (1774–1782) shows that foreign merchants who wanted to keep shops and sell retail were required 'to settle here, to accept their taxation' (*să se aşeze aici, să-şi ia dajdia*), in other words, to establish permanent residence in Wallachia and to pay their share of taxes.[72] A similar practice can be seen across the Carpathians in the lands of the Habsburg Monarchy. For example, by a decree of 1741, Empress Maria Theresa ruled that Ottoman subjects might receive the right to conduct their business affairs without restrictions of any kind only if they brought their families with them to Hungary. Then in 1769, she conditioned the trading activity of Ottoman subjects on permanent residence and an oath of subjecthood to the empress.[73] To encourage them to settle in the territories of the crown and to contribute to the development of their new 'homeland', she issued the Act of Naturalization in 1774, followed in 1781 by the Edict of Tolerance, which contributed to the settlement and integration in local society of the Balkan Orthodox population.[74] These measures offered the Greeks an opportunity to receive civil rights and to become members of the economic elite.[75]

How did all these foreigners put down roots in the host country? What was involved in passing from the status of foreign subject to that of princely, and implicitly Ottoman, subject? How did all these foreigners influence material culture and consumption in southeastern Europe? In the following chapters, I shall try to analyse the status of subject as it is captured in the archive documents. It is a question that has only tangentially received the attention of researchers.[76] Somewhat more attention has been devoted to the 'Muslims' or 'Ottoman subjects' of Muslim faith who settled or tried to settle in the Principalities.[77]

---

72 V.A. Urechia, *Istoria românilor* (Bucharest: 1891), I, 97–98, 12 July 1776.

73 Olga Katsiardi-Hering and Ikaros Madouvalos, 'The Tolerant Policy of the Habsburg Authorities Towards the Orthodox People from Southeastern Europe and the Formation of National Identities (18th–early 19th Century)', *Balkan Studies*, 49 (2014), 25–26; Suraiya Faroqhi, *Artisans of Empire. Crafts and Craftspeople Under the Ottomans* (London: 2009), 144–145.

74 Katsardi-Hering and Madouvalos, 'The Tolerant Policy of the Habsburg Authorities', 26.

75 Katsardi-Hering and Madouvalos, 'The Tolerant Policy of the Habsburg Authorities', 26.

76 Jean D. Condurachi, *Câteva cuvinte asupra condiţiei juridice a străinilor în Moldova şi Ţara Românească până la Regulamentul Organic* (Bucharest: 1918); Cotovanu, *Migrations et mutations identitaires.*

77 Mustafa A. Mehmet, 'Despre dreptul de proprietate a supuşilor otomani în Moldova şi Ţara Românească în secolele XV-XVIII', *Cercetări istorice*, III (1972), 65–81; Maria Matilda Alexandrescu-Dersca, 'Despre regimul supuşilor otomani în Ţara Românească în veacul al XVIII-lea', *Studii. Revista de istorie*, XIV/1 (1969), 661–672; Maria Matilda Alexandrescu-Dersca Bulgaru, 'Sur le mariage entre les Turcs ottomans et les Roumains (XVe–XIXe siècles)', *Recherches sur l'histoire des institutions et du droit*, 6 (1981), 15–17; Maria Matilda

In what conditions could a foreigner become a local subject, following the stages of social-juridical integration? Firstly, we should not automatically assume that a foreigner operating in the Principalities would want to settle in the host country. They might pursue their activity there while still depending on another sovereign power, might speak another language than Romanian (or Greek), might adhere to a faith other than Orthodoxy, and might still consider themselves to belong to a foreign space. Permanent residence and payment of taxation were the criteria that transformed a foreigner into a subject, binding them to their country of adoption.[78] But as I have mentioned, the process of integration and assimilation into the fabric of the host country depended very much on the process of identification undergone by every foreign candidate for subject status. The diversity in the socio-economic standing of the foreigners, as it emerges from the sources, points to the inequality in their means of access to integration in society. It seems to have been easier for a favourite arriving in the retinue of a prince to work his way into the princely council by way of administrative office, to marry the daughter of a wealthy boyar, and then to be recognized as himself a member of the boyar class. He included in his process of identification the prestige of the prince, who could ease his path towards integration.

A Greek shoemaker, on the other hand, arriving in Bucharest from Salonica, had first to rent a workshop and stall, and to win the trust of neighbours, clients, and residents of the district in order to find himself a wife chosen from among his business associates.[79] Once married, he could buy a stall, in addition to what came in his bride's dowry, enter the shoemaker's guild, win the right to sell retail, and start to build a family, a lineage, a house, a fortune, an inheritance.[80] It should be added that the wealth of the foreign merchant who had become a subject was protected. The prince had no right to confiscate the

---

Alexandrescu-Dersca Bulgaru, 'Sur le régime des ressortissants ottomans en Moldavie (1711–1829)', in Cristina Feneşan (ed.), *Seldjoukides, Ottomans et l'Espace Roumain* (Istanbul: 2006), 439–480.

78 Cotovanu, *Migrations et mutations identitaires*, 428. Lidia Cotovanu emphasizes that it was fiscal domicile that transformed a foreigner into a local subject, and Orthodox faith that gave him access to juridical structures, while the linguistic aspect was less important. Ibid., 440.

79 There was no clear delimitation between master craftsman and trader. For example, the shoemaker (*cavaf*) made shoes, but also sold them.

80 Also in the eighteenth century, there was competition between 'native' merchants (or those already settled with fiscal residence in Moldavia or Wallachia) and foreign merchants regarding respect for the commercial rights. See the document of 1 January 1731, Iaşi, issued by Prince Grigore Ghica, in which he tries to resolve a dispute between the two camps, giving the 'foreign' merchants the right to sell goods retail in exchange for a

goods of a foreigner who died without heirs in the host country.[81] This is made clear in a document issued by Prince Constantin Ipsilanti (1802–1806): 'when it should happen that some Christian merchant dies without true heirs, let no one be free to take and sell his things and his merchandise, but let the *staroste* [master of the guild] with guardians go to put a seal on the goods and whatever there is, and when it is set in a place under seal, make known to the prince all that is left, and let it remain thus until the masters come who are entitled to take those things.'[82]

All the same, the process was not as simple as it might appear. To be recognized as a member of the class of great boyars, a candidate had to be Orthodox (though there were exceptions); to hold considerable wealth; to speak Romanian (or 'Moldavian') and Greek; to acquire boyar etiquette and luxury garments; and to adhere to the daily sociability specific to the rank and position. When they analysed the status of boyar in occupied Oltenia (1718–1739), the Austrians came up against the stubbornness of the boyars, who linked their privileges and their entitlement to posts in the administrative apparatus to the holding of extensive properties and the antiquity of their lineages. When the Austrians asserted that there were no nobles in Wallachia, and wrote that '[boyar] means a person who himself occupies one of the most important offices at court and whose ancestors have been in uninterrupted possession of such court positions,' the boyar counsellors of the Austrian administration proposed a classification, dividing the boyar class into three levels and insisting that those included in the first 'are of superior origin, of lineage that is old and always in the most prominent offices.'[83] The same idea was reiterated in the reforms of Prince Constantin Mavrocordat (1735–1741), who linked boyar status to administrative office, in spite of the opposition of the boyars themselves.[84] In this context, displaying a luxurious lifestyle became a sign of social

monthly payment. Ioan Caproşu (ed.), *Documente privitoare la istoria oraşului Iaşi. Acte interne* (Iaşi: 2001), vol. IV, 81–82.

81 By way of comparison, in the Ottoman Empire, the property of foreigners was protected under the capitulations. If a foreigner died, his property reverted to the heirs named in his testament; in the absence of a testament, it was inventoried and entrusted to the relevant consul or ambassador to be kept until the heirs appeared. Edhem Eldem, *Capitulations and Western Trade. Western Trade in the Ottoman Empire: Questions, Issues and Sources*, in Suraiya Faroqhi (ed.), *The Cambridge History of Turkey*, vol. 3, *The Later Ottoman Empire, 1603–1839* (Cambridge: 2006), 283–335.

82 BAR, MS 242, f. 15–16, 1 June 1803.

83 Şerban Papacostea, *Oltenia sub stăpânirea austriacă (1718–1739)* (Bucharest: 1998), 145–146.

84 Paul Cernovodeanu, 'Mobility and Traditionalism: The Evolution of the Boyar Class in the Romanian Principalities in the 18th Century', *Revue des Etudes Sud-est Européennes*, 24/3 (1986), 249–257.

distinction for a society that had not known noble titles or ranks. The elegance and etiquette introduced by the Phanariots constituted an important reference point, and the ruling elite entered a competition of social representation, investing its fortunes in clothes, banquets, carriages, and jewellery. The display of social status through fashion and manners was part of the process of differentiation and social distinction.[85]

The shoemaker, hat-maker, and petty trader could merge into the mass of the urban population; as a rule, their inclusion in the fiscal register was at their own request as they attempted to put down roots. The political authorities in Moldavia and Wallachia had neither the financial nor the human resources to supervise the mobility of the population. Most of the time, they relied on the role of the local community in exerting social control. Craftsmen and merchants joined guilds according to their occupations, and were under the control of the master of the guild.[86] The master supervised not only the training of journeymen, but also collective fiscal responsibility, by collecting individual contributions.[87] They all tacitly followed a path towards assimilation and aggregation in the local structures, by way of the stages already mentioned above, which applied and can be traced in other European towns too: practising a trade, entering a guild, marrying into an honourable family.[88]

Foreign women appear periodically in the archival sources, but information about their integration and assimilation is scanty. By examining the granting of citizenship rights to women in medieval and modern Italy, Simona Feci has shown that they managed to combine the advantages of their place of origin with those of their new residence, maintaining their material and symbolic

---

85 For the Romanian boyar class and the construction of identity through luxury and fashion, see Constanţa Vintilă-Ghiţulescu, 'Shawls and Sable Furs: How to be a Boyar under the Phanariot Regime (1710–1821)', *European Historical Yearbook*, 20 (2019), 137–158.

86 On the organization of guilds and the importance of religion in their structuring, see Suraiya Faroqhi, 'Understanding Ottoman Guilds', in Suraiya Faroqhi and Randi Deguilhem (eds.), *Crafts and Craftsmen of the Middle East. Fashioning the Individual in the Muslim Mediterranean* (London: 2005), 3–40.

87 On the way in which Greek merchants were integrated in Moldavia in the seventeenth and eighteenth centuries, see also Laurenţiu Rădvan, 'Foreign Merchants in Iaşi (17th–18th centuries)', *Istros*, 18 (2012), 453–480; Eugen Pavelescu, *Economia breslelor în Moldova* (Bucharest: 1939).

88 Wolfgang Kaiser, 'Extranéités urbaines à l'époque moderne', in Pilar González-Bernaldo, Manuela Martini and Marie-Louis Pelus-Kaplan (eds.), *Etrangers et sociétés. Représentations, coexistences, interactions dans la longue durée* (Rennes: 2008), 78; Roberto Zaugg, 'Entre diplomatie et pratique judiciaries: la condition des étrangers sous l'Ancien Régime napolitain', *Revue d'histoire maritime*, 17 (2014), 322–323.

interests.[89] In Moldavia and Wallachia, we cannot speak of citizenship as such, as the notion did not yet exist. However, the documents refer to the 'right of the city', in other words, the right of residence in the city, which often came with a series of fiscal privileges.[90] This was granted directly by the prince, after a thorough investigation of the social and economic situation of the applicant. The temporary character of the prince's rule meant that the privileges he granted ended with his reign, and a new application had to be made to the next ruler in order to preserve or extend them. Being excluded from political life, women were not entitled to hold office in the administrative or judicial apparatus. Many of them did not practise a profession and were not involved in commerce (unless through taking over the business of a deceased husband), with the result that they appear in the historical sources mainly as wives, daughters, or mothers. As such, women played a role behind the scenes, directing the political game from the shadows.[91] As the number of surviving documents increases, so women become more present in the archives, and their role in constructing trans-border networks becomes more and more evident. From the second half of the eighteenth century, and even more in the nineteenth, women seem to make up for their earlier invisibility, contributing by their presence in correspondence and in family archives to the tracing of a material culture that was necessary for the upholding of social distinctions and specific to the process of identification. Women thus emerge from the shadows of anonymity, expressing and displaying themselves, with a visibility that is a boon to the researcher. Widows and spinsters help us to understand how women managed to integrate themselves in the social fabric and to face the challenges posed by their new residence with its local judicial and fiscal systems. Emerging from the protective framework of the family, these women had to struggle alone for day-to-day survival and to maintain the social position that they owed to their descent and their education.

---

89 Simona Feci, 'Mobilité, droits et citoyenneté des femmes dans l'Italie medievale et moderne', *Clio. Histoire des Femmes*, 43 (2016), 47.

90 See the case of the Canela sisters, who came from Istanbul to Bucharest, where they built a stone house for themselves in the Șerban Vodă district. Prince Grigore Ghica granted them the right of residence in the city, with a series of fiscal privileges and exemptions. ANIC, Mitropolia Ţării Româneşti, CDLXXIII/1, 27 November 1748.

91 See in this connection Leslie Peirce, *Beyond Harem Walls: Ottoman Royal Women and the Exercise of Power*, in Dorothy O. Helly and Susan M. Reverby (eds.), *Gendered Domains. Rethinking Public and Private in Women's History* (Ithaca, NY – London: 1992), 40–55.

Sudiţi and Protégés

After the peace of Küçük Kaynarca and the establishment of consulates in Iași and Bucharest, a new social and juridical category appeared: the *sudiţi*. The foreign powers opened these consulates for the purpose of protecting their subjects' business activities on the territory of the Principalities. Extending the provisions of the capitulations to include their subjects, Russia, the Habsburg Empire, Prussia, France, and Britain created the category of *sudiţi* (from the Italian *sudditi*): foreigners who enjoyed privileges and protection.[92] The economic, juridical, and personal privileges held by these individuals in comparison with the general population led to the 'procurement' of this status by various means, and the development of a sub-category of protégés. Félix Colson, secretary of the French consulate in Bucharest, and later secretary to the boyar Ion Câmpineanu, makes clear the boundary between the two groups: 'The consuls have subordinates of two classes; *immediate* subjects, that is, subjects of the Empire that they represent, or else protégés, that is, subject to the jurisdiction and coming under the protection of the consul, by virtue of treaties or abusively.'[93] In other words, *sudiţi* were foreigners living on the territory of the Principalities and under the protection of their respective consulates, while protégés were locals (Moldavians, Wallachians, Jews, Armenians, Greeks, Bulgarians) or foreigners who did not have consular representation who put themselves under the protection of a foreign consulate operating in the Principalities. Under pressure from the consulates, a Chancellery for Foreign Affairs [*Logofeţia Pricinilor Străine*] was set up in each of the two Principalities, with responsibilities including resolving litigation of '*sudit* with *raia* [*re'aya*]' or '*sudit* with *sudit* of different protection.'[94] Exactly when these departments were founded in Wallachia and Moldavia remains unclear. For Wallachia there is as yet no study on the subject, but if we are to believe the disposition given by Prince Ioan Caragea, the Chancellery for Foreign Affairs in that principality was in operation from the end of November 1812.[95] In the case of Moldavia,

92 Stela Mărieş, *Supuşii străini din Moldova în perioada 1781–1862* (Iaşi: 1985).

93 'Les consuls ont des subordonnés de deux classes; *sujets* immédiats, c'est-à-dire sujets de l'Empire qu'ils représent, ou bien, *protéjés*, c'est-à-dire soumis à la jurisdiction et relevent de la protection du consul, en vertu des traités ou par abus.' Félix Colson, *De l'Etat présent et de l'avenir des Principautés de Moldavie et de la Valachie, suivi des traits de la Turquie avec les puissances européennes* (Paris: 1839), 249.

94 ANIC, Fond Manuscrise, Ms. 1073, f. 1, 30 November 1812.

95 ANIC, Fond Manuscrise, Ms. 1073, f. 2, 29 November 1812; See also Marcel-Dumitru Ciucă, 'Logofeţia Pricinilor Străine din Ţara Românească', *Revista Arhivelor*, LXVIII, 3 (1991), 367–379.

Stela Mărieş maintains that the Chancellery was founded sometime between 1777 and 1780.[96]

The privileges enjoyed by protégés led to an arbitrary growth of this category, membership of which allowed one to escape the provisions of Wallachian, Moldavian, and Ottoman fiscal legislation. Both the Porte and the rulers of the Principalities tried to stop, or at least to control the chaotic expansion of the number of protégés, but with little success until the second half of the nineteenth century, with the passing of laws regarding naturalization and citizenship.[97]

Foreigners, whether Phanariots, merchants, artisans, doctors, or teachers were the agents of change in southeastern Europe. Transiting empires, they made possible the circulation not only of goods but also of knowledge, and became a model for the communities that hosted them temporarily or permanently.

Content and Structure

Each chapter will focus on a particular theme, through the intermediary of one central figure. The first chapter will deal with all those 'foreigners at the princely court'. What did it mean to be in the service of a Phanariot prince, a bey, or a pasha? The office of princely secretary (*secretar domnesc*) has received very little attention in Romanian historiography in particular and Balkan historiography in general. There are, of course, numerous individual biographical-documentary studies, but few prosopographic analyses such as I propose in this book. A prince or a pasha of any importance would be surrounded by doctors, teachers, secretaries, and diplomatic agents from various corners of Europe. French, German, Italian, or Ragusan, these individuals came to occupy an important position in the entourage of a ruler by virtue of their knowledge. The Phanariot rulers managed to gather around themselves an intellectual elite that they transported from the banks of the Bosphorus (Istanbul) to those of the Dâmboviţa (Bucharest) or the Copou Hill (Iași), some

96 Mărieş, *Supuşii străini din Moldova*, 40.

97 For the Ottoman Empire, see Ariel Salzmann, 'Citizens in Search of the State: the Limits of Political Participation in the Late Ottoman Empire', in Michael Hanagan and Charles Tilly (eds.), *Extending Citizenship, Reconfiguring States* (New York: 1999), 37–66; Frank Castiglione, '"Levantine" Dragomans in Nineteenth Century Istanbul: The Pisanis, the British, and Issues of Subjecthood', *Journal of Ottoman Studies*, XLIV (2014), 169–195; Will Hanley, 'What Ottoman Nationality Was and Was Not', *Journal of the Ottoman and Turkish Studies Association*, 3, 2 (2016), 277–298.

of whom subsequently followed them into their political exile, while others were scattered among other European courts or turned towards more financially advantageous positions. The creation of such a structure would have been impossible without the bureaucratic reorganization of the Ottoman Empire and the development of a Foreign Affairs service.[98]

From the Italian Anton Maria del Chiaro to the Ragusan Stefan Raicevich, from the Frenchman François-Thomas Linchou to his compatriot Georges Mille, all these figures fulfilled essential functions in the service of their masters and left rich accounts of the society of the time. Some of them, however, went further and pursued strategies of integration in the local community, trying to settle, to establish a home, a family, to insert themselves into local networks, investing in social relations and the acquisition of the ranks or insignia necessary for acceptance. The case of François-Thomas Linchou is a special one, through which I shall attempt to decipher the social and political mechanism used in the construction of a multiple belongings and allegiances. By way of Thomas-François Linchou, secretary to Prince Constantin Racoviță, I shall examine the strategies that could be applied to insert oneself into the local community, and how this community reacted towards a 'foreigner'.[99]

In the second part, I shall again traverse and transgress imperial borders to follow the construction of the career of a high Ottoman dignitary. The chapter on Ianache Văcărescu seeks to elucidate the career-building and status-building strategies of a man who achieved high office. I shall analyse the important role played by material culture in affirming and maintaining such a status. At the same time, his example helps us to understand the struggles of such high office-holders to survive and prosper in a 'foreign' environment with different social norms and codes. Also relevant in this connection are the letters of exiles in Brașov in 1769–1772, during the Russian–Ottoman War.[100]

With the third part, we descend to the ranks of the common people and of the numerous Orthodox Christian 'refugees'seeking a secure social position in the Principalities. Greeks, Bulgarians, Serbs, and Russians travelled through the Principalities in the course of their professional and commercial activity.

---

98 See Carter V. Findley, 'The Legacy of Tradition to Reform: The Origins of the Ottoman Foreign Ministry', *International Journal of Middle East Studies*, 1 (1970), 224–357; Virginia Aksan, *An Ottoman Statesman in War and Peace: Ahmed Resmi Efendi, 1700–1783* (Leiden: 1995), 12–23.

99 A short version of this chapter was published under the title '"Le Coquin Grec" vs. "le Véritable François": Being a foreigner in the Danubian Principalities in the Eighteenth Century', in *Cromohs* (*Cyber Review of Modern Historiography*), 21/2017–2018, 91–105.

100 A short version of this chapter was published under the title: 'A Wallachian Boyar in Emperor Joseph II's Court', in *Journal of Early Modern History*, 2019, 341–362.

Artisans and merchants, these 'Greeks', as they were generically named on account of their Orthodox faith, preferred to develop their businesses on the imperial peripheries, gradually becoming indispensable suppliers of goods for the local elites. Some of them ventured into large-scale trans-imperial commerce, linking Vienna and Leipzig with Istanbul; others were content with small cross-border trade, settled in centrally-placed towns, and invested in the education and professional training of a second generation. Such is the case of Dimitrie Foti Merişescu, Epirot through his father, Wallachian by birth (born in Bucharest), Moldavian in his professional trajectory. He will help us to understand the role of a trans-imperial network in advancement and social ascent.[101]

With old age approaching, hounded by her own children in interminable court cases, wearied by a difficult marriage, Elena Hartulari (née Plitos) decided to write her memoirs, setting down on paper the unhappy course of her life. Her husband's career, the ranks he obtained, and the wealth he accumulated are presented and explained through the prism of the major contribution she brought due to her belonging to a patronage network. Apart from the fact that Elena Hartulari is the only woman in Moldavia or Wallachia to have left such a detailed account of her everyday life, her journal is also the only one that gives a detailed description of the social and political networks that were active in Moldavia in the early nineteenth century. Assiduously contested by her own children as the legitimate possessor of an immense fortune accumulated by her husband, their father, Elena Hartulari resorted to this explanatory and justificatory action, in which she underlines the role played by women in the social ascent of men. My analysis is helped by the discovery in the Archives in Iași of an immense quantity of hitherto unpublished documents concerning Iorgu Hartulari's business dealings and posts. A first-generation Greek, Iorgu knew how to manoeuvre his father-in-law's network in order to enter the entourage of Prince Mihail Sturdza. As the prince's right-hand man, Iorgu took over the business of leasing monastic estates (both dedicated and non-dedicated), and succeeded in making himself indispensable. The surviving documents reflect very well the ability of this office-holder, who interacted with various imperial officials (Stephanos Vogorides, the bey of Samos, the patriarch of Constantinople, the patriarch of Jerusalem, Kapudan-pasha Mehmed, Prince Mihail Sturdza, boyars and wealthy merchants) to build an immense fortune entirely from speculation.

101 A short version of this chapter was published under the title: 'I believe in stories: The journey of a young boyar from Bucharest to Istanbul in the early nineteenth century', in *Turcica*, (50) 2019, 285–317. All of the three chapters introduced in this book have been revised and enriched with new information and documents.

PART I

Foreigners at the Phanariot Court

CHAPTER 1

Foreign Secretaries and Phanariot Princes

Map 1 Map of Eastern Europe cc. 1750. Made by Michał Wasiucionek.

There is an almost complete lack of research regarding the functioning of the Phanariot administration in the eighteenth century. Apart from certain stereotypes that have developed concerning the princely secretaries in Phanariot chancelleries, relatively little is known about their activity, about the manner of their recruitment, or even about the bureaucratic structure within a princely chancellery. In this chapter, I shall focus particularly on the princely secretaries of the Phanariot period, but also I shall extend my investigation to take in other foreigners serving in the private space of the princely courts, employed as teachers of the princely offspring, as personal physicians, or simply as intellectuals involved in the sharing of specific knowledge. Their inclusion in the same category as secretaries may be justified by the fact that many of them were similarly used for diplomatic missions.

The category of princely secretaries is relevant for an understanding of how a foreigner could succeed in penetrating the fabric of a local administration and in occupying a place in a network in such a way that he might keep his job even after his patron was removed from power. At the same time, the careers of these secretaries help us to examine the links between geographical belonging, religion, and loyalty in the shaping of a political identity and in social acceptance. In the course of their employment, foreign secretaries circulated from one post to another, from one region to another, passing through the service of ambassadors, pashas, Phanariot princes, and local elites. Secretaries may be seen as a vehicle for the transmission of knowledge, information, and experience, and as the creators of geo-spatial connections linking western Europe, the Principalities, and the Ottoman Empire. Recent research dedicated to these intermediaries helps us to understand how they moved between different cultures and how they managed to cope with the normative rules that applied.

I shall focus first on recruitment criteria, in an attempt to see how and why only certain European scholars managed to occupy this position. In the second part of the chapter, I shall turn my attention to the manner of their integration in the Wallachian and Moldavian chancelleries and the relations they established within the local elites. Finally, I shall try to analyse the way in which knowledge circulated by way of the texts, maps, books, objects, travel accounts, conversations, and oral descriptions that passed from one secretary to another and then to members of the host society. I shall conclude with a case study that can help us to understand how the fate of these secretaries might sometimes be very closely tied to that of their patrons.

Education, Letters of Recommendation, Networks

The professional training of a secretary generally took place in the intellectual circles of western Europe. Pisa, Venice, Florence, Rome, Padua, Paris, Uppsala, and Berlin are just some of the centres where applicants for the post of secretary or physician to a Phanariot prince could claim to have received university education or simply schooling. Another place where a young man received training was the family, as may easily be observed in cases where the profession of secretary and diplomatic agent was handed down from one generation to the next. The family would then employ all its leverage for his education to be completed at the *Ecoles des Jeunes de Langues* in Paris and Istanbul.[1] A diploma from these institutions provided significant symbolic capital, but

1 The members of the Mille family began their education within the family. Jean and Pierre went on to be 'jeunes de langue' in Paris and Istanbul. See Andrei Pippidi, 'Notules Phanariotes. I: Panagiodoros', in *O Eranistis*, 15, 1 (1979), 104. See also Paul Mason, *Histoire du commerce français dans le Levant au XVIIIe siècle* (Paris: 1911), 145–149.

it was not sufficient for obtaining a post; the candidate also needed experience, as many recommendations as possible, and above all, membership of a network. The archaeologist and numismatist Domenico Sestini has left us an important account of the steps he followed in order to enter a network. Born in 1750 in Florence, Domenico left for the Orient after finishing his studies, in search of a job. He had already visited part of Italy and had written about Sicily before his arrival in Smyrna, in 1777–1778, and then in Istanbul. However, he was aware that in order to obtain a post, education needed to be backed up by the support of protectors. Thus, on his arrival in Istanbul, he began making courtesy visits, in the hope of entering the European diplomatic network of Pera with the help of the letters of recommendation that he carried in his satchel. Some he had gathered on the way, while passing through Smyrna, from the French consul, Claude-Charles de Peyssonnel, and the Dutch consul, Daniel-Jean de Hochepied, but it was Alexander Stakieff, the Russian ambassador in Constantinople, who opened the doors of diplomatic homes to him. Like Sestini, Stakieff was a lover of plants, and he had known the botanist Linnaeus. This common factor—Carl Linnaeus—brought them together, as they realized that they shared the same values and tastes: 'This Minister introduced me the same day to M. Tort, the Dutch chargé des affaires, to whom he was so good as to present me, as well as to the minister or priest of his Church, M. Ribe by name. He then told me that he would also introduce me to a Swedish traveller, M. Bjornsthol by name, who had for some years been in these lands, to study there the peoples who inhabited them.'[2] In fact he had already met the Swedish traveller and orientalist Jacob Jonas Björnståhl in Florence: 'As this Swedish traveller had met me in Florence, and as we had often spoken on various literary subjects, and as I had let him know my projects and my views, I conjectured that this Scholar would thus have a pretext for speaking about me, subsequently, with a certain interest, in the various houses of the Ministers, where his talents had procured him entrance, and where he was at the same time welcome.'[3] Being talked about was just as important.

2 'Ce Ministre me fit faire le même jour la connoissance de M. Tort, chargé des affaires de Hollande, à qui il voulut bien me présenter, ainsi qu'au Ministre, ou prêtre de son Eglise, qui se nommait M. Ribe. Il me dit ensuite qu'il me ferrait encore connaître un voyageur suédois, nommé M. Bjornsthol, qui se trouvait, depuis quelques années, dans ces contrées, pour y faire des observations sur les peuples qui les habitent.' Domenico Sestini, *Lettres de monsieur l'abbé Dominique Sestini, écrites à ses amis en Toscane, pendant le cours de ses voyages en Italie, en Sicile et en Turquie*, trans. Jean-Claude Pingeron (Paris: 1789), III, 56–57.

3 '[C]omme ce voyageur suédois m'avait connu à Florence, & que nous avions souvent parlé sur divers sujets de littérature & que je lui avais fait connaître mes projets & mes vues, je conjecturais que ce Savant aurait alors un prétexte pour parler de moi, dans la suite, avec un

The Italian doctor Antonio Lucci remarked on Sestini's arrival in the house of the Neapolitan representative Count Guglielmo Maurizio Ludolf, with the result that the young man was invited to dinner.[4] Within a short time, Sestini was acquainted with a part of the European diplomatic personnel in Istanbul, through recommendations, visits, luncheons, and banquets to which he was invited.[5] He met and conversed with Sir Robert Ainslie, the British ambassador; François-Emmanuel Guignard, comte de Saint-Priest, the French ambassador; Karol Boskamp, envoy extraordinary of Poland to the Porte and Kajetan Chrzanowski, secretary of the Polish legation; and Ulric Celsing, the Swedish envoy, the secretary, and the chaplain of the Swedish representation. Any person could be of value to him, both as a connection and intellectually. With some he went on trips of historical, numismatic, or botanical discovery around Istanbul, trips that he later described in letters sent to 'friends' in Tuscany. Indeed, travel correspondence was a very fashionable literary genre in the period.[6] In Jacob Jonas Björnståhl, to whom, as mentioned above, he was bound by their shared passion for the world of plants and their taste for antiquity, he found a good adviser to direct him along the way to finding a patron.[7]

Networks were woven around shared affinities, tastes, and values; debates were animated by generous luncheons and accompanied by countless coffees and narghiles. It was science that drew them together in solidarity, building friendships both strong and profitable. Once he had entered a network, the candidate had to maintain his presence with visits or gifts. Domenico Sestini tells how he went to Pera twice 'to pay court to various Ministers.'[8] He always called on Jacob Jonas Björnståhl, to remind him of his situation and to reiterate his request to find him a post (*'pour qu'il pût me procurer une place décente*

certain intérêt, dans les différentes maisons des Ministres, où ses talents lui avaient procuré l'entrée, & où il était en même-temps bien venu.' Sestini, *Lettres*, 58.

4 Sestini, *Lettres*, 59.

5 For Istanbul as a centre of diplomacy, see Emrah Safa Gürkan, *Early Modern Istanbul as a center of Diplomacy*, https://www.academia.edu/15465678/Early_modern_Istanbul_as_a_Center_of_Diplomacy [accessed 14.05.2021].

6 Alex Drace-Francis, 'A Provincial Imperialist and a Curious Account of Wallachia: Ignaz von Born', *European History Quarterly*, 36(1), 2006, 61–89; Wendy Bracewell, Alex Drace-Francis (eds.) *Under Eastern eyes. A Comparative Introduction to East European Travel Writing on Europe* (Budapest: 2008).

7 Catharina Raudvere, 'The Pedagogical Virtues of Comparison. Jacob Jonas Björnståhl in Constantinople 1776–79', in Ib Friis, Michael Harbsmeier and Jørgen Bœk Simonsen (eds.), *Early Scientific Expeditions and Local Encounters. New Perspectives on Carsten Niebuhr and 'The Arabian Journey'. Proceedings of Symposium on the Occasion of the 250th Anniversary of the Royal Danish Expedition to Arabia Felix* (Det Kongelige Danske Videnskabernes Selskab: 2013), 149–160.

8 He was still living on the ship that had brought him to Constantinople.

auprès de quelques Seigneurs'), but also because he was eager to learn, to find out more about the 'ways and customs of the Turks.'[9] In the end, Domenico Sestini put himself under the protection of Count Ludolf, who offered him a 'shelter' in time of plague. Sestini attended to the count's two sons, to whom he had to transmit '*plusieurs genres d'érudition*' and helped them to perfect their 'Tuscan'. The post had been intermediated by the Swedish special envoy at the Porte, whom Sestini called his 'mediator', following the repeated interventions of his friend and protector Jacob Jonas Björnståhl.[10]

Patrons and Clients: Princely Secretaries Between Phanariot Greeks and French Ambassadors

When Markos Katsaitis arrived in Iaşi, in the autumn of 1742, he met at the court a small group of 'scholars' in the service of the prince: Exupère Joseph Bertin, the prince's first physician, a member of the Paris Academy; Jean-Etienne Liotard, the prince's painter; the Marquis de Magnan, charged with political matters; and Petru Depasta, the prince's second physician.[11] In common to all four was that the prince had recruited them from the shores of the Bosphorus. The physician Bertin had been recommended to Prince Mavrocordat by the comte de Castellane, French ambassador to the Porte.[12] At the same time, Jean-Etienne Liotard had been in Istanbul, where he had won fame among the European diplomats and merchants.[13] The same ambassador Castellane had recommended Liotard to Prince Mavrocordat. The three were employed for the immediate needs of the court: Markos Katsaitis informs us that the marquis de Magnan was from Constantinople, and had served 'in Moscow under Tsar Peter, in England, in Vienna, and at other courts.' His area of responsibility was the foreign affairs of prince Mavrocordat, a charge for which he had been recommended by his qualities: 'he had several languages, and was well versed in problems of state and in the affairs of princes.'[14] Petru Depasta, in

9 Sestini, *Lettres*, 63.

10 Sestini, *Lettres*, 197.

11 Markos Antonios Katsaitis, 'Călătorie de la Constantinopol la Iaşi şi de la Iaşi la Bucureşti în anul 1742', ed. & trans. D. Limona, in Dumitru Limona, *Negustorii 'greci' şi arhivele lor comerciale*, ed. Loredana Dascăl (Iaşi: 2016), 391–494.

12 Vasile Mihordea, 'Un medic frances la curtea lui Constantin-vodă Mavrocordat, doctorul Bertin (1741–1743)', *Revista istorică*, 4–6 (1933), 139–155.

13 Kristel Smentek, 'Looking East: Jean-Etienne Liotard, the Turkish Painter', *Ars Orientalis*, 39 (2010), 84–113.

14 Katsaitis, 'Călătorie', 418.

addition to his medical duties, was also engaged on writing a biography of Prince Mavorcordat,[15] a work which he indeed completed.[16] We may observe that the French ambassador to the Porte played an important role in recruiting the 'intimate' personnel around the Phanariot princes. As I shall demonstrate below, the case of Constantin Mavrocordat is not unique[17]. Roland Puchot Des Alleurs, ambassador of France to the Porte from 1747 to 1754, recommended to Prince Constantin Racoviță both the physician Giuseppe Antonio Pisani and François-Thomas Linchou, who became his Frankish-language secretary.[18] It was also due to the advice of French ambassadors to the Porte that Jean-Baptiste Linchou and Pierre de La Roche became secretaries to Phanariot princes.

With the installation of Phanariot princes in Wallachia and Moldavia, the prince brought with him a qualified staff to serve his private needs: tutors, physicians, painters, men of letters, who carried out various duties, drafting correspondence, compiling histories of the region, elaborating law codes. The practice of using foreign secretaries was not specific to the Phanariots. The Ottoman Empire and Western chancelleries made use of foreign staff in their administration, especially in the conduct of foreign affairs. Before the Phanariots, the princes of Wallachia had employed foreign interpreters in their chancelleries and some of them had engaged personal secretaries to administer their private business.[19] However, it was the Phanariots who promoted the post and its importance, continually surrounding themselves with cultivated foreigners. Apart from the immediate utility of such functionaries, these secretaries also helped to propagate the Phanariot princes' image as refined and educated men, distinguished by their elegance, their manners, and their

15 Sorin Grigoruţă, 'Un doctor ieşean din a doua jumătate a veacului XVIII: Dracache Depasta', *Anuarul Institutului de Istorie 'A.D. Xenopol*, XLVII (2010), 33–47.

16 Petru Depasta, 'Constantin-vodă sau scrisoarea faptelor vrednice de pomenire întâmplate în Dacia sub Constantin Mavrocordat', in Constantin Erbiceanu, *Cronicari greci care au scris despre români în epoca fanariotă* (Bucharest: 2003), 295–335.

17 Constantin Mavrocordat ruled many times in Wallachia (1730, 1731–1733, 1735–1741, 1744–1748, 1756–1758, 1761–1763) and Moldavia (1733–1735, 1741–1743, 1748–1749, 1769).

18 Vasile Mihordea, *Politica orientală franceză şi ţările române în secolul al XVIII-lea (1749–1760)* (Bucharest: 1937), 174.

19 I would mention here the Italian-language secretary Anton Maria Del Chiaro, who worked for Prince Constantin Brâncoveanu (1688–1714), but who enjoyed neither the position nor the intimacy of an eighteenth-century secretary. Del Chiaro wrote *Istoria delle moderne rivoluzioni della Valachia* (Venice: 1718). A first step towards the creation of the post was made by Vlad Boţulescu, secretary and personal advisor to prince Ştefan Cantacuzino (1714–1716). Ovidiu Olar, 'Logofătul de taină. Viaţa, aventurile şi traducerile lui Vlad Boţulescu de Mălăieşti', in Vlad Boţulescu de Mălăieşti, *Scrieri*, eds. Emanuela Timotin, Ovidiu Olar (Bucharest: 2013), 13–37.

knowledge. They had already succeeded in standing out as a distinct group in the Ottoman administration through the holding of important functions[20]. As dragomans, high officials of the Patriarchate of Constantinople, and princes of Moldavia and Wallachia, the Phanariots skilfully wove links that extended across empires and gave them access to substantial resources. Within this trans-border network was the network developed with the European embassies in Istanbul, among which the particular relationship with the French embassy stands out. Ambassadors and princes constituted the visible peak of the network, under which a web of trans-border patronage unfolded.[21] The cooperation extended over more than a century, structuring the network and its modes of functioning. Relations within the network were cemented by reciprocal favours, exchanges of gifts and information,[22] while good rhetoric protected the honour of each patron, kept pride under control, and instituted a certain type of behaviour that was promoted and accepted by ambassadors and Phanariots alike. Secretaries and diplomatic agents were the intermediaries who kept this patronage network alive, bearing gifts, information, objects, and knowledge to and fro, and consolidating a certain type of trust. At the same time, it may easily be observed that the secretaries developed multilateral relations that went beyond the two patrons. Passing from one patron to another, leading a mobile life, the secretaries cultivated various networks and experienced multiple loyalties.[23] Sharon Kettering has clearly shown the

---

20 On the education of the Phanariots see Nir Shafir, 'Phanariot Tongues: The Mavrocordatos Family and the Power of the Turkish Language in the Eighteenth-Century Ottoman Empire', *Oriente Moderno*, 101, 2021, 181–220.

21 For patrons and clients, see Wasiucionek, *The Ottomans and Eastern Europe*; Sharon Kettering, 'Patronage in Early Modern France', *French Historical Studies*, 17, 4 (1992), 839–862; Sharon Kettering, 'Patronage and Kinship in Early Modern France', *French Historical Studies*, 16, 2 (1989), 408–435.

22 The gifts that circulated between Phanariot princes and ambassadors included barrels of wine, baskets of apples, fine textiles, furs, clocks, horses, carriages, and books. To these may be added the small favours that implied protection and hospitality for recommended clients, interventions, writing letters of recommendation, procuring goods, etc. See Ioan C. Filitti (ed.), *Lettres et extraits concernant les relations des Principautés roumaines avec la France (1728–1810)* (Bucharest: 1915), Des Alleurs to Giovanni Calimachi, dragoman of the Porte, 24 June–15 September 1753, 231, 238, 249–251, 288, 295, 301, 322, 326, 329, 332. For the use of gifts in diplomatic ritual, see Barbara Stollberg-Rilinger, *Zur moralischen Ökonomie des Schenkens bei Hof (17.-18. Jahrhundert)* in Werner Paravicini (ed.), *Luxus und Integration: Materielle Hofkultur Westeuropas vom 12. bis zum 18. Jahrhundert* (Munich: 2010), 187–202; Sharon Kettering, 'Gift-Giving and Patronage in Early Modern France', *French History*, 2 (1988), 131–51.

23 For diplomacy in the modern period, see the three special issues of *Journal of Early Modern History* dedicated to this subject: 2016 (4), 'Diplomacy and Cultural Translation in the Early Modern World'; 2016 (1), 'The Art of Embassy: Objects and Images of Early

difficulty of applying such words as *patrons*, *clients*, and *fidelity* in researching the French networks of the modern period. Although commonly used in English, these terms tend to have economic connotations in French (and indeed in Romanian), while the subjects under examination used a completely different vocabulary to denote the relations among themselves.[24] The secretaries' correspondence was drafted principally in French and Italian, and they used such words as: *ami*, *amitié*, *fidelité*, *loyalité*, *maître*, *serviteur*, *domestique*. In order to determine the nature of the relations between the members of a network, I shall make use of other sources in addition to diplomatic correspondence, which, although it has been reappraised and included in the category of self-narrative documents, needs to be supplemented by other elements to clarify the nature of patronage relations.[25]

The French embassy to the Porte was the principal provider of secretaries and other qualified persons. This may be explained by the privileged diplomatic position that France enjoyed in the first half of the eighteenth century and its need to monitor the information sent by the Phanariot princes to the Porte; to supervise the passage through the Principalities of diplomatic correspondence between France, Poland, and the Ottoman Empire; and to construct 'a sophisticated network of political influence and contacts within the Ottoman bureaucracy and ruling élite.'[26] This reality led to the active involvement of French diplomats in engaging the Phanariots in the collection of information for the Ottoman Empire through the intermediary of diplomatic agents. The French language was another factor to France's advantage, given that it had become not only the language of diplomacy but also that of culture, replacing Italian, which was now in decline after its period of triumph in the seventeenth century.

As it would have been difficult to find in Iași or Bucharest staff qualified in the knowledge of foreign languages, the Phanariots sought to recruit them from

---

Modern Diplomacy'; and 2010 (6): 'Italian Ambassadorial Networks in Early Modern Europe'. See also the special number of *International History Review*, 2018: 'Eurasian Diplomacies Around 1800: Transformation and Persistence'. See also E. Natalie Rothman, *The Dragoman Renaissance. Diplomatic Interpreters and the Routes of Orientalism* (Ithaca, NY: 2021).

24 Kettering, 'Patronage', 848–849.

25 Christine Vogel, 'Diplomatic Writing as Aristocratic Self-Fashioning: French Ambassadors in Constantinople', in Tracey A. Sowerby, Joanna Craigwood (eds.) *Cultures of Diplomacy and Literary Writing in the Early Modern World* (Oxford: 2019), 192.

26 Edhem Eldem, 'French Trade and Commercial Policy in the Levant in the Eighteenth-Century', *Oriente Moderno*, 18(79), 1 (1999), 29.

Istanbul.[27] Indeed, they were themselves no strangers to foreign languages, as many of them had previously held the post of dragoman to the Porte. They were aware of both the importance of linguistic ability and the value of information in the games of diplomacy.

The recruitment of secretaries thus took place within a network. Some of the secretaries recommended were personal acquaintances of the French ambassador, while others merely sought assistance, invoking the rhetoric of their entitlement to enjoy the protection of the 'French nation'. For example, François-Emmanuel Guignard, Comte de Saint-Priest, ambassador of France to the Porte, proposed to the newly appointed prince of Wallachia Nicolae Caragea (1782–1783) no less than three candidates: his personal physician, one of his dragomans, and a young French protégé. Each of these three 'clients' occupied a different position in the ambassador's circle of acquaintances, as may be observed from the 'laudation' drafted for each of them in turn. In the first place was the personal physician: Jaoul, 'François de nation', is presented as one of the best of physicians, whose training is vouched for by 'le premier médecin de Mdr. le duc d'Orléans, chancelier de l'Université de Montpelier,' where he had studied. The physicians of Pera could offer guarantees for Jaoul, while the ambassador considered him 'un homme profond dans son art', dedicated to study. When the dragoman Nicolas Dandolo asked the ambassador to intervene before the prince 'to procure him a post in Wallachia,' he did his duty as the protector of all the French in the Levant and put in a good word for him. In third place was a young Frenchman, recommended for the position of secretary 'for the French language and Latin,' and who would be able to draft the prince's correspondence with 'Hungary and Poland.'[28] The ambassador did not know him personally, but he knew his family, and so he could vouch for the good name of the 'boy', who would come straight from Paris, while the others were in Istanbul and could join the princely suite on its way to Bucharest. Indeed, Ambassador Saint-Priest sums up this hierarchy among his clients: 'Your Highness will easily appreciate that the last two [recommendations]

---

27 For the system of education in the principalities in the eighteenth century and the first half of the nineteenth, see Alex Drace-Francis, *The Making of Modern Romanian Culture. Literacy and the Development of National Identity* (London: 2006).

28 The recommendation shows how the linguistic landscape was changing in the region. The chancellery of Moldavia, for example, employed Polish and Hungarian secretaries to draft correspondence with these two countries throughout the seventeenth century. But the eighteenth century was leaning towards French, and the Phanariots entered into the logic of diplomacy. Gheorghe Lazăr, 'Les logothètes de la chancellerie princière de la Valachie (XVIIe siècle). Considérations préliminaires pour une recherché prosopographique', *Istros*, XX (2014), 601–619; Silviu Văcaru, *Diecii Țării Moldovei în prima jumătate a secolului al XVII-lea* (Iași: 2006).

touch me much less than the first.'[29] Reputation and honour are essential elements in the drafting of a letter of recommendation. The above example shows very clearly how the functioning mechanisms of a good reputation extended over the whole family, governing all its members. In other words, the reputation of a family counted just as much as an individual reputation.

Nicolae Caragea turned down the first two proposals: he already had a physician, Georzaky Skulida, who had served the Caragea family for many years; in addition, the British ambassador had been much quicker with his recommendation, so that, 'unable to refuse,' the prince had already accepted 'Mr Weber for languages.' He accepted the young Frenchman, but asked 'to be well informed regarding his talents and knowledge.'[30] On his arrival in Bucharest, Nicolae Caragea did not wait for the young man to come from Paris, but kept on Pierre de La Roche, who had served as princely secretary and diplomatic agent under Grigore Callimachi,[31] for whom he maintained connections with Poland, and Alexandru Ipsilanti (1774–1782), and who would remain in the post under Mihai Suţu (1783–1786). Pierre de La Roche had long been under the protection of Ambassador Saint-Priest, with whom he was in direct contact because of his important missions in Poland.[32]

The French diplomatic representation to the Porte was not alone in putting forward prospective agents or secretaries for the Moldavian and Wallachian courts. In fact, it was through the Phanariot princes' personal relations with foreign diplomatic representatives in Istanbul that men qualified for such missions were brought to their attention. From the above example it may be observed that there was competition among European ambassadors to place their loyal candidates in the service of the Phanariot rulers.

Belonging to a network or having the recommendation of an acquaintance within the patron's circle were not sufficient. Personal chemistry also played

29 'V.A. distinguera aisément que les deux dernières me touchent bien moins que la première.' Filitti, *Lettres*, Saint Priest to Nicolae Caragea, prince of Wallachia, Constantinople, 21 January 1782, 240–241.

30 Ibid. 241–242. Prince of Wallachia Nicolae Caragea to St Priest, Fanal, 19/21 January 1782.

31 In July 1762, when Ruggiero Giuseppe Boscovich arrived in Iaşi, in the company of Ambassador James Porter, he was met by Pierre de La Roche, whom he described as 'the prince's secretary for French and Italian correspondence' and a native of Aix. He also wrote that he had heard from others that La Roche was 'a man of great politeness and of mature judgement', of 'the greatest honour', that he was the trusted servant of Prince Callimachi and that 'he did not become mixed up in the intrigues of the Greeks', which ensured that he kept his post, not being 'brought down' as happened to others. Ruggiero Giuseppe Boscovich, *Giornale di un viaggio da Costantinopoli in Polonia dell'Abate Ruggiero Giuseppe Boscovich, con una sua relazione delle Rovine di Troja* (Bassano: 1784), 115.

32 Filitti, *Lettres*, 246.

a part in obtaining a post so 'intimately' bound to the person of the prince. Markos Katsaitis had many of the qualities of a princely secretary. Born into a noble family in Corfu,[33] he had studied law in Venice, where he had developed a passion for geography and had published a book in the field.[34] To complete his education, he had travelled through Italy and then to Smyrna and Constantinople. Here he had made the acquaintance of Iancu Mavrocordat, the brother of the prince of Moldavia, Constantin Mavrocordat, who had suggested that he should go to Iași and apply for the job of court historian. To avoid a marriage that he no longer desired,[35] Markos accepted the proposal. He joined the suite of Constantin Cantemir, a gentleman of Moldavian princely stock who was travelling in the same direction and headed for Moldavia. In support of his candidacy, he had obtained three letters of recommendation: one from the prince's brother, Iancu Mavrocordat, and two from the prince's *capuchehaias* (diplomatic representatives). All these must have impressed Constantin Mavrocordat. Himself erudite, given to study, and well versed in the languages of the day, the prince welcomed Markos with high expectations. However, the audience opened with a gaffe: 'I began by making a speech in Italian, to inform him verbally of the motive that had brought me to his Court and to beg him to grant me his protection, but after two sentences he interrupted me, asking me why as a Greek I did not use my mother tongue … I answered that being educated in Italian schools and having connections since my childhood with Venetian nobles, functionaries, and other Italians, of whom our land is full … and after I had travelled much through Italy, my mother tongue was almost unaccustomed and foreign to me.'[36] The episode is very interesting, bringing together political subjecthood and ethnic identity: Katsaitis is Greek, but a Venetian subject from Corfu and seeking employment in Ottoman territory. Dressed as he was in his French suit and skilfully handling rhetoric in Italian, it had not occurred to Katsaitis that the Greek Mavrocordat would not give the same interpretation to his strategy of self-fashioning and would invite him directly to be Greek by the use of their mother tongue.

33 He was born on 28 September 1717 into a Greek noble family registered in the 'Golden Book' of the Ionian nobility, the son of the lawyer Ioannis Katsaitis.

34 *Geografia in dialogo, con moltissime notizie istoriche cronologiche* (Venice: 1738).

35 Markos Katsaitis had become engaged in May–June 1742 to the daughter of the former Venetian consul Francesco Cortazzi. However, as a result of a fire in Smyrna, Cortazzi lost a large part of his wealth, and in these circumstances, Katsaitis no longer wished to proceed with the marriage. Limona, 'Markos Antonios Katsaitis: Călătorie', 416.

36 Katsaitis, 'Călătorie', 413. For an English version see Marco Antonio Cazzaiti 'A Venetian Greek in the Ottoman Balkans', trans. Maria Kostaridou and Alex Drace-Francis, in: Wendy Bracewell (ed.) *Orientations. An Anthology of East European Travel Writing, ca. 1550–2000* (Budapest – New York: 2009), 49–50.

After the audience, there followed other meetings in which the young man was subjected to 'interviews' by the prince and by his grand *cămăraş* (chamberlain), both of whom had previously read Katsaitis's geographical book and other 'unpublished compositions'. While the prince analysed the candidates 'file', Katsaitis made repeated visits to cultivate all those who might be of use in supporting his candidacy: the grand *vornic*; the *aga* Paleologul, a close friend of the prince; the grand *cămăraş*; Petru Depasta, physician and friend of the prince; the Divan-Effendi; and the 'foreigners' with whom he had already established amicable relations (Liotard, Magnan, Bertin). Markos Katsaitis lost out through his constantly repeated assertion that his noble status 'did not permit him to profess any profession', still less to seek a salary from the prince for compiling the required history. Katsaitis's arrogance displeased Constantin Mavrocordat, and he did not insist when the young man took offence at the salary he was offered (50 groschen). Although he had been urged to propose a suitable remuneration, Katsaitis had refused, hoping to be generously rewarded for his efforts. Moreover, he had enquired as to the salaries and privileges received by the other foreigners he had met at the court. Highest paid of all was the physician Bertin, who received '6,000 groschen or 12 bags per year, apart from gifts, board and lodging.' In second place was Petru Depasta, with 230 groschen per month, followed by the marquis de Magnan with a monthly salary of 130 groschen.[37] The latter had made Katsaitis aware of his discontent at his treatment at the court of Iași and of the jealousies within the group. As such, Katsaitis considered Mavrocordat's offer to be demeaning, and he preferred to leave.

Rivalry and envy between the members of the group of foreigners could also result in failure to obtain a post. In 1776, after the sudden departure of Lionardo Panzini, Prince Alexandru Ipsilanti of Wallachia took steps to employ a secretary and teacher of Italian for his sons. From Constantinople, Domenico Sestini was recommended to him, a Florentine with studies in the classics and archaeology. This seemed an 'advantageous proposal' to Sestini, who held a similar post at the Neapolitan diplomatic representation, and he made haste to leave for Bucharest.[38] In October 1779, Domenico Sestini presented his letters of recommendation to Prince Ipsilanti, but the secretary's post was not to be his.[39] Stefan Raicevich held up Sestini's appointment for eight months, until the latter, despairing of ever receiving the post, took advantage of the

---

37 Katsaitis, 'Călătorie', 418, 425.

38 Domenico Sestini, *Viaggio da Costantinopoli a Bukoresti fatto l'anno 1779 con l'aggiunta di diverse lettere relative a varie produzioni ed osservazioni Asiatiche* (Rome: 1794), 1.

39 Sestini, *Lettres*, 50–51.

passage of the Ludolf brothers to leave Wallachia. Franz Joseph Sulzer, invited by the same Alexandru Ipsilanti to occupy the position of professor of law and to be involved in the drafting of a law code, found himself in a similar situation. After two years, in 1776, his collaboration with Ipsilanti was terminated without any explanation, leaving Sulzer to speculate as to the attitude of the prince, who 'had not kept his word to me and to others ... on the advice of other Europeans, flatterers with interests.'[40]

Numerous people circulated through this network, bearing with them letters of recommendation and hopes of obtaining advantageous posts at the courts of the Phanariot princes. They were of quite diverse professions and ethnicities. Merchants and men of letters stand out among the mass of clients and relations delivered to the Phanariots. French, Italians, and Greeks predominated among the various ethnicities. Nevertheless, it was the princes' right to choose those best fitted to the post and with whom they could relate socially and culturally. Being selected for a position and remaining in it depended on the loyalty and trustworthiness of the secretary, who would have access to many secrets concerning the prince and his family.

What Did a Secretary Do?

In his *History of Dacia*, Dionisie Fotino writes that it is the grand *postelnicie* that deals with the foreign policy of the Romanian Principalities, with the grand *postelnic* himself, as head of this department, being 'properly speaking, the prince's minister of external affairs.' Thus 'the entire prince's correspondence with Constantinople, with the pashas of the cities over the border, and with other regions abroad through him [i.e. the grand *postelnic*] is sent and through him receives answers.' The grand *postelnic* had under him: the *polcovnic* (commander) of riders, the head of the couriers who were sent to Constantinople; the *lipku-agasi*,[41] the head of the couriers sent to other regions of Europe; the agents sent on missions; the second *postelnic*; the third *postelnic*; and twelve lesser *postelnics*. All correspondence from or to the prince passed through the hands of the grand *postelnic*. For this reason, writes Dionisie Fotino, the prince

40 Franz Joseph Sulzer, *Geschichte des transalpinischen Daciens, das ist der Walachey, Moldau und Bessarabiens. Im Zusammenhange mit der Geschichte des übrigen Daciens als ein Versuch einer allgemeinen dacischen Geschichte mit kritischer Freyheit entworfen*, vol. 3 (Vienna: 1781), 80–81.

41 From the Turkish *lipkan*, initially meaning a Tatar soldier serving as a courier, and then extended in meaning to denote an official courier.

appointed to this high office an 'intimate' and 'capable' boyar.[42] High offices had a fixed salary, varying according to the duties involved in the job, to which were added a series of privileges. There has yet been no study of the chancellery of the *postelnicie*. It is not known whether the grand *postelnic* had a good knowledge of languages, which would be useful in drafting correspondence. From the list of officeholders who occupied this position during the eighteenth century, two things may be noted: the prince would appoint a close friend; and this friend would be a 'Levantine Greek' from the shores of the Bosphorus.[43]

The prince also had, however, a private chancellery headed by a grand *grămătic* (secretary), with a second *grămătic* serving under him.[44] The term *secretar domnesc* (princely secretary) has entered Romanian usage as a translation from the French 'secrétaire du prince' or 'secrétaire princier', which suggests that these secretaries were bound to the person of the prince, performing their duties withing the private chancellery and thus assimilable to the post of *grămătic*. This hypothesis is based both on the manner in which these secretaries were recruited and on the duties that were assigned to them. Referring to their secretaries, the princes used various terms, according to the language in which a letter was written. We find the following: *secrétaire, officier, maggiordomo, mio aulico, agent*. The secretaries in their turn referred to themselves as *secrétaire, chargé des Affaires Etrangères, agent*, or as heading the department of Foreign Affairs.[45]

Frankish-language secretaries were primarily responsible for the drafting of the prince's personal and diplomatic correspondence, handling Italian, French, and Latin. François-Thomas Linchou's work for Prince Constantin Racoviţă also included translating gazettes arriving from Europe.[46] The Phanariot princes paid to have gazettes brought from Sweden, France, and Prussia. Their content was systematized, translated, and then sent on to Istanbul, imprinted with the interpretation the patron desired. 'His Highness is obliged, following

42 Fotino, *Istoria Generală a Daciei*, 282–283.

43 Theodora Rădulescu, *Sfatul domnesc şi alţi mari dregători ai Ţării Româneşti din secolul al XVIII-lea. Liste cronologice şi cursus honorum* (Bucharest: 1972).

44 Fotino, *Istoria Generală a Daciei*, 309.

45 See Jean Mille's letter to Giuliani of 12 September 1763, in which he declares: 'il a plus à Son Altesse de me mettre à la tête des Affaires Etrangères'. Nicolae Iorga (ed.), *Documente privitoare la familia Callimachi* (Bucharest: 1903), II, 334.

46 Periodicals saw considerable development in the eighteenth century and were a principal source of information in the context of diplomatic tensions and international conflicts. French-language gazettes appeared all over Europe, with the Gazette d'Amsterdam establishing itself as a model. See François Moureau, *La plume et le plomb. Espaces de l'imprimé et du manuscrit au siècle des Lumières*, Paris (Paris: 2006); Pierre Rétat (ed.), *La Gazette d'Amsterdam, miroir de l'Europe au XVIIIe siècle* (Oxford: 2001).

the orders that he has from the Porte, to forward all dispatches addressed to him, but he is master in giving them the cast that he judges the most convenient,' François-Thomas Linchou wrote to the French resident in Warsaw, Durant, on 10 March 1757.[47] He likewise assured ambassador Vergennes that he respected the instructions received from Durant in the modelling of reports sent to the Porte.[48] Ambassador Des Alleurs recommended that his agents slip 'les bonnes insinuations' into the ears of those for whom they worked and on whom they could exert influence.[49] From the secretaries' correspondence it is clear that they maintained close relations with their patrons. With such intimate access, some secretaries came to hold considerable powers, which they made use of to intervene in the interpretation of the news that they collected.

While this activity constituted the core of their job, the secretaries were also given other greater or lesser duties according to the fidelity they demonstrated towards their patrons. François-Thomas Linchou, Jean-Baptiste Linchou, Georges Mathieu Mille, and Pierre de La Roche were faithful diplomatic agents of their princes (but also of the French ambassadors), sent on missions to collect information in Poland, the Crimea, or Russia. Their linguistic and social abilities enabled them to travel across empires, putting their expertise to use in their employers' service. As transcultural intermediaries and imperial agents, the secretaries played an essential role in the conduct of political relations between the Phanariots and the Ottoman Empire. Indeed once the thrones of Wallachia and Moldavia were assigned to Phanariots, their secretaries were everywhere and in considerable numbers. As such, the secretaries were employed both on diplomatic activity and on the prince's private activity, becoming involved in the education of the prince's sons, whom they initiated in the study of foreign languages and with whom they shared their knowledge of various sciences. For example, Daniel Fonseca became personal physician to prince Nicolae Mavrocordat by a 'transfer' arranged by the French ambassador, Jean-Louis d'Usson marquis de Bonnac on 20 March 1719: 'We hereby declare that, without prejudice to the position that we have permitted him to take as

47 'Son Altesse est obligée, suivant les ordres qu'elle a de la Porte, d'envoyer toutes les expéditions qu'on lui adresse, mais elle est maîtresse de leur donner la tournure qu'elle juge la plus convenable.' Archives des Affaires Etrangères, Paris, Correspondance Politique, Pologne, Supplément, vol. 10, f. 353. See also Mihordea, *Politica orientală franceză*, 66.

48 Filitti, *Lettres*, 212. Linchou to Vergennes, Iaşi, 16 March 1757: 'Son Altesse est obligée par devoir et par les ordres qu'il ne cesse de recevoir de la Porte, de luy faire passer les expéditions qu'il reçoit de Pologne, mais il en modère beaucoup le sens par la tournure qu'il y donne, et dont je luy ay fourni à mon arrivé icy le plan, qui est conforme aux instructions que m'a donné M. Durand, là-dessus.'

49 Filitti, *Lettres*, 322, 325.

Physician to the Prince of Wallachia, we keep for him that of physician to the embassy of His Most Christian Majesty at Constantinople and, moreover, we hold and maintain him in absence as in presence under the powerful protection of His Majesty.'[50] After seventeen years in the service of France, Daniel Fonseca took the road to Wallachia, where he was employed as a physician, but also as a secretary due to his political abilities.[51] He served Nicolae Mavrocordat until 1722, when he returned to Constantinople. Some sources state that Daniel Fonseca was not only physician and secretary, but also teacher of French and Italian to the princely offspring.[52] Another example is provided by François Recordon, son of the merchant Pierre François Timothée Recordon, born in Rances, Switzerland, in 1795. His arrival in Bucharest in 1815 was not by chance: his father was already there, developing his business.[53] A graduate in 'belles-lettres et philosophie', the son did not follow in his father's footsteps, but found employment as French-language secretary to the Phanariot prince Ioan Caragea. His activity was particularly focused on correspondence with the banks in Geneva where the prince kept his savings. Recordon kept in contact with Caragea after the latter's flight from Wallachia in 1818, and in 1812 he published in Paris his impressions from his time in the principality in the form of letters.[54]

As I have shown above, the secretaries dealt with the affairs of their patrons, carrying out a series of activities, from the drafting of diplomatic correspondence to trafficking in information, favours, and money, from moulding and educating the princes children to procuring luxury items. Information and the search for information played an essential role in winning the patron's

50 '[N]ous déclarons, par ces présentes, que, sans préjudice de la qualité que nous lui avons permis de prendre de Médecin de M. le Prince de Valaquie, nous lui conservons celle de médecin de l'ambassade de Sa Majesté Très Chrétienne à Constantinople et, plus, le tenons et maintenons absent comme présent sous la puissante protection de Sa Majesté.' Eudoxiu Hurmuzaki (ed.), *Documente privitoare la istoria românilor* (Bucharest: 1897), I_1, 444.

51 Vasile Mihordea, 'Un agent politic al ţărilor noastre: Daniel Fonseca', *Revista Istorică*, XXIX, 1–6 (1943), 93–132. See also Andrei Pippidi, 'Mysticisme et rationalism au Phanar: le cas de Daniel de Fonseca', in idem, *Hommes et idées du Sud-Est européen à l'aube de l'âge moderne* (Paris, Bucharest: 1980), 237–252.

52 Saumery (Pierre Lambert de), *Mémoires et avantures secrètes et curieuses d'un voyage du Levant* (Liège: 1732), II, 206–207.

53 Pierre Recordon's business activities must have been successful, as in November 1818 he could afford to buy an inn with eight shops in the Arhimandritului district from the grand *logofăt* Constantin Dudescu.

54 François Recordon, *Lettres sur la Valachie ou observations sur cette province et ses habitants écrites de 1815 à 1821 avec la relation des derniers événements qui y ont eu lieu* (Paris: 1821).

favour.[55] The mere recording of this information was not sufficient; it had to be delivered as quickly as possible so as not to lose its value. For this reason, there was frequent competition between the Phanariot princes to be first to deliver information to their great patron, the sultan. Possession of information enabled one not only to use it to consolidate the network and strengthen the fidelity of its members, but also to manipulate it, imposing the desired interpretation.[56] Rivalries between the princes impacted on the activity of their secretaries, who thus became involved in the political game. For example, the rivalry between the Racoviţă and Ghica families can be seen played out at the level of their secretaries, as Linchou and Mille, struggling to please their respective patrons, anticipated and sabotaged one another's moves.[57]

In spite of their ubiquity and utility, the job of secretary was not turned into a formal office with rules of operation and specific recruitment procedures. In historical works written during the eighteenth and early nineteenth centuries, the job is not mentioned as such. On the contrary, the secretaries and auxiliary personnel at the princely court appear in the narration of events only when their activity becomes a focus of conflict. This would seem to support the hypothesis that secretaries were intrinsically bound to the person of the Phanariot prince and had no interest in projecting such a post as part of the administration of the two provinces.

Adapting and Adopting a Way of Life

In Iaşi or Bucharest, the secretaries and other foreign staff in the service of the prince carried out their activities at the princely court. As soon as their patron was installed, the secretaries had to find accommodation, to learn the rules of their country of adoption, to adjust to culinary habits and vestimentary rules, and to learn the language. Little information is available regarding the accommodation rented by secretaries, tutors, agents, or indeed cooks during their period of service. For those closest to him, the prince would offer lodgings near

55 For the importance of news, see also Ovidiu Cristea, 'Ştirea—"Marfă de lux". Mărturii veneţiene din primele decenii ale secolului al XVI-lea', *Revista Istorică*, 14, 3–4 (2003), 195–209.

56 Wasiucionek, *The Ottomans and Eastern Europe*, 105–111; Filippo de Vivo, *Public Sphere or Communication Triangle? Information and Politics in Early Modern Europe*, Massimo Raspocher (ed.), *Beyond the Public Sphere. Opinions, Publics, Spaces in Early Modern Europe* (Bologna and Berlin: 2012), 115–136.

57 The chronicler Enache Kogălniceanu attributes to Enacache Mille an important role in the death of his compatriot François-Thomas Linchou. Pseudo-Enache Kogălniceanu, *Letopiseţul Ţării Moldovei de la domnia întâi şi până la a patra domnie a lui Costandin Mavrocordat vv.* (1733–1774), ed. Aurora Ilieş and Ioana Zmeu (Bucharest: 1987), 105–107.

the princely court, as can be seen in the case of the physician Bertin. In the summer of 1762, the secretary La Roche made considerable approaches to his friend in Warsaw, marquis Francesco Crescenzo Giuliani, with a view to procuring 'a good and perfect French cook' with knowledge of 'patisserie, rotisserie, stews, preserves, pies, and sweets.' For this service, Giuliani was repaid with an ermine fur, an angora shawl, and a piece of *ghermeşut* silk. The cook, who arrived, after a series of delays, in the autumn of the same year, accompanied by his full collection of gastronomic utensils, received an annual allocation of 800 piastres and an apartment in the vicinity of the princely court.[58] Proximity to the court was an important factor in renting accommodation.

The foreigners in the service of the Phanariots constituted a distinct group who gravitated around the princely court. The language barrier and difference in clothing separated them, for a time, from the population of the city. As Catholics or Protestants, the secretaries attended the churches opened in Bucharest and Iași to serve the members of the various 'nations' present in Wallachia and Moldavia. Some of them showed an interest in the condition of these places of worship and took advantage of their position to bring pressure to bear on the prince and on high-ranking diplomatic agents, calling for urgent intervention in favour of their communities. The diplomatic correspondence preserves countless requests for intervention to protect the Catholic or Protestant 'communities', to repair churches, to erect new places of worship, to acquire the instruments necessary for the conduct of worship, or to appoint and send clergy. These actions show the secretaries' connection to the local communities, through their assumption of a confessional belonging and their involvement in improving local structures of day-to-day usefulness. Identification by confessional belonging meant an underlining of difference in relation to the majority and an acceptance of this difference that was necessary in everyday coexistence.

All the same, they gradually adopted the social practices of the country in which they were carrying out their activity. Through the intermediary of forms of sociability at the princely court, some of them built connections with the local elites, in the attempt to increase their income, to consolidate their position, and to find new patrons. From his short stay in the Moldavian capital, Markos Antonios Katsaitis gives us essential information about the group of secretaries in the service of Prince Constantin Mavrocordat. Katsaitis often took lunch or dinner in the company of the three aforementioned foreigners,

58 Iorga, *Documente Callimachi*, II, 292–293, 301. See also the letter of 23 August 1762, in which La Roche writes: 'ce cuisinier aura d'ailleurs son appartement pour soy et pour sa famille, tout auprès de son palais' (p. 298).

the physician Bertin, the marquis de Magnan, and the painter Liotard. On Sunday, 17 October 1742, he writes: 'I went for lunch to marquis de Magnan's, where I dined with much pleasure with M. Bretagni and M. Liotard, being treated after the French manner with the highest refinement.'[59] The same Katsaitis tells how, while waiting for Constantin Mavrocordat's decision on his candidacy, he made courtesy visits to the local elite, in the hope of finding protectors and building a network if he was to stay in Moldavia, and also to socialize. He went on visits almost every day, invited or uninvited; when he found no one at home, he did not lose heart, but headed to another house, and thus managed in a short period of time to weave a network embracing the prince's circle of scholars and branching out to include the Turkish secretary (the Divan Effendi), the grand *postelnic*, the grand *cămăraş*, the grand *aga* (chief of police), the grand *vornic* (interior minister and chief judge) and the grand *vistier* (treasurer). Together or separately, they socialized by way of meals, served sometimes in the French and sometimes in the Turkish manner, or simply over coffee, sherbet, and narghiles.[60]

Katsaitis was in no hurry to adopt the Ottoman garb of the boyar elite and the court. On the contrary, he was proud of his French costume, and mentioned it whenever necessary.[61] The presence of 'French' clothes was no novelty either for the Ottoman Empire or for its peripheries.[62] Domenico Sestini describes the reaction of the Muslim population of Istanbul, who insulted or even threw stones at those dressed in the European style and wearing 'hats'.[63] Sestini did not adopt Ottoman costume because he did not consider it at all comfortable. Even when he left for Wallachia, he preferred to 'disguise' himself as a Tatar for protection on the long post road.[64] Sestini might find Ottoman costume 'uncomfortable' and lacking in grace, but Jean-Etienne Liotard adopted it, and did not abandon it even when he arrived in the world of French fashion.

The secretaries built their own networks and relations, establishing long-lasting friendships. Pierre de la Roche speaks with sadness of his parting from the *postelnic* Nicolae Suţu, who had left for Constantinople in the spring of 1762. 'A friend too generous and too loyal [for me] not to wish to enjoy, if not his conversation, at least his correspondence,' he writes, on 16 March 1762, from

59 Katsaitis, 'Călătorie', 430.
60 Katsaitis, 'Călătorie', 430.
61 Katsaitis, 'Călătorie', 411.
62 Matthew Elliot, 'Dress Codes in the Ottoman Empire: The Case of the Franks', in Suraiya Faroqhi and Christoph K. Neumann (eds.) *Ottoman Costumes: From Textile to Identity* (Istanbul: 2005), 103–123.
63 Sestini, *Lettres*, 113.
64 Sestini, *Viaggio*, 4, 6.

Iași, to Giuliani, trying to console him and to console himself.[65] The same La Roche was eager to show his own utility, offering to help the boyars to procure luxury goods or items of everyday usefulness.[66] The secretaries copied the model of their patrons and resorted to gifts, favours, and services to consolidate relations. La Roche's friendship with Giuliani was reinforced by frequent exchanges of gifts or small services. For example, on 8 November 1762, he sent Giuliani 'a little honey and cheese from our regions' (i.e. Moldavia), knowing that this was something that the latter wanted.[67]

These mediators or 'brokers', as Natalie Rothman calls them, were masters in handling a language of transcultural politeness. Courtesy was an important ingredient in maintaining relations. Educated in a language of diplomatic politeness, the secretaries were very cautious when they spoke about their masters. They carried out orders, even if these proved to be contradictory or tried the patience and goodwill of others. Pierre de La Roche was often critical of those he served and among whom he carried out his activity and led his life. His criticisms could be interpreted as a manner of apologizing to cover the caprices of the boyars and princes in whose name he requested various goods. When the prince had second thoughts about the purchase of some dogs from Saxony, which had already been ordered, La Roche wrote of the 'inconsistency and variable character' of the Greek nation, which obliged him to renounce and to cancel what had seemed good a few days previously. He criticized the Greeks who made 'pirouettes and changed their disposition' without realizing that they were 'abusing the goodwill of friends'; they 'are very generous in promises, but unfortunately tend not to keep their word.'

La Roche knew that in order to survive he needed not only the goodwill and protection of the prince, but also the protection and friendship of his correspondent in Warsaw who, exasperated by so many requests and cancellations, might have broken off relations with him. To build another bridgehead would have meant time and trust. He chose to protect himself, the 'humble servant', who was only following a prince's orders, the prisoner of a changeful nation: 'I have had to live for six years with the most unreliable nation' where 'people

65 'Un ami trop généreux et trop loyal pour ne pas souhaiter de jouir, sinon de sa conversation, du moins de sa correspondance', Iorga, *Documente Callimachi*, II, 278.

66 Iorga, *Documente Callimachi*, II, 284, 291, 296. See his correspondence (5 July 1762) with Giuliani with a view to procuring seeds of rare flowers and other plants from the 'Hamburg catalogue' for the grand *vistier*. The assiduity with which he sought to carry out this service shows how necessary it was to cultivate powerful protectors among the local elite.

67 Iorga, *Documente Callimachi*, II, 303.

change with the wind,' he wrote to Giuliani on 7 March 1763.[68] Even while gossiping behind their backs, he continued to keep on good terms with everyone. The rhetoric of his letters was addressed to another diplomat, marquis Giuliani, who had lived among Greeks and Turks and should be understanding when he made requests, cancelled them, and then renewed them on behalf of others.

La Roche's personal interventions in diplomatic correspondence bear witness to how he experienced his role, caught up as he was in the fabric of diplomacy. He strove to take full advantage of his position as intermediary, corresponding with important members of the network. Often he overstepped his function, promoting himself and underlining his own role in bringing a mission to a successful conclusion, in ensuring a service was carried out, in procuring certain items. He carefully pursued his own interests in relation to his patrons. Only by simply making himself useful, indeed indispensable, would he have a chance of keeping his post when the prince, who was merely a temporary patron, was no longer in power. Proceeding in this way, he served his patron, while at the same time meticulously building a bridgehead for the future. After the deposition of Prince Grigore Callimachi, he managed to keep his position as secretary and diplomatic agent under Prince Grigore Ghica in Moldavia (1764–1767, 1774–1777) and Wallachia (1768–1769), and later under Nicolae Caragea (1782–1783) and Mihai Suțu (1783–1786) in Wallachia. He was one of the longest-serving princely secretaries, who knew how to make himself indispensable through his services and the relations he established, especially with Poland, and how to pass from one prince to the next. Despite the length of his activity, La Roche did not attempt to put down permanent roots, and there is (as yet) no evidence that he had any wish to settle, to build himself a *home* in Moldavia or Wallachia.[69] He preferred to retire to Poland. There his son, Kasimir, carried on his father's diplomatic activity, as secretary of the French Legation.[70]

Other secretaries did, however, right from the beginning of their employment, build the networks and 'recipes' that would enable them to anchor themselves in the local social fabric. On arrival in Iași or Bucharest, they sought ways of enhancing their income by continuing the commercial activity in which they had been engaged before taking the post of secretary, speculating on the economic information that came to them from the surest source of all

68 Iorga, *Documente Callimachi*, II, 297, 310, 311, 312.

69 In 1786, Jeremy Bentham found him in Bucharest, together with his wife. E.D. Tappe, 'Bentham in Wallachia and Moldavia', *Slavonic and East European Review*, 29, 72 (1950), 69.

70 Andrei Pippidi, *Documente privind locul românilor în Sud-estul Europei* (Bucharest: 2018), 257.

(the princely court) to embark on a series of profitable activities. The local elite was a model of success, which they imitated by buying properties and then obtaining positions in the local administration. I shall take as an example here the Mille family, as the surviving documents allow us to follow their strategies of integration.

The Mille family wove a network in which the principal connections were those of kinship. The members of the family tried first to anchor themselves in the imperial diplomatic networks and then to put down roots in the world that they served. A scion of a French family settled in the Levant, Georges Mathieu Mille was the son of Joseph Mille, dragoman and vice-consul in Chios, and grandson of Esprit Mille, who had also held the post of consul in Chios. In 1716, Mille was appointed second dragoman at Thessaloniki, and from there he passed into the service of Grigore Ghica, who ruled successively in Moldavia (1726–1733; 1735–1741; 1747–1748) and Wallachia (1733–1735; 1748–1752).[71] On 16 August 1752, the French ambassador Des Alleurs wrote the following about him: '*Le sieur* Mille, French by origin, currently in the service of the prince of Wallachia. Apart from the fact that the family of *le sieur* Mille has provided dragomans and consuls to Chios who have well deserved [recognition] from the state, he has enjoyed for over forty years the confidence of the prince of Wallachia [and] has rendered on every occasion to the nation services for which my predecessors have often expressed to him their satisfaction.'[72] According to Anne Mezin, Georges Mille married a Moldavian woman, Catherina, with whom he had a number of children. On the basis of the documents, I have been able to identify five of them: Jean, George, Pierre,[73] Catherine, and Louise. In 1749, he sent his wife and daughter to Constantinople. He sought the protection of the ambassador and his wife for his family in the most bombastic terms possible. On this occasion, we find out that Louise was married to Pierre Cingria.[74] In Constantinople, where he himself later withdrew, Catherine's marriage was planned in 1754 to Alexandre Philibert Deval, first dragoman of France to the Porte. Marriages within the

71 For the Mille family, I have found useful the index compiled by Anne Mezin for the National Archives in Paris. I am grateful to Mrs Mezin for making this information available to me.

72 Mihordea, *Politica orientală franceză*, 72, cites Des Alleurs's letter to Rouillé, Archives Nationales, Paris, Fond Affaires Etrangères, Correspondance Consulaire, Constantinople, vol. 55.

73 Mentioned by Anne Mezin in her index as the son of Georges Mathieu Mille (born around 1734), for whom his father requested a place in 1748 among the 'jeunes de langue'.

74 On 10 September 1749, Georges Milles (the father) sent to ambassador Des Alleurs an account of money spent on the repatriation of French deserters in Wallachia, which was to be presented 'to his son-in-law, M. Cingria.' (Filitti, *Lettres*, 272).

diplomatic network were an important strategy, designed to consolidate networks and promote member's interests.[75] The Mille family developed numerous connections in Moldavia and in the Ottoman Empire, which offered them access to resources and protection, and forged speculative links that could provide the levers necessary in order to quickly find a new patron, in a time when political alliances were changing. In cultivating trans-border connections and multiple loyalties, the Milles never put their interests solely in the hands of one patron. On the contrary, the members of the family proved their creativity and flexibility in adapting to the social and political contexts in which they carried out their activity.

After their father's withdrawal, Jean and Georges Mille remained in the service of the Ghica family, pursuing diplomatic careers. Ambassador Vergennes wrote to the prince of Moldavia, Constantin Racoviță, on 21 February 1756 as follows: 'Your Highness will find in the new principality MM. Jean Mille and Georges Mille,[76] his brother, who are already known to Your Highness, [...] good Frenchmen, [... but also] the brothers-in-law of M. Deval, one of my dragomans.'

On this occasion, when the prince was changed, the secretaries, who had been in the service of the Ghica family for decades, needed interventions of this sort to enable them either to continue their activity or to withdraw safely to Constantinople, where their father was.[77] The prince of Moldavia replied several months later that the Mille brothers were free to remain in the principality, especially as 'the elder is married in this country.'[78] It was Jean Mille who was married in Moldavia, and whom the previous ruler, Matei Ghica (1753–1756) had raised to the rank of *staroste* (governor) of Cernăuți (Chernivtsi). He had received this post thanks to the intervention of the French embassy, but also as a result of 'his services'.[79] This was the beginning of the career of Jean Mille

75 For example, Pietro Gian Nagni married the daughter of Johann Benedict Lochmann, surgeon and diplomatic agent in Iaşi. After peregrination between Paris, Bucharest, and Constantinople, Lochmann chose to settle in Iași, to marry a Moldavian woman, Catrina, and to build himself a *home* and a life in Moldavia. An important step towards integration in the fabric of Moldavian society may be seen in his naming his children after relatives on their mother's side: Ștefan and Anița were named after his brothers-in-law, but the others—Petru, Ioan, Maria, Zmaranda, and Anton—were given names that seem more Moldavian than Bohemian in origin. For more details, see Sorin Grigoruţă, *Boli, epidemii şi asistenţă medicală* (Iaşi: 2017), 112–121.

76 They are not mentioned in Anne Mezin's list. But since one of the sons bears the name of his father, Georges Mathieu, it is clear that there has been a confusion.

77 Filitti, *Lettres*, 384–385.

78 Filitti, *Lettres*, 388, Racoviţă to Vergennes, Iaşi, 13/24 April 1756.

79 Filitti, *Lettres*, 432–433, Iaşi, 24 July/4 August 1755, Mathieu Ghika to Vergennes.

in Moldavia. In his short Moldavian reign, Scarlat Ghica (1757–1758) offered him the office of grand *paharnic*, but Jean Mille continued hold the office of *staroste* of Cernăuţi and to serve as a diplomatic agent.[80] In this capacity, he played an important role in the mediation of the conflict between Poland and the Crimean Khanate (1763), and his diplomatic ability was much appreciated and praised.[81]

Settling in Moldavia, Jean Mille married Safta, the daughter of Andrei Rosetti and Maria (née Sturza).[82] Through this matrimonial strategy, he became related to two of the leading boyar families of Moldavia: the Rosettis and the Sturzas. Both his father-in-law, Andrei Rosetti, and his wife's grandfather, Sandu Sturza, were in the forefront of Moldavian politics, holding important offices in the princely divan.[83] But above all, these boyars had great wealth and were part of a network of relations that connected the leading families of Moldavia among themselves.[84] The basis of Mille's Moldavian life was established by the considerable dowry that he received on his marriage to Safta: this enabled him to enter the ranks of the Moldavian elite, to buy properties and then to claim access to prestigious and lucrative administrative offices. Of course the assistance of his two patrons—the Ghica family and the French ambassador—was essential. But such assistance was equally manifest in the case of François-Thomas Linchou, who did not have the same success. Under the protection of the Ghica family, princely secretary Jean Mille became Moldavian boyar Enacache Millo. This was how Ruggiero Giuseppe Boscovich found him in 1762 when he returned from Istanbul in the company of British ambassador James Porter.[85] Enache (or Enacache) Millo told the Ragusan Boscovich that his sister was married to 'Signor Cingria of Ragusa', a rich merchant in Constantinople.[86] Boscovich discovered that 'the Greek boyar by birth' had 'French origins', being named Mille, and that 'he knows well the Italian language and the French.'

80 Filitti, *Lettres*, 436.

81 Pierre–Michel Hennin to Grigore Callimachi, Warsaw, 30 April 1763 and 30 June 1763, in Pippidi, *Documente*, 250–255. For this episode see Dariusz Kołodziejczyk, *The Crimean Khanate and Poland-Lithuania* (Leiden: 2011), 205.

82 Mihai-Bogdan Atanasiu, *Din lumea cronicarului Ion Neculce. Studiu prosopografic* (Iaşi: 2015), 500.

83 Atanasiu, *Din lumea cronicarului Ion Neculce*, 82.

84 See also Elena Bedreag, 'Descendenţa şi averea marelui vornic Iordache Ruset', in Dan Dumitru Iacob (ed.), *Avere, prestigiu şi cultură materială în surse patrimoniale. Inventare de averi din secolele XVI–XIX*, Iaşi, Editura Universităţii 'Alexandru Ioan Cuza', 2015, 157–203.

85 For the passage of the British ambassador, see also the letters of La Roche to Giuliani, 21 June 1762 and 28 June 1762, Iorga, *Documente Callimachi*, II, 288–289.

86 Boscovich, *Giornale*, 151.

His marriage to 'a wealthy heiress' had brought him 'much wealth' and 'great influence with the princes.'[87] Having become a 'Greek boyar', Mille constructed an important career as an office-holder; he was rewarded with the office of grand *spătar* after a successful mission to Poland,[88] and then rose step by step to that of grand *ban*.[89] His offspring married into the local boyar class, thus consolidating connections with the local network and gradually distancing themselves from their French origin.

When Matei Millo (1814–1896) dedicated himself to acting, the family were against his decision, considering that it did not befit the 'boyar' origins of the Milles.[90] After just two generations and a succession of alliances within the Moldavian boyar class, the members of the Mille (Millo) family believed themselves to be long-established boyars. It was thus easier for them to find Matei, who had studied dramatic art in Paris (1840–1845), a post as 'artistic director' at the newly-founded National Theatre in Iași (15 February 1846) than to agree to his following a profession that was not compatible with noble standards.[91]

Jean Mille had managed to penetrate the social fabric of the country that had received him, adopting the identity of a Moldavian boyar. Of course we must also take into account the ability of this Frenchman to act in tenacious pursuit of his own interests. Marriage into the ranks of the local elite was an essential step in the fashioning of a new belonging and identity. I have not found any record of Enacache Millo's conversion to Orthodoxy, but it may be presumed that he took this step too. I believe that his successful integration in the ranks of the local elite would have been greatly facilitated by his embracing the faith of the majority.

From Secretary to Consul

The post of princely secretary often served as a springboard towards a more important position and as an opportunity to form business relations. For this reason, the secretaries tried to gain their masters' trust as much as possible, proclaiming their subservience and loyalty. While some were interested in

87 Boscovich, *Giornale*, 127.

88 Iorga, *Documente Callimachi*, II, Mille to Giuliani, 26 August/6 September 1763.

89 Ioan Caproşu (ed.), *Documente privitoare la istoria oraşului Iaşi* (Iaşi: 2005), VI, 441, document of April 1763, in which Enacache Millo is grand *ban* in the divan of Grigore Callimachi.

90 Matei Millo was the son of Vasile Millo and Zamfira Prăjescu, and the great-grandson of Enache Millo.

91 Mihai Vasiliu, *Istoria teatrului românesc* (Bucharest: 1971).

adopting a Wallachian or Moldavian identity, others merely used the position to advance their own careers. From secretary to consul (or diplomatic agent) was but a short step; it took only favourable circumstances and active advocacy of the necessity of such a position. François-Thomas Linchou made remarkable and repeated efforts to have a French consulate set up in Iași or Bucharest, underlining how useful the presence of a consul would be for the development of the business activities of the 'French nation' in the Principalities.[92] However political circumstances were not favourable: the Ottoman Empire still had a strong interest in its peripheries, and French merchants could not yet see sufficient commercial openings in the Principalities for them to support his project.[93] On the other hand, it can be plausibly argued that the French secretary in the service of the prince represented France's interests in the Principalities sufficiently well for there to be no need of an official institution. For example, Pierre de La Roche was 'unmasked' first by *comis* (master of the horse) Enache Kogălniceanu, who stated that, when La Roche was sent by Prince Grigore Callimachi to Poland, 'he met with the French envoy and what that envoy told him, that he wrote too to the prince that he had heard.'[94] His rival, Stefan Raicevich, accused him of having very close relations with the French ambassador, to whom he never stopped sending reports.[95] The hypothesis is strengthened by the relations of subordination and fidelity described by Alexandre Maurice Blanc de Lanautte, comte d'Hauterive.

92 I reproduce here only one of his numerous interventions in favour of the establishment of a consulate: 'Comme je reconnois une grande utilité qu'il y eut un François établi icy avec titre de Consul, pour que, dans le cas d'un changement de Prince, les affaires puissent avoir leur cours par cette voie, comme à présent, dans l'incertitude que le Prince qui succèderait seroit dans les mêmes dispositions que celuy d'aujourd'hui … Sur quoy j'auray l'honneur de dire à Votre Excellence, que pour peu que ce Consul sceut se ménager icy les bonnes grâces du Prince résignant, il auroit la même facilité qui existe à présent, tant de donner les nouvelles au Prince, que de faire passer les expéditions avec la même sureté et facilité que nous faisons passer aujourd'hui: outre qu'il pourroit entretenir la Cour de Jassy dans des bonnes dispositions'. F. Linchou à Vergennes, Jassy, 19/30 August 1756, Filitti, *Lettres*, 192–193.

93 For the activity of the French consuls and their utility in defending and protecting the interests of French merchants, see Arnaud Bartolomei, Guillaume Calafat, Mathieu Grenet et Jörg Ulbert (eds.), *De l'utilité commercial des consuls. L'institution consulaire et les marchands dans le monde méditerranéen* (*XVII*^{e}*–XX*^{e} *siècle*) (Rome-Madrid: 2017), https://books.openedition.org/efr/3293 [accessed 20.05.2020]. See also the special issue, 'De l'intérêt d'être consul en Méditerranée, XVIIe–XXe siècle', Silvia Marzagalli and Jörg Ulbert (eds), in *Cahiers de la Méditerranées*, 98 (2019).

94 Kogălniceanu, *Letopisețul*, 129.

95 Hurmuzaki, *Documente*, XIX/1, 81, Raicevich to Kauniz, 22 November 1782.

D'Hauterive began his career in 1784 as librarian of the French embassy in Constantinople, under the protection of the new ambassador Marie-Gabriel-Florent-August de Choiseul-Gouffier.[96] When Alexandru Mavrocordat-Firaris became prince of Moldavia (1785–1786), d'Hauterive was recommended for the position of first secretary. After being instructed by the ambassador, and before leaving for Iași, d'Hauterive wrote to Charles Gravier de Vergennes, the French Secretary for Foreign Affairs, assuring him that he would 'remain the king's most zealous servant' and that he would spare no effort to obey 'orders received'. Among other things, he was instructed to be attentive to 'anything that seemed to him useful,' and, using a cipher, to communicate it either to the ambassador or directly to the secretary of state.[97] The loyalty of these secretaries was rewarded by France with substantial pensions in recognition of the services they rendered.[98] In other words, the French secretaries in the service of the princes seem to have substituted in the role of consul, leading to a lack of interest in officially establishing a consulate.

The peace treaty of Küçük Kaynarca (1774) opened new opportunities for those with ambitions in politics by giving Russia the right to set up consulates throughout the territory of the Ottoman Empire. The opening of the Black Sea to commercial navigation under the same treaty was another circumstance favourable to the establishment of consulates in the Principalities, and contributed to a growth in commercial interest in the Black Sea.[99] The first Russian consul, Serghei Lazarevici Laskarev, was sent to Bucharest in 1782,[100] enabling Russia to increase its influence over the Principalities.[101] The arrival of Laskarev in Bucharest provided a good occasion for Stefan Raicevich to bring up the

96 This is how he appears in the report of Consul König of 3 May 1785, Hurmuzaki, *Documente*, X, 21.

97 See d'Hauterive's letter to Vergennes, Constantinople, 10 February 1785, in Vasile Mihordea, 'De Hauterive, secretar domnesc în Moldova (1785)', *Revista Istorică*, 1–3 (1935), 40.

98 Alexandre-Maurice d'Hauterive received a salary of 1,200 de livres per annum, while Pierre de la Roche was rewarded with a pension of 4,000 livres per annum (Mihordea, 'De Hauterive, secretar domnesc', 38, 41). Daniel Fonseca was paid 2,000 livres per annum by France and received a similar income from the Mavrocordats. See Villeneuve's letter to Maurepas, Constantinople, 16 November 1730, in Mihordea, *Un agent*, 128 and Hurmuzaki, *Documente*, I_1, 459.

99 For the issue of the Black Sea, see Constantin Ardeleanu, 'The Opening and Development of the Black Sea for International Trade and Shipping (1774–1853)', *Euxeinos*, 14 (2014), 30–52; Constantin Ardeleanu, *The European Commission of the Danube, 1856–1948. An Experiment in International Administration* (Leiden: 2020).

100 Stela Mărieş, *Supuşii străini*, 30–39.

101 Victor Taki, *Limits of Protection: Russia and the Orthodox Coreligionists in the Ottoman Empire* (Pittsburgh: 2015), 1–79; Roderic H. Davison, 'Russian skill and Turkish imbecility': The Treaty of Kuchuk Kainardji reconsidered', *Slavic Review*, 35, 3 (1976), 463–483.

subject of the usefulness of a consulate to defend the economic and commercial interests of the Habsburgs. Apart from his obvious personal ambition, Raicevich was trying to find a new position for himself, as the abdication of Prince Alexandru Ipsilanti had left him without his post of secretary, in which capacity he had served from 1774 to 1782. Appointed secretary for Frankish languages, he had gradually won the prince's trust and had become involved in the education of his offspring, thus eliminating Domenico Sestini and Franz Joseph Sulzer, who had applied for a similar position. When he was sent to Vienna to bring back his master's sons, Raicevich used the opportunity to promote himself and advance his interests. He asked Chancellor Wenzel Anton von Kaunitz to open a consulate in Bucharest, with himself as first consul. Sulzer had done the same, writing a paper on the subject in the hope that he would be rewarded by Vienna with a consul's post in Bucharest.[102] However, where Sulzer had failed, Raicevich succeeded. He was an Ottoman subject (born in Ragusa in 1739), but that did not stop him actively arguing for the setting up of an Austrian consulate in Bucharest, speculating on the favourable international circumstances.[103] Described by his contemporaries as ambitious and very arrogant,[104] Raicevich tenaciously constructed the position he so much

102 Writing in German, Sulzer argued for the necessity of protecting the commercial activities that had been developed on the territory of the Principalities by the foundation of a consulate to defend and protect the rights of subjects of the Habsburg Empire. Sulzer proposed himself as the most suitable person for the position on the basis of the relations that he had succeeded in establishing in the Principalities and the knowledge he had accumulated over the years. Franz Joseph Sulzer, *Geschichte des transalpinischen Daciens, das ist der Walachey, Moldau und Bessarabiens. Im Zusammenhange mit der Geschichte des übrigen Daciens als ein Versuch einer allgemeinen dacischen Geschichte mit kritischer Freyheit entworfen*, vol. 3 (Vienna: 1781). See also *Călători străini despre ţările române*, eds. Maria Holban, Maria Magdalena Alexandrescu-Dersca Bulgaru, Paul Cernovodeanu (Bucharest: 2000), X/1, 460–461.

103 For the Ragusans and their involvement in commercial and diplomatic activity in the Principalities, see Andrei Pippidi, *Rapports de Raguse avec les pays roumains*, in idem, *Hommes* 65–124. For the development of diplomatic relations between the Habsburgs and the Ottomans, see David do Paço, 'Une collaboration économique et sociale: consuls et protecteurs des marchands ottomans à Vienne et à Trieste au XVIIIe siècle', *Cahiers de la Méditerranées*, 98 (2019), 57–74.

104 Jeremy Bentham met him in Bucharest and appreciated him for his knowledge but also wrote acidly of his desire to be held in honour by others: 'His good qualities are tinctured with a certain hauteur which might be spared ... Some have accordingly given him the name of *Joseph 3rd* and in consideration of his method of treating the Transylvanians that depend on him, the Agent *Coups de Baton*. By his own account you would suppose the reverse to be the case; to reconcile the two, conceive him fond of governing and making liberal use of both engines, at least as to the exterior, as I can testify.' E.D. Tappe, 'Bentham in Wallachia and Moldavia', 69.

desired, striving to make himself as useful as possible to Chancellor Kaunitz and Vice-Chancellor Philipp von Cobenzl, not only by drafting detailed reports, but also by showing a real interest in protecting Austrian business and Austrian merchants in the Principalities. For all this, he was rewarded merely with the position of imperial agent on 30 September 1783, only to be removed from the post in February 1786 precisely because of his boundless ambition, expressed in exaggerated pomp. It was his successor, Franz Leopold von Metzburg, who would be directly appointed imperial consul in 1786.[105] The appointment by the Habsburg Empire of an imperial agent or secretary, as they are termed in the diplomatic correspondence, spurred Prussia's desire to intervene and to counter the influence of its rivals—Russia and the Habsburg Empire—by appointing a consul in 1784, in the person of Ernest Frederick König.[106] He too had started out in the position of secretary and Latin teacher to the princely offspring, as Raicevich himself wrote in a report to Chancellor Kaunitz.[107] The information was intended to underline yet again the necessity of confirming him as consul and not merely consular agent. France and Britain were slower to follow the example of Russia, the Habsburg Monarchy, and Prussia, and did not recruit from the ranks of the princely secretaries. Constantin Stamati, the first French consul, though educated in Paris, was Greek and an Ottoman subject, and as such he was rejected by the Ottoman Empire immediately after his appointment in 1795,[108] while Britain appointed no consul until 1803, and then only in order to avoid being left out of the political and diplomatic games of the period.[109]

105 For Stefan Raicevich, see Cristian Luca, 'Il raguseo Stefano Ignatz Raicevich, diplomatico dell'impero e promotore del progetto di espansione Asburgica alla foce del Danubio', *Annuario dell'Istituto Romeno di Cultura e Ricerca Umanistica di Venezia, XII–XIII, 2010–2011* (Bucharest: 2015), 157–169; Stela Mărieş, 'Activitatea lui Ignaţiu Ştefan Raicevich, primul consul al Austriei în Ţările Române (1782–1786)', *Cercetări Istorice*, VI (1975), 123–140.

106 On the appointment of König, see the patents issued by Frederick II and the correspondence in ANIC, Microfilme RDG, Rola 46, c. 4–29, August–November 1784.

107 Hurmuzaki, *Documente*, XIX/1, 227, 14 December 1784, Iaşi.

108 Constantin Stamati would be replaced by Emile Claude Gaudin, secretary of the French Embassy to the Porte. Hurmuzaki, *Documente*, Supliment I_2, 112–115.

109 Paul Cernovodeanu, 'Înfiinţarea consulatului englez în Ţările Române (1803) şi activitatea sa până la 1807', *Revista română de studii internaţionale*, V, 1 (1971), 139–162.

Cultural Intermediaries and Knowledge Transfer

The world of the secretaries was a melting pot where knowledge of all sorts could be transmitted in all directions: orientalists, numismatists, archaeologists, botanists, poets, and historians could be found working as secretaries, teachers, physicians, and sometimes even merchants in order to maintain themselves while dedicating themselves to scholarship. Through their correspondence, travel journals, and books we may form a picture of the diverse knowledge that circulated from one to another and then to the patrons they served, to the offspring of those patrons, and to the local elites. The secretaries' correspondence reveals the transfer of knowledge in the fields of geography, history, literature, architecture, and even gastronomy. Together with knowledge, objects also circulated. From one part of the empires to another, there was a movement of papers, books, gazettes, antiquities, scientific knowledge, scientific apparatus, recipients for various experiments, kitchen utensils, fashions, and tastes.

I shall make use of several examples to underline the mobility of knowledge and objects across empires. Secretary Pierre de La Roche was the intermediary through whom a camera obscura was procured for Prince Grigore Callimachi (1761–1764). He wrote in this connection to his friend, marquis Francesco Crescenzo Giuliani, who had returned a few months before to Warsaw after spending years in the Ottoman Empire. As the prince wanted 'une chambre obscure pour son amussament,' he mandated La Roche to write and ask Giuliani 'if it would be possible for the components to be found that would enable him to make one.' And he enumerated those components: 'the two mirrors and the optical glass which together serve to bring the objects outside into the camera obscura,'[110] with the 'glasses' required to be 'so perfect in their structure that they may represent the exterior objects naturally and in their true colours.'[111] The business of the camera obscura features in a number of letters over a period of months. On 3 March 1762, in a reply to Giuliani, La Roche expresses surprise that details have been given about the object but not about the price, and he asks insistently for at least an approximate figure.[112] When the camera obscura set out on its journey to Moldavia, both the prince and his secretary were quick to write to Giuliani, thanking him and

---

110 'les deux miroirs et le verre d'optique, qui servent ensemble à porter dans la chamber obscure les objets du déhors.'

111 'si parfaits dans leur structure, qu'ils réprésentassent au natural et avec leurs veritables couleurs les objets exterieurs.' Iorga, *Documente Callimachi*, II, 271, La Roche to Giuliani, Iaşi, 18 January 1762.

112 Iorga, *Documente Callimachi*, II, 276.

giving him five pieces of cloth for his efforts.[113] But the story of the camera obscura did not stop here. It arrived in Iași with some damage due to the poor roads. On 6 July 1762, Grigore Callimachi took advantage of the presence in the city of the scholar Ruggiero Giuseppe Boscovich to ask him for details about the use of the camera. Armed with other instruments ('a telescope three feet long, after Dollond's new invention' and three small prisms), used to study the planet Venus and 'sunspots and eclipses,' Boscovich gave an astronomy lesson in the prince's cabinet. Present were Pierre de La Roche, an unnamed boyar who spoke good Italian and French, and the prince's brother, Ioan Callimachi, all of them curious 'to see how all these instruments are used.' In particular, Boscovich spoke about the transit of Venus, which was the subject that most preoccupied the scientific world that year. His interlocutors seem to have had some grounding in the field, and they showed an ability to handle the instruments he presented and to maintain conversation on the topic which led him to exclaim, 'We all felt as among friends.'[114] Astronomy was one of the sciences in fashion at the time, a passion of crowned heads as well as scholars. At the Princely Academy in Iași, for example, three years later, in 1765, Iosipos Moisiodax was teaching the subject, following the theories of Galileo Galilei and Isaac Newton, of whom he was a follower.[115]

Francesco Giuliani, who had dealt with the procurement of the camera obscura, was himself a 'savant italien', as the French translator of Domenico Sestini's letters describes him. Giuliani had spent the greater part of his life in the Levant, where he had held the post of dragoman. He had made use of his experiences to write a multi-volume history of the Ottoman Empire, though this had not enjoyed the success he had hoped for.[116]

On 13 September 1762, Pierre de La Roche had another request: '15 geographical maps, the largest, the most exact, and the most recent,' printed on 'good paper,' 'luminous and distinct,' and to be made up of 'three world maps, three

---

113 Iorga, *Documente Callimachi*, II, 280. Grigore Callimachi to Giuliani, Iaşi, 1 April 1762: 'Veuillez bien agréer, Mr., comme un gage de mon souvenir, ces cinq pieces d'etoffe de nos contrées, que je vous envoye, en attendant quelque autre chose qui merite d'avantage votre attention'. See also La Roche to Giuliani, 10 May 1762 (ibid., 283).

114 Boscovich, *Giornale*, 136–137.

115 Kitromilides, *The Enlightenment as Social Criticism*, 1992, 144–145; Andrei Pippidi, 'L'accueil de la philosophie française du XVIIIe siècle dans les Principautés Roumaines', in Andrei Pippidi. *Byzantins, Ottomans, Roumains. Le Sud-Est Européen entre l'héritage impérial et les influences occidentales* (Paris: 2006), 295–296.

116 Sestini, *Lettres*, 398–399. For Giuliani's works, see Klaus Tuchelt (ed.), *Türkische Gewänder und Osmanische Gesellschaft im achtzehnten Jahrhundert: Facsimile-Ausgabe des Codex 'Les portraits des differens habillemens qui sont en usage à Constantinople et dans tout la Turquie' aus dem Besitz des Deutschen Archäologischen Institutes in Istanbul* (Graz: 1966).

Asias, three Europes, three Africas and three Americas.'[117] Ioan Callimachi, the brother of prince Grigore Callimachi, also made use of La Roche to procure either *Diarum Europaeum* or the *Encyclopédie*.[118] (The work of Jacques Hommey, *Diarum* was described as 'a compilation of gazettes concerning what happened at the beginning of the eighteenth century.'[119]) In an age of enthusiasm for numismatics, Jean Mille helped Pierre-Michel Hennin, the French resident in Warsaw, to obtain ancient coins. In exchange, Hennin, who is best known today for his correspondence with Voltaire, gave Mille encouragement and advice regarding the making of a map of Moldavia.[120] It should be added that once settled in Moldavia and established as the boyar Enacache Millo, the same Jean Mille took an interest in the archaeology of his adoptive homeland, scouring the country in search of antiquities and studying old chronicles.[121]

The secretaries drew on a wide range of knowledge, transmitted by way of correspondence and through journeys to different regions of the empires. At the same time, they put into circulation goods and objects of knowledge: books, maps, scientific instruments. Constantin Mavrocordat made use of his secretaries, and also of the French ambassadors to the Porte, to procure the books he needed directly from Paris.[122] Books were traded like any other item, holding commercial value for merchants and intellectual value only for princely and other customers interested in literary and scholarly matters. Seekers of rare books or manuscripts wandered the roads of empires in the hope of spectacular discoveries.[123] In this context, libraries prove to have been one of the destinations visited by curious travellers, who would rummage through shelves and chests and express their satisfaction or disappointment at the 'goods' they discovered.

---

117 Iorga, *Documente Callimachi*, II, 299.

118 Iorga, *Documente Callimachi*, 301, 303.

119 *Nouveau dictionnaire historique, ou histoire abregée de tous les Hommes qui se sont fait un nom par des Talens, des Vertus, des Forfaits, des Erreurs* (Caen: 1786), IV, 448.

120 Hennnin to Mille, 22 September 1763, Warsaw. Pippidi, *Documente*, 258. For Pierre-Michel Hennin, see the special issue 'Dialogisme culturel européen au siècle des Lumières. Relations épistolaires de P.M. Hennin avec M.P.G. Chabanon, J.B. de la Borde et F. Tronchin', *Musicorum*, 13 (2012).

121 Boscovich, *Giornale*, 151.

122 Vasile Mihordea, 'Biblioteca domnească a Mavrocordaţilor', *Analele Academiei Române. Memoriile Secţiunii Istorice*, XXXII, 16 (1940), 359–371.

123 For the circulation of books in the Ottoman context, with particular attention given to the Mavrocordats, see Radu G. Păun, 'Réseaux de livres et réseaux de pouvoirs dans le sud-est de l' Europe: le monde des dragomans (XVIIe–XVIIIe siècles)', in Frédéric Barbier, Istaván Monok (eds.), *Contribution à l' histoire de l' Europe: réseaux du livre, réseaux des lectures* (Budapest: 2008), 63–107.

Before taking up their posts, secretaries did their homework. They collected information from a variety of works that circulated in the academic milieu to which they belonged. From the memoirs, journals, and letters in which they recounted their Wallachian and Moldavian experiences, we may get a glimpse of what they read. Among the works mentioned are Dimitrie Cantemir's *Description of Moldavia* and *History of the Ottoman Empire*.[124] Domenico Sestini, for example, cites Cantemir's *History* when he tries to give historical significance (and authority) to his discoveries of archaeological sites in his travels.[125] Sestini is not alone in using scholarly works published in the period as a primary and reliable source of information. Other likewise took their inspiration from Cantemir, but also from other texts of the time, sometimes repeating their errors and omissions as the travel narrative became a highly appreciated literary genre.[126] At times, secretaries engaged in polemics on historical themes, citing and criticizing one another. The work of Jean-Louis Carra (1742–1793) aroused heated discussion at the time, influencing the style and writing of his contemporaries Sulzer and Raicevich.[127] Carra was princely secretary to Grigore Ghica III, prince of Moldavia (1764–1767, 1774–1777) and of Wallachia (1768–1769), who ended up decapitated on the sultan's orders in 1777, the year in which his secretary published in Bouillon his *Histoire de la Moldavie et de la Valachie*. Carra himself was to meet the same fate as his patron, though in quite different circumstances, as a victim of the turmoil of the French Revolution.[128]

At the same time, the works of these secretaries, doctors, and teachers fashioned the image of Wallachia and Moldavia in Europe. Through their writings, they offered information to all those who passed through the Principalities on their way to Constantinople. Apart from diffusing information of practical utility, some of them insisted on historical, economic, and social details, arousing the interest of a public attracted by adventure or by business opportunities. Carrying out their activity around the princely courts, the secretaries were

124 For Cantemir, see Ovidiu-Victor Olar, 'Dimitrie Cantemir', in David Thomas and John Chesworth (eds.), *Christian-Muslim Relations. A Bibliographical History*, vol. 14. Central and Eastern Europe (1700–1800) (Leiden: 2020), 304–322.

125 Sestini, *Lettres*, 70–71.

126 On travellers and the pitfalls of their texts, see Wendy Bracewell, 'Arguing from Experience: Travelees versus Travellers in Early Modern Exchanges', *Renaissance Studies*, 33, 4 (2019) 548–567.

127 For the Carra, Sulzer, Raicevich polemic, see Alex Drace-Francis, '"Like a member of a free nation, he spoke without shame": foreign travellers as a trope in Romanian cultural tradition', in Corinne Fowler, Charles Forsdick and Ludmila. Kostova (eds.), *Travel and ethics: theory and practice* (New York: 2021), 183–203.

128 See Ştefan Lemny, *Jean-Louis Carra (1742–1793). Parcours d'un révolutionnaire* (Paris: 2000).

direct participants in the political life of the Principalities, which they tried to place in a historical and geographical context, collecting historical information and informing themselves about the past. The presence of these secretaries at the princely courts transformed Bucharest and Iași into centres of interaction, of cultural transfer, in which different ideas and cultures met. Given that boyars did not travel to the West for fear of being punished by the Porte, it was the secretaries who provided them with information about events in Europe, about fashions and scientific knowledge. It was they too who took charge of the education of the young and their training in the spirit of eighteenth-century values. Of course their contribution was on a small scale, but it laid the foundation of practices that would become more evident in the early nineteenth century.

The Adventure and Danger of the Foreign

The fate of these princely secretaries was closely bound to that of their patrons. Few of them managed to remain in the job after the removal from office of the prince who employed them, and even fewer passed from one prince to another. Normally the deposition of the Phanariot prince meant the end of the secretary's post: some chose to accompany their employer back to Constantinople, as was the case of François-Thomas Linchou, who remained each time with his patron, Constantin Racoviță, now in Moldavia, now in Istanbul, now in Wallachia.[129] The fall of the patron into disgrace threw a shadow of doubt over the activity of the camarilla around him. As secretaries were part of this entourage, they shared their patron's fate. When prince Grigore Callimachi (1767–1769) was arrested on the sultan's orders, so was his secretary, Pietro Nagni.[130] The pressure was considerable, and the threat of Turkish invasion

129 Compare the fate of the physician and diplomatic agent Fotache, in the entourage of Constantin Mavrocordat, who was imprisoned in Istanbul when his master was deposed. Sorin Grigoruţă, 'Aspecte din viaţa şi activitatea unui doctor de la curtea lui Grigore al III-lea Ghica. Doctorul Fotache', *Anuarul Institutului de Istorie 'A.D. Xenopol'*, LI (2014), 81–91.

130 Iorga, *Documente Callimachi*, II, 383–384, the report to Everhardt, 3 July 1769. From the same report, we learn that Grigore Callimachi was to be decapitated on 9 September 1769. It is not recorded whether Nagni was punished. Later, Nagni took the place of Pierre de La Roche, in Moldavia. La Roche had left for the Hague to be treated for a medical problem and had remained in Warsaw as diplomatic agent for the same prince.

and the permanent fear of deposition led some to give up before completing their contracts. This was the case of Lionardo Panzini, employed by Alexandru Ipsilanti (1774–1782) as teacher of Italian to his sons Constantin and Dimitrie. Panzini left Wallachia after two years, scared by the rumour that the prince was about to be deposed.[131] Others fell victim to the intrigues of the princely court, in which they had become caught up. Such was the fate of the Italian physician Giuseppe Antonio Pisani, who arrived at the court in Iași in the summer of 1751, called to attend to the prince's wife, Sultana Racoviță. In December 1752, the patient's condition deteriorated, and she died. Pisani found himself thrown into the middle of the rivalries at the court between various favourites of the prince. Before long, the doctor was accused of poisoning Lady Sultana and was thrown into prison. The French secretary, François-Thomas Linchou, who had arranged Pisani's employment, fell into disgrace and was marginalized for a time. The historian of the times notes, 'They say this Frenchman was the occasion of the death of the prince's wife in his first reign, with a doctor whom he had brought and had introduced to the court, giving him praise for his learning.'[132] Once back in favour with the prince, Linchou asked Count Heinrich von Brühl, who was close to Augustus III of Poland, to intervene to save Pisani.[133] Another intervention in favour of the doctor, who was kept in irons by Racoviță, came from the French ambassador, Des Alleurs, who indicated that he was willing to employ him as his personal physician. Pisani's fate is lost in the diplomatic correspondence between Istanbul, Bucharest, and Warsaw, leaving it uncertain whether Racoviță released him as he claimed. He was not alone in finding himself in such a situation. Being both physician and diplomatic agent at the same time put one in a somewhat dangerous position because of the double distrust that could accumulate. Both roles involved handling information that was inaccessible to others and working with intimate secrets. Suspicions became acute in the presence of doctors, and death was closer than glory.[134]

131 *Călători străini despre țările române*, eds. Maria Holban, Maria Matilda Alexandrescu-Dersca Bulgaru, Paul Cernovodeanu, Ion Totoiu (Bucharest: 2000), vol. X/1, 210–226.

132 Kogălniceanu, *Letopisețul*, 72–73.

133 Vasile Mihordea, 'Giuseppe-Antonio Pisani, medicul lui Constantin Racoviţă', *Revista Istorică*, 22, 7–9 (1936), 247, annexes I and II, Linchou to Giuliani, Iaşi, 14/25 May 1753, Linchou to Bianconi, Bucharest, 25 August/5 September 1753.

134 Compare the harsh fate of Toma Testabuza, who served the Phanariot prince Grigore Ghica as physician and diplomatic agent, as described not only by the chronicles of the time, but in internal documents: 'We also inform you that His Highness Grigorie vodă being deposed, and there being in His Highness's service one Toma Tesabuza the physician, he came here for a few days, and he being under the emperor's suspicion, we found

Disputes between secretaries and their masters arose quite frequently, and patrons were called on to mediate and arbitrate. On 22 February 1782, Etienne Ménard complained to the French ambassador, Saint-Priest, that his master, Alexandru Ipsilanti, whom he had 'served for five years,' had thrown him in prison when he was preparing to leave for Istanbul. The prince, who had just been removed from office, claimed that this was at the ambassador's request. From prison, Ménard appealed to his protector, emphasizing that 'he had had nothing to be reproached for either in France, or in Constantinople, or in Wallachia.' On the contrary, Ipsilanti had not given him his pay for the last three months and owed him 300 piastres. And now, when he had found another post, in the service of M. Cullely in Constantinople, he was prevented from leaving.[135] The bond between master and servant was dissolved by the failure to respect contractual obligations, and the protector intervened to protect his client and to attenuate dissensions within the network.[136]

Along the roads of the empires, we find many other individuals who had set out in search of fortune and adventure. It was said of the physician Bertin that he returned from Wallachia rich; the same was said of Raicevich[137]. Such rumours fed the ambitions and dreams of adventurers drawn to the Orient in search of easy enrichment. The diplomatic correspondence makes frequent reference to these people caught between empires, asking for help or, on the contrary, denying their own identity and claiming imagined identities. Without a network and group solidarity, it was hard to gain access to the riches of the East.

ourselves with two of the emperor's men and a strong command for us, wherever he might be to hand them over to his envoys, to do as they had been commanded. And so, we handed him over, and immediately they took him down to the princely garden, to the pavilion, and there they cut off his head, skinned it according to their custom, and took it to carry to the Porte. For which we inform you too of this situation, that you may know how it happened.' Letter of Captain Radu Pravat to the grand *ban* Manolache Lambrino, Bucharest, October 1741. The document is preserved in the archives of the Museum of the Municipality of Bucharest, inv. 25159. A similar fate befell another doctor, Fotache, who was accused of contributing to the assassination of Grigore Ghica III by having an understanding with the Turkish envoy sent to kill him. See Sorin Grigoruţă, 'Doctorul Fotache', 81–91.

135 Filitti, *Lettres*, 526–527, 22 February 1782, Etienne Ménard to Saint-Priest.

136 See Saint-Priest's letter to Ipsilanti in Ménard's favour, Constantinople, 4 March 1782, Filitti, *Lettres*, 242–243.

137 Mihordea, "Un medic frances la curtea lui Constantin-vodă Mavrocordat", 139–155.

Secretaries and Boyars: Foreigners and Their Reception

On 22 May 1835, Ioan Lochmann received a sort of diploma of social recognition on the part of the metropolitan of Moldavia and the leading boyars of the country. The document described the faithful service rendered to Moldavia by the surgeon and diplomatic agent Johann Benedict Lochmann. His son, Ioan, born on Moldavian soil to such a noble and worthy father, had shown himself worthy in his turn, struggling with plague and cholera, keeping his apothecary's shop open and helping all the sick, not for his own interests (*'mijlocire de alijveriş'*) but as a duty to his country (*'însărcinare pământească'*).[138] A striking aspect of the document is the discrepancy between the modesty of its content and its grandeur of its authentication. The text is written on paper, with no sophisticated introduction, no ornamentation in cinnabar or highlighting of particular words. And yet it is authenticated with seventeen seals in red wax (two of which have fallen off). Beside each seal is the signature of a boyar, a holder of high office in the government of the country, starting with the metropolitan of Moldavia, Veniamin Costache. I believe the purpose of the document is to grant social recognition to the apothecary of Iași, whose papers had been destroyed in the great fire that devoured the Moldavian capital in 1827.[139] The boyars were testifying that Ioan Lochmann had become 'noble' and naturalized not by holding a high office, but by virtue of his worthiness, of his recognition and acceptance by those among whom he lived.[140] It is clear that the documents has a great visual impact, and was also conceived to be displayed and pointed out.[141]

Lochmann and Mille began their strategies of integration in approximately the same period: the mid-eighteenth century. Both chose insertion into the Moldavian community by way of marriage to a local spouse. Marriage, followed by integration in a network, helped them to promote themselves and to build a career, a home, a family, a lineage. Social acceptance came at different

138 The document makes reference to the epidemics of plague and cholera in the years 1829–1834.

139 For the fire of June 1827 that caused great damage in Iaşi, see also Postelnicul Manolachi Drăghici, *Istoria Moldovei pe timp de 500 de ani pînă în zilele noastre*, ed. Andrei Pippidi (Bucharest: 2017, 241).

140 SJAN, Iaşi, Documente, 156/71. I am grateful to Sorin Grigoruţă for taking a photograph of the document available to me.

141 I am grateful to Marian Coman for suggestions and discussions regarding this document.

Fig. 1 Diploma of social recognition of Ioan Lochmann apothecary from Iaşi, 22 May 1835, National Romanian Archives, Iaşi. Photograph by Sorin Grigoruţă.

rates and depended on the social networks they managed to access: faster and more easily for Mille, who opted for the path of administrative office, slower for Lochmann, who chose to pursue an independent profession. Having the status of diplomatic agent was an important instrument in penetrating a network and then in building the connections necessary to access social and economic resources.

I have tried in this chapter to reconstruct the networks and relational spaces of the princely secretaries by tracing their individual trajectories and the cultural and historical context in which these developed. The need, characteristic of the eighteenth century, for information and communication opened the way to mobilities: people, objects, ideas, recipes, remedies, albums, gazettes, and books circulated and contributed to the development of a new sort of knowledge. What counted in the selection of these secretaries? Religion, linguistic abilities, patronage or loyalty? Many of the foreign secretaries were French, Italian, Ragusan, German, Greek, or Jewish. Most were Protestant or Catholic, and thus Christian, but that did not make them the same as the Orthodox Phanariots. Religion was an important element in the process of identification, but not so important in the recruitment of a secretary. Linguistic abilities and protection were the fundamental instruments for access to a position in the Phanariot administrative hierarchy.

Nevertheless, conversion might come to serve a pragmatic role in the process of social recognition.[142] Mille and Lochmann sensed this; they married Orthodox women and had their children baptized in the majority faith. Once settled on Moldavian soil, they began to build a home there, developing and pursuing step by step a strategy of integration, copying the model of the host society by investing in properties and administrative offices. This facilitated their integration and acceptance. Other foreigners remained foreign, perceived and described as such for as long as they limited themselves to carrying out their duties, maintaining social distance. We have seen how critical Pierre de La Roche was of the 'Greeks' he served, whom he describes as 'different' in their attitude, religion, and behaviour. The same attitude can be seen in other secretaries who pendulated between two worlds, assuming fluid identities[143] according to the context or their own interests, but taking off the 'mask' when they felt themselves safe and among 'their own'. The Wallachian and Moldavian world in which they lived for a while received them to the extent that they involved themselves in civic life. As skilled competitors in winning favours on the part of the princes, they were looked at askance for their difference, mixing religion, ethnicity, and sometimes profession. Labelled 'papists', 'Franks', 'Germans', 'Italians', 'foreigners', they were judged through the prism of difference, accentuating suspicion, lack of loyalty, parvenu attitude, intrigue. Identified by their language, and not 'by their claimed quality of subjects of the king of France,' they would be accepted to the extent of their involvement in the life of the local community.[144] It was belonging to the local community (by language, marriage, the right to buy property, taxation) that completed the process of integration and acceptance.

---

142 See on this topic Natalie E. Rothman, 'Becoming Venetian: Conversion and Transformation in the Seventeenth-Century Mediterranean', *Mediterranean Historical Review* 21 (2006), 39–75.

143 Cemal Kafadar, *Between Two Worlds* (Berkeley: 1995), 4, 19–21, 26–28, 141.

144 Benjamin Landais, 'Être français dans le Banat du XVIIIe siècle', *Etudes Vauclusiennes*, no. 84, 2019, 50.

CHAPTER 2

Princely Secretary François-Thomas Linchou

'I beg you, my Lord, since this Greek is truly a rascal who is trying to slander my brother, who is a true Frenchman, to obtain from the Porte a counter-*ferman* ordering this Greek to be brought back to Constantinople, where my brother will appear without fail to make known the justice of his cause.'[1] The words are those of François-Thomas Linchou, secretary to the prince of Wallachia, Constantin Racoviţă,[2] and they are addressed to the French ambassador to the Porte, Charles Gravier comte de Vergennes. In 1752, Joseph Linchou, through the Linchou Company, entered into an association with the Greek candle-maker Sterio to set up a candle factory in Iaşi. The Linchou Company brought capital to this venture, while Sterio contributed his experience as a master candle-maker and his connections in the network of Moldavian guilds and in political circles. The venture never came to fruition, but it unleashed a major political, economic, and diplomatic scandal, which was to spread beyond the borders of Moldavia, involving the Ottoman Empire and France. Considerable correspondence was generated around this diplomatic dispute,[3] correspondence that can help us to understand not only the status of foreigners in the Ottoman Principalities but also the manner in which individuals fashioned themselves and others according to their surroundings and immediate interests. Moreover, these insights allow us to see how symbolic or material resources (such as honour, prestige, gifts, and social networks) were handled on multiple social and political fronts in order to negotiate social status or membership within a specific social group.

I am particularly interested in the metamorphoses undergone by the Linchou family in the course of a little over a century (between 1740 and 1850): from Linchou to Lenş and Linche de Moissac, between Marseilles, Istanbul,

1 'Je vous prie, Monseigneur, que, puisque ce Grec est un véritable coquin et qui cherche de faire une avanie à mon frère qui est véritable françois d'obtenir de la Porte un contre-firmanat qui ordonne de ramener ce Grec à Constantinople, où mon frère se rendra sans faute pour faire connoître la justice de sa cause.' in Filitti, *Lettres*, 153, 23 September/4 October 1755.

2 Constantin Racoviţă reigned as prince several times in Moldavia (1749–1753, 1756–1757) and Wallachia (1753–1756, 1763–1764).

3 For earlier comparative studies on transregional dispute/scandal see Tolga U. Esmer, 'Notes on a Scandal: Transregional Networks of Violence, Gossip, and Imperial Sovereignty in the Late Eighteenth-Century Ottoman Empire', *Comparative Studies in Society and History*, 58, 1, (2016), 99–128.

Bucharest, and Paris, from Moorish converts to *true* Frenchmen, from Levantine merchants to Wallachian office-holders, ending up as the French comtes de Moissac. For the purposes of this chapter, however I shall limit myself to the first member of the Linchou family who opens this file of manoeuvring of multiple identities: François-Thomas Linchou.[4]

Pour l'honneur de la nation: From French Linchou to Ottoman Subject

François-Thomas Linchou was born in Marseilles early in the eighteenth century, into a family of French merchants, the son of Maurice Linchou and Catherine Roux, and the brother of Jean-Baptise, Joseph-Marie, and Pierre-François.[5] He arrived in Istanbul around 1739 as representative of the French company Manaire,[6] and was involved there in trade and later in diplomacy on behalf of the French embassy.[7] From this position, he managed to become integrated in the Phanariot network, and became close to the Racoviţă family.[8] As diplomatic agent of Prince Constantin Racoviţă (1699–1764), François-Thomas Linchou carried out intense diplomatic and commercial activity, which is recorded in a rich correspondence. This correspondence reveals his gradual development of relations of friendship and clientelism with

4 See Marian Coman, *François-Thomas Linchou (1720–1760)*, in *Călători străini despre ţările române*, Suplimentul II (Bucharest: 2016), 253–258.

5 Information about this family is offered in M. André Borel D'Hauterive, 'Notice Historique et Genealogique sur la Maison de Linche', *Revue Historique de la Noblesse*, publiée par M. André Borel D'Hauterive, tom II (Paris: 1841), 365–373.

6 AN.AE, Paris, Fond Consulats. Mémoires et Documents. Affaires Etrangères, AE/B/III/253, ff. 3–4. See also the index 'Linchou' elaborated by Anne Mézin. I would like to express my gratitude to her for offering me the unpublished index.

7 See also Christine Vogel, 'The Caftan and the Sword. Dress and Diplomacy in Ottoman–French Relations Around 1700', in *Fashioning the Self in Transcultural Settings: The Uses and Significance of Dress in Self-Narratives*, ed. Claudia Ulbrich and Richard Wittmann (Würzburg: 2015), 25--45; Maurits H. van den Boogert, 'Intermediaries par excellence? Ottoman Dragomans in the Eighteenth Century', in *Hommes de l'entre-deux. Parcours individuals et portraits de groups sur la frontière de la Méditerranée (XVIe–XXe siècle)*, ed. Bernard Heyberger and Chantal Verdeil (Paris: 2009), 95–114.

8 Constantin Racoviţă took refuge in the house of Thomas Linchou in Constantinople when he was pursued by the sultan's men after the deposition and imprisonment of his father Mihai Racoviţă, prince of Wallachia (1741–1744). As a reward for Linchou's assistance, Racoviţă offered him the post of secretary when he received the throne of Moldavia in 1749, and wrote in this connection to Des Alleurs, the French ambassador in Constantinople, whose agreement was necessary. See Mihordea, *Politica orientală franceză*, 174.

different political and commercial circles in Istanbul: the French diplomatic representation and the Phanariot elite. This latter group held important offices at key points in political decision-making: the Ottoman court, the Orthodox Patriarchate, and the Moldavian and Wallachian diplomatic representations in the Ottoman Empire.[9] For each, François-Thomas Linchou offered his services in the procurement of luxury goods: information for everyone, porcelain tableware for the sultan's mother, greyhounds or wine for the French ambassador, greyhounds and thoroughbred horses for diplomats, gold thread for *Madame la Princesse*, gold tobacco cases and perfumed tobacco for the prince, amber for the narghiles of the boyars, among other wares. His position in the service of the prince enabled him to support the cause of the Franciscan missionaries in Moldavia, who wanted to build a church—a position which indeed was also supported by repeated interventions on the part of the French ambassador Des Alleurs[10]—not to mention his most important mission, which is apparent in every letter: to keep the prince on the side of France.

While François-Thomas Linchou remained in this field of diplomacy, the family, through its representation 'Linchou & Compagnie' or 'Linchou père et fils', was pushed forward both for the occupation of 'posts in the Levant'[11] and in Levantine commerce. When his patron, Constantin Racoviţă, became ruler of Moldavia or Wallachia, Linchou went with him as princely secretary, a post which he used to advance his family's position in Balkan commerce and to obtain commercial privileges. Thus, between 1749 and 1758, we find his father and brothers sometimes in Bucharest, sometimes in Iaşi, and sometimes in Galaţi, setting up the first French companies in the Principalities (1753 in Galaţi and 1754 in Bucharest),[12] trading in wax, honey, salted meat, hides, wine and wool, or handling the transit of porcelain, coffee, tobacco, horses, greyhounds, paper, mirrors, and clocks.[13]

9 On this topic see Christine Philliou, *Biography of an Empire: Governing Ottomans in an Age of Revolution* (Berkeley: 2011).

10 See the correspondence between Linchou and Des Alleurs on this subject in the summer of 1751 in Filitti, *Lettres*, 34–42.

11 Filitti, *Lettres*, 82–84: 7/18 December 1752.

12 The (failed) attempt of the Linchou brothers to establish commercial links between France and the Principalities was recorded by Claude-Charles de Peyssonnel, French consul in the Crimea, Cana and Smyrna between 1753 and 1782. In 1758, Peyssonnel visited Moldavia in the company of Pierre-François Linchou. See Claude-Charles de Peyssonnel, *Traité sur le commerce de la Mer Noire* (Paris: 1787), vol. 2, 207–209.

13 'Linchou et fils' were working in Constantinople on 22 May 1750 when Maurice Linchou's involvement was mentioned in a commercial litigation regarding the selling of 36 bal-lots of wool. Balthazard-Marie Emerigon, *Traité des assurances et des contrats à la grosse* (Marseille: 1784), vol. I, 323.

Wax, Honey, and Cattle

Wax, honey, cattle, livestock, butter, and leather were the most sought-after products of Moldavia and Wallachia. For a better understanding of the nature of the business ventures of François-Thomas Linchou and his family, let me introduce at this point some details regarding the economic potential of these territories as presented in various foreign reports and in fiscal documents issued in the course of the eighteenth century.

It was not by chance that the Linchou family turned their attention towards the wax trade. Consular reports and memoranda, to which François-Thomas Linchou had access in his capacity as princely secretary, informed him about the economic potential of the two provinces: 'La Valachie fournit la plus belle cire,' says a memorandum of 1751. The document was compiled at the request of the Levant merchants, as is made explicit from the start, where it is stated that 'La nation française de Constantinople,' wishing to establish commercial links with Moldavia and Wallachia, has gathered 'les informations et les connaissances les plus exactes.' French fabrics ('nos draps londrins seconds'), satin, coffee, sugar, and indigo might be exported to the Principalities. An experiment had even been made which showed that *draps londrins seconds* sold very well. The financial benefits offered by the commercialization of local products are also mentioned: 'la Moldavie fournit la cire, et cette marchandise serait pour les Français le retour le plus avantageux.'[14]

However, it was not only France that showed an interest in the wax trade. As is noted in the memorandum, the Ragusans had for decades been exporting wax through Trieste to Venice.[15] From Venetian diplomatic correspondence of the spring of 1744, we learn of the moment of crisis generated by the rise in price of the wax brought from Wallachia. On 18 March 1744, Wallachian wax is described as 'tanto comune e necessario' in Venice. The quarantine taxes and transit restrictions established by Empress Maria Theresa pushed up the price

14 See the memoirs of 1751, AAE, Paris, Correspondence Politique, Turquie, Suppl. 15, ff. 86, 89. Documents published also in Hurmuzaki (ed.), *Documente* (Bucharest: 1897) I_1, 608–610.

15 A memorandum of 1751, drafted in Constantinople, 'Commerce des Ragusains, Allemands et Polonais', notes that 'Bosnia, Wallachia, and Moldavia are open to the Ragusans who come and buy hides and wax, competing with the Hungarians and the Poles. They then sell cloth from Poland and Leipzig, which is much tougher and less fine than *nos londrins seconds*.' AAE, Correspondence Politique, Turquie, 15, f. 75.

considerably,[16] and attempts were made to find new centres of procurement.[17] However, it was the Ottoman Empire that had the greatest interest in procuring these 'common but necessary' products from Wallachia and Moldavia at the lowest possible prices. The French memorandum mentions that the head of customs ('le Grand douanier') had drafted an order obliging all merchants to sell wax and hides only in Istanbul. The reference is to the *ferman* of Sultan Mahmud I of 30 December 1750/8 January 1751 (1164 evâil-i safer), commanding the Ottoman authorities in Rumelia, Ochakov, and Bender, and the princes of Moldavia and Wallachia to ensure that the merchants of the Porte could procure large quantities of wax, suet, wool, honey, and pastırma from the Principalities. In addition, it forbade sale of cattle, wax, honey, suet, and wool to 'enemy territories,'[18] and includes information about those involved in diverting these important goods towards such territories: 'For some years, some have appeared among the monopolisers, among the Giaours and among the Jews, and they, relying on certain persons and giving them bribes, act in such a way that the merchants of the Porte of my joy, do not get the aforementioned goods, but they themselves buy them and transport them, and sell them in the Hungarian, and German, and Venetian, and Ragusan lands.' The *ferman* enumerates the Armenian, Bosnian, Jewish, Ragusan, and Venetian merchants who, with the complicity of the princes and other office-holders, were procuring the goods mentioned at much higher prices than the Ottoman merchants, and thus were preferred by the producers.[19]

We do not know to what extent the sultan's *ferman* was respected.[20] The French memorandum refers to Ragusan merchants who had managed to

16 After the outbreaks of plague in 1738–1739, which spread from Moldavia and Wallachia into Transylvania, a Sanitary Commission was set up to enforce quarantine measures on the borders. The requirement to spend time in quarantine and to pay a tax led many to find less legal methods of crossing the borders. By the ordinance of 14 January 1744, new measures were taken against those who were undermining the quarantine. At the same time, in order to avoid abuses on the part of customs officers, a single tariff was instituted for the 'disinfection' of the goods that were to pass through quarantine. Ioan Moga, 'Politica economică austriacă şi comerţul Transilvaniei în veacul XVIII', *Anuarul Institutului de Istorie Naţională*, VII (1939), 138–139.

17 See the correspondence between the doge of Venice and Ambassador Contarini at the Porte, with a view either to finding new areas from which to bring salt (Poland, Saxony, and Bohemia are proposed) or ways of having these measures relaxed by making approaches to Count Windischgrätz, the governor of Vienna. Hurmuzaki, *Documente*, 9/1, 685–689.

18 Valeriu Veliman (ed.), *Relaţiile româno–otomane, 1711–1821. Documente turceşti* (Bucharest: 1984), 315–319.

19 Veliman, *Relaţiile româno–otomane*, 318.

20 The princes themselves were involved in this trade, variously taking the side of the Ottoman merchants or of the 'giaours' according to their interests. For example, on

subvert the Porte's command,[21] and it was not only the Ragusans who were involved in undermining the rules: those known as 'Greek merchants' had also managed to get their goods to Trieste and Venice, taking the risk of assuming false identities and other illicit practices.[22]

Documents which have been preserved concerning the activity of the 'Greek' merchant Constantin Malache—successive testaments, dowry contracts, and accounts ledgers—provide an insight into his commercial activities between 1741 and 1770. Foremost among these was trading in wax, which brought him considerable income. Settled initially in Sibiu (Hermannstadt), Constantin Malache then chose Râmnicul Vâlcea as his place of residence and the base of his commercial activities.[23] This Wallachian town had the advantage of being close to Sibiu, and enabled him to gather wax from the surrounding area. His business operated with the help of family members (a brother and an uncle) and through the creation of a network linking Râmnicul Vâlcea to Sibiu, and from there to Trieste and Venice. On 22 February 1750, to make sure that the network was functioning, Constantin Malache left for Venice. On this occasion, fearing lest his 'untimely death' on the long and unfamiliar journey leave his wife and his two children (a son and a daughter) poor and without inheritance, he drew up his first testament. In March of the following year, however, Malache returned from Venice, though he offers no details about his journey there or about his commercial network; in subsequent years, still obsessed with the risk of 'untimely death on the road', Malache drew up further testaments and dowry documents, in which he included information about his business dealings and the goods he had bought on this journey. The wax road went by land on the route: Râmnic–Bran (where there was a

---

15 June 1755, the princely larder bought a considerable quantity of wax from merchants in Moldavia, and then sent it, through the merchant Mustafa Hagi Emir, to the market in Constantinople (BAR, Fond Documente Istorice, XII/34, 35, 36).

21 Hurmuzaki, *Documente*, I/1, 609.

22 On this topic see Daniele Andreozzi, 'Croissance et économie licite, illicit et informelle à Trieste au XVIIIe siècle', in Marguerite Figeac-Monthus, Christophe Lastécouères (eds.), *Territoires de l'illicite et identités portuaires et insulaires. Du XVIe siècle au XXe siècle* (Paris: 2012), 173–188.

23 We know nothing about Constantin Malache's identity. It is possible that he came from the region of Epirus, together with his brother Chirică and his mother, and that he settled first in Sibiu and moved from there to Wallachia. He was merely one link in a vast network of 'Greek' merchants engaged in cross-border trade. See Gheorghe Lazăr, *De la Râmnic la Veneţia şi Sfântul Mormânt. Catastiful negustorului Constantin Malache (secolul al XVIII-lea)*, in Laurenţiu Rădvan (ed.), *Oraşe vechi, oraşe noi în spaţiul românesc. Societate, economie şi civilizaţie urbană în prag de modernitate (sec. XVI-jumătatea sec. XIX)* (Iaşi: 2014), 79–89.

lazaretto)–Sibiu–Trieste–Venice.[24] The wax was transported in barrels or sacks, and stocked in 'bundles', either in its natural state or separated from the honey. In Venice, the trade was controlled by the Greek merchant Duka Tsoukalas (Romanian 'Ţucala'), who sold the wax and then distributed the takings. As well as wax, Constantin Malache developed trade in hides, butter, honey, salt, and morocco leather, which he sent either only as far as Sibiu or further on to Trieste or Graz. When his son, also called Constantin, was older, he sent him with goods 'and to learn' first to Graz and then to Venice.[25] Unfortunately, Constantin Malache gives us no indication as to how he managed to steer his way between Sultan Mahmud's *ferman* and the Transylvanian quarantine.[26]

Wax was one of the most sought-after products, but the Principalities also offered butter, honey, cattle, and hides. Many other reports draw attention to this wealth of resources, which would bring huge profits if the products could be commercialized. It was this prospect that spurred François-Thomas Linchou to venture into the wax trade, while through the trading house he opened in Galați, his family dealt in many other products that were eagerly sought by Ottoman and Ragusan merchants alike.

Claude-Charles de Peysonnel writes in his *Traité sur le commerce de la mer Noire* (1787) that the Linchou brothers had erected in Galați a sort of manufactory for the preservation of ox meat. Large cattle were easy to procure at low prices, and so was salt. As such, the Linchou enterprise sought to develop 'une branche de commerce très importante', which would bring France 'un grand benefice.' The prepared meat was to be either exported to France or sold on the spot to the locals. To this end, the brothers had obtained permission to bring their 'saleurs' (makers of salt-dried meat) from France.[27] This idea of exporting preserved meat was taken up again several decades later by other entrepreneurs,

---

24 To give just two examples of how he records his journey on the wax road in his record book: '7 March 1759: 6,114 *ocas* of wax with all expenses to Bran, in the lazaretto at Bran rent for the sacks, expenses to Trieste,' which brought him an income of 7,359.84 thalers; '24 April 1760: 3,642 *ocas* of wax, 30 sacks, with all expenses to Trieste, 12 lei per sack,' which brought him an income of 5,528.18 thalers. See Gheorghe Lazăr (ed.), *Catastife de negustori din Ţara Românească (secolele XVIII–XIX)* (Iaşi: 2016), 30–32.

25 Lazăr, *Catastife de negustori*, 17–67.

26 Through the commercial Companies in Sibiu and Brașov, many other 'Greek' merchants traded in wax, procuring it from the Principalities to be sold in Trieste, Venice, or Vienna. Dumitru Limona, *Negustorii 'greci' şi arhivele lor comerciale*, ed. Loredana Dascăl (Iaşi: 2016).

27 Peyssonnel, *Traité sur le commerce de la mer Noire*, II, 199.

developing more sophisticated procedures but taking advantage of the same cheap raw materials.[28]

Linchou's Commercial and Diplomatic Dealings

The Linchou family acted on the basis of privileges that they were continually requesting from the prince and from the French ambassador in Constantinople, and François-Thomas Linchou was able to keep these connections active by means of a steady supply of information.[29] Trade in information and goods managed to enrich the Linchou brothers, but it also created a permanent dependence on their Phanariot patron and protector and on his networks. In their commercial dealings, the Linchou brothers succeeded in engaging the interest both of Prince Constantin Racoviţă and of the French ambassador to the Porte, other diplomatic personnel, and the French Levant merchants. The diplomatic correspondence provides information that helps us to reconstruct the numerous connections between the Linchou brothers and other French merchants operating in the Levant, Poland, or the Crimea and sharing the same commercial interests.

Furthermore, the Linchou company chose not become integrated in the Balkan trading network that dominated the trade routes linking the Principalities to the Ottoman Empire, Russia and the Habsburg Monarchy, but to create its own network,[30] thus irritating various social and commercial interests. In this venture, the family banked on their status as 'Frenchmen'.[31]

---

28 Constantin Ardeleanu, 'A British Meat Cannery in Moldavia (1844–1852)', *Slavonic and East European Review*, 90/4 (2012), 671–704.

29 See the Report of the French ambassador Des Alleurs, on January 1754, about the importance of the Principalities for the transit of information between Paris and Constantinople. AAE, Correspondence Politique, Turquie, 127, ff. 22–41.

30 Among other documents, see 'Recommandation pour une maison de commerce à Constantinople à la famille de S. Linchou', written by M. Potocki in Lublin, 2 December 1754, and sent to the French ambassador in Constantinople. AAE, Correspondence Politique, Turquie, 127, f. 356.

31 When he became secretary to prince Constantin Racoviţă, Linchou's 'fidelity' was checked by the French authorities, as from an ordinary French merchant in Constantinople, he had become an important piece in the games of French diplomacy. The secretary of state for Foreign Affairs, Louis Philogène Brûlart, marquis de Puysieulx, asked Vincent de Lusignan, the commissioner for the Navy to check whether or not Linchou was Provençal. The commissioner's reply was that: 'il y a à Marseille une famille de négociants nommée Linchou que je connois. Je crois que le jeune homme qui est auprès de l'hospodar de Moldavie étoit cy devant négociant à Constantinople'. Mihordea, *Politica orientală franceză* , 181.

To be French was more important and more useful than to be a subject of the prince of Moldavia, and thus a *re'aya*, paying taxes to the Ottoman Empire (or, as it is expressed in the correspondence, 'to the Grand Seigneur', in other words, the sultan).

François-Thomas Linchou, at the helm of this operation, is the most visible and the most vocal. Linchou's 'self-fashioning' is constructed and deconstructed according to personal and contextual interests. François-Thomas insists on being defended by 'the honour of the French nation,'[32] but mixes with local boyars in pursuit of Moldavian offices; he asks for it to be set down in black and white that he is French, while wishing to come closer to the local elite through a marriage of convenience.

But how did others relate to this status? Did they bow before his claimed French superiority? The status of being French had no great relevance for the native elite, unless it was backed up by a powerful patron. On his arrival at the court in Iaşi in 1749, princely secretary François-Thomas Linchou tried to protect his business interests by accepting an administrative office. He acquired the position of grand *sluger*,[33] and became *Leinţul franţuju* (Linchou the Frenchman) to the boyar elite.[34] While his holding of an office annoyed the 'native' wing of the boyars, his closeness to Constantin Racoviţă, through his function as princely secretary, upset the Greek faction in the Prince's entourage: 'The free access that I have to His Highness at whatever hour arouses the jealousy of most of His Highness's boyars, who do not know the reason for this free access.'[35] On top of that, the arrival of his family in Moldavia annoyed everybody. When he first came to Moldavia, François-Thomas was accompanied by his brother Pierre-François, who continued the family's business activity

32 On 'French Nation' from Istanbul see Edhem Eldem, *French Trade in Istanbul in the Eighteenth Century* (Leiden: 1999), 204–210. For the use of the term 'nation' in the past, see Eric R. Dursteler, *Venetians in Constantinople: Nation, Identity, and Coexistence in the Early Modern Mediterranean* (Baltimore: 2006).

33 His appointment may have been connected to his commercial activities, as the grand *sluger* was responsible for the distribution, on the part of the princely court, of meat and candles to boyars and foreigners who enjoyed this right. With the reforms of Prince Constantin Mavrocordat, the office of grand *sluger* lost its traditional content, and its holder received specific duties from the prince. See Fotino, *Istoria Generală a Daciei*, 292–293.

34 Pseudo-Enache Kogălniceanu, *Letopiseţul Ţării Moldovei de la domnia întâi şi până la a patra domnie a lui Costandin Mavrocordat vv. (1733–1774)*, ed. Aurora Ilieş and Ioana Zmeu (Bucharest: 1987), 50.

35 'l'accès libre que j'ay auprès de Son Altesse à quelle heure que ce soit excitent la jalousie de la plupart de boyard de Son Altesse, qui ignore les raisons de ce libre accès.' Filitti, *Lettres*, 59. Constantin Racoviţă considers him 'one of the closest and most faithful office-holders'; AAE, Correspondence Politique, Turquie, vol. 127, f. 307, 20 July 1754.

under the cover of minor jobs offered by Prince Racoviţă, so as not to irritate the local elite. The financial gain to be obtained from the intermediate trade between Moldavia and Istanbul, and above all the consolidation of Thomas's position, encouraged other members of the family also to hasten to Moldavia. The Greeks and the boyars 'never cease to say that I seek to fill Moldavia little by little with Frenchmen,'[36] François-Thomas writes from Iaşi on 4 June 1753 to the French ambassador to the Porte, Roland Puchot Des Alleurs.[37] At the time he was trying to delay the coming of his father to Iaşi, after his brothers had long since descended on the Principalities. In any case, he writes, if his father arrived in Moldavia, he would quickly realise that 'merchants are so despised there, as are all those who are not attached to the principality.'[38] This contempt is shown in the way that a series of rules of good conduct are disregarded in the presence of foreigners precisely in order to underline the difference of status: 'The Greek boyars regard the merchants who are in the country with much contempt, because they leave them [standing] in front of them without having them cover their heads or sit down.'[39]

As he stubbornly insisted on remaining a foreigner, adhering neither to one faction nor to the other, François-Thomas fell into disfavour with the grand *postelnic*, Iordache Stavarache.[40] A Greek personage, the holder of an important office concerned with the handling of foreign affairs, Iordache Stavarache was supported by his father-in-law, Manolache Geanet, the *capuchehaia* (i.e., the diplomatic agent) of the Phanariot prince at the Ottoman court. By incurring Stavarache's disfavour, François-Thomas thus lost (for a while) much of his influence with Constantin Racoviţă, who was dependent from a diplomatic point of view on his *capuchehaia*. *Linţu* the Frenchman, raised to the rank of

36 'ne cessent de dire que je cherche à remplir la Moldavie peu à peu de François.' Filitti, *Lettres*, 58–61.

37 He held the post from February 1747 to 23 November 1754, when he died in Constantinople. See AAE, Correspondance Politique, Turquie, vol. 127, ff. 433–434.

38 'Les marchands y sont si méprisez, comme aussi tous ceux qui ne sont pas attachés à la principauté.' Filitti, *Lettres*, 89.

39 'Les boyards grecs regardent avec beaucoup de mépris les marchands qui se trouvent sur le pays, puisqu'ils les laissent devant eux sans les faire couvrir ni les faire asseoir.' Filitti, *Lettres*, 59.

40 Iordache Stavarache was one of the most influential Greek office-holder who came to Moldavia in 1749 in the suite of Prince Constantin Mavrocordat; soon afterwards, he invited his brother Ianache and his father-in-law Manolache Geanet to join him. For a long time, the three of them managed to monopolize important administrative offices (*spătar, kaymakam, capuchehaia*), remaining from one prince to the next and amassing a substantial fortune together with the confidence of the princes and of the high office-holders. In 1765, Iordache fell into disgrace in the eyes of the sultan. He ended up being hanged and his entire fortune confiscated. Iorga, *Documente Callimachi*, I, 23–25.

grand *sluger*, had landed between the political factions that were struggling for precedence in their relations with the prince.[41]

The boyars in their turn accused him of arrogance: 'He had become very impudent and paid no regard to anyone,' wrote the chronicler Enache Kogălniceanu.[42] It should also be added that his being given a new office, that of grand *vameş* (i.e. head of customs), which was much more profitable than that of grand *sluger*, created tension among the boyars who had been pushed aside by a foreigner: 'The disgrace of M. Linchou was produced by jealousy for his being favoured and for his being the Prince's head of customs, which takes a lucrative and important charge away from someone of the Moldavian nation, who cannot without envy or regret see it filled by a foreigner,' writes the French ambassador.[43] Beyond the inherent envy provoked by his holding such a high office, the testimonies of contemporaries present François-Thomas Linchou behaving in an authoritarian manner, proud of the position he held, and which he used to obtain profits and privileges. Abbot Sinadon describes '*Linciu* the papist' as being arrogant, influential and powerful. The abbot confesses, on 24 October 1764, that only his fear of this powerful figure has made him turn a blind eye to some illegal purchases of estates: knowing 'what man was *musiu Linciu*,' 'the *vameş* of His Highness Constantin Racoviţă,' who always acts with 'arrogance' and 'force.'[44] The abbot's 'fear' adds a new element to the definition of the foreigner: the religious dimension. Linchou was a Catholic, a 'papist'. However, what abbot Sinadon's account emphasises is the *vameş*'s marginality within the local elite, which he tried to enter by immoral means, using his

41 This rivalry has been interpreted by Romanian historiography in ideological terms, acquiring either social or national significance. In fact the boyar groupings defined as 'Greek' or 'native-born' were made and unmade according to immediate interests. For details on the conflicts in the time of Constantin Racoviţă, see Mihai Mîrza, 'Revolta boierilor moldoveni din vara anului 1750: Reconstituire factologică, ipoteze, semnificaţii', in Cristian Ploscaru and Mihai-Bogdan Atanasiu (eds.), *Elitele puterii, puterile elitelor în spaţiul românesc (secolele XV–XX)*, (Iaşi: 2018), 257–289.

42 Kogălniceanu, *Letopiseţul*, 70. The chronicler notes the conflict between the Frenchman and the Greek office-holders around the prince, introducing the presumption that he was the cause of the death of grand *postelnic* Lascarache Geanet: 'It is said that he was poisoned and that the occasion was a Frenchman, namely Linţă, who was in the service of the prince, because in many respects Lăscărache could not stand him, for he became very impudent and paid no attention to anyone' (Ibid., 71).

43 'La disgrâce du Sieur Linchou est produit par la jalousie de sa faveur et de ce qu'il est douanier du Prince, ce qui ôte une charge lucrative et principale à quelqu'un de la nation moldave, qui ne peut sans envie ni regret la voir remplir par un étranger.' AAE, Correspondance Politique, Turquie, Suppl. 15, ff. 282, Des Alleurs to Broglio, 16 August 1753, Constantinople.

44 *Documente Iaşi*, V, 532–533, 538–540.

concubine's connections to acquire estates which would have otherwise been subject to pre-emption rights.

François-Thomas Linchou took a further step towards social integration when his patron moved to the throne of Wallachia: marriage. Marriage was the most accessible method of social integration into a network. Practised successfully by the vast majority of the 'Greeks' who arrived in the Principalities in the suite of the Phanariot princes, marriage proved useful to both parties: the newcomer acquired social recognition among the native boyars, which gave him the right to settle in the Principalities, to buy properties, and to enter into the political game even after the removal of his political patron; the boyars in their turn were brought closer to the power group around the Phanariot prince.

On his arrival in Bucharest, in 1753, François-Thomas Linchou kept not only the job of princely secretary, but also his influence with Constantin Racoviţă, since he now received the office of grand *cămăraş*.[45] Caught up in complexities of politics and administration, and not knowing how much longer he would be tarrying in the Principalities, the Frenchman tried to create a new belonging for himself and to obtain the social recognition and support of the native elite. As such, he sought to follow a path of proven efficiency, namely marriage.[46] His betrothal to Ancuţa Sturza, the daughter of the Moldavian boyar Sandu Sturza, had taken place already during his residence in Moldavia. The lineage of the Sturza boyars was a very important one, possessing not only enormous wealth but also important positions in the social hierarchy[47]. François-Thomas Linchou judged that the engagement would be very advantageous for him: 'On my departure from Moldavia, as an advantageous marriage presented itself, both materially and because of the family, in the person of Cucoană [Lady] Ancuța Sturza, a relative of His Highness, I was engaged before my departure from Moldavia.'[48] His betrothed's father had held the highest positions in the political apparatus, serving in turn as grand *ban*, grand *spătar* and even

45 Filitti, *Lettres*, 173. The *cămăraş* was responsible for the salt mines, and belonged, administratively speaking, to the 'prince's household'. Fotino, *Istoria*, 309.

46 As we have seen in the previous chapter, his rival, Jean Mille, secretary to prince Grigore Ghica, married Safta Rosetti, the niece of the boyar Sandu Sturza. He thus could see before his eyes the success of this strategy.

47 For details regarding the boyar Sandu Sturza see Mihai-Bogdan Atanasiu, *Din lumea cronicarului Ion Neculce. Studiu prosopografic* (Iaşi: 2018), 498–507.

48 'À mon départ de Moldavie, s'étant présenté un mariage de convenance, soit par l'avantage du bien, aussi bien que de la famille, en la personne nommée Kokone Ankocha Sturdge, parente de Son Altesse, je me suis fiancé avant mon départ de Moldavie.' Filitti, *Lettres*, 169.

caimacan[49], and he was known to be close to Mihai Racoviţă, the father of Constantin Racoviţă. The alliance would have included Linchou in one of the most powerful boyar families and would have brought him even closer to the Racoviţă lineage, from which princes had been recruited for the thrones of the two Principalities. The marriage that he requested with such insistence, two years after the celebration of the betrothal, also had a very practical aim: the protection of the business interests that he had left in Iaşi on his move to Wallachia.[50] He thus had much to gain.

The materialisation of the marriage, however, raised problems. These were far more political than religious in nature. The confessional difference between the Orthodox Ancuţa Sturza and the Catholic François-Thomas Linchou is nowhere mentioned, and the betrothal had already been celebrated without this minor detail proving an impediment.[51] It was not here that the problem lay, therefore, but rather in the status of the two persons: Ancuţa Sturza belonged to the boyar elite and was a Moldavian subject under the authority of Prince Matei Ghica, and implicitly, that of the Ottoman Empire; as such, she needed a permit of passage and the prince's agreement for the marriage to be finalized. François-Thomas Linchou was a mere merchant, a French subject resident in the Levant, and would have to submit to the laws of France.[52] The ambassador of France in Istanbul was agreeable to a compromise, promising that he would 'turn a blind eye' if the marriage took place, but he pointed out that 'no French person in the Levant can marry without the agreement of the Minister [of the Navy].' In other words, the French diplomatic representative in the Levant might tolerate the match, but he asked Linchou to write directly to the Minister of the Navy specifying his reasons for disregarding the 'general rule.'[53] As he had left a considerable quantity of unsold wax in Moldavia

49 Grand *ban* (a title of Slavonic origin) was the highest office in the political hierarchy of Moldavia and Wallachia; the grand *spătar* (from Greek *spathários*) was the official responsible for handling the military affairs of the principality, while the *kaymakam* carried out the duties of interim ruler, handling administrative duties in the absence of the prince. See Fotino, *Istoria*, 265–266, 275–276.

50 Filitti, *Lettres*, 376.

51 According to Orthodox canon law, such an alliance is forbidden. See *Îndreptarea legii (1652)* (Bucharest: 1962), 179–180.

52 For the matrimonial strategies of French merchants in the Levant see Edhem Eldem, 'The French *Nation* of Constantinople in the Eighteenth Century as Reflected in the Saints Peter and Paul Parish Records, 1740–1800', in Patricia M.E. Lorcin and Todd Shepard (eds.), *French Mediterraneans: Transnational and Imperial Histories* (Lincoln, NE—London: 2016), 131–159.

53 Filitti, *Lettres*, 165–166. The understanding shown by Vergennes may be explained by the fact that he himself was in a similar relationship. Unable to marry Anne Testa, née

in the care of his brothers, François-Thomas desperately needed this marriage in order to prevent the confiscation of his goods and the ruin of his trading activity.[54] His argumentation hinges on the fluidity of the borders of the Levant: Moldavia and Wallachia belong to Christendom, not to the Levant.[55] As such, he was a Frenchman sent on a mission to the prince of Wallachia with the agreement of the king, who should take into account the services rendered and grant him this favour: 'I therefore presume that the Court will do me the kindness of not disapproving a marriage that is advantageous to me.'[56] This was the status that he needed now: a Frenchman in a Christian country, not a Frenchman in the Levant. But he also needed to belong to the local boyar class, in the interests of social integration.

All these forms of status were turned to his advantage when necessary: 'Permit me, my lord, to point out to you that there are some differences between me and the other Frenchmen who are settled in the Levant, given that I am here with the knowledge and even the approval of the Court; furthermore, one may regard this country as part of Christendom and excluded from the Levant. Besides, my residence here is uncertain, and it may be that I shall be obliged to remain here a very long time.'[57] Social differences constituted another weak point in the contract: François-Thomas Linchou was a mere functionary in the service of Prince Constantin Racoviţă, while Ancuţa Sturza belonged to the highest rank of the Moldavian boyar class and was related to

---

Vivier, the widow of a Genoese doctor from Pera, he was to live in concubinage until 1768. Marriage would result in his being called back from his post. For more details see Orville T. Murphy *Charles Gravier, Comte De Vergennes: French Diplomacy in the Age of Revolution, 1719–1787* (New York: 2009), 167–170.

54 From his letter to the ambassador, it emerges that he had invested a considerable sum of money in the wax business (19,000 piastres), which, with the return of Constantin Racoviţă to Moldavia, he hoped, somehow, to recover. See his letter of 27 March 1757. At this point, not only would he have lost out if Constantin Racoviţă had not regained his throne, but so would a number of other merchants and diplomats who had invested considerable sums in the wax trade. (Filitti, *Lettres*, 217).

55 On the Levant see Marie-Carmen Smyrnelis, *Une société hors de soi: Identités et relations sociales à Smyrne aux XVIIIe et XIXe siècles* (Paris: 2006); Oliver Jens Schmitt, *Les Levantins. Cadres de vie et identities d'un groupe ethno-confessionnel de l'Empire Ottoman au 'long' 19e siècle* (Istanbul: 2007).

56 'Je présume donc que la Cour me fairont la grâce de ne point désapprouver un mariage qui m'est avantageux.' Filitti, *Lettres*, 169–170.

57 'Permettes-moi, Monseigneur, de vous représenter qu'il y a quelques différances entre moy et les autres François qui sont établis en Levant, attendu que je suis icy avec la connoissance et même l'approbation de la Cour; outre qu'on peut regarder ce pays comme une partie de la Chretienneté et exclue du Levant. D'ailleurs ma résidence icy est incertaine, et il se peut que je sois obligé d'y rester un très long temps.' Filitti, *Lettres*, 169–170, 5 January 1757, Bucharest.

the most important boyar families; indeed she was a first cousin of the same Constantin Racoviţă. In the interests of social equilibrium, François-Thomas insistently requested that he be granted a noble title by the king of France, Louis XV, emphasising his merits in the service of the kingdom.[58]

Like all expatriates, François-Thomas Linchou and his brothers acquired a certain amount of linguistic, legislative, and administrative knowledge, which they put to use in daily life. From this point of view, it would be interesting to know several small details regarding their everyday social life: what sort of language did François-Thomas use to communicate with the locals; what sort of clothes did he wear; what sort of house did he have; and with which circle of friends and acquaintances did he socialise in Iaşi and Bucharest?

On 19 December 1756, François-Thomas Linchou wrote to the French ambassador in Poland, Charles-François de Broglio suggesting that he intervene before the king regarding the establishment of a consulate in the Principalities.[59] The idea was not new: it had been raised by other French subjects who had tried to do business in Moldavia and Wallachia and had realised the necessity of diplomatic protection through a consulate. François-Thomas, however, was more insistent and more argumentative, out of highly personal motives. After petitioning the count de Vergennes for the setting up of a consulate,[60] he then urged de Broglio, who was in Paris, to request a French consul in Moldavia.

Fariba Zarinebaf has presented numerous other cases of conflict between French, Greek, and Muslim merchants, underlining the necessity of consular intervention to protect French subjects.[61] She also notes the weak authority of the ambassadors, who were unable to impose respect for the articles of the capitulations (*ahdname*).[62] This is easy to observe in the peripheral territories of the Ottoman Empire, where French merchants were far from the authority of the sultan, and also from the protection offered by embassies or consulates. The protection of foreign merchants (especially French) who under the *ahdname* of 1740 had been accorded the right to travel and trade in the

58 AAE, Correspondance Politique, Pologne, vol. 250, f. 529. 'Les lettres de noblesse contribueront beaucoup à terminer mon mariage avec la cousine germaine du prince qui seroit très avantageux', 19 December 1756.

59 AAE, Correspondance Politique, Pologne, vol. 250, ff. 528–529.

60 AAE, Correspondance Politique, Pologne, vol. 250, ff. 330–333, 1 July 1756, Linchou to Broglio.

61 Fariba Zarinebaf, *Mediterranean Encounters. Trade and Pluralism in Early Modern Galata* (Berkeley, CA: 2018), 202–204, 210–219. See also Mathieu Grenet, 'Consuls et "nations" étrangères: état des lieux et perspectives de recherche', *Cahiers de la Méditerranées*, 93 (2016), 25–35.

62 Zarinebaf, *Mediterranean Encounters*, 215.

Black Sea region was becoming a necessity.[63] Thomas Linchou discovered for himself how hard it was for a foreigner who was neither an Ottoman subject nor an Orthodox Christian merchant to survive, let alone carry on business by the Black Sea.[64] Corruption, clientelary relations, inter-faith connections, and patronage frequently figure in his correspondence as factors that interfered with economic activity. For all these reasons, Thomas Linchou insisted on the need for a consul, and even proposed a person for the job: his brother, who had been in Iaşi for six years and spoke 'the language of the country'.[65]

Elsewhere, Maurice Linchou describes his and his sons' integration in Moldavian society as making good progress. 'We are quite well, as if we were in the middle of France,' he writes on 11 September 1753 to Ambassador Des Alleurs. At the same time, speaking of one of his sons, he presents him as 'known and respected by the whole people,' and especially by 'the commandant here [in Galaţi] and his servants.'[66] The reality behind Maurice Linchou's claim is confirmed by other first-hand accounts from the time: François-Thomas and Joseph had managed to establish social relations with some members of the local boyar class. Even if officially and within their group, the boyars complained that the French were taking their posts, some of them were nevertheless trying to maintain contact with these men who enjoyed the protection and favour of the prince. A note in an expenses ledger informs us that Joseph and François-Thomas Linchou had lent the grand *vistier* (treasurer) Toader Paladi 8,000 lei, a considerable sum, which they recovered by instalments: 'to Iozăf [Joseph], the brother of *Musulinţul* [Monsieur Linchou] the *sluger* what he had to take' and '96 lei and 60 bani, he gave to *Musulinţul* the *sluger* out of 8,000 lei which he gave as a loan.'[67] François-Thomas Linchou the grand *sluger* and Toader Paladi the grand *vistier* were members of the princely council and often met at the court of Prince Constantin Racoviţă. Trade in wax needed the approval of the grand *vistier*, so it was more than necessary to cultivate good relations with him.

Having lived for a time in Istanbul, the Linchou family were familiar with the oriental costume worn in the Principalities and used it for protection against any hostility and to ease their social integration. Such vestimentary duality was accepted in the period, and served a person's immediate interests,

63 Zarinebaf, *Mediterranean Encounters*, 142.

64 Filitti, *Lettres*, 193, François Linchou à Vergennes, Iassy, 19/30 August 1756.

65 AAE, Correspondance Politique, Pologne, vol. 250, ff. 528–529.

66 Filitti, *Lettres*, 91–93.

67 Mihai Mîrza, 'Socotelile vistiernicului Toader Palade cu diecii de vistierie, după un catastif de la mijlocul secolului al XVIII-lea', *Ioan Neculce. Buletinul Muzeului de istorie a Moldovei*, XVI–XVIII (2012), 126, 132.

especially when the nature of their profession required them to travel through various empires. Even the French ambassador, Vergennes,[68] adopted oriental costume, and so did the Linchou brothers, adapting to their surroundings. The adoption of a specific local costume facilitated their access to the trading networks by means of which they formed business connections. For example, in the spring of 1754, when Constantin Racoviţă decided to send him to Warsaw, François-Thomas Linchou asked one of his brothers who was in Istanbul 'to send him clothes *à la française* by the intermediary of a *capuchehaia* who will undertake to send them quickly.'[69] Similarly, knowledge of the Romanian language (and presumably also Greek) helped them to communicate and, most importantly, to conduct business. Thus, François-Thomas Linchou (and the whole family) took essential steps in the process of identification, adopting the lifestyle specific to the social elite among whom they pursued their activity. In Iaşi, François-Thomas began a 'family' life, living with a certain Vasilica, through whom he bought vineyards and estates in Bucium, a village close to the city.[70] As his concubine (*ţiitoare* as the documents label her in Romanian), Vasilica followed Thomas on his journeys between Iaşi and Bucharest, as Prince Constantin Racoviţă moved from one capital to the other.[71] Speaking the language of the country, adopting the costume of the local elite, buying estates, and living with a local woman, had not François-Thomas Linchou assimilated all the criteria that designated him as an Ottoman subject (*re'âyâ*)?

Re'âyâ *v.* françois

Returning now to the candle business, it should be explained that the artisan of the Linchou business ventures was in the first place François-Thomas Linchou. As the political and diplomatic interface for the commercial dealings of the Linchou Company, François-Thomas got involved in and in fact took charge of the solution of this dispute. The litigation ended up being presented in Iaşi before the Prince, in Giurgiu before the kadı, in Bucharest before the vizier and the aga, and in Constantinople before the Divan. The venture brought to light invented identities, forged documents, networks, and favours, used now by one side, now by the other. At present, I can only give the point of view expressed

68 See the portraits of the French consul and his wife by Antoine de Favray in the Pera Museum.

69 Filitti, *Lettres*, 100.

70 Another document, of 15 November 1753, speaks of 'musiu Liţii' who had vineyards in Iaşi, purchased when he was grand *sluger*. Caproşu, *Documente*, V, 502–503.

71 Caproşu, *Documente*, V, 532–533.

by the Linchou family in their voluminous correspondence with the ambassador of France in Istanbul, as I do not yet have access to more documents that would complete the picture.[72]

It seems that six months after the establishment of the candle factory, Joseph Linchou, one of the brothers, was unhappy with the progress of the venture. Consequently he closed the factory and confiscated all the goods in the shop in order to recover the money he had invested: 'Seeing that Sterio was squandering the capital, because of his bad behaviour, Joseph Linchou withdrew all the goods that were to be found in the shop in order to recover his capital and put the business in order.' Sterio owed 538 piastres. He did not have the money, and thus ended up in the debtors' prison. From this point on, a long revenge fell upon the Linchou brothers: Sterio fabricated a receipt according to which Joseph owed him 3,407 piastres, the sum of all the goods delivered in the course of their collaboration but never paid for. He claimed that he had been given the receipt by Pierre-François in Rusçuk (Ruse), in the presence of a number of other merchants, signed and sealed in the name of his brother Joseph.[73] On the basis of this 'document', the Linchou brothers were dragged all over the Empire, sometimes in irons, often blackmailed, suffering violation of the privacy of their home in the middle of the night, and sent into exile or subjected to the humiliation of the confiscation of their property. Each time, the key point of defence concerned identity: when Sterio brought the case before the sultan, Joseph Linchou was cited as a *re'âyâ* with business on Moldavian territory, while his brother, the experienced François-Thomas requested a *ferman* stating that Joseph was French, and thus benefitted from protection.[74] According to the capitulations concluded between France and the Ottoman Empire,[75] a French subject could not be dragged out of his home, as had happened to Joseph: 'The *çavuş* (executive agent) came into Linchou's house to seize him, which is contrary to the capitulations, for the house of a

72 Despite searching a considerable number of Romanian archive fonds, I have been unable to find information about the Greek candlemaker Sterio. I have, however, found similar cases, which can provide information about how such litigation proceeded.

73 See Thomas Linchou's exposition to Ambassador Vergennes, in which he summarizes the hearing that took place in Bucharest in the presence of the kadı of Giurgiu. As Sterio could not bring witnesses to testify to the presence of Pierre-François in Ruse, and the supposed receipt ('billet') was signed in Greek and not in French, Vizier Agassi (?) gave an *ilam* in favour of Pierre-François Linchou. Sterio was undeterred and set off for Istanbul. Filitti, *Lettres*, 161–162, Bucharest, 16/27 November 1755.

74 The use of the term: 'raya ou zimmi' bothered Vergennes who wrote to Thomas Linchou from Constantinople on 1 October 1755. Filitti, *Lettres*, 155.

75 Maurits H. van den Boogert, *The Capitulations and the Ottoman Legal System: Qadis, Consuls and Beratlis in the 18th Century* (Leiden: 2005).

Frenchman may not be entered no matter where he is in Turkey.'[76] The *çavuş* sent by the Imperial Divan had even, François-Thomas believed, violated the laws of Moldavia, which stated 'that he may not enter any house and that he must read the *ferman* before the Prince and request the person sought by the Porte.'[77] Without respecting either the capitulations or the laws of Moldavia, the imperial *çavuş* had taken Joseph in irons, after he had been cited repeatedly to stand opposite Sterio before the Imperial Divan, a treatment which François-Thomas judged to be 'contraire à l'honneur de la nation françoise.'[78] More than that, the honour of the Prince of Moldavia was injured by such a violent intrusion, which had resulted in aggressive behaviour towards the officials who requested that the Moldavian laws be respected. 'The Greeks say,' writes François-Thomas, 'that a subject (*re'âyâ*) would have resolved this matter by now, even if he had not enjoyed protection' as a French subject did, and that 'Sterio would have received exemplary punishment.'

The very reputation of France had been affected by the prolongation of the matter, and by the non-involvement of the ambassador in the protection of the French and the defence of their rights. 'The eyes of Moldavia are on us, curious to see what direction this matter will take,' declaimed François-Thomas, ceaselessly invoking 'the honour of the nation' and implicitly 'the honour of the French.'[79] The rhetoric of the Frenchman's defence is obvious. In fact, Christian merchants from Moldavia and Wallachia, Ottoman subjects, often appealed to the judgement of the Imperial Divan when they were unhappy with the sentences or mediation offered by the local authorities, thus providing an occasion for the repeated interference of Ottoman envoys in the justice system.[80]

---

76 'Le chaoux est venu dans la maison de Linchou pour l'y prendre, ce qui est contraire aux capitulations, puisqu'on ne peut entrer dans la maison d'un François dans quelque endroit de la Turquie que ce soit.' See Filitti, *Lettres*, 394–395. Thomas Linchou is here citing the article of the *ahdaname* of 1740 which stipulates that 'any undue violence or oppression against French subjects would be punished'. See Zarinebaf, *op. cit.*, 143.

77 Filitti, *Lettres*, 394–395.

78 Filitti, *Lettres*, 394–395.

79 Filitti, *Lettres*, 394–395.

80 According to the *ferman* issued by Sultan Mahmud I on 16 October 1746, litigation between Christians in Wallachia was to be judged by the local courts in the first instance; if the parties were not satisfied with the decision, they could appeal to the kadı of Giurgiu. This is confirmed in another document of 13/22 August 1760, when it was specified that cases would be judged in Bucharest in the presence of the kadı of Giurgiu and under the supervision of the prince of Wallachia. In Mustafa A. Mehmed (ed.), *Documente turceşti privind istoria României*, vol. I (1455–1774) (Bucharest: 1976), 258–259, 270–271.

The French diplomatic representation intervened in the conflict, trying to counter the financial pretentions of the Greek Sterio (who in the meantime been joined by another Greek by the name of Dimitraki) both through constant communication with the Linchou brothers, offering them information and advice and producing the documents they needed, and through numerous approaches to the Ottoman authorities. Nevertheless, François-Thomas Linchou judged their interventions insufficient and ineffective. 'I take the liberty of telling Your Excellency that it is most disgraceful that a Frenchman should be exposed to such a business and the dragomans not give him any warning, in spite of the orders given by Your Excellency,' he writes on 19 April 1756, after finding out that Sterio had dropped his accusations against his brother Pierre-François and directed them against him, and had managed to obtain a *ferman* of the Porte for him to be brought to Istanbul as a debtor of the sum of 3,047 piastres, which he refused to pay, relying on the protection of Prince Racoviţă. He had had to learn of the accusations against him from the prince's *capuchehaias*, who had striven to prevent such a *ferman* being sent.[81] He wrote that the stakes concerned not only the Linchou brothers, but France itself, which must prove to its subjects, and to other nations, that it was capable of fighting and defending its citizens: 'We are waiting here [Iaşi] to see end of it, to know the credit that our nation has with the present government.'[82] The affair came to an end in the autumn of 1756, when the three brothers—Pierre-François, Joseph-Marie and Jean-Baptiste—returned to Iași, while their elder brother was in Poland, in the service of the 'nation'.[83] I have not yet found information as to whether the brothers managed to recover the 3,047 piastres handed over to the *çavuş* when François was taken in irons; however it is clear that François-Thomas Linchou did not succeed in recovering the 700 piastres he had paid to the kadı of Giurgiu for the *ferman* given in their favour by the vizir Agassi. The whole affair had cost him not only money but also time spent on the road to Istanbul to prove his innocence, while his real business, trading in wax, stagnated. For this reason, the unexpected removal from power of Constantin Racoviţă on 14 March 1757, after a year on the throne of Moldavia,

81 Filitti, *Lettres*, 180. In his letter of reply, Vergennes assures Linchou of all his support, but advises him that: 'tout François attaqué pour une dette vraye ou fausse qui excède 4000 aspres ne peut être tenu de se deffendre qu'au Divan de Constantinople'. He recommends that Linchou should not insist but should comply and come to defend himself before the situation becomes more serious. (Filitti, *Lettres*, 182–183).

82 'On attend icy d'en voir la fin pour connaître le credit que nottre nation a auprès du gouvernement present.' Filitti, *Lettres*, 185.

83 Filitti, *Lettres*, 408.

caught him unprepared and with his business activities dispersed and unprotected.[84] A year later, François-Thomas and Jean-Baptiste Linchou were still in Iași, trying to recover their money, to pay their debts, and to withdraw to Istanbul, impelled by the hostile attitude of the new prince, Scarlat Ghica, who did not want them in the country. Vergennes insistently asked Ghica to offer them the necessary protection and assistance so that they might 'terminer les affaires qui les ont conduit en Moldavie' and withdraw safely.[85]

Honour, rights, protection were words that fashioned the identity of a Frenchman. For François-Thomas Linchou, the capitulations were above any law; in fact, he shared the opinion of other Westerners regarding 'the primacy of the capitulations'.[86] The status of *re'âyâ* was invoked only to obtain privileges or to force the resolution of a conflict. François-Thomas's attempt to combine his two identities, enjoying only the advantages of each, ultimately cost him his head.

On 14 March 1760, François-Thomas Linchou was decapitated before Sultan Mustafa III, accused of grave offence to the Empire in his desperate attempt to restore Constantin Racoviță to the throne of Moldavia.[87] The French embassy proved unable to give a definite answer to the Reis Effendi's questions: 'Was Linchou a genuine Frenchman; was his service to the prince compatible with this status; and had he ever paid tribute to the Grand Seigneur'?[88] The Frenchman's death on the 'scaffold' took the French embassy in Istanbul by surprise. It had not had time to build a defence, or even to know the charges.

84 See Jean-Baptiste Linchou's letter of 25 March 1757, in which he presents to Vergennnes the state of the family's business and their debts to a number of French merchants who were demanding their money now that the family's protector had withdrawn to Istanbul and the new prince was asking them to liquidate their business as quickly as possible and leave Moldavia. Filitti, *Lettres*, 214–216.

85 Filitti, *Lettres*, 440–442.

86 Van den Boogert, *Capitulations*, 21.

87 See the report of the Polish interpreter Francesco Giuliani sent from Constantinople to Count Heinrich von Brühl on 18 March 1760. Iorga, *Documente Callimachi*, II, 249. The death of the Frenchman Linchou was also noted by the British ambassador to the Porte, James Porter: 'A Frank residing at Constantinople, who threw himself as a dependant on a deposed Vaywode, and who thought himself sufficiently protected, ventured to send a scheme to his correspondent in Moldavia for exciting that people to rebel against the Vaywode in possession, accompanying it with severe reflection on the Turkish government; he sent it by what he esteemed the securest conveyance. His letter, notwithstanding his precaution, was intercepted, and he lost his head near the Seraglio: no solicitations could save him'. James Porter, *Observations on the Religion, Law, Government and Manners of the Turks* (Dublin: 1768), vol. 1, 186.

88 AAE, Fond Correspondence Politique, Turquie, vol. 136, f. 68.

According to Ambassador Vergennes, Linchou had fallen prey to his own intrigues, wishing 'to make himself useful to Prince Constantin Racoviţă, to whom he had linked his fate.' Getting involved in a series of 'schemes', Linchou had apparently written a number of letters that were somewhat damaging to the Ottoman court, claiming that he had the agreement of the grand vizier.[89] It was the interception of the letters that led to his decapitation, confirming his character as an 'adventurer', and thus merging him with the 'Greeks' of the Empire, who were often so described in diplomatic correspondence.[90]

However, Linchou had made so many efforts to fashion a Moldavian status for himself, albeit only for the sake of privileges, that rumour had already assigned to him the identity of a 'rebel Moldavian boyar', far from that of an honourable Frenchman.[91] 'Dass sie ihn nicht als einen Franken sondern als einen aufrührerichen moldauer Boyaren ansähen, der das Leben verwirket hätte,' writes Schwachhein, the Viennese ambassador, to Chancellor Kaunitz, on 18 March 1760.[92] If, in the eyes of the Turks, Linchou had put on the clothes of a rebel Moldavian boyar, to his conationals, the French Levant merchants, he had become an immoral 'Greek', who had dishonoured the French nation by his behaviour and as such deserved to die. In their petition, the French merchants expressed their concern with the inability of their king to protect his subjects. They stated that, together with his Greek clothes, Linchou had taken up tastes, manners, and morals such as only Greeks are capable of, going so far as to maintain a harem in the Moldavian capital.[93] This behaviour had separated him from the honour of the French nation, noted the French merchants in the memoir, hiding behind the anonymity of the group.

89 See 'Relation du supplice de S. Linchou condamné comme traître et sediciuex par la Porte', written by the first dragoman of the French Embassy, Deval, and attached to a letter of 17 March 1769. AAE, Fond Correspondence Politique, Turquie, vol. 136, f. 66–70; AN. Correspondance Consulaire. Constantinople, AE/B/I/437, ff. 9–10, 13–14.

90 On this topic see the memoir 'Caractère des gens du pays, leur commerce', AAE, Correspondence Politique, Turquie, Suppl. 15, ff. 105–107, 1751, Constantinople.

91 *Comis* Enache Kogălniceanu, witness and chronicler of the events, also places him in the Moldavian boyar class ('he had entered the ranks of the boyars'), listing the offices he held, but also mentioning his trading in wax, justified by the need 'to feed his three younger brothers'. Kogălniceanu, *Letopiseţul*, 105.

92 Iorga, *Documente Callimachi*, II, 410.

93 'On a souffert que le Sieur Linchou se vouat au service d'un Prince Grec de Moldavie, eut serrail de femmes dans la capitale de la province, et déshonnorât enfin le nom français.' Mihordea, *Politica*, 527.

As Stephen Greenblatt has pointed out, such constant adoption of new 'masks' would inevitably lead to 'some loss of self.'[94] Although repeatedly invoking 'the honour of being French,' François-Thomas Linchou seems to have had difficulties in his attempts to integrate himself in the community of French merchants in the Levant. They claimed that he had become a veritable Greek, since not even the Turks could distinguish him any more from the other subjects of the Empire.[95] After the tragic event, the French authorities tried to distance themselves from the 'adventurer' Linchou, who had linked himself too closely to the 'Greek prince,'[96] and thus by his behaviour forfeited any claim to French consular protection.[97]

François-Thomas Linchou donned the clothes of identity according to context and interest, adapting to the times but always seeking protection behind 'the honour of the French nation.' Others would categorise him sometimes as *Moldavian*, sometimes as *Greek*, starting from the exterior and public manifestations of this French subject in search of social recognition.

*

On 20 December 1842, the Collège Archéologique et Généalogique de France accepted the titles of nobility presented by Phillipe Jean-Baptiste de Linche for admission as a titular member.[98] Phillipe Linche (or Linchou), the nephew of

94 Stephen J. Greenblatt, *Renaissance Self-fashioning: From More to Shakespeare* (Chicago: 1980), 2–9.

95 'Il semble que l'habit donne les goûts, les manières, et souvent les mœurs de ceux qui les portent dès que les Turcs ne nous distinguent plus, ils ne sont pas fâchés de punir sur un Français travesti l'insolence apparente d'un Grec qui devant eux ose de méconnaître.' Mihordea, *Politica*, 527. On his death in 1760, François-Thomas Linchou had a single son from a relationship with a woman from Istanbul. This natural son would inherit all his wealth. (Iorga, *Documente Callimachi*, II, 411, no. 30).

96 On 10 October 1762, Ambassador Vergennes wrote to the French ambassador in Poland, Antoine-René de Voyer, marquis de Paulny: 'La mort du Sieur Linchou, nous est étrangère, celui-ci ayant pris le service d'un prince Grec et s'étant mal adroitement engagé dans des intrigues très criminelles il en a ètè la triste victime.' AAE, Correspondence Politique, Pologne, vol. 273, f. 632.

97 On 3 May 1760, Etienne-François de Choiseuil wrote to Vergennes: 'Vous avez fait, Monsieur, tout ce qui pouvoit dépendre de vous pour sauver le Sieur Linchou, mais il faut convenir que le crime dont il a été accusé et dont il a en quelque sorte fait l'aveu au Sieur Deval meritoit le supplice auquel il a été condamné. Nous ne pouvons pas exiger que l'article 22 de nos capitulations avec la Porte, renouvelées les 28 mai 1740 soit applicables aux crimes de lése Majesté et de trahison en matière d'Etat.' AAE, Correspondence Politique, Turquie, vol. 136, f. 98v.

98 BNF, Fond Roumain 6. Documents généalogiques et administratifs relatifs aux familles de Linche et Carpinişanu (1570–1855), f. 300.

François-Thomas Linchou,[99] had succeeded where his uncle had failed: he had reached the highest level of the Wallachian boyar class, married a boyaress and accumulated a vast fortune. The likeness of Filip Lenș has been preserved for us thanks to the painter Ida Fielitz (1847–1913). In 1888, she recopied the portrait of the famous boyar, probably from the visual archive of the family members settled in Paris. Appointed a *dikaiophylax* of the Great Eastern Church in 1821, Filip Lenș had managed skilfully to work his way into Phanariot cross-border networks, taking advantage of his French roots, the support of the French consul Hugot, and the protection of his patron, Constantin Filipescu, who introduced him into the circles of the princes Ioan Caragea (1812–1818) and Grigore Ghica IV (1822–1828). His path to the highest offices was thus opened up. He served as grand *vornic* (interior minister), grand *vistier* (treasurer), and *logofăt* (chancellor) of Justice, and dreamed of attaining the rank of prince of Wallachia. Having become a boyar and high office-holder, with a mansion on the main artery of Bucharest, the Mogoşoaia Road,[100] Phillipe (Filip) returned to his French noble roots, traceable back to the Linche de Moissac branch.[101] The painting captures all his pride and grandeur, while his costume and general self-presentation link him to his Ottoman allegiance. The dog at his feet is the symbol of fidelity—shared of course among his various patrons, Greek, Wallachian, Ottoman, Russian, and French.

The Linchou case speaks of the multiple processes of identification that individuals could use to traverse and adapt to empires. The distinction between locals (*pământeni*) and outsiders (*străini*) highlights a complex network of identity and belongings in which the boundaries of 'Greekness',

99 Philippe was the son of Jean-Baptiste Linchou, who settled in Wallachia after the death of his brother, first as a teacher of foreign languages and then as secretary at the court of Alexandru Ipsilanti (1774–1782). The identity of his mother is uncertain. Jean-Alexandre Vaillant names a certain Maria Hodivoaianu, whom he believed was a freed slave of the great boyar Constantin Filipescu, in whose entourage the young Filip Lenş grew up (Jean-Alexandre Vaillant, *La Roumanie, ou Histoire, langue, littérature, orographie, statistique des peuples de la langue d'or, Ardialiens, Vallaques et Moldaves, résumés sur le nom de Romans* (Paris: 1844), vol. 2, 311.

100 In 1829, Filip Lenș was listed as born in Bucharest, aged 52, holding the title of *postelnic*, with a house on the Mogoșoaia Road, in the Yellow district, at number 376. See Ioan C. Filitti, *Catagrafie oficială de toţi boierii Ţării Româneşti la 1829* (Bucharest: 1929), 17. The house exists to this day, under the address Calea Victoriei 133 and is managed by the Writers' Union of Romania. Despite being one of the oldest and most beautiful mansions in Bucharest, it currently houses a casino.

101 The first part of this Linchou file, deposited in the Bibliothèque Nationale de France on 22 July 1929, by Alexandre de Linche de Moissac, gathers documents from the years 1570–1650 regarding the connections of the Linche family with Moissac. See BNF, Fond Roumain 6, ff. 1–47.

Fig. 2
Ida Fieltz (1847–1913) – Filip Lenş (Philippe Linche) (1779–1853) – great logothete, 1888, National Museum of Art, Bucharest.

'Moldavianness' or 'Frenchness' appear somewhat fluid. The Orthodox Christians of the Ottoman Empire, such as Sterio the Greek, the candle-maker, integrated relatively quickly into Moldavian and Wallachian society because of their faith and political proximity, and were assimilated into the social fabric, while Christians of different confessions (Catholic, Armenian, or Protestant) bore the mark of difference. This was the situation of the Linchou family, who succeeded in integrating by way of commerce but would never manage to penetrate the social fabric of the community. Ultimately, François-Thomas Linchou adapted to every situation, trying to make as much profit as possible for himself and his family. It was this adaptability[102] that was held against him from all sides, the adaptability that helped him to survive, but that negated the attributes of a distinct French nation in the Levant.

102 See Ian Coller, 'East of Enlightenment: Regulating Cosmopolitanism between Istanbul and Paris in the Eighteenth Century', *Journal of World History* 21/3 (2010), 447–70.

PART II

Loyalty and Subjecthood in the Eighteenth Century

CHAPTER 3

Phanariots and Boyars at the Borders of Empires

'The Prince Has Died and at His Mourning We Should Rejoice.'[1]

In 1711, at Stănileşti on the River Prut, not only was the fate of two great empires at stake, but also the destinies of those who had positioned themselves on one side or the other, following their masters and confirming or renouncing their loyalties. The defeat of Russia and its ally, the little principality of Moldavia, led to the exile of Prince Dimitrie Cantemir and the boyar faction that had joined him in this adventure. Ion Neculce, Grand *Hatman*[2] of Moldavia, was among the boyars who followed his master and patron to Russia. A close advisor of the prince of Moldavia, he had been among the supporters of his plans to enter an alliance with Russia. Once in Russia, Neculce thought of the homeland he had left behind, of the fortune going to waste in his absence, and of the positions of power he had held, and requested permission to return to Moldavia. Dimitrie Cantemir interpreted the boyar's wish as a form of insubordination and refused to give his consent. At the same time, returning to Moldavia was itself problematic: in following Cantemir, Neculce had shown himself to be unfaithful not only to the new prince, but also to the sultan. With frequent changes of ruler and conflicts between the surrounding great empires, the eighteenth century in Wallachia and Moldavia was a time of numerous positionings, wanderings, and re-fashionings of notions of loyalty, belonging, and social status.

In this part, I propose to explore the relation between office, social status, and loyalty. First of all, I shall examine the social and political ascent of boyars to the highest offices in the princely council through the prisms of belonging, social status, and loyalty. I shall then focus on the manner in which a social status was identified and fashioned in relation to the position of power held at a certain moment in southeast European circles. I shall show how the process of self-fashioning contributed to the underlining of social prestige and the propagation of a social representation designed to uphold the boyars' pretensions to social advancement. I shall close with a case study intended to mirror the fluid identities and loyalties assumed by the southeast European elites.

1 Iordache Golescu, *Scrieri alese*, ed. Mihai Moraru (Bucharest: 1990), 132.

2 The highest-ranking military officer, commander of the Moldavian army.

© CONSTANŢA VINTILĂ, 2022 | DOI:10.30965/9783657704873_004

In Search of the Greeks

The taking over of the thrones of Wallachia and Moldavia by the Phanariots changed the political and social paradigm of the elites. Even if what is generally known in historiography as the Phanariot regime seems actually to have been installed much earlier, it is true that the eighteenth century brought important changes regarding the structure of the games played on the political stage.[3] The local elites faced two types of challenge in defining their social status and political loyalties: the significant infusion of new individuals into the social fabric and the social reforms launched by Constantin Mavrocordat.

But let us start from the beginning. Before Dimitrie Cantemir's withdrawal to Russia in 1711, and the decapitation of Constantin Brâncoveanu in 1714, political groupings competed among themselves for influence and power in the proximity of the princes. These groupings were structured according to immediate interests, political affinities, and relations of kinship. Although they might define themselves as 'native' (*pământeni*) boyars, in opposition to the 'Greek' boyars, an analysis of their ethnic structure shows that in fact it was external factors rather than geographical belonging that counted most in the formation of social and political alliances. The most conclusive example is provided by the political conflicts of the second half of the seventeenth century, in which the 'native' party was led by the Cantacuzino family, while the Băleanu family headed the 'Greek' party. In short, the descendants of the Byzantine Cantacuzinos, who had rapidly and recently become 'local boyars', were *defending* their country of adoption, while 'old boyar families' had made themselves 'foreign' by their alliances with the 'Greeks', whose ideas and interests they had adopted. The rhetoric of these political factions is best reflected in the writing of the chroniclers, who offered an interpretation of events favourable to the grouping to which they belonged.[4] Detailed analysis shows that the two camps could in no way be divided by ethnicity and that it was shared interests that gave rise to the formation of factions in the political arena.[5] The boyar class, divided into great boyars and petty boyars, had its own

---

3 Andrei Pippidi, 'Aux origines du regime phanariote en Valachie et Moldavie', *Revue des études sud-est européennes*, XI, 2 (1973), 353–355; Andrei Pippidi, 'Phanar, Phanariotes, Phanariotisme', *Revue des études sud-est européennes* XIII, 2 (1975), 231–239.

4 Radu Popescu, *Istoria domnilor Ţării Rumâneşti*, ed. Mihail Gregorian (Bucharest: 1984); *Istoria Ţării Româneşti de la octombrie 1688 până la 1717. Cronica Anonimă*, ed. Constantin Grecescu (Bucharest: 1959).

5 This aspect has benefitted from ample treatment by researchers. See in this connection Andrei Pippidi, *Tradiţia politică bizantină în Ţările Române în secolele XVI–XVIII* (Bucharest: 2001); Bogdan Murgescu, '"Fanarioţi" şi "pământeni": religie şi etnicitate în definirea

criteria of social definition and recognition, which gave access to important offices in the princely council and, as such, to material and symbolic resources. The great boyars defined themselves by their claims to ancient lineage and their holding of large landed estates. These criteria ensured them the right to expect high positions in the princely council and in the administration of the Principalities. In fact, both in Wallachia and in Moldavia, the great boyars were grouped around just a few dozen families. Matrimonial strategies had helped them to maintain their power and their status as a privileged caste. In the course of the seventeenth century, new figures, preponderantly of Balkan origin, had penetrated the inner circles of power and carved out a path to the high offices that brought income and social prestige. In an analysis of the situation in Moldavia, Radu Păun has shown that the proportion of 'Greco-Levantines' who managed to enter the ranks of office-holders in the princely council amounted to between 20 and 25 percent of the total number of council members.[6] It was much the same in Wallachia, with some princes supporting the social and political ascent of individuals of different ethnicity as a reward for fidelity and services rendered. At the same time, the princes created their own political alliances and 'reservoirs of fidelity'[7] in order to remain in power for as long as possible. They rewarded their favourites for 'their faithful services to the prince and to the country' with high offices and sometimes with estates, confiscated from those they considered treacherous (*hain*). Once they had established fiscal residence and were incorporated in a taxable category, they became subjects of the prince, even if their social and cultural integration might take generations.[8]

The term 'Greeks', as it appears in the contemporary historical sources, in fact covers a population of diverse regional belongings, but bound together by the Orthodox faith and the use of the Greek language in their commercial

identităţilor în Ţările Române şi în Imperiul Otoman', in Bogdan Murgescu, *Ţările Române între Imperiul Otoman şi Europa Creştină* (Iaşi: 2012); Radu G. Păun, 'Some remarks about the historical origins of the "Phanariot phenomenon" in Moldavia and Wallachia (16th–19th centuries)', in Gelina Harlaftis and Radu G Păun (eds.), *Greeks in Romania in the Ninetheenth Century* (Athens: 2013), 47–94; Wasiucionek, *The Ottomans and Eastern Europe*; Constantin Iordachi, 'From Imperial Entanglements to National Disentanglement: The 'Greek Question' in Moldavia and Wallachia, 1611–1863', in Roumen Daskalov, Tchavdar Marinov (eds.), *Entangled Histories of the Balkans*, vol. I: *National Ideologies and Language Policies* (Leiden: 2013), 67–148. Cotovanu, *Migrations et mutations identitaires*.

6 Radu G. Păun, 'Les grands officiers d'origines gréco-levantine en Moldavie au XVIIe siècle. Offices, carrières et stratègie de pouvoir', in *Revue des Etudes Sud-est Européennes*, XLV, 1–4 (2007), 155.

7 Ibid.

8 Cotovanu, *Migrations et mutations identitaires*, 478–548.

and financial dealings.[9] Some historians have preferred to refer to them as 'Greco-Levantines', a concept that enables the integration of categories such as the Ragusans or the Italianized Slavs alongside Orthodox Christians from the Balkans (Greeks, Albanians, and Vlachs or Aromanians) among the individuals who played a role on the political stage of the Principalities.[10]

The eighteenth century saw a rise in the number of 'Greeks' present in the Principalities, some coming in the retinue of the Phanariot princes and other simply in search of a better life. We shall repeatedly encounter this population in the course of this book. In the present chapter, I introduce those at the apex of the pyramid, those who came in the entourage of Phanariot princes and set in motion the repositioning of the local boyars. The 'Greco-Levantine' infusion changed the rules of the game in a region already dominated by political instability. The conflicts between different groupings transgressed frontiers, give rise to fierce competition for support and influence. Weaving multiple cross-border networks, the newcomers played on multiple levels, positioning themselves according to the resources available at a particular moment. Members of important families—Ruset, Ispilanti, Suțu—integrated themselves in the local ruling elite by way of administrative office, marriage, and the purchase of large estates, while other members continued to extend their connections using the same methods in the Ottoman Empire, showing solidarity and offering each other economic and political support at key moments. With regard to the administrative structure, we may observe a preference for 'Greco-Phanariots' in the offices of grand *postelnic* and grand *spătar* and grand *hatman*. The preference lies in the close connection between these posts and the prince; to keep control over them, the prince would prefer to appoint someone close to himself.[11] He thus ensured that the new appointee was loyal to him and would

9 Radu G. Păun, 'Les Gréco-Levantins dans les Pays Roumains: voies de penetration, étapes et strategies de maintien', *Studia Balcanica*, 25 (2006), 304–316; Konrad Petrovsky, '"Those Violating the Good, Old Customs of Our Lands": Forms and Functions of Graecophobia in the Danubian Principalities, 16th–18th Centuries', in Hakan T. Karateke, H. Erdem Çipa and Helga Anetshofer (eds.), *Disliking Others: Loathing Hostility, and Distrust in Premodern Ottoman Lands* (Brighton: 2018), 187–218.

10 Radu G. Păun, 'Stratégies de famille, stratégies de pouvoir: les Gréco-Levantins en Moldavie au XVIIe siècle', in Ionela Băluţă, Constanţa Vintilă-Ghiţulescu, Mihai-Răzvan Ungureanu (eds.), *Social Behaviour and Family Strategies in the Balkans (16th–20th Centuries)/ Comportaments sociaux et stratégies familiales dans les Balkans (XVIe–XXe siècles)* (Bucharest: 2008), 17. See also the terminology proposed by Ştefania Costache, *At the End of Empire: Imperial Governance, Inter-Imperial Rivalry and 'Autonomy' in Wallachia and Moldavia (1780s–1850s)*, PhD, University of Illinois (Urbana-Champaign: 2013), 8–9.

11 See Dan Berindei, Irina Gavrilă, 'Analyse de la composition de l'ensemble des familles de grands dignitaires de la Valachie au XVIIIe siècle', in *Comunicaciones al XV Congresso Internacional de las Ciencias Genealógica y Heráldica* (Madrid: 1983), 73–74.

not someday turn against him, forming an alliance with his rivals. However, the most important office in the princely council, that of grand *vistier* (treasurer), was held mostly by local boyars, although it was through this office that the prince controlled the financial resources of the country. Even if they came accompanied by a support group, the Phanariot princes tried all the time to recruit clients from among the local elite, gaining their fidelity by the offer of offices and privileges. The appointee to the office of grand *vistier*, for example, was not just any boyar. In accepting the office, the boyar was also accepting a collaboration with the prince and his close associates through his inclusion in their network. His obedience and loyalty were conditional on his being kept in office. In these conditions, the local boyars played the Phanariots' game for the advantages of such a position. Moreover, the grand *vistier* was chosen from among the wealthiest local boyars, those with sufficient resources to enable them to cover shortfalls in the treasury, should the need arise.[12]

Some of the Phanariots went further and put into operation matrimonial strategies and alliances of spiritual affinity to consolidate a network and to make loyalties more secure. By means of marriage, they acquired the right to buy properties in Wallachia and Moldavia and introduced themselves into the local network of alliances of clan and affinity. The sale of real estate was regulated by the *custom of the land*, patrimonial property being protected by a right of pre-emption (*protimisis*). Should part of an inheritance be for sale, relatives had priority, and only after their refusal could it be sold to the other potential buyers, 'strangers' from outside the community.[13] All the same, such a sale posed problems in the long term, for a relative had the right to change their mind and invoke their right of pre-emption later, thus undoing the deal. Analysis of the documents shows that such sales were almost always contested, and the 'stranger' who had entered the patrimonial community by way of purchase might end up being pushed out and given their money back.

The second challenge, alluded to above, concerns the administrative reforms promoted by Prince Constantin Mavrocordat. Mavrocordat bound the quality of nobility to the holding of high office: only those who held functions in the administrative apparatus were considered noble; for their service, the

12 See in this connection the fate of the grand *vistier* Nicolae Dudescu, who ended up paying out of his own fortune considerable sums demanded by the Phanariot princes. He was repeatedly either imprisoned or exiled, and forced to ransom himself with numerous bags of gold pieces. The same happened to the grand *vistier* Mihai Cantacuzino, who was given the task of 'gathering' large sums to cover not only the tribute due to the Porte, but also the regular financial demands of the Phanariots. See Mihai banul Cantacuzino, *Genealogia Cantacuzinilor*, ed. Nicolae Iorga (Bucharest: 1902), 121–157.

13 *Instituţii feudale din Ţările Române. Dicţionar*, eds. Ovid Sachelarie and Nicolae Stoicescu (Bucharest: 1988), 391.

holders of functions were recompensed with a salary.[14] The introduction of salaries under Constantin Mavrocordat's reforms, together with the assimilation of the boyars into an administrative system, both clearly bureaucratizing and modernizing measures, increased the boyars' preoccupation with their posts and their dependence on those holding political power. The boyars accepted Mavrocordat's reforms but did not give up the criteria of social differentiation that had applied until then: the antiquity of one's lineage and the holding of landed estates. In fact, competition stimulated the production of the necessary instruments for social and political legitimation and appealing to the past of one's lineage was one of these. As Petr Mat'a has shown, 'invented pedigrees, origin myths and legends of genealogical descent' were 'key features of aristocratic identity.'[15] The Moldavian and Wallachian ruling elites embroidered legendary kinships and used them not only to underline their social position, but also for political legitimation. In fact the process had begun long before, and was stimulated by the Austrian occupation of Oltenia. Obliged to present documents in support of their noble rank, the boyars had begun an assiduous process of refashioning identity, reaching further and further back into the past and connecting themselves to branches of various cross-border noble lines. The process reached its apogee in the nineteenth century, when every kindred of any antiquity and wealth considered itself duty-bound to produce a 'family book' accompanied by a family tree extending as far as possible in time and space. I shall not insist here on this very important aspect regarding identity formation, except to remark that, as Petr Mat'a has noted, historians have striven to denounce falsehoods and seek truths,[16] and yet the phenomenon, seen in the social and political context of the period, offers valuable insights into the definition of household and kinship.

Contemporary sources tell us that the local boyars had no grounds for fear, given that only a quarter of the holders of high offices were 'Greeks'. However, this did not mean that the boyars did not feel threatened by the presence of the foreigners who came to Moldavia and Wallachia in the company of the Phanariots, and who proved to be unfair competitors for access to the highest

14 Şerban Papacostea, 'La grande charte de Constantin Mavrocordato (1741) et les réformes en Valachie et en Moldavie', in *Symposium « L'Epoque phanariote »* (Thessaloniki: 1974), 365–367; Gheorghe Brătianu, 'Două veacuri de la reforma lui Constantin Mavrocordat, 1746–1946', *Analele Academiei Române Memoriile Secţiunii Istorice*, 3d ser., XXIX (1946), 395–461.

15 Petr Mat'a, 'The false Orsini from over the Alps: Negotiating aristocratic identity in late medieval and early modern Europe', *Römische historische Mitteilungen*, 55 (2013), 155.

16 Petr Mat'a, 'The false Orsini', 157.

levels of power. Ion Neculce, a boyar and a contemporary chronicler of this situation, expresses his viewpoint perhaps better than anyone:

> Thus I consider with my foolish mind: when God wants to make it so there will be no rust on iron and no Turks in Tsarigrad, and so wolves will not eat sheep in the world, then perhaps there will be no Greeks in Moldavia or in the Land of Walachia either, nor will they [the Greeks] be boyars, and nor will they be able to devour these two lands as they devour them [now ...] Fire you put out, water you dam and divert in another direction, when the wind blows you get out of the way, take shelter, and rest, the sun goes into the clouds, the night with its darkness passes and there is light again; But the Greek has neither mercy nor goodwill, nor justice, nor sincerity, none of these, nor the fear of God.[17]

The Greeks described by Neculce in his chronicle are Orthodox Christians, a little more skilful in handling money and business deals than the Moldavians. As Radu G. Păun observes, direct access to administrative offices eased the path of outsiders to 'high society',[18] providing them with an important lever in the competition for economic resources. As favourites of the princes, the 'Greeks' received functions without having to follow a *cursus honorum* or to be connected to civic life by way of property-owning or other economic activities. In the absence of detailed research on the matter, it is difficult to know who really held power within the princely court. Who took political decisions? Which office-holders in the prince's inner circle really had the power of decision and influence in the princely council? The grand *ban* and the grand *vornic* were the most prestigious offices in the princely council, but were they also the ones that held the power of decision? Each prince displaced the centre of decision-making towards the members of the network to which he belonged. Control was kept over resources by appointing close associates to key offices. Economic resources were gathered from the sale of salt, wax, butter, animals, and skins, from the exploitation of mines, and from the collection of taxes and customs duties. More often than not, the prince would lease the exploitation of the salt mines to members of his network, and would give importance to administrative offices according to the persons appointed to them and not their place in the hierarchy. At the same time, the prince was constrained to use the existing human resources to cover all the posts necessary for the functioning of the state, and this meant appealing to the local boyars. As in the case of Russia, there was no middle class in Moldavia and Wallachia, no rural or

17 Ion Neculce, *Opere. Letopisețul Țării Moldovei și O seamă de cuvinte*, ed. Gabriel Ștrempel (Bucharest: 1982), 301.

18 Păun, *Stratégies de famille*, p. 20.

urban bourgeoisie to supply the functionaries needed if administrative activities were to be carried out.[19] Recruitment was from the ranks of the boyar class, but the prince was able to choose the office-holders that he needed, gratifying them with favours and privileges to compensate for the relatively small salary. Such strategies were always available to a prince, and kept the local boyars dependent on the discretion and mercy of their master. Furthermore, the prince's right to choose his office-holders is mentioned in the numerous *fermans* issued by the Ottoman Empire either to resolve local conflicts or to strengthen the princely prerogatives.

The Curialization of the Boyars

'Never did he leave Bucharest to go to his villages,' writes Mihai Cantacuzino about Iordache Crețulescu, who held the office of grand *vornic* for twenty-seven years (1719–1746) in spite of changes of ruler and of the political factions at the apex of government. The portrait sketched by Mihai Cantacuzino shows the boyar's extraordinary capacity to adapt to the political and economic thinking of the age. We do not know what Iordache Crețulescu had read, or whether he simply saw how to speculate on the changes of the times, embracing them and adapting to meet them. First, he understood very quickly that landed estates constituted an important economic and symbolic capital, but that in order to maintain them it was necessary to have financial resources and power. Second, after the decapitation of his father-in-law, Constantin Brâncoveanu, in 1714, he realized that the centre of power had shifted towards the Phanariots, who needed loyal functionaries skilled in exploiting the province, not boyars proud of their dignity (*ighemonicon*), refined but conflictual and unreliable.[20] It was said of him that he served all the princes with the same devotion and loyalty, keeping as distant as he could from political intrigue, but as close as he could to the princely courts; that he maintained a balance between his job and his private life ('he never spoke in his home about anything of what happened at Court or in the homes of others'); and that he displayed moderation, even

19 For comparisons with the Russian boyar class, see Marc Raeff, 'The Bureaucratic Phenomena of Imperial Russia, 1700–1905', *American Historical Review*, 84, 2 (1979), 399–411.

20 Iordache Creţulescu was married to Safta, the daughter of Constantin Brâncoveanu and Marica. For details, see also Mariana Lazăr, 'Spre lumea "de dincolo", trecând împreună prin lumea pământeană. Marele vornic Iordache Creţulescu şi soţia sa, domniţa Safta Brâncoveanu', in Mircea Ciubotaru, Lucian, Valeriu Lefter (eds.), *Mihai Dim. Sturdza la 80 de ani. Omagiu* (Iaşi: 2014), 799–822.

frugality both in his family life and in his public appearances ('very economical with household expenses he was, and his servants poorly dressed; money on loan he would never give, even at threefold interest'), preferring to live in seclusion, surrounded only by his family.[21] The boyar's behaviour was conditioned by the new political circumstances and by the competition for resources.

As Michał Wasiucionek has observed, departure from the capital involved a considerable risk: the absent boyar might be discredited by his opponents.[22] It was also in order to have access to information that the Moldavian and Wallachian boyars became curialized and tried to remain in the proximity of the princely courts. Gradually the boyars left the residences they had erected on their estates and built houses in the capitals, as close as possible to the centre of power.[23] By the middle of the eighteenth century, the phenomenon had become so alarming that the princely authorities took measures. In 1765, Prince Ștefan Racoviță demanded that the boyars 'without posts' leave Bucharest to attend to their estates and their property in the provinces. He threatened with banishment those found in the city 'spending and ruining themselves only to acquire some post or other.' The measure cannot have been effective, as the prince himself acknowledged that he could not 'judge' the insubordinate boyars, but only frighten them with the threat of 'punishment'.[24]

In the early years of the nineteenth century, the British consul William Wilkinson noted the abandoning of estates and country houses by the boyars in order to be present in the capitals:

> They hardly ever visit their country possessions, which some let our for several years, for much less than their real value, when they find customers who are willing to pay the whole amount of rent in advance. They build fine country-houses which they intend never to inhabit, and which, in a few years, fall into ruin. The most delightful spots in their beautiful country have no power to attract them, neither is it at all customary with them to quit the town residence at any season of the year.[25]

Neglected or left in the hands of tenants, the estates upheld the fame and grandeur of a great boyar, but did not supply him with economic resources. Hence

---

21 Cantacuzino, *Genealogia*, 372–373.

22 Wasiucionek, *The Ottomans and Eastern Europe*, 43.

23 George D. Florescu, *Din vechiul Bucureşti. Biserici, curţi boereşti şi hanuri între anii 1790–1791 după două planuri inedite* (Bucharest: 1935).

24 Valentin Al. Georgescu, Emanuela Popescu (ed.), *Legislaţia urbană a Ţării Româneşti, 1765–1782* (Bucharest: 1975), 235.

25 William Wilkinson, *An Account of the Principalities of Wallachia and Moldavia: With Various Political Observations Relating to Them* (London: 1820), 137–138.

the continual need to hold high offices, and to arrange the political stage in such a way that these positions would remain in the family. The nobility thus came to be attached to functions and not to persons, as the French diplomat Charles Bois-le-Comte observed in his report to count Henri de Rigny.[26] The struggle for positions in the princely council and opposition to numerous ennoblements (grants of titles without the effective content of an administrative office) seemed perfectly legitimate. This rendered the Wallachians 'ungovernable', but also gave them the 'strength' always to hold the 'reins of administration' and political power[27]; less interested in this 'rush' for offices were the Moldavians, the boyar and memorialist Nicolae Suțu writes:

> The Moldavian boyars, much more attentive to their material interests, concern themselves much more with the exploitation of their lands than with seeking administrative offices. For this reason, they have always been more independent and have known how to resist the power of their rulers when public interest required it. The Wallachians were more malleable and more inclined to pull all sorts of strings for the occupation of administrative offices, and thus less docile.[28]

But before Suțu, the French consul Charles-Frédéric Reinhard had also noticed this difference.[29] His observation is repeated by Wilkinson:

> The Boyars in Moldavia, like those in Wallachia, are the great land-proprietors; but they bestow much more of their attention and time to the improvement of their estates, which they make their principal source of riches.[30]

Lack of interest in their estates increased the boyars' dependence on the positions offered by the prince and implicitly on political power. 'Waiting for the mercy of the ruler,' writes Dinicu Golescu at the start of the nineteenth century, 'we are merely born and rot in the city.' This waiting 'for some five or ten

26 *Călători străini despre țările române în secolul al XIX-lea*, eds. Paul Cernovodeanu and Daniela Bușe (Bucharest: 2007), III, 124; See also Gheorghe Platon, Alexandru Florin Platon, *Boierimea din Moldova în secolul al XIX-lea. Context european, evoluție socială și politică* (*Date statistice și observații istorice*) (Bucharest: 1995), 69, note 42.

27 *Călători străini în secolul al XIX-lea*, III, 124.

28 Nicolas Soutzo, *Mémoires du Prince Nicolas Soutzo, grand-logothète de Moldavie, 1798–1871*, ed. Panaïoti Rizos (Vienne: 1899), 356; See also Gh. Platon, Al. F. Platon, *Boierimea din Moldova*, 69.

29 *Călători străini în secolul al XIX-lea*, I, 254–255.

30 Wilkinson, *An Account of the Principalities*, 138.

years, or till our turn comes' was not easy, and led to a total abandoning of their estates, of their true wealth, in favour of the desire to 'rule'.[31]

'For Him to be Again Alpha and Omega': Patronage and Kinship

The Phanariots came to their thrones accompanied by an entourage, and they offered key posts to close associates so as to hold onto their power as long as possible and be sure that the resources at their disposal were exploited as effectively as possible. The newcomers relied in the first place on the protection offered by their patron. Direct and immediate access to administrative office came, however, with a vulnerability: dependence on the goodwill of the patron, in this case the prince, who in his turn depended on the goodwill of the Porte. In these conditions, the 'Greeks' had to find levers that could enable them to build stability and to ensure a future for themselves.

Before arriving in Iași or Bucharest, they created for themselves transborder support networks to help them to obtain positions. The Phanariots knew no territorial limits, building networks as wide-reaching as possible, and their mastery of foreign languages helped their self-advancement. The cultivation and maintenance of as many personal relations as possible was directed towards the structuring of a network in which patrons and clients offered one another mutual support in the promotion of common interests. The local boyars appealed to the antiquity and prestige of their lineages as grounds for receiving administrative offices, but these two criteria were not sufficient when it came to appointments to important posts. It was matrimonial strategies that contributed to the construction of connections that were durable and profitable in the long term. Ion Neculce offers as an example the boyar Iordache Ruset (Rosetti), who became one of the most powerful men in Moldavia: 'Iordache thought that again he would bring Mihai-vodă from Tsarigrad, to make him prince here in this country, that he might again *be alpha and omega*, just as he was before princes sent by the Turks ruled.'[32] The moment of this

31 Dinicu Golescu, *Însemnare a călătoriii mele, Costandin Radovici din Goleşti făcută în anul 1824, 1825, 1826*, ed. Mircea Iorgulescu (Bucharest: 1977), 116. The hypothesis is also supported by the historians Gh. and Al. F. Platon. In a very detailed analysis for Moldavia, they observe that the boyars of Wallachia were much more tied to administrative functions and ranks, which constituted to a large extent their economic support, while the Moldavian boyars managed to maintain a degree of independence due to their involvement in the exploitation of their estates (Gh. Platon, Al. F. Platon, *Boierimea din Moldova*, 87).

32 Neculce, *Letopiseţul Ţării Moldovei*, 557–558.

intervention is very important: 1711, when Dimitrie Cantemir opted for Russia and Tsar Peter I to the detriment of the Ottoman Empire, which had, after all, appointed him to the throne of Moldavia. In this moment of testing of faith and loyalties, the boyars aligned themselves according to their own interests and political and social attachments. Iordache Ruset had opposed the alliance with Peter, ably manoeuvring his relations and influence among the boyars, Phanariots, and Ottoman dignitaries to bring his nephew, Mihai Racoviță to the throne.[33] His intrigues aroused the fury of the tsar, who had him arrested and imprisoned him in Kyiv for two years.[34]

How did Iordache Ruset manage to amass so much power? What political and social levers did he make use of in his ascent? The figure I shall now focus on is one among many 'Greek' office-holders who managed to hold immense power at a particular moment, and in what follows I shall try to identify the means by which this was possible.

The roots of the Ruset (Rossetos, Rosetti) lineage go back to thirteenth-century Genoa, whence it seems that one Ioanes Rossetos left for Constantinople, where he married, converted to Orthodoxy, and so managed to enter the ranks of the Byzantine aristocracy.[35] However it is only from the seventeenth century that we have concrete and verifiable data, starting with Laskaris Rossetos, grand logothete of the Patriarchate of Constantinople, married to Bella, daughter of Ioan Cantacuzino. According to Radu Rosetti, he was the father of Constantin the *cupar*[36] and Antonie Ruset, the founders of the Ruset lineage in Wallachia and Moldavia.[37] According to Eugène Rizo-Rangabé, however, Constantin the *cupar* was not the son of Laskaris Rossetos, but merely a contemporary of his, who held various offices in the service of the princes of Wallachia and Moldavia and succeeded in acquiring great influence at the Porte.[38] Iordache

33 Mihai Racoviţă was the son of Ion, grand *vornic* of Moldavia. Ion's sister, Safta was married to Iordache Ruset.

34 He would be released in 1714 at the intervention of his son's father-in-law, Constantin Brâncoveanu.

35 Radu Rosetti, *Amintiri. Ce am auzit de la alţii. Din copilărie. Din prima tinereţe* (Bucharest: 2013), 19; Radu Rosetti, *Familia Rosetti.* I. *Coborâtorii moldoveni ai lui Lascaris Rousaitos* (Bucharest: 1938), 56; See Andrei Pippidi, 'Date noi despre Roseteşti şi pământurile lor la sfârşitul secolului al XVIII-lea', *Carpica*, IV (1971), 331–341; Andrei Pippidi, 'Originele familiei Rosetti şi confirmarea unei mărturii a lui Neculce', *Anuarul Institutului de Istorie şi Arheologie "A.D. Xenopol"*, XX (1983), 275–180.

36 So called because he held the office of *cupar*, a minor post with responsibility for the princely beverages. His sons would also be known as 'Cupăreştii'.

37 Rosetti, *Amintiri*, 20.

38 Eugène Rizo-Rangabé, *Livre d'or de la noblesse phanariote en Grèce, en Roumanie, en Russie et en Turquie, par un phanariote* (Athènes: 1892), 113.

Ruset began his career in Wallachia, building, together with his four brothers, a network that extended its tentacles as far as Istanbul. Married to Maria, daughter of Prince Eustratie Dabija and sister of Dafina, the wife of Prince Gheorghe Duca, he invested energy, time, money, and influence to bring favourable rulers to the thrones of the two countries. Manole (Manolache), Scarlat (Scarlatache), Lascar (Lascarache), and Mihai (Mihalache) Ruset acted together with him. The first two represented the interests of the princes at the Porte in the role of *capuchehaia* (diplomatic agent), while the other two were active on the political arena, sometimes in Moldavia and sometimes in Wallachia, marrying their offspring into local boyar families, and laying the foundations of a network that would enable them to hold political control.[39] When Maria died, Iordache Ruset married Ecaterina, the daughter of Nicolae Racoviță and aunt of Mihai Racoviță.[40] This marriage introduced him into another trans-border network, and also brought him a significant dowry. Iordache Ruset settled permanently in Moldavia, and with the help of Ecaterina's dowry, he began to build a landowning empire, assiduously buying village after village. In order to root himself as deeply as possible in his country of adoption, he skilfully developed a matrimonial policy for his family, marrying his sons and daughters into some of the most distinguished boyar families in Wallachia and Moldavia. By 1710, he was a target of hatred, fear, and envy. The boyars expressed their discontent and unease in a letter addressed to Nicolae Mavrocordat:

> Iordachi the *vornic*, being here a man foreign to the country, with the help of his brothers who were *capuchehaia*s to the imperial Porte, has ruined our whole country, changing frequently the princes who were not pleasing to him, thus incurring very heavy expenses, without the country knowing. Similarly he has trodden over and disregarded all the boyar houses, completely ruining most of them.[41]

Nicolae Mavrocordat loathed Iordache Ruset for this ability to grasp any opportunity, diligently weaving networks of kinship by placing his sons, daughters, and grandchildren in wealthy and politically influential families. The real reason for his hostility, however, was the fear that, Ruset, in collaboration with his brothers based in Istanbul, was plotting to have Mavrocordat deposed and his nephew, Mihai Racoviță, put on the throne. Although he discovered a series of

39 For the political careers of these brothers, see Nicolae Stoicescu, *Dicţionar al marilor dregători din Ţara Românească şi Moldova* (Bucharest: 1971), 436–440.

40 Mihai Racoviţă occupied the throne of Wallachia twice (1730–1731, 1741–1744) and that of Moldavia three times (1703–1705, 1707–1709, 1716–1726).

41 *Cronica Ghiculeştilor. Istoria Moldovei între 1695–1754*, eds. Nestor Camariano and Ariadna Camariano-Cioran (Bucharest: 1965), 67–69.

compromising letters in Ruset's house, Mavrocordat was afraid to punish him with death. He staged a treason trial coordinated by Metropolitan Ghedeon of Moldavia, supported by the boyar faction who were faithful to him. 'The law condemns him to death,' wrote the metropolitan, but the prince commuted the death penalty to having his tongue cut out, because Ruset had defended himself by saying that all the evidence brought against him was mere 'lies'. Even this sentence he could not carry out. 'Several of the Greek boyars, close to the prince, went again to him and begged him not to apply that punishment,' writes the chronicler of the events of the time.[42] What is striking is the repeated attempts ('again') to eliminate Ruset from the political game. As on every occasion, the family and transborder network intervened, showing its power and influence.

In contrast to Iordache Crețulescu mentioned above, who was loyal to all princes, Iordache Ruset was loyal only to his own interests, aligning himself according to the context and the immediate utility of a relationship. His interests lay in installing and maintaining on the Moldavian throne a member of his network, a patron who would repay his services with access to economic resources. Mihai Racoviță met these criteria and so Ruset's efforts and those of his network were focused on this end, though it was only in 1716 that Racoviță obtained the throne of Moldavia. According to the chronicles of the time, he repaid the efforts of the Ruset brothers, giving them his full confidence and power: 'What he wanted, what he commanded, that Mihai *vodă* did,' writes a contemporary of Iordache Ruset.[43]

Ion Neculce, belonging to the opposing side, had every reason to characterize Ruset as the 'source of all evils' in Moldavia, judging as treason the decisions of his rival to align himself according to immediate interests, but acknowledging his extraordinary ability to find a way out of any situation. Of Iordache Ruset's decision to resolve his open conflict with Prince Constantin Brâncoveanu by a marriage, he writes:

> At least he was a wise man, and his nature was that of a Greek greedy for honour; he took no account of God, nor of shame in the eyes of people, nor of punishment, nor of what might come after. And straight away he made the engagement

---

42 Ibid., 69.

43 Mihail Kogălniceanu, *Cronicele Romȃniei sau Letopisețele Moldaviei și Valahiei* (Bucharest: 1872), II, 278–280. On favourites and the great power that they might exert, see the excellent study by Günhan Börekçi, *On the Power, Political Career and the Patronage Networks of the Ottoman Royal Favourites* (*late Sixteenth and Early Seventeenth Centuries*) https://www.academia.edu/38073778/On_the_Power_Political_Career_and_Patronage_Networks_of_the_Ottoman_Royal_Favourites_Late_Sixteenth_and_Early_Seventeenth_Centuries [accessed 12.09.2020].

> and agreed to cast off the Cantemirs. Brâncoveanu asked Antioh *vodă* to [let him] give him his daughter and to cast off the friendship of the Cupărs, and he [Antioh] did not agree; and he [Ruset], when he had the chance, immediately agreed happily.[44]

The move was well thought-out, for by the marriage of his firstborn Nicolae to Brâncoveanu's daughter Ancuța, Ruset was appeasing a conflict and bringing a rich and important ruler close to him. Of course the alliance raised problems: the Cantemirs and the Brâncoveanus were deadly enemies.[45] Antioh Cantemir remained faithful to his office-holder, refusing the matrimonial alliance proposed by Brâncoveanu in order to protect his subject and adviser.[46] Iordache Ruset, however, had no reservations about betraying his master. He sensed which way the wind was blowing and directed his attention to the most powerful figure of the moment. Dimitrie Cantemir would assign him an important role in his allegorical history of the conflict between the Cantemirs (Antioh, the son of the Elephant, and Dimitrie, the Unicorn) and Brâncoveanu (the Raven). Written in Istanbul in the years 1703–1705, after the death of the author's father, Constantin Cantemir (1693), the *Hieroglyphic History* (*Istoria ieroglifică*) describes the rivalries between the various political factions seeking to take power in Moldavia (the land of quadrupeds), Wallachia (the land of birds), and the Ottoman Empire, (the empire of fish). Iordache Ruset takes the form of the Leopard in the land of animals, while his brother Scarlat Ruset is the chameleon, capable of changing according to its prey. When Dimitrie Cantemir was finishing the writing of the *Hieroglyphic History*, his brother Antioh took the throne of Moldavia for two years (1705–1707).[47]

On his death (probably around 1720), Iordache Ruset left one of the greatest fortunes in Moldavia, which he divided among his sons and daughters. But above all, he had managed to lay the foundations of an extensive and influential family network, making alliances with the most powerful families of Moldavia.[48] By means of this network, the Ruset family dominated the Moldavian political scene throughout the eighteenth century, modifying

44 Neculce, *Letopisețul Țării Moldovei*, 430–431.

45 It seems that the alliance was mediated by the patriarch of Jerusalem, Chrysanthos Notaras. Kogălniceanu, *Cronicile României*, II, 274.

46 At this point, Iordache Ruset held the office of grand *vistiernic* under Antioh Cantemir. Stoicescu, *Dicționar*, 436.

47 Dimitrie Cantemir, *Opere fundamentale*, vol. I (*Divanul. Istoria ieroglifică. Hronicul vechimei a româno-moldo vlahilor*) (Bucharest: 2003).

48 Elena Bedreag, 'Descendența și averea marelui vornic Iordache Ruset', in Dan Dumitru Iacob (ed.), *Avere, prestigiu și cultură materială în surse patrimoniale. Inventare de averi din secolele XVI–XIX* (Iași: 2015), 157–203; Elena Bedreag, '"La vrerea me este să-i dau au

its identity and integrating perfectly in the Moldavian environment. In the course of a generation, the family's Greekness was lost, and they adopted a Moldavian identity. Already by the middle of the eighteenth century, the Ruset kindred had managed, by way of marriage, to enter the ranks of the great boyar families of Moldavia, and were considered to belong there. Their name was changed from Ruset to Roset, and then, in the early nineteenth century, the legends of their Italian origin led to its being changed to Rosetti.[49] In 1856, when Constantin Sion was compiling the book of the Moldavian boyars, he questioned both the Greek and the Italian origins of the Rosettis. Known for the virulence of his criticisms of the 'Greeks', Sion proved more than generous in the case of the Rosettis. Indeed, he even justified and accepted their Greek origin, which no longer seemed so bad once it was lost in the mists of time: 'If these Rosettis who are great boyars are also Greeks, they came to our country long ago, for 200 years have passed since they were raised to high ranks.'[50]

The above case highlights the importance of a family network for social advancement and active participation in the political arena. The economic resources of the Principalities were limited, and the system of succession resulted in their being divided with each new generation. Written law (the *Pravilă*) and custom provided for the transmission of estate to all rightful heirs in Moldavia, men and women alike. In Wallachia, only men could receive equal shares in the estate, while women received a dowry on marriage. In the case of boyar families, the dowry was often very substantial, and might be considered an important part of the paternal patrimony, In these conditions, the patrimony crumbled. Even if the heirs received significant shares of the estate, they were obliged to enter the political game in order to amass a patrimony of their own, which would then be shared among the members of their families. Ultimately, to borrow Valerie A. Kivelson's conclusion, this system of succession was 'a way of life', which the elites did not regard passively, but sought to make use of in order to build up their own wealth.[51] By rationally thought-out matrimonial strategies, the boyars constructed for themselves the levers necessary for access to the political arena, and from there, to economic resources. From among the members of the family, trustworthy figures were recruited who could be inserted into key posts and who could be relied on at any time.

---

ba dintr-ale mele lucruri". Diata marelui vornic Iordache Ruset', in Mircea Ciubotaru, Lucian-Valeriu Lefter (eds.), *Mihai Dim. Sturdza la 80 de ani. Omagiu* (Iaşi: 2014), 571–586.

49 Rosetti, *Familia Rosetti*, 25.

50 Constantin Sion, *Arhondologia Moldovei. Amintiri şi note contimporane. Boierii Moldovei* (Bucharest: 1973), 222–223.

51 Valerie A. Kivelson, 'The Effects of Partible Inheritance: Gentry Families and the State in Muscovy', *The Russian Review*, 53, 2 (1994), 206.

Trust was an important ingredient in the construction and maintenance of a network.[52]

Iordache Ruset had made sure of a future for himself, anchoring himself permanently in a 'homeland'. By buying estates, building houses for himself in Moldavia, marrying his children into the native elite, and participating actively in the political life of the country, Ruset had won the right to be considered 'Moldavian'.

Identification and Loyalty

In the face of this aggressive campaign of self-promotion, the local boyars had no option but to adapt, to learn, and then to fight back using the same methods. I opened this chapter with Ion Neculce, grand *hatman* of Moldavia, who witnessed the rise of the Phanariots and of Greek office-holders in the principality in the first half of the eighteenth century. Born in Moldavia around the year 1672, the son of the *vistier* Neculce and Catrina Cantacuzino, Ion Neculce had the privilege of belonging to a network of family solidarity that spread out towards Wallachia and the Ottoman Empire. Although the Byzantine ancestry of the Cantacuzinos was continually asserted to add to the prestige of the lineage, their ethnicity had been lost along the way through integration and assimilation among the boyar families. Their Greek origins were ignored, while they obstinately insisted on the prestige of imperial descent. The 'Greeks' criticized by Neculce were in fact his competitors in the political arena, recently arrived with the Phanariot prince, and thus much better placed than he and the other Moldavian boyars were. Through direct connections, these 'Greeks' obtained important offices directly and immediately. It was with them that Neculce had his quarrel. The others, settled for a generation or two, with houses, families, and estates, were accepted as already part of the social fabric.

Nevertheless, our interest in Neculce focuses on his period of exile, to bring to light the different forms that allegiance could assume.[53] Returning to 1711, it must be emphasized that Ion Neculce, grand *hatman* of Moldavia, had been one of the leading supporters of the alliance with Russia.[54] When the war took

52 Wasiucionek, *The Ottomans and Eastern Europe*, 45.

53 Roland Mousnier, 'Les concepts d' « ordres » d' « états », de « fidélité » et de « monarchie absolue » en France de la fin du XVe siècle à la fin du XVIIIe', *Revues Historique*, t. 247, Fasc. 2,502 (1972), 289–312; Antoni Mączak, *Unequal Friendship. The Patron-Client Relationship in Historial Perspective* (Frankfurt am Main: 2017).

54 For the stages in the course of the war, see Virginia H. Aksan, *Ottoman Wars, 1700–1870. An Empire Besieged* (London: 2007), 90–98.

an unexpected turn and the Ottomans won, the *hatman*'s fate too was sealed. In the same situation were another 4,000 people: great boyars with their families (24), lesser boyars with their families (448), servants, soldiers, and members of the princely family.[55] During his stay in Kyiv in October 1711, Cantemir had to face the first cracks in his people's fidelity.[56] A number of boyars, including Neculce, asked leave to remain in Kyiv and wait for a suitable moment to return to Moldavia. The prince had gone to some effort to get Peter I to grant his boyars and servants posts and means of subsistence in their new homeland. Early in 1712, many of them indeed received estates and serfs, each according to his rank, in the regions of Novomlisk, Balakleika, Kolodezhna, Dvurechny Kut, and Kursk.[57] Ion Neculce refused to accept the grant of property, and repeated the same request to be allowed to return to Moldavia. When Cantemir refused his request, Neculce appealed to the Tsar, who gave him a favourable answer: 'If he does not want to settle, let him have his will: God help him to go where he wishes, for he is not my slave.'[58] In appealing to Peter, Neculce was highlighting the new status he had assumed from the moment he entered Russia: that of one under the Tsar's protection. His patron, Dimitrie Cantemir had lost his exclusive power and capacity to offer services to his clients.[59] Leaving such a relationship was more than justified from the point of view of Neculce, who pragmatically noted his patron's powerlessness to build a future:

> And the prince dreams that he is still powerful, as in his own country, when he is prince, and wants to keep it so, to upset those boyars, and he does not consider the service they have done him, that they have abandoned their homes, which he has no understanding of.[60]

Of course he is referring to the relations between himself and Dimitrie Cantemir, which deteriorated from the moment he declared himself dissatisfied with exile and with the new power relations. Furthermore, the new social

55 A list of the boyars who followed Dimitrie Cantemir can be found in Ion Neculce, *Letopiseţul Ţării Moldovei*, 602. For an exhaustive list, see Mihai-Bogdan Atanasiu, 'Bucuroşi Muscalilor şi Greşiţi Prealuminatei Porţi. Oamenii Măriei Sale Dumitraşcu Vodă Cantemir, pribegi la Harkov', in Cristian Ploscaru, Mihai-Bogdan Atanasiu (eds.), *Elitele Puterii-Puterea Elitelor în spaţiul Românesc (secolele XV–XX)* (Iaşi: 2018), 243–256.

56 On Cantemir, see Ştefan Lemny, *Cantemireştii. Aventura europeană a unei familii princiare din secolul al XVIII-lea* (Iaşi: 2013), 133–145.

57 Atanasiu, *Neculce*, 70.

58 Neculce, *Letopiseţul Ţării Moldovei*, 618.

59 Kettering, 'Patronage', 845.

60 Neculce, *Letopiseţul Ţării Moldovei*, 620.

and political context does not favour a father's dreams of greater things for his sons:

> So, as for my life, it was as it was, but [I cared] more for my children, what they would be left with, that they would just be soldiers; while in other high noble offices there is not room for the sons of some [exiles] as for these.[61]

Peter I's reforms had created the necessary premises for the absorption of new members into the ranks of the 'Russian nobility', but had also prepared the ground for better competition. The table of ranks opened the way to noble privilege and status for soldiers and capable functionaries in the imperial administration.[62] However it was a way that seemed long and unpredictable.

According to Neculce, obedience and loyalty towards a ruler should be limited to the borders of the country and the duration of his rule:

> Which, brother Moldavians, I beg you to bear in mind, to teach yourselves, and to guard yourselves. However much is honourable towards a prince, it is good to serve him with justice, for from [God] too you have payment. And with the prince never to go into exile, no matter what, and not only in a foreign country but neither to Tsarigrad to go with him, you being Moldavian. You should serve him in your own country, for foreigners seek only to pity and to honour the prince, but the boyars who are in exile with him are as nothing.[63]

Tsarigrad and the Ottoman Empire are not assimilated to 'foreignness', but fix the status of the Moldavian as Orthodox Christian and Ottoman subject. This status of 'Ottoman subject' remained attached to the boyar and brought and carried with it an inherent ground for suspicion. The fear that the boyars might quickly change their loyalty to the Tsar for loyalty to the sultan was expressed both by Dimitrie Cantemir and by the Russian generals. Cantemir denounced his boyars for having an understanding with the 'Turks', while the Russian generals did not want powerful competition in Kharkhiv, and thus made the Tsar aware of their suspicion that the Moldavian prince might make peace with the sultan at any time, as others had done before him.[64] Moreover, cooperation with Russia brought as a consequence the annulment of the protection offered

61 Ibid. 619.

62 Nancy Shields Kollmann, *The Russian Empire, 1450–1801* (Oxford: 2017), 428.

63 Neculce, *Letopisețul Țării Moldovei*, 620.

64 Ibid., 615, 617.

by the sultan according to the terms of the capitulations, and might lead to the arrest or even enslavement of the boyars.[65]

Neculce's exile and his regaining of the sultan's trust lasted nine years. Family solidarities and transborder networks worked together to obtain the sultan's forgiveness. Without this, a boyar could not safely cross the Moldavian border. As *capuchehaia*s, princes, and viziers were bombarded with more and more letters and gifts for the winning of forgiveness, so the boyar would advance closer and closer to the border. Exile had brought with it the confiscation of his wealth, as a punishment for betrayal, and its redistribution among the other competitors. They in their turn would do what they could to keep the renegade beyond the border, similarly, making use of money and networks to prevent forgiveness. Such was the case of Neculce, whose wealth had been confiscated and shared out by Nicolae Mavrocordat among other boyars who had here he embarked on the process of winning the trust of the new prince, recovering his wealth, remaking his alliances, and regaining his place in the networks of power. A 'face-washing', as Neculce put it, was necessary for him to regain his social position and to introduce his sons into circles of power.[66]

In 1720, when he launched the process of recovering his estates, Ion Neculce set down the nature of the relations between patron offered him their loyalty.[67] However, Mavrocordat himself, together with the other Phanariot prince, Mihai Racoviță, helped to obtain a *ferman* of forgiveness from the sultan. Mavrocordat's volte-face can only be explained by his need for allies within the country when he regained the throne of Moldavia. The *ferman* arrived at the end of 1719 and Neculce returned to his 'homeland', wand client, between master and subject, establishing the framework in which they operated and the obligations of each party. Accused that he had been influential in the decision to enter an alliance with Russia, Neculce defended himself, emphasizing that 'he had been no more than the servant who served his master rightly,' obeying him and being faithful to him as his office and honour demanded. He could have no power of decision in such a relation ('nor was he anyone with power'), given his position in the political hierarchy.[68] Speaking about the events of 1711, the document recounts in detail the relations of the boyars with their various

65 Will Smiley, *From Slaves to Prisoners of War. The Ottoman Empire, Russia and International Law* (Oxford: 2018), 26. See also Viorel Panaite, 'The Re'ayas of the Tributary Protected Principalities: The Sixteenth Through the Eighteenth Centuries', *International Journal of Turkish Studies*, 9, 1 (2003), 79–104.

66 Neculce, *Letopisețul Țării Moldovei*, 625.

67 Iulian Marinescu, 'Documente relative la Ioan Neculce', *Buletinul Comisiei Istorice a României*, IV (1925), 1 august 1712, 43–45.

68 Marinescu, *Documente*, 49, [1720].

patrons, showing the rapidity and pragmatism with which loyalties might shift according to immediate material ends.[69]

Loyalties and disloyalties were proven or disproven with every reign; the new prince punished some but forgave the majority. Forgiveness was an aspect of princely mercy, by means of which he ensured future allegiances. Moreover, a prince could not govern when there were significant groups of boyars scattered through the neighbouring empires who might at any time come together and complain to the sultan, thus contributing to his removal from the throne.[70] Forgiveness thus also had a practical dimension: it kept subjects close so that they could be supervised and controlled. In its turn, the Ottoman Empire granted collective forgiveness after every conflict. Preoccupied with the economic capacity of its subjects, it urged them to return to their homes, to work their land, and to pay their taxes.[71] Different objectives converged towards the social pacification that could ensure the human resources necessary for the political and economic process.

Waiting for Peace: Subjecthood as an Oriental Embroidery

On 15 June 1773, Zoiţa Brâncoveanu sent Empress Maria Theresa an oriental embroidery together with the following letter of thanks:

> Madame, It is only after obtaining the permission of His Imperial Majesty, our August Emperor, that I take the liberty of presenting the first fruits of my work to Your Sacred Royal and Imperial Majesty. As these are oriental effects, I believe that Your Majesty will be pleased to accept them from *a most obedient subject*. It is all worked by my hand to give an idea of Turkish work. I shall be happy if Your Majesty will be pleased to receive it favourably. Ever recommending myself to her powerful protection, I shall glory in being, with the most

69 Kettering, 'Patronage in Early Modern France', 844.

70 Dimitrie Cantemir writes that a skilful ruler who knows how to introduce himself into the Ottoman networks of influence may at any time counter any complaint with gifts to the great ones of the moment. Cantemir, *Descrierea Moldovei*, 74–75.

71 Such an amnesty also took place after the Russian–Ottoman war of 1711, when 'the most exalted Porte, after the return of the Muscovites, at once to all showed mercy and pardoned everyone of all their wrongdoings that they might return to their lands and be tax-payers as they had been before'. Marinescu, *Documente*, 56. After almost every war, *fermans* of amnesty were issued for the Christians of Moldavia and Wallachia, either collectively or individually. See, for example, the *fermans* of 4/14 November 1774, 2/12 May 1792, and 9/19 June 1793, which speak of the pardoning of 'boyars and rayas' and the 'forgetting' of wrongs committed in time of war. Mustafa A. Mehmet (ed.), *Documente turceşti privind la istoria României* (Bucharest: 1983), vol. II, 2–4; (1986), vol. III, 31, 46–47.

> profound respect, the most humble and most obedient servant and *faithful subject*. Zoitza B. De Brancovanis. Wife of Emanuel.[72] [emphasis mine]

The letter and the embroidery left the city of Kronstadt (Brașov) in Transylvania, for Vienna.[73] Emanuel (Manolache, Manuil) Brâncoveanu likewise wrote a letter, this time to Chancellor Kaunitz, announcing and praising the gift as something that 'cannot be found in Europe, but only among the oriental nations.'[74] By this gesture, he was showing his gratitude for the most important service with which the empress had rewarded him: the granting of a passport. The process had taken more than three years, and had involved an assiduous correspondence in which he affirmed his fidelity to the imperial crown. Why did Brâncoveanu now need such a gesture of gratitude? What happened to the status of subject in wartime? Was it suspended? By examining an important body of correspondence preserved in the archives in Vienna, I shall try to analyse the multiple facets of the status of subject, as it appears in the writing of the actors involved: Wallachian boyars, the Austrian authorities, and the Russian authorities.

The eighteenth century was marked by the exile of various groups of boyars in Poland, Russia, the Habsburg territories, and the Ottoman Empire. The wars fought in the region were the cause of most such flights and led to many families seeking refuge elsewhere. The Moldavian boyars withdrew especially to Poland or Russia, while those from Wallachia preferred Transylvania. For their protection, some made efforts to seek powerful patrons among the tsars, kings, and emperors, offering them their allegiance and taking oaths of loyalty. The process did not prevent them remaining also Ottoman subjects. In an age of permanent insecurity, protection was necessary to ensure one's survival. The Cantacuzinos, Bălăceanus, Brâncoveanus, and Văcărescus were just a few of the great boyar families that assiduously cultivated relations with the crowned

72 'Madame, Ce n'est qu'après avoir obtenu la permission de Sa Majesté Impériale, notre Auguste Empereur, que je prends la hardiesse de présenter les prémices de mes ouvrages à Votre Majesté Sacrée Royale Impériale. Comme ce sont des effets orientaux, je crois que Votre Majesté voudra bien les recevoir comme partant d'une sujette très soumise. Le tout est travaillé de ma main pour donner une idée des ouvrages Turcs. Je me trouverai heureuse si Votre Majesté veut bien l'accueillir favorablement me recommandant toujours sous sa puissante protection, je me ferai gloire d'être avec le plus profond respect. La plus humble et la plus obéissante servante et fidele sujette. Zoitza B. De Brancovanis. Epouse d'Emanuel'.

73 See HHStA, Moldau-Walachei I/26, Brancovan (1767–1777), f. 41.

74 HHStA, Moldau-Walachei I/26, Brancovan (1767–1777), f. 40, 15 June 1773.

heads round about, seeking and managing to obtain noble titles.[75] On the basis of these titles, family members sought protection, asylum, passports, and other favours, invoking their obedience and fidelity over the decades to the values of the empires.[76]

The Russian–Ottoman war of 1768–1774 brings a situation of this sort to the foreground.[77] The moment is captured in a number of sources, giving us access to a variety of opinions both about the event itself and about the positions expressed regarding the social and political status of the members of the elite.[78] Two contemporaries record the event, each from a different position: *ban* Mihai Cantacuzino, writing the history of his family, supports the pro-Russian wing among the boyars[79]; Ianache Văcărescu, writing a history of the Ottoman Empire, supports the pro-Ottoman wing.[80] At the same time, the correspondence of the refugee boyars in Transylvania provides further material for an analysis of behaviour and of the definition of a social status in relation to social and political circumstances. The Russian–Ottoman war divided the political class according to their affinities and interests. The Cantacuzinos tried to gather around them as many boyars as possible dedicated to the Russian cause. The Russian advance into Moldavia aroused the hopes of Christians (encouraged by the propaganda of Russia, which presented itself as the defender of all Christians[81]) and opened doors for numerous opportunists who profited from the war, as Ianache Văcărescu observed:

75 See the transcription of these diplomas, passports, and other privileges in Cantacuzino, *Genealogia*, 259–283.

76 HHStA, Moldau-Walachei I/26/Vaccaresculi (1772–1773) and Brancovan (1767–1777).

77 Aksan, *Ottoman Wars*, 129–159.

78 For the Russian–Ottoman war, see also two contemporary accounts in V.A. Urechia, 'Istoria evenimentelor din Orient cu referinţă la principatele Moldova şi Valahia din anii 1769–1774 de biv-vel stolnicul Dumitrache', *Analele Academiei Române. Memoriile Secţiei Istorice*, t. X (1887–1888), 398–417; and Dionisie Eclisiarhu, *Scrieri alese. Hronograf. Predoslovii*, ed. Natalia Trandafirescu (Bucharest: 2004). The archimandrite Venedict, member of the Moldavian delegation also wrote a travel diary. See Drace-Francis, *Traditions of Invention. Romanian Ethnic and Social Stereotypes in Historical Context* (Leiden: 2013), 99–102.

79 Mihai Cantacuzino, *Genealogia Cantacuzinilor*, ed. Nicolae Iorga (Bucharest: 1902).

80 Ianache Văcărescu, *Istoria Othomanicească*, ed. Gabriel Ştrempel (Bucharest: 2001).

81 Mihai Cantacuzino introduces into his history a translation of the printed manifestos ('tălmăcire a manifestelor tipărite') that Russia distributed among the Orthodox Christians of the Balkans. Cantacuzino, *Genealogia*, 161–167. On this subject, see Victor Taki, *Limits of Protection: Russia and the Orthodox Coreligionists in the Ottoman Empire* (Pittsburgh: 2015), 1–79.

> All Christians who did not ponder on what had happened, and who were not steeped in knowledge of political direction, considered that Russia would lift from the world, or at least from Europe, all Turkish rule. Some out of ardour for the law, others out of an appetite for glory, and others for the love of plunder became Russian soldiers.[82]

The boyars on the side of Russia sent a delegation, headed by *ban* Mihai Cantacuzino and Nicolae Brâncoveanu, to Saint Petersburg to declare their fidelity to the empire. Ferdinand William Ernest von Solms wrote from Saint Petersburg on 10 April 1770 that 'the delegates from Moldavia and Wallachia, clergy and nobles, have arrived here and the day before yesterday they had a solemn audience with His Imperial Majesty, in the course of which they formally recognized the subordination of their provinces to the sceptre of Russia.' Among them, Solms recognized the metropolitan of Moldavia, the principal bishops and archimandrites, and the boyars Cantacuzino and Brâncoveanu at their head, both 'maintaining that they are descended from old Greek emperors.'[83] In his turn, Mihai Cantacuzino recounts in great detail the splendid reception that the Moldavian and Wallachian delegations enjoyed in the presence of Empress Catherine II.[84] As Victor Taki notes, by accepting the protection of Russia, the boyars were seeking to consolidate their own position in relation to the Phanariot princes and the Ottoman Empire.[85] Many of them would receive important offices in the administration of their countries under Russian occupation (1768–1774), but at the end of the war they would have to go into exile in Russia to escape the wrath of the sultan.

Ianache Văcărescu, who at the time held the office of grand *vistier*, deftly managed to avoid inclusion in the delegation, and took refuge in Brașov, in Transylvania. For political reasons and seeing things through the prism of the network of which he was part, he remained faithful to the Ottoman Empire, and tried to make himself useful and to respond whenever his involvement was solicited.

However, if the positions of the Cantacuzinos and the Văcărescus were clear, Nicolae and Emanuel Brâncoveanu wavered. After his return from Saint Petersburg to Iași, Nicolae Brâncoveanu came into conflict with the Russian army stationed there, as a result of which he decided to take refuge in Brașov,

---

82 Văcărescu, *Istoria*, 103.

83 Nicolae Iorga (ed.), *Acte şi fragmente cu privire la istoria românilor adunate din depozitele de manuscrise ale Apusului* (Bucharest: 1896), vol. 2, 27.

84 Cantacuzino, *Genealogia*, 181–184.

85 Taki, *Limits of Protection*, 8.

where he had a house and several estates.[86] The insecurity generated by the armed conflict led numerous other boyars to leave the conflict zone and take refuge over the mountains in Brașov. It cannot have been easy for the administration of the city to handle the influx of population from south of the Carpathians, a pretentious and demanding group. Accustomed to enjoying privileges and prestige in their homeland, the boyars tried to maintain these in their migration, to demand them, and indeed to insist on them.[87]

The case of the Brâncoveanus is important as an example of this game of *self-fashioning* and underlining of social status despite the conditions of exile. The Brâncoveanus requested and obtained diplomas as princes of the Holy Roman Empire. Constantin Brâncoveanu, prince of Wallachia (1688–1714), had received the title of Prince of the Empire from Emperor Leopold I on 30 January 1695, with the right to buy properties in Transylvania where he could take refuge in case of war.[88] Later, his grandson, Constantin Brâncoveanu (1707–1752) took steps to have this title renewed, so that his sons, Nicolae and Emanuel might request and obtain the reconfirmation of the title of 'Prince'.[89] As refugees in Brașov, waiting for peace, Nicolae and Emanuel Brâncoveanu invoked whenever they had occasion the fidelity of their lineage to the Habsburg Monarchy, and above all to the emperor. In the name of this fidelity, they considered themselves entitled to expect protection and help in difficult situations, especially when they were on the territory of their patron. On 20 September 1772, Emanuel Brâncoveanu writes from Brașov:

> I claim very respectfully at the foot of the sacred throne of Your Imperial Majesties the protection that my ancestors enjoyed in Your States. The fidelity with which they always served this Empire to the point of shedding their blood

86 The Brâncoveanu family had properties in Braşov, Poiana Mărului, and Berivoiu, and at Sâmbăta de Sus, where they had built a residence and a church. Vezi Ştefan Meteş, *Moşiile domnilor şi boierilor din ţările române în Ardeal şi Ungaria* (Arad: 1925, 81–89); See also the document of 20 November 1761, in which Constantin Brâncoveanu writes to the city of Braşov about his house there. On 1 May 1762, the city authorities informed him that an officer had been quartered in his house. Hurmuzaki, *Documente*, XV/2, 1719, 1720.

87 In December 1771, Ianache Văcărescu and other boyars complained to the governor of Transylvania about the insults and mistreatment to which they had been subjected by the people of Brașov. Hurmuzaki, *Documente*, XV/2, 1737.

88 Nicolae Iorga, 'Les diplômes impérieux de Constantin Brâncoveanu, prince de Valachie', *Revue historique du sud-est européen*, XIV, 7–9 (1937), 177–186.

89 Paul Cernovodeanu, 'Coordonatele politicii externe a lui Constantin Brâncoveanu. Vedere de ansamblu', in Paul Cernovodeanu, Florin Constantiniu (eds.), *Constantin Brâncoveanu* (Bucharest: 1989), 123–138.

> on the occasions that arose, leads me to hope that I shall obtain my just demand from the magnanimity of Your August Majesties.[90]

In this petition ('*placet*' he calls it in the text) addressed both to Empress Maria Theresa and her son, Joseph, Brâncoveanu maintains that it is precisely this fidelity that has led to the requisitioning of his wealth in Wallachia.[91] At this moment, the patrons become the rulers asked to protect their 'subjects':

> Your Majesties deign to order that I be supplied with a certificate and passport to cross into my homeland so as to be recognized as a subject and member of your Empire, that in this quality no violence be done to me during my stay in Wallachia, that I may be able to enjoy in peace my revenues, and the permission to return here when I find it appropriate.[92]

Requesting protection or financial support was no mere whim. Both Russian and Ottoman soldiers resorted to looting as soon as they entered Wallachia and Moldavia, and boyar houses were always the first targets.[93] In an agrarian economy, the means of storing wealth were limited. Part of a boyar's fortune would be tied up in jewellery and clothing; otherwise, the wealth of these boyars consisted in the grain, cattle, honey, wax, and skins in which they traded, and above all in the income from the posts they occupied. In wartime, all these no longer produced anything, leaving the boyars to survive for months or years on what they had managed to store or from the sale of future harvests. In exile, the great boyars were keen to display a lifestyle that reflected their rank and position, investing in appearances. The goods necessary for survival and to uphold their rank were there to be purchased, as Brașov was an important commercial centre. Some took the risk of incurring expenses that they subsequently

90 'Je réclame très respectueusement au pie[d] du trône sacré de Vos Majestés Impériales la protection dont mes ancêtres ont joui dans Vos Etats. La fidélité avec laquelle, ils ont toujours servi cet Empire jusqu'à répandre leur sang dans les occasions qui se sont présentées, me font espérer que j'obtiendrai ma juste demande de la magna[ni]mité de Vos Augustes Majestés' HHStA, Moldau-Walachei I/26/Brancovan, f. 21.

91 At this point, the peace negotiations were in progress in Bucharest. The Russian delegation, led by General Aleksey Mikhailovich Obreskov, was lodged in the house of Emanuel Brâncoveanu in the Sfântul Spiridon district. Urechia, 'Istoria evenimentelor', 416.

92 'Vos Majestés daignent ordonner que je sois muni d'un attestat et passeport pour passer dans ma patrie à fin d'être reconnu sujet et membre de votre Empire, qu'en cette qualité, il ne me soit pas fait de violence pendant mon séjour en Valachie, que je puisse jouir tranquillement de mes revenus et la permission de m'en revenir ici lorsque je le trouve à propos.' HHStA, Moldau-Walachei I/26/Brancovan, f. 21.

93 Urechia, 'Istoria evenimentelor', 370–373. On the difficulties of feeding the Ottoman army during the Russian–Ottoman War, see Virginia Aksan, 'Feeding the Ottoman Troops on the Danube, 1768–1774', *War & Society*, 13, 1 (1995), 1–14.

could not cover, thus giving rise to conflicts.[94] In this context, the Brâncoveanu brothers introduce and insistently make use of three key words: 'protection', 'fidelity', 'subject'. These words acquire multiple meanings as the brothers experience the 'fatalities' of war and the deprivations of exile.[95] It should be mentioned that shortly before the outbreak of war, the Brâncoveanu brothers had quarrelled over the division of their paternal patrimony. Dissatisfied at the solution offered by the Divan of Wallachia, Nicolae and Emanuel appealed to the mediation of the kadı of Giurgiu. Kadı Ilyas transcribed into a *hoğet* the reconciliation of the parties, at the same time recording details of the history of the family.[96] Through kadı Ilyas, Nicolae Brâncoveanu asked the 'High Porte of the Devlet' to turn the *hoğet* into a *ferman* to reinforce the reconciliation between the brothers.[97] As I have shown elsewhere, the Christians of the principalities were not shy of appealing to the Ottoman authorities to resolve legal conflicts when they felt wronged by the decisions of the princely authorities. In so doing, they were implicitly recognizing the authority of the Ottoman Empire and claiming the protection due to its subjects.

In 1770, Nicolae and Emanuel Brâncoveanu requested the right to reside on the properties they owned in Brașov and at Sâmbăta de Sus for the duration of the war. The government of Transylvania granted them this right, as it did to other families or individuals fleeing from the path of war.[98] The Brâncoveanus, however, were eager in all circumstances to underline the old connections and the fidelity that bound them to the Emperor, making them stand out from the general mass of refugees. Chancellor Kaunitz recognized their quality of 'princes of the Empire' and used the designation in all their correspondence, but he made a distinction between the form and the content of this title. It was

94 See the conflict between Emanuel Brâncoveanu and the merchant Gavril of Şcheii Braşovului, 23 July 1771, in Hurmuzaki, *Documente*, XV/2, 1737.

95 In Brașov, Nicolae Brâncoveanu was accompanied by his wife, Maria, the sister of Ianache Văcărescu, and a minor son, Constantin, while his brother, Emanuel Brâncoveanu, came with his wife, Zoe Sturza, and four children, as he declares in one of his petitions. In addition, there were relatives, clients, and servants. HHStA, Moldau-Walachei I/26, Brancovan, f. 38.

96 Emanuel Brâncoveanu tells how his brother Nicolae raised him, fed him, and arranged his marriage, following the death of their father when he was still a minor. After his marriage, on the urging of relatives, he started legal proceedings against his brother, claiming a larger share of their paternal inheritance. See the document of 12 November 1768 in *Documente turceşti*, vol. I, 309–310.

97 Ibid., 311, document of 13 November 1768.

98 On 28 May 1770, the governor of Transylvania wrote to the city of Braşov, requesting it to provide shelter and hospitality for the Brâncoveanu and Dudescu families and for monks taking refuge because of the war. Hurmuzaki, *Documente*, XV/2, 1735–1736.

an honorary title that implied only relatively superficial clientelary relations. In a first phase, the Brâncoveanus made use of the weak sense of the words 'protection' and 'fidelity', without making any reference to the quality of 'subject'. The context was their conflicts with the 'Greek' merchants from whom they had bought goods on credit and who were now pursuing them even within the city of Brașov.[99] Indeed the Brâncoveanus were not the only ones in this situation, as we may notice in the letter sent to Chancellor Kaunitz by Nicolae Brâncoveanu, in which he offers explanations regarding the fate of the exiles:

> The Russians have pillaged every great house since we started wandering about, so to speak, here and there, [and we are] even very embarrassed in the upholding of our rank. Moreover, at present, with our goods confiscated by the Russians, and we resolved to wait here for bread, so receiving none of the income of our estates, even if the pretensions of these people are just, by what channel might we satisfy them?[100]

For this reason, in the name of the Wallachian boyars, refugees in Brașov, Brâncoveanu draws Kaunitz's attention to the fact that the boyars enjoy 'the protection of His Imperial Highness', a protection requested so they may be 'in peace', and that they cannot be judged according to the laws of 'the imperial courts of Transylvania', which are so different from those of Wallachia.[101] The Wallachian boyars here make reference to the unwritten law of hospitality, but also to the imperial protection that they have sought both collectively and as individuals. They request the postponement of any trial till the end of the war, as the cases are within the competence of the courts of Wallachia, whose *subjects* they still are. In his response, Kaunitz does not go beyond the game of rhetoric, assuring the refugees that he is trying to make their stay as pleasant as possible. No more than that![102]

The prolongation of the war, and above all the breakdown of the peace negotiations at Focșani and Bucharest, led the Brâncoveanu brothers (and

---

99 On the Greek merchants and the commercial companies of Sibiu and Brașov, see Mária Pakucs, '"This is their profession". Greek merchants in Transylvania and their Networks at the End of the 17th century', *Cromohs: Cyber Review of Modern Historiography*, 21 (2017–2018), 36–54.

100 'Les Russes pillèrent chaque grande maison, depuis errant, pour ainsi dire, ça et la même forte embarrasse pour soutenir notre rang; de plus à présent, tous nos biens confisqués par les russes, nous étant résolus d'attendre ici la pain, ainsi ne recevant point de revenus de nos terres quand bien même les prétention de ces gens-là fussent justes, par quel Canal pourrions nous les contenter?' HHStA, Moldau-Walachei I/26, Brancovan, f. 13.

101 HHStA, Moldau-Walachei I/26, Brancovan, f. 14, 15 January 1772, Kronstadt.

102 HHStA, Moldau-Walachei I/26, Brancovan, f. 15, 3 February 1772, Vienna, Kaunitz to Nicola de Brancovano.

implicitly the other boyars too) to seek pertinent solutions to get out of the financial impasse in which they found themselves.[103] Even though they had fled because of the war, their status was uncertain. Their actions were interpreted differently by the boyars who had stayed at home, by the Russian authorities in control in Moldavia and Wallachia, and by the Ottoman authorities. Their fate was intrinsically bound to the empire that had offered them shelter. Even if there were nuances in the way their 'desertion' was regarded, ultimately 'perfidy' was on the lips of all. As in the case of Neculce presented above, the boyars wanted to help themselves to the wealth of the Brâncoveanus, while the Russian and Ottoman authorities pursued them to punish them for the disloyalty they had shown. In this new context, the brothers reconsidered the concepts of fidelity and protection, trying to obtain as much as they could to protect themselves.

Tempting fate, Nicolae Brâncoveanu went back to Moldavia to attend to the administration of his estates, according to his own declaration.[104] However, the Russian authorities arrested him, accusing him of engaging in secret correspondence in favour of the Ottomans. Meanwhile, Sultan Mustafa III had issued a *ferman* in which he threatened to enslave the prince, boyars, and clergy who had collaborated with Russia.[105] Whose subject was Nicolae Brâncoveanu? Where should he turn for help and protection? He had gone to Saint Petersburg and had met Empress Catherine II, to whom he had sworn obedience and loyalty, thus betraying his status as an Ottoman subject[106]; then he had chosen exile and Habsburg protection, betraying his oath of fidelity to Empress Catherine. The Habsburgs, however, had granted him far too little to survive, thus obliging him to head for Moldavia in search of economic resources. The only thing he could do in his 'captivity' in Iași was to write letters

103 In 1771, Nicolae Brâncoveanu mortgaged his estate at Sâmbăta de Sus to the merchant Dumitru Marcu for a period of five years. On 20 February 1794, the two were still engaged in litigation, the one demanding the return of the mortgaged estate, and the other, the repayment of the loan with interest. Urechia, *Istoria românilor*, VI, 562–567.

104 In his letter to Kaunitz, Nicolae Brâncoveanu complains that he has been in 'captivity' for nine months in Iași, detained on the orders of Count Pyotr A. Rumyantsev, commander of the Russian army, although the latter had promised him verbally and in writing that he would give him freedom to look after his estates. In order to be allowed to leave, Nicolae Brâncoveanu claimed that he was 'sujet de leur Majestés Impériales'. As Rumyantsev was not impressed by the claim, Brâncoveanu asked to be 'requested as one of the subjects of the Empire' in order to be able to return to Transylvania. HHStA, Moldau-Walachei I/26, Brancovan, f. 18–19, 11 September 1772.

105 Smiley, *From Slaves to Prisoners of War*, 26.

106 See the oath of subjecthood to Empress Catherine II taken by the Moldavian and Wallachian boyars in Hurmuzaki, *Documente*, VII, 7, 81, 21 August 1770.

to his protector, Chancellor Kaunitz, trying to establish his status as an 'imperial subject'. He was joined in this by his brother Emanuel, who had similarly been obliged to return to Wallachia both for financial reasons and because of litigation. Between 11 September and 24 October 1773, Kaunitz and Empress Maria Theresa were deluged with letters and gifts by which the Brâncoveanus' *subject* status in relation to the Habsburg Monarchy was fashioned. Their quality of imperial *subjects* was upheld by appealing to the uninterrupted *fidelity* shown by the brothers' ancestors, who had been attached to the values of the Habsburgs and had spilled their blood when it was called for, serving the empress whenever this was needed. The references are all general, not specifying any particular instances of loyalty.[107] Were these affirmations sufficient to justify their request for protection, asylum, loans, interventions, passports, and ultimately the recognition of their status of *subjects*? The empress had received other requests for asylum, protection, and even loans from the other refugee boyars in Brașov.[108] And while she had made a general offer of protection and asylum, she had diplomatically refused all other requests.

The Brâncoveanus' insistence bore fruit in the end, however, and on 29 April 1773, Emanuel was sent a passport and a report by the governor of Transylvania certifying that he was in litigation with his father-in-law Dimitrie Sturza and, as such, had to go to defend his interests.[109] It is in this context that Zoița Brâncoveanu sent her thanks, offering Maria Theresa an 'oriental embroidery' and declaring herself the empress's 'faithful subject'. For his part, Emanuel Brâncoveanu, after receiving the passport, did likewise, signing this letter with 'le très humble et obeissant valet et sujet'.[110]

What was the significance of this passport? Did it automatically give him the quality of Habsburg *subject*? How did others interpret the *subjecthood* so much

107 On the nobility of the Habsburg Empire and its attributions, see Judson, *The Habsburg Empire*, 51–102.

108 On 7 October 1774, after the end of the war, the Wallachian boyars wrote a letter of thanks to Empress Maria Theresa for the 'asylum' she had provided. I find it interesting how the boyars reinvent their names in order to match the world of their exile. The signatures on the document identify them as: Thomas de Kretzulesculis (Toma Crețulescu), Demetréus de Racovitza (Dimitrie Racoviță), Rodolphe de Vaccaresculi (Rudolf Văcărescu), Ioanes de Vaccaresculi (Ianache Văcărescu), George de Saul (Gheorghe Saul), and Ioanes de Iuliani (Ioniță Iuliani). HHStA, Moldau-Walachei I/26, Vacaresculi, f. 1–3.

109 He was granted this passport in response to his application of 7 April 1773, in which he requested the following: a loan to be able to survive in Brașov until the end of the war, a passport, the right of asylum for his wife and four children for the period of his absence, and an attestation that he was an 'imperial subject'. HHStA, Moldau-Walachei I/26, Brancovan, f. 38–39.

110 Ibid.

invoked by the Brâncoveanus? In the late eighteenth century, the passport was still a valid instrument to ensure the possessor a safe journey from one named place to another named place. The fact of its being issued by an important person gave it weight.[111] In his reading of Casanova, Valentin Groebner notes that the passport rather offered 'prestige' to its holder, helping them to cross borders by partaking of the renown of the person who had issued the document.[112] Emanuel Brâncoveanu likewise emphasizes the prestige of the document he holds, writing to Count Pyotr A. Rumyantsev that his passport has been signed by Empress Maria Theresa herself: 'Her Majesty, my Sovereign, has been pleased to supply me with a passport signed with her own hand.'[113] The passport has not been preserved, so we cannot be sure what it looked like and what it may have contained. Most likely, it took the form of a letter specifying the name of the holder, the purpose of his journey, and the route. Nor do we know whether the document actually was signed by Maria Theresa. Barbara Stollberg-Rilinger has shown that the empress tried hard to direct her subjects to the local authorities, carrying out a series of administrative reforms to establish the steps to be followed in responding to a petition, and thus relieving the imperial chancellery of many requests that could be dealt with at local level.[114] Indeed Kaunitz (or rather his chancellery) noted in his responses that some requests fell within the competence of the local authorities and that he had thus sent them back to the government of Transylvania. Together with the passport, Emanuel Brâncoveanu had requested a certificate that he was a 'member and subject of this empire so as to be recognized as such'[115]; so had his brother Nicolae.[116] However, the certificate never came. For all that, the Brâncoveanus considered themselves 'imperial subjects' because this was the status that they needed at that moment. It is very interesting how individuals define themselves, interpreting power relations in response to aspirations, needs, and social and political circumstances. In this particular case, the

---

111 Martin Lloyd, *The Passport: The history of Man's Most Travelled Document* (Kent: 2008), 23. On this subject see also John Torpey, *The Invention of the Passport. Surveillance, Citizenship and the State* (Cambridge: 2000).

112 Valentin Groebner, *Who Are You? Identification, Deception, and Surveillance in Early Modern Europe* (New York: 2007), 227.

113 'Sa Majesté, ma Souveraine a bien voulu me munir d'un passeport signé de sa propre main.' HHStA, Moldau-Walachei I/26, Brancovan, f. 52.

114 Barbara Stollberg-Rilinger, 'Maria Theresa and the Love of Her Subjects', *Austrian History Yearbook*, 51 (2020), 7–9. See also Barbara Stollberg-Rilinger, *Maria Theresia. Die Kaiserin in ihrer Zeit. Eine Biographie* (Munich: 2017).

115 'membre et sujet de cet Empire afin d'être reconnu comme tel'. HHStA, Moldau-Walachei I/26, Brancovan, f. 19–20.

116 HHStA, Moldau-Walachei I/26, Brancovan, f. 18.

Brâncoveanus were also taxpayers in the Habsburg Empire by virtue of the properties they owned there, although they only very seldom resided on these properties. Up until 1770, however, they had emphasized only the prestige of the title they held of 'Prince of the Holy Roman Empire', a title that eased their way to doing business with the commercial elite of Transylvania, by serving to reinforce their credibility.[117] Their engagement in the process of self-definition was determined by the insecurity generated by the war and the need to adapt to the new power structures.

The gift offered by Zoița Brâncoveanu did not remain without a response either: in the name of the empress, Kaunitz thanked her for the gift and offered her a porcelain box and 500 ducats to purchase 'whatever may please her', with the justification that 'Her Majesty does not know the princess's tastes.'[118] Reciprocity of gifts and services was one of the keys to the maintenance and proper functioning of relations of patronage.[119]

Russia, through its representatives in Bucharest and Iaşi, was not impressed by the status of Habsburg *subjects* claimed by the Brâncoveanus. Nicolae was kept in 'captivity' in Iași, while his brother Emanuel wrote energetically requesting freedom of movement by virtue of his quality as a *subject*, pleading his blamelessness ('I have no secret correspondence and nor have I been involved in the movements of either the imperial Russian army or the Ottoman one'), and invoking the alliances between Austria and Russia, which should ensure him 'an inviolable asylum in his homeland.'[120] Count Rumyantsev wrote back drily, and only after the third letter, from the camp on the Ialomița, that if Emanuel fulfilled 'the duties of a good citizen,' he would be protected.[121] However, Rumyantsev only responded after an entire arsenal of connections and influences had been set in motion. Again, Kaunitz had been approached to put in a good word with Baron Vincent Freiherr von Barco,[122] with the Russian ambassador in Vienna, Dmitry Mikhailovich Golitsyn, with the commander of the Russian army, Prince Alexander Mikhailovich Golitsyn, and with Rumyantsev.[123]

117 In a letter to the imperial chancellery, Emanuel Brâncoveanu provides details about his financial deals in Vienna and his money deposited in Viennese banks. See HHStA, Moldau-Walachei I/26, Brancovan, f. 44, 3 July 1773.

118 HHStA, Moldau-Walachei I/26, Brancovan, f. 46, August 1773.

119 Sharon Kettering, 'Gift-Giving and Patronage', 131–51.

120 HHStA, Moldau-Walachei I/26, Brancovan, f. 14 July 1773, Brâncoveanu to Rumyantsev. See also his letter to the same of 12 June 1773.

121 HHStA, Moldau-Walachei I/26, Brancovan, f. 26 July 1773.

122 General in the Austrian imperial army. In 1772, he was in Iaşi, sent to take part in the peace negotiations that took place in Focşani and Bucharest.

123 HHStA, Moldau-Walachei I/26, Brancovan, f. 25, 26, 27, 30, 32.

In the summer of 1774, the Russian–Ottoman war ended with the signing of the peace treaty of Küçük-Kaynarca. The actors involved over the last six years (1768–1774) were now negotiating the positions they would occupy in the new structures.[124] The Wallachian boyars as a group had requested a special status within the Ottoman Empire similar to that of Ragusa, but Russia's interests in the region were quite different.[125] Thus, the Principalities returned under Ottoman domination, even if they had obtained certain regional advantages.[126] The fate of the boyars too was shaped by the new political circumstances created by the peace treaty. Mihai Cantacuzino went into exile, paying the price of his fidelity to Russia[127], while Ianache Văcărescu returned to Bucharest, where he would long occupy the political stage. As for the Brâncoveanus, on 9 October 1774, Emanuel thanked Chancellor Kaunitz and Empress Maria Theresa in his usual bombastic style for the protection and help they had given him: 'I leave these states, my heart penetrated by the most vivid gratitude, leaving my rights under the protection of Your Majesty.'[128] Although they had properties in Transylvania, the Brâncoveanus only used them as a place of refuge for limited periods of time. Thus they did not hold the status of residents of the Empire. Moreover, we do not know how and to what extent they paid taxes for these properties, or whether they enjoyed certain privileges on the basis of having the title of 'Prince' and thus belonging to the aristocracy.[129] Under these conditions, their relations were built not with the Empire that should have protected them in their quality as subjects and taxpayers, but on

124 For the peace negotiations, see Virginia Aksan, *An Ottoman Statesman in War and Peace: Ahmed Resmi Efendi, 1700–1783* (Leiden: 1995), 167–169.

125 Taki, *Limits of Protection*, 22–23. See also Brian L. Davies, *The Russo-Turkish War, 1768–1774. Catherine II and the Ottoman Empire* (London: 2016).

126 Viorel Panaite, 'Wallachia and Moldavia according to the Ottoman Juridical and Political View, 1774–1829', in Antonis Anastasopoulos and Elias Kolovos (eds.), *Ottoman Rule and The Balkans, 1760–1858. Conflict, Transformation, Adaptation* (Rethymno: 2007), 21–44.

127 Here is Mihai Cantacuzino's statement: 'Mihai Cantacuzino, who alone had remained responsible for looking after his house and his brothers, knowing after these two congresses what followed, how Moldavia and Wallachia would remain again under the Turks, and considering that their families would not be able to live in Wallachia without fear and without danger, decided they should go to Saint Petersburg and try their luck.' Cantacuzino, *Genealogia*, 190–206.

128 '[J]e pars de ses Etats, le cœur pénétré de la plus vive reconnaissance, en laissant mes droits sous les auspices de Votre Majesté.' HHStA, Moldau-Walachei I/26, Brancovan, f. 64.

129 On the fiscal system in the Habsburg Monarchy, see Peter Rauscher, 'Comparative Evolution of the Tax Systems in the Habsburg Monarchy, c. 1526–1740: The Austrian and the Bohemian Lands', in Simonetta Cavaciocchi (ed.), *La Fiscaltà nell'economia Europea, secc. XIII–XVIII/ Fiscal Systems in the European Economy from the 13th to the 18th Centuries* (Firenze: 2008), 291–320.

an individual basis, as they cultivated well-chosen relations with certain key figures in political life, whose protection and influence they managed to enjoy as clients.[130] This protection and the status of imperial subjects helped them to survive at a very difficult moment, enabling them to keep their families safe in wartime. Concern for the protection of their families is reiterated obsessively in the writings of all the actors involved in the political events of the moment. The family was the principal factor of support in the political arena, and the protection of one's progeniture ensured a future.[131]

The experience of exile did not end in 1774, however. Back in Wallachia, Nicolae and Emanuel Brâncoveanu took advantage of the relative peace in the region to get involved in political life. During the eight-year reign of Prince Alexandru Ipsilanti (1774–1782), they were among many who received posts in the Divan: Nicolae was raised to the rank of grand *vistier*, while his brother was appointed grand *vornic*.[132] A new war in the region (1787–1792) and the eccentric policies of Prince Nicolae Mavrogheni (1786–1790) led to the exile of boyars suspected of having other political visions. Thus, the Brâncoveanu brothers, together with other boyars, arrived in Nikopol, offered as a sort of hostages by Mavrogheni to the Ottoman Empire. They made use of their Brașov experience to weave new networks of protection. In exile in Nikopol, they directed their correspondence and their leverage towards Istanbul. Taking advantage of his relations with Alexandru Ipsilanti, who had been appointed Prince of Moldavia, Emanuel Brâncoveanu managed to obtain an order (Tk. *buyuruldu*) of Prince Selim (the future Sultan Selim III) permitting him to withdraw together with his family and a doctor (Djurdjaki by name) to Arnabud (Arbanasi) in the region of Târnovo, where they could live, troubled by no one, till the end of the war.[133]

130 By their reforms, both Maria Theresa and Joseph II contributed to the redefinition of the subject, providing the legal levers for the transformation of the individual into a 'citizen'. At the same time, loyalty went through the same process of evolution, with political writings linking it to the homeland and to the assumption of civic responsibilities. See Judson, *The Habsburg Empire*, 49–51; R.J.W. Evans, Austria, *Hungary, and the Habsburgs. Central Europe c. 1683–1867* (Oxford: 2006), 60–62.

131 Nicolae Brâncoveanu lost his only son in Brașov; he died at the age of about two. Nicolae was to have no other children. Dan Berindei, 'Urmaşii lui Constantin Brâncoveanu şi locul lor în societatea românească. Genealogie şi istorie', in Paul Cernovodeanu, Florin Constantiniu (eds.), *Constantin Brâncoveanu* (Bucharest: 1989), 275–285.

132 Theodora Rădulescu, *Sfatul domnesc şi alţi mari dregători ai Ţării Româneşti din secolul al XVIII-lea. Liste cronologice şi cursus honorum* (Bucharest: 1972), 118, 120–122, 128–129, 299, 301, 304, 322.

133 Document of 26 September 1788, *Documente turceşti*, II, 310.

A few years later, in order to feel 'in safety within the High Devlet', Nicolae Brâncoveanu bought a house at Arbanasi. With the help of Prince Alexandru Moruzi (1793–1796), on 27 July 1793, he obtained a *berat* by which he was granted a series of privileges as recognition of 'service and devotion' shown to the High Devlet. For the length of his stay in Arbanasi, he and his sons (if he had sons in the future) would be 'exempt from the *cizye* required by *shari'a* law and from the *variz* and from the ordinary taxes and corvées'; they had the right to wear whatever clothes they wanted and yellow footwear or whatever slippers they wanted; their house could not be used as a billet for soldiers and no one had the right to enter it by force; they and their servants enjoyed the right to travel freely in the Empire keeping their clothing; and in dangerous places they were entitled to the assistance of local chiefs.[134] The Brâncoveanus continued to orient themselves according to the political context and their needs, trying to protect themselves by invoking loyalty and subjecthood, even if the patrons were different.

*

Local elites fought a bitter struggle for political supremacy. Their attempt to remain in the political arena, to hold onto their privileges, or to participate in the redistribution of resources inevitably led to their involvement in all sorts of conflicts and political struggles. For this reason, all too few families managed to escape imprisonment, exile, persecution, or confiscation of goods. Of course the fate of the political elites of Moldavia and Wallachia was not unique in the region.[135] In this struggle for supremacy, boyars sought to expand their networks and to increase the number of their patrons in the regional competition for power. Some of them sought to oscillate between different subjecthoods that they could invoke as required, while others displayed multiple allegiances in order to protect their families, their wealth, and implicitly their interests. The search for a home and a stable environment, propitious to personal development, was not based on chance. The examples given above are more than eloquent. Not only 'Greeks' felt the need for a 'homeland' where they could build a future in safety'; so did Wallachians and Moldavians. Iordache Ruset, Ion Neculce, Nicolae Brâncoveanu, Emanuel Brâncoveanu, and Mihai

134 Documente turceşti, III, 48–50.

135 For a comparison, see Dean J. Kostantaras, 'Christian Elites of the Peloponnese and the Ottoman State, 1715–1821', *European History Quarterly*, 43, 4 (2013), 628–656; Martha Pylia, 'Conflicts Politiques et Comportements des Primats Chrétiens en Morée, avant la Guerre de l'independence', in Antonis Anastasopoulos and Elias Kolovos (eds.), *Ottoman Rule and The Balkans, 1760–1858. Conflict, Transformation, Adaptation* (Rethymno: 2007), 137–148.

Cantacuzino pragmatically analysed the opportunities offered by the powers in the region. While Iordache Ruset found or managed to create the necessary conditions for rooting his future in Moldavia, the same cannot be said of Ion Neculce and his future in Russia. Neculce made a practical comparison of the Russian and Moldavian worlds and the place that he could occupy in each of the two societies. Embracing a military career did not seem an adequate future for his sons.[136] He understood that only collaboration with the Phanariot princes would bring wealth and peace, summing it all up in the sentence: "I have seen no boyar thriving of those who put themselves in conflict with the prince."[137]

Nor did the Habsburg Empire turn out to be the 'homeland' the Brâncoveanus were seeking. Rather, the advantages obtained from the protection it offered operated better at a distance than through direct enrolment in a strict subject–ruler relation. The Cantacuzinos, on the other hand, like the Cantemirs seventy years previously, chose the 'soldier's life' offered by the Russian Empire, while at the same time negotiating their positions and status.

I opened this chapter with a line from a play written (around 1821) by the great boyar Iordache Golescu: '*The Prince has died and at his mourning we should rejoice.*'[138] The line illustrates better than anything the tensions between the Phanariot princes and the ruling elite at the end of the eighteenth century. The change of rulers might be a bad moment for those already in power, but it could be a new beginning for all the rest.

136 On the Russian elite and its rights and obligations, see John P. LeDonne, *Absolutism and Ruling Class. The Formation of the Russian Political Order, 1700–1825* (Oxford: 1991).

137 Neculce, *Letopisețul Țării Moldovei*, 656.

138 Iordache Golescu, *Scrieri alese*, 132.

CHAPTER 4

A Wallachian Dignitary at the Crossroads of Empires: Ianache Văcărescu

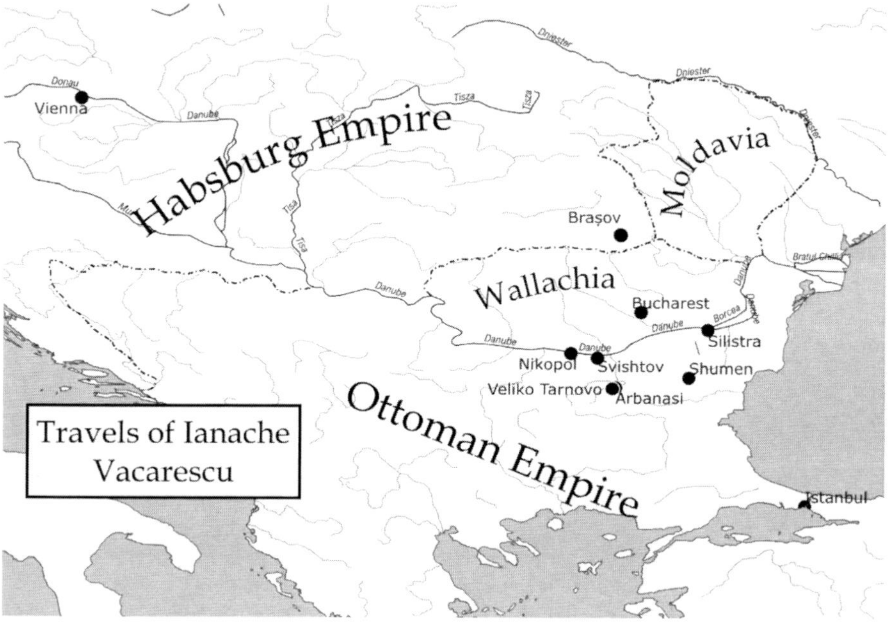

Map 2 Travels of Ianache Văcărescu, cc. 1770–1796. Made by Michał Wasiucionek.

In the winter of 1782, Ianache Văcărescu, Grand *Vistier* (treasurer) of Wallachia, set out on a secret mission to the imperial court of Vienna. The two sons of Prince Alexandru Ipsilanti (1774–1782) had run away from home in search of adventure in the wondrous realms of Europe. After the establishment of Phanariot rule in the Principalities, princes and boyars preferred to avoid crossing the border to the West, although no official interdiction limiting their freedom of movement was ever pronounced.[1] In other words, the journeys of the political elite were directed for a century towards the Ottoman Empire. Braşov (German *Kronstadt*) and Sibiu (German *Hermannstadt*), in Habsburg Transylvania, were only temporary refuges in times of war, where boyar

1 Regarding the right to circulate freely and the memoranda drafted by the boyars on this matter, see Vlad Georgescu, *Istoria ideilor politice româneşti (1369–1878)* (Munich: 1987), 215.

families might find a safe haven for a matter of months, or on occasion years, depending on the duration of the war and military occupation.

In this chapter I seek to show how Văcărescu,[2] in his capacity as an office-holder in the prince's administration, an Ottoman subject, and a diplomatic agent, mediating between Istanbul and Vienna, made use of the knowledge and abilities that he had accumulated in the course of his meetings and travels. What kind of cultural intermediary was Văcărescu?[3] Fortunately for historians, he wrote about his diplomatic experiences, describing the journeys in which he was involved, and providing details about the people he met, in his *History of the Most Puissant Ottoman Emperors*, which long remained in manuscript.[4] Although this purports to be a chronicle of the sultans and viziers who built the Ottoman Empire, in fact it proves, at least in its second part, to be an autobiographical journal. As a model, he had the history written by Dimitrie Cantemir, *Historia incrementorum atque decrementorum Aulae Othomanicae* (1716), which he used and quoted.[5]

---

2 Also known by the diminutive 'Ienăchiță' in Romanian historiography.

3 Recent contributions have demonstrated the role of diplomatic agents, interpreters, dragomans, and other 'brokers' in mediating contacts between the Ottoman domains and western Europe in the early modern period, see David Do Paço, 'A Social History of Trans-Imperial Diplomacy in a Crisis Context: Herbert von Rathkeal's Circles of Belonging in Pera, 1779–1802', *International History Review* 40, 5 (2018), 3–22; David Do Paço, 'Trans-Imperial Familiarity: Ottoman Ambassadors in Eighteenth-century Vienna', in Tracey A. Sowerby and Jan Hennings (eds.), *Practices of Diplomacy in the Early Modern World, c. 1410–1800* (London: 2017), 166–184; Natalie Rothman, *Brokering Empire: Trans-Imperial Subjects between Venice and Istanbul* (Ithaca, NY: 2012); Francesca Trivellato, *The Familiarity of Strangers: the Sephardic Diaspora, Livorno, and Cross-Culture Trade in the Early Modern Period* (New Haven, CT: 2009).

4 The full title of the history is: *Istorie a prea puternicilor împăraţi otomani. Adunată şi alcătuită pă scurt de dumnealui Ianache Văcărescu dicheofilaz a bisericii cei mari a Răsăritului şi spătar al Valahiei. Începându-se în vremea prea puternicului împărat sultan Abdul Hamid* I *la văleatul bijretu 1202 şi mântuiroriu 1788 în Nicopoli a Bulgariei. Şi s-a săvîrşit în zilele prea puternicului împărat sultan Selim III la văleat 1794 şi 1208 în luna lui Şeval* (*History of the most puissant Ottoman emperors, gathered and put together in brief by his lordship Ianache Văcărescu, dikaiophylax of the great Church of the East and spătar of Wallachia. Begun in the time of the most puissant emperor Sultan Abdul Hamid* I, *the Year of the Hijra 1202 and of the Saviour 1788, in Nikopol in Bulgaria. And it was finished in the days of the most puissant emperor Sultan Selim III in the year 1794 and 1208 in the month of Shawwal*). For this study, I have used the most recent critical edition of the works of Ianache Văcărescu. See Ianache Văcărescu, *Istoria Othomanicească*, ed. Gabriel Ştrempel (Bucharest: 2001).

5 Dimitrie Cantemir's work was first printed in English translation as *History of the Growth and Decay of the Othman Empire* [...] *by Demetrius Cantemir, late Prince of Moldavia* (London: 1734), then in French, *Histoire de l'Empire Othoman où se voyent les causes de son Aggrandissement et de sa Decadence par S.A.A. Demetrius Cantemir, Prince de Moldavie* (Paris: 1743) and German, *Geschichte des osmanischen Reiches nach seinem Anwachsen und Abnehmen, beschrieben von*

The scholarship on southeastern Europe and the Ottoman Empire as seen through the prism of travel narratives is abundant, while other studies have investigated the journeys of Ottoman subjects in the direction of 'Europe'.[6] Văcărescu's journal is all the more important in that so far it seems to be the only one of its kind from the Romanian Principalities. I would like to approach the text by way of its author and to analyse his interaction with the 'others': 'Frenchmen,' 'Germans', or 'Europeans', as he calls them. This investigation is particularly important given Văcărescu's description of his encounters as a self-described 'Turk' with other 'Europeans'. How does he see 'Europe', and what does he retain from his travels and interactions? In many respects, his account of a diplomatic mission to Vienna parallels that of Ottoman ambassadors' experiences there, thus providing an important addition to the topic of such encounters.[7] Other aspects of the mission refine our knowledge regarding the role of Ottoman Christian subjects and the way they interacted with the Sublime Porte.[8] Therefore, the aim of the present chapter is to examine how Văcărescu employed the knowledge and manners acquired throughout his travels in both Ottoman and Habsburg empires to fashion his social status and to establish the connections necessary for career advancement.

Life and Family Background

Ianache Văcărescu (1740–1797) came from an old Wallachian boyar family whose existence is recorded already in the sixteenth century.[9] His father, Ştefan Văcărescu, held an important office in the princely council, that of grand

---

Demetrie Kantemir (Hamburg: 1745). For Dimitrie Cantemir, see Ştefan Lemny, *Les Cantemir: l'aventure européenne d'une famille princière au XVIIIe siècle* (Paris: 2009).

6 Wendy Bracewell and Alex Drace-Francis (ed.), *Under Eastern Eyes: A Comparative Introduction to East European Travel Writing on Europe, ed.* (Budapest: 2008). Fatma Müge Göçek, *East Encounters West: France and the Ottoman Empire in the Eighteenth Century* (New York: 1987); Robert Dankoff, *An Ottoman Mentality: The World of Evliya Çelebi* (Leiden: 2006); Frédérick Hitzel, *Prisonnier des infidèles: Un soldat ottoman dans l'Empire des Habsbourg* (Arles: 1998); and Hanna Dyâb, *D'Alep à Paris: Les pérégrinations d'un jeune Syrien au temps de Louis XIV*, trans. Paule Fahmé, Bernard Heyberger, and Jérôme Lentin (Arles: 2015).

7 Carter Vaughn Findley, 'Ebu Bekir Ratib's Vienna Embassy Narative: Discovering Austria or Propagandizing for Reform in Istanbul?', *Wiener Zeitschrift für die Kunde des Morgenlandes* 85 (1995), 41–80; and Virginia Aksan, *An Ottoman Statesman in War and Peace: Ahmed Resmi Efendi, 1700–1783* (Leiden: 1995).

8 Virginia H. Aksan and Veysel Şimşek, 'Introduction: Living in the Ottoman House', *Journal of Ottoman Studies* 44 (2014), 1–8.

9 In the course of the eighteenth century, members of the Văcărescu family sought to construct a prestigious genealogy for themselves that would tie them to Wallachia's founding dynasty, see Biblioteca Academiei Române (hereafter BAR), Fond Manuscrise MS 305, f. 3v.

vornic.[10] At the same time, Ştefan was a man with an interest in literary pursuits, and this was reflected in the education of his son. Education did not traditionally have much importance for political advancement: boyars had access to important offices in the princely council according to their rank and the clientelary networks to which they belonged. This changed, however, after the intervention of Prince Constantin Mavrocordat, who ordered that no boyar's son could hold office unless he went to school and learned Greek.[11] Ianache, who was a child at the time, began his education under the influence of this prince's 'Enlightenment' ideas. Much has been written and countless hypotheses have been put forward regarding his education.[12] I shall not go into detail here but merely recall an episode that was to contribute to his later writings. In 1763, Grand *Vornic* Ştefan Văcărescu was poisoned by Prince Constantin Cehan Racoviţă while at his country house in Valea Orlei, Prahova county.[13] His son, Ianache, took refuge in Constantinople, seeking help lest he suffer the same fate. Through his marriage to Elena Rizo, Ianache had an important connection in the Ottoman Empire in the person of his father-in-law Iacovaki Rizo, an office-holder and the prince's diplomatic representative (*capuchehaia*) at the Porte, who had important contacts in the world of the Phanar.[14] According to his own account,[15] his stay in Constantinople was a profitable one; for more than a year he studied Turkish in the company of the secretary of the imperial divan, Halil Hamid, who was to become vizier in 1783. The family archive, with its maps, books, treatises, grammars, and dictionaries testifies to Ianache's linguistic ability. He had a good knowledge of Greek, Turkish, Italian, and German, and made use of these skills in his political and diplomatic ascent to become a key figure in negotiations between the Phanariot princes, the Sublime Porte, the Russian Empire, and the Habsburg Empire.[16]

---

10 Cornel Cârstoiu, *Ianache Văcărescu: Viaţa şi opera* (Bucharest: 1974), 36–38. The post of grand *vornic* was equivalent to a minister of justice.

11 See the anaphora of May 9, 1746: V.A. Urechia, *Istoria Şcoalelor* (Bucharest: 1892), I, 14.

12 Cârstoiu, *Văcărescu*, 52–56; Văcărescu, *Istoria Othomanicească*, xix–xxii. His career in the Ottoman service shows parallels with those of other high-ranking Christian and Ottoman officials of this period. See, for instance, Fatih Yeşil, 'How to Be(come) an Ottoman at the End of the Eighteenth Century', *Journal of Ottoman Studies*, 44 (2014), 123–139; and Philliou, *Biography of an Empire*.

13 Alexandru Odobescu, *Opere*, vol. 2 (Bucharest: 1967), 53.

14 Frequently mentioned in diplomatic correspondence, Iacovaki Rizo was a very influential figure and member of a network that covered the European embassies in Pera, Hurmuzaki, *Documente*, VII, 20, 134, 172, 269, 280, 291; IX: part 2, 113.

15 Văcărescu, *Istoria Othomanicească*, 219.

16 In addition to this history of the Ottoman Empire, Ianache Văcărescu wrote the first grammar of Romanian, printed simultaneously in Râmnic and in Vienna (1787), compiled (probably) bilingual German–Romanian (BAR, MS. 1392) and Turkish–Romanian dictionaries (BAR, MS 1393), and wrote poetry.

Ianache Văcărescu married three times, his fathers-in-law being dragomans and princes, holders of important offices at the court of the sultan and the Patriarchate of Constantinople. Following the death of his first wife (Elena Rizo) in September 1780, Ianache married Elena Caragea, the daughter of Iordache Caragea, *tercüman* at the court of Constantinople, in December 1781. He was unlucky this time too, as Elena died seven months later; his third marriage, in September 1782, was to Ecaterina Caragea, the daughter of dragoman and prince of Wallachia Nicolae Caragea.[17] He himself held high offices in the Wallachian state (grand *spătar*,[18] grand *vistier*, grand *ban*[19]), all the time being a leading member of the princely council (*divan*).

Circulation of Objects, Circulation of People: Ottoman Coffee v. European Coffee

Around 1780, the boyar elite followed Ottoman fashion and etiquette: costume, behaviour, cuisine, and sociability were all strongly influenced by Constantinople. The predominance of the Ottoman model is confirmed by travellers who arrived in the Romanian capitals. Fashion, imposed by the political regime, proved to be an indispensable of expression of subjecthood in the context of Phanariot rule. At the same time, through its opulence and luxury, this Ottoman costume served a process of self-fashioning.[20] Ianache Văcărescu helps us to understand this process of construction of the self, which may be reconstituted both through his writings of an autobiographical character and, visually, with the help of his portraits.[21]

17 Sturdza, *Grandes Familles de Grèce, d'Albanie et de Constantinople*, 257, 259. Although they belonged to the same branch of the family. Iordaki and Nicolae were only distantly related. Iordaki was the son of the grand dragoman Charles Caradja. He was doctor and grand logophoros to the Patriarchate in Constantinople, and grand dragoman, and was married to Sultana Mavrocordat, the daughter of the Phanariot prince Ioan Mavrocordat. Nicolae was the son of Constantin Caradja and Zafira Soutzu, and held the office of grand dragoman before later becoming prince of Wallachia. See Rizo-Rangabé, *Livre d'or de la noblesse phanariote*, 37–39.

18 Literally sword-bearer, the high office-holder in charge of the armed forces and the police.

19 Governor of Oltenia, the highest office in the princely council.

20 In recent research, the term 'Ottomanization' has been proposed to explain the rapid adoption of Ottoman costume by the Christian population on the borders of the Ottoman Empire. See Michał Wasiucionek, 'Conceptualizing Moldavian Ottomanness: Elite Culture and Ottomanization of the Seventeenth-Century Moldavian Boyars', *Medieval and Early Modern Studies for Central and Eastern Europe*, 8 (2016), 39–78.

21 See his portraits drawn by Anton Chladek.

Fig. 3
Anton Chladek (1794–1882) – Ienăchiţă Văcărescu, 1852–1858, National Museum of Art, Bucharest.

Our information about the daily life of holders of high office at this time, about the organization of their mansions or their interior decoration and furniture, is relatively scanty, especially for the eighteenth century. Because of the wealth of detail regarding material culture and luxury consumption that it offers, the Văcărescu family archive and library have become an essential source for a reconstruction of the lifestyle of a high office-holder of this period.

Văcărescu's mansion, situated in the vicinity of the princely court, was organized according to Ottoman models.[22] His journeys, whether on diplomatic missions or simply seeking refuge in time of war, took him to Braşov, Vidin, Silistra (Silistre), Nikopol, Rhodes, Constantinople, and Vienna. People and objects would influence his lifestyle and behaviour, and would mould his thinking and his manners.[23]

22 Grigore, Bishop of Argeş provided a description of the mansion, calling it worthy of a great pasha: see Odobescu, *Opere*, vol. 2, 75–77. For the manner in which the house of a Turkish pasha was organized, see the interesting analysis made by Hedda Reindl-Kiel, 'The Must-Haves of a Grand Vizier: Merzifonlu Kara Mustafa Pasha's Luxury Assets', *Wiener Zeitschrift für die Kunde des Morgenlandes*, 106 (2016), 179–221.

23 For example, Văcărescu's mansion in Băneasa just outside Bucharest, built around 1784–1785 following the boyar's return from Braşov, was inspired by 'German' models, as stipulated in the contracts he had signed with mason Johann Ratner and carpenter Theodor

The Russian–Ottoman War (1769–1774), in which he played a prominent part, took him first on a mission and then into exile in Braşov. Here he met for the first time the young sovereign Joseph II. The meeting brought together two different social and political models, and the behaviour of Văcărescu, a high office-holder now in exile, was adapted and modelled to take account of the new context. Here is what he writes:

> In this year, 1773, May, the Emperor of the Romans Joseph II, wishing to go to Galicia and Lodomeria, to the lands that he had then obtained, crossing the borders of Transylvania came to Braşov, where he stayed for three days and did us Romanian boyars who were guests there great honour, for as soon as he arrived at the mansion prepared for him, he at once sent his Imperial Majesty's doctor to us, where we were all gathered in my lodgings [...], and invited us to come the next day at ten o'clock for him to give us an audience.[24]

The audience took place as announced, providing Ianache with a good occasion to showcase his abilities by providing 'dragoman service to the boyars in the Italian language.' Highly proficient in the language of diplomacy, Ianache Văcărescu pushed himself into the proximity of the Emperor, who invited him to accompany him to the ball held in honour of the Wallachian boyars taking refuge in Braşov: 'Signor Văcărescu,' said the emperor, 'I invite you and put you to the trouble of doing me this evening the service of an interpreter.' Ianache's answer was one befitting an experienced diplomat: 'Bowing, I replied to him that this was the happiest night I had encountered in the world since I was born.' He continued: 'and so, taking him by the left arm, I was in this service and honour until an hour after midnight, allowing no boyar or lady to go without asking some question.'[25]

His three days spent in the company of Emperor Joseph II, together with his several years of exile in Braşov (he would leave the city in September 1774) contributed to the remodelling of Ianache's tastes and manners. On July 16, 1773, he compiled a list of purchases that reflects the influence of objects and

---

Janos. See Nicolae Iorga (ed.), *Studii și documente cu privire la istoria românilor*, vol. 3 (Bucharest: 1901), 79–80.

24 Văcărescu, *Istoria Othomanicească*, 116.

25 Ibid., 117. Emperor Joseph II noted (June 6, 1773) this social encounter with the Romanian boyars who had taken refuge in Braşov: 'Hernach giengen wir in die Gessellschaft zum General Eichholz so alle Boerinnen und Griechinnen eingeladen hatte. Er scheinet ein alter wohlgedienter Mann zu seÿn, der ziemlich gut informiret ist, von hiesigen Gegenden. Es waren etlich und 20. Griechinnen, alle magnifique angelegt, und welche mitsammen theils spieleten, theils so sitzeten, aber keine einzige konnte eine Sprache als griechischen und wallachisch. Ich redete mit den Herrn eine.' *Călătoria împăratului Iosif al II-lea în Transilvania la 1773*, ed. Ileana Bozac and Teodor Pavel (Cluj: 2017), 629.

the new lifestyle on his conduct. He asked for a series of items of tableware to be procured direct from Vienna, among them: soup bowls, metal trays, dishes, spoons, forks, knives, jugs, cups, sugar bowls, trays, plates, salt cellars, candlesticks, and candelabra, all of silver or porcelain. What gives this list its significance is not the quantities involved but the eye of our boyar, who has looked at length at the object, has been impressed, and now wishes to enrol in a trend, convinced of the validity and grandeur of the model to be followed. Nothing is left to chance, and 'Europe' becomes the keyword. The metal trays must be large, slightly oval, with handles 'as is usual there in Europe.'[26] Ianache had not yet been as far as 'there in Europe,' but only to Braşov, where he had often been invited to dine in the houses of local notables. The objects induce another manner of serving dinner, another perspective on sociability over coffee, another ceremony of the aesthetic exhibition of cuisine. We thus find very detailed requirements that imply certain gestures, bodily self-control, certain manners, and a different type of behaviour. For example, he asks that 'the forks be with three prongs, that is, in the form of those of the English type.' The salt is no longer to be poured on the table but contained in a silver salt cellar; the mustard gets a jug, and also a little spoon; the oil also has its jug, because 'that is how the Europeans do it.' It would appear that, up till this date, the fork was absent from the tables of boyars in Wallachia and Moldavia.[27] Ottoman influence, which became permanent and dominant with the establishment of the Phanariot rule, led to the loss of this object of civility to which Norbert Elias attributed a special significance in the propagation of good manners.[28]

The same requirements are found with regard to the ritual of coffee-drinking. Ianache Văcărescu asked for 'European cups and in no circumstances Turkish coffee-cups.' They should be accompanied by 'a "proportion" jug too for milk' and a sugar bowl from which the sugar will no longer be taken with the fingers but 'as the Europeans do with tongs, who take the sugar and put it in the cup.'[29]

---

26 See the list in Mihai Carataşu, *Documentele Văcăreştilor* (Bucharest: 1975), 59–61.

27 An analysis of dowry lists and inventories for the period 1700–1800, finds forks present in the dowry lists of the children of Prince Constantin Brâncoveanu (1688–1714), included in the item '12 pairs of knives, with their forks and spoons.' It cannot be said with certainty that forks were in regular use. The princely family could be an exception. After this date, however, the expression is simply '12 pairs of silver knives and spoons', under the heading 'Silverware'. The fork reappears in the context of the Russian military occupations in the nineteenth century. See Constanţa Vintilă-Ghiţulescu, *Patimă şi desfătare. Despre lucrurile mărunte ale vieţii cotidiene în societatea românească, 1750–1860* (Bucharest: 2015), 140–147.

28 Norbert Elias, *La civilisation des mœurs* (Paris: 1973), 180.

29 Carataşu, *Documentele*, 59–61.

To understand these changes, let us consider the way in which coffee was served in a boyar salon, as experienced by the German doctor Andreas Wolf, around 1784:

> The master of the house claps his hands (this is a usual signal which replaces the bell used in our country), and, at once, the reception room is filled with servants. The housemaid, usually a Gypsy, brings on a silver tray a glass of fresh water, together with a pretty bowl, containing the so-called *dulceaţă*. This she hands over to the lady, who then serves each guest by hand. Because this is the first sign of the honours, regardless of the day or season, to refuse would signify a lack of good manners. The guest thus takes a good spoonful, and then drinks as much water after it as he desires. Meanwhile the coffee-bearer appears with his tray, on which sit the jug of coffee and the cups with their supports. The coffee is served unfiltered, and usually [prepared] without sugar, as I have seen among the Turks. The mistress of the house holds out in her hand a cup of coffee to each guest; in that moment the pipe-server approaches and offers to each in turn a pipe lit right then.[30]

Coffee was an important ingredient, part of a ritual of socialization practised both at the princely court and at the courts of the boyars. However, coffee was not offered alone: copying the Ottoman model, it was associated with *dulceaţă* (fruit conserve), sherbet, and the indispensable pipe.[31] Ianache Văcărescu was moving towards the Viennese model, which transformed only the coffee, by adding milk and sugar, but not the ritual of socialization.[32] For this 'Viennese model', he needed different objects: 'European cups', tongs, sugar bowls, and milk jugs, which he ordered insistently from his Viennese supplier.[33] All this silverware was to be 'suitable in weight, neither too heavy nor too light, but as is customary these days among the nobility in Europe.' And it should fit inside a trunk 'lined with fabric inside and [covered] with leather and bound with thick iron wire.'[34]

---

30 Andreas Wolf was a Transylvanian Saxon, a doctor at the princely court of Moldavia. He came to Moldavia in 1780 and stayed at the court until 1783. In 1784 he was in Wallachia, returning to Moldavia in 1788–1790 and 1796–1797. See Andreas Wolf, *Beiträge zur einer statistich-historischen Beschreibung des Fürstenthums Moldau* (Sibiu: 1805), 218–219. See also Maria Holban, Maria M. Alexandrescu-Dersca Bulgaru, Paul Cernovodeanu (eds.), *Călători străini despre ţările române*, Bucharest: 2000, vol. X/1, 1267.

31 For the coffee ritual see Vintilă-Ghiţulescu, *Patimă şi desfătare*, 149–157.

32 David Do Paço shows how coffee became part of a ritual of diplomatic meetings between Turks and Austrians in 'Comment le café devient viennois. Métissage et cosmopolitisme urbain dans l'Europe du XVIIIe siècle', *Hypothèses 2011: Travaux de l'École doctorale d'histoire* (Paris: 2012), 351.

33 Carataşu, *Documentele*, 59–61.

34 Carataşu, *Documentele*, 59–61.

All of these objects were commissioned to perform the practices of sociability specific to Brașov. Prince Nicolae Brâncoveanu, also in exile, stated that social status had to be upheld everywhere and in all circumstances.[35] While this imperative was complicated by their temporary residence in a foreign country, the consciousness of rank overrode any difficulties. In order to maintain his social prestige, on March 6, 1773 Văcărescu requested a loan of 8,000 florins from Chancellor Kaunitz, at the same time stressing his 'humiliation' at being forced to do so.[36]

In the end, Braşov proved to be the stage on which the actors of the two great empires met, interacting through dialogue and socialization, exchanging ideas and above all cultural values. Significantly, Văcărescu provided the emperor with information and with his vision of the Ottoman Empire and of the political situation in its peripheral regions. As a translator and interpreter, he mediated the differences between the two cultural environments.[37]

In shalwar and işlic to Vienna[38]

As was mentioned at the beginning of this study, the flight of the sons of the Wallachian Prince Alexandru Ipsilanti to 'the lands of Europe' triggered a diplomatic scandal.[39] As Ottoman subjects, Constantin and Dimitrie could cross the border only if the sultan gave his accord, which was almost unthinkable given that their father held the position of prince of Wallachia.

Prince Ipsilanti went to considerable effort in the hope of bringing his sons home before the news reached Istanbul. An intense diplomatic correspondence took place with the court of Vienna,[40] with a view to having the wayward sons

35 HHStA, Moldau-Walachei I/26/ Brancovan, f. 13, 15 January 1772. See also Chapter 1.

36 The chancellor dismissed the request, arguing that 'l'Impératrice-Reine' had to give priority to her subjects, whose interests had to take precedence over those of foreigners in the distribution of privileges and money (April 19, 1773, Vienna). HHStA Moldau-Walachei I/26/Vaccaresculi, f. 39–40; See also Andrei Pippidi, *Documente privind locul românilor în Sud-estul Europei* (Bucharest: 2018), 266–267.

37 It is unclear whether Văcărescu was the recipient of a letter that arrived from Vienna on November 15, 1777. Written in German, it provides a detailed description of social events in the Habsburg town, see BAR, fond Documente Istorice, CCCI/49.

38 *Işlic*: the tall, fur-trimmed hat worn as a mark of status by a Wallachian or Moldavian boyar.

39 The event attracted such popular interest that the story was quickly versified and circulated in the alleys of market towns in the form of a poem. See *Cronici şi povestiri româneşti versificate* (*sec. XVII–XVIII*), ed. Dan Simonescu (Bucharest:1967), 221–224.

40 HHStA, Moldau-Walachei I/26, Ipsilanti (1775–1793), 9–11, ff. 30–40, Türkei, II/77, ff. 55–57.

extradited, while the young men's tutor, Ignatius Stefan Raicevich, was sent on their trail.[41] As for the runaways themselves, Constantin and Dimitrie Ipsilanti, aged nineteen and seventeen respectively, wrote to Friedrich von Preiss, chief of the imperial army in Transylvania, and to Emperor Joseph II that their flight had been hastened by 'the bad treatment they suffered from their parents', that their lives and those of all Christians were always insecure in Turkey, that they wanted to study in Vienna, the most enlightened place in Europe, and that they put themselves at the service of the Emperor, for whom they were prepared to lay down their lives.[42] In an age in which travel was perceived as a means of education, especially in the case of young noblemen, the attitude of the Austrian authorities was somewhat encouraging. Neither General Preiss nor Chancellor Kaunitz nor even Emperor Joseph II seemed in any hurry to give orders for the young men to be sent back to Wallachia.[43]

Afraid that he might lose his head, Prince Ipsilanti sent a new mission to track down his sons, this time a much more impressive one, consisting of Metropolitan Grigorie of Wallachia, Bishop Filaret of Râmnic, Grand *Ban* Dumitrache Ghica, and Grand *Spătar* Ianache Văcărescu—almost half of the princely council—in the hope that they could 'urge the enlightened young gentlemen to come back.'[44] For the boyars of Wallachia, the Ipsilanti boys' exploit could only be interpreted as 'a criminal flight' that 'compromised their father forever' and destroyed 'the tranquillity and safety of our country', as Văcărescu stated in his letter to General Preiss, asking the latter to stop the young men in Transylvania.[45] We are thus faced with two different systems of thought: Joseph II and his diplomatic representatives speak of 'individual will' and personal liberty, and Văcărescu of 'submission and fidelity towards the Porte' and total obedience to their father.

The court of Vienna became the grand stage on which the Wallachian office-holder played the role of wealthy boyar, polyglot diplomat, and elegant gentleman.[46] He attracted the gaze of those around because he was a 'Turk',[47]

41 Hurmuzaki, *Documente*, VII, 331.

42 Hurmuzaki, *Documente*, VII, January 8, 1782, 339–340.

43 Hurmuzaki, *Documente*, VII, January 8, 1782, 339–340.

44 Văcărescu, *Istoria Othomanicească*, 127. On 'Ottoman Vienna' at the end of eighteenth century, see David Do Paço, *L'Orient à Vienne au dix-huitième siècle* (Oxford: 2015).

45 Hurmuzaki, *Documente*, VII, 345, January 13, 1782, Cronstat.

46 Ianache arrived in Vienna on January 25, 1782.

47 On the use of the denomination 'Turk' see Palmira Brummett, 'You Say "Classical", I Say "Imperial"', Let's Call the Whole Thing Off: Empire, Individual, and Encounter in Travel Narratives of the Ottoman Empire', *Journal of Ottoman Studies* 44 (2014), 21–44.

or defined himself as such, and above all because he was a 'foreigner' of startling opulence.

Prince Kaunitz introduced him into the Viennese atmosphere:

> He took me by the hand and went out into the assembly room, where were gathered all the ambassadors of the courts and the most brilliant ladies in Vienna. I made the acquaintance of them all and they greeted me with affection and with honour … Prince Kaunitz found the occasion to praise the sable furs in which I was dressed (for the Europeans habitually speak casually of these things, and to people they have met for the first time). And at that assembly the ladies undid my sash, to see my shawl.[48]

Everything gave off an air of extravagance: Lahore shawl, sable furs, diamond ring, silk *anteri*[49] and brocaded *fermene*,[50] hanjar inlaid with precious stones, and *sahtiyan* leather slippers. The Wallachian official on a diplomatic mission was the living image of what a 'Turk' ought to be. He quickly became the star attraction of the salons, enjoying the company of Prince Kaunitz, Grand Duke Paul of Russia, French ambassador Louis August Le Tonnelier de Breteuil,[51] Vice-chancellor Philipp von Cobenzl, the Spanish ambassador, and Archduke Maximilian.[52] The boyar entered into the logic of Viennese protocol, paying visits of courtesy and greeting: 'I went to all the ambassadors to greet them with notes and when I returned to my lodgings to dine all the ambassadors came to me to greet me with notes.'[53]

Expensive furs were very important for the maintenance of prestige. Their very high price turned them into luxury objects, often forbidden under sumptuary laws, and at the same time important gifts in diplomatic relations.[54]

---

48 Văcărescu, *Istoria Othomanicească*, 129–130.

49 A long robe.

50 A short, embroidered jacket, worn over the *anteri*.

51 Văcărescu emphasized the attention and respect he received from French ambassador Breteuil, who tried to ingratiate himself with the 'Sublime *Devlet*'. Upon grasping the underlying reason for this 'abundance of ceremonies' on Breteuil's part, Văcărescu responded to him as to 'a Turk', causing the diplomat 'much satisfaction'. Văcărescu, *Istoria Othomanicească*, 131.

52 On Vienna as a diplomatic centre see David do Paço, *The Political Agents of Muslim Rulers in Central Europe in the 18th century*, in *Christian-Muslim Relations. A Bibliographical History*, vol. 14: *Central and Eastern Europe, 1700–1800*, eds. David Thomas and John Chesworth (Leiden: 2020), 39–55.

53 Văcărescu, *Istoria Othomanicească*, 131.

54 Donald Quataert, 'Clothing Laws, the State and Society in the Ottoman Empire, 1720–1829', *International Journal of Middle Eastern Studies* 29, no. 3 (1997), 403–425; Hedda Reindl-Kiel, 'Luxury, Power Strategies and the Question of Corruption: Gifting in the

Prince Kaunitz insisted on knowing the price of the sable furs that decorated Ianache's *cüppe*,[55] and then asked him to offer advice on the pricing of some gifts: 'He said to me: "Let me show you a sable fur that the Crown Prince of Russia gave me and I pray you tell me its price." He brought the fur and put it on the billiard table.' The situation was problematic, as that the Wallachian official wore furs much more expensive and more beautiful than those received by his Viennese host, so he saved himself by means of the rhetoric of diplomacy: 'I answered him that neither by sunlight nor at night can sable furs be priced properly. This fur, however, taking into account the place from which it was given and the place to which it was given, is priceless. And I, even if I had seen it by day, do not have the skill to price it.'[56]

Văcărescu again becomes a 'Turk' when he enters the palace of Emperor Joseph II, which he describes in lavish details, impressed as he was by 'the pavilion with marble pillars supported on the backs of lions,' by 'the curtains that hang from the baldachin worked with gold,' by 'the folded draperies with metallic thread,' by the pearls decorating them, by the guards, the swords, the multitude of rooms, of cabinets, etc.[57] It is a meeting of two different worlds: Joseph II, the adept of ceremony simplified as far as possible,[58] and Văcărescu, the adept of Ottoman diplomatic protocol:

> As I went in through the door, I saw the Kaiser in the middle of the room, on his feet and without a hat, and taking two steps forward I knelt down in the Turkish manner, and after putting my head on the ground, when I wanted to raise it, I found myself with the Kaiser's hand on my head; he said to me that he did not require this ceremony and I should rise, and when I wanted to kiss his hand, he pulled it away.[59]

Ottoman Elite (16th–18th Centuries)', in Yavuz Köse (ed.), *Şehrâyîn. Die Welt der Osmanen, die Osmanen in der Welt, Wahrnehmungen, Begegnungen und Abgrenzungen: Festschrift Hans Georg Majer* (Wiesbaden: 2012), 107–120.

55 A long felt coat, often lined and trimmed with fur.

56 Văcărescu, *Istoria Othomanicească*, 130. A similar scene can be found in the account of Ebu Bekir Ratıb, Ottoman ambassador to Vienna in 1792. This time, the scene focused on Prince Kaunitz and his horse-riding skills. See Findley, 'Ebu Bekir Ratib's Vienna Embassy', 65. For Kaunitz's behaviour, see Franz A. Szabo, *Kaunitz and Enlightened Absolutism 1753–1780* (Cambridge: 1994), 20–35.

57 Văcărescu, *Istoria Othomanicească*, 133.

58 Barbara Stollberg-Rilinger, *Les vieux habits de l'empereur. Une histoire culturelle des institutions du Saint-Empire à l'époque moderne* (Paris: 2008), 312. For Joseph II and court ceremonial, see Derek Beales, *Joseph II: Against the World, 1780–1790* (Cambridge: 2013).

59 Văcărescu, *Istoria Othomanicească*, 133.

Ottoman protocol, as performed by Văcărescu, suddenly became insignificant and rather embarrassing when the Emperor withdrew the hand that was about to be kissed.[60]

In Wallachia, the boyars followed Ottoman protocol, kissing the prince's hand and/or the hems of his robes as a form of respect and of recognition of hierarchies.[61] Meanwhile, in 1787, Emperor Joseph II issued an imperial decree forbidden kneeling, considering that it was 'not a fitting form of behaviour from one human being to another and should be reserved for God alone.'[62] Prostration, kneeling and kissing of hands and feet were part of a cultural code put into practice in the Ottoman Empire and respected strictly on its peripheries, at the borders between rival empires.[63]

The audience lasted more than two hours. Joseph II argued the case for individual free will, imperial hospitality, and political asylum for young men who wanted to study and to travel freely, stressing that the young princes might be advised to return home but under no circumstances forced to do so.[64] The Wallachian office-holder, an Ottoman subject, asked for no more and no less than their expulsion by force, emphasizing that his whole career depended on the success of this diplomatic mission:

> Besides the effort that to my great honour and praise I have made to come, I will lose what little reputation and standing (*ypolipsis*) I have in all the principality of Wallachia, where to the sorrow I feel on account of these happenings is added that of being incapable of carrying [my mission] to a conclusion and being unable to obtain justice even from the very justice itself that you are, your Imperial Majesty.[65]

---

60 In the meantime, events had taken a new turn in Wallachia. Alexandru Ipsilanti had given up the throne and had named Ianache Văcărescu as *kaymakam*. Văcărescu, *Istoria Othomanicească*, 135.

61 In Wallachia, 'the custom of kissing the prince's hand as a sign of subservience would be abolished only on July 21, 1834, by a princely decree sent to all departments, ANIC, Fond Achiziţii Noi, MMMXXXIX/1; SJAN/Vâlcea, Fond Prefectura Judeţului Vâlcea, 35/1834; SJAN/Buzău, Fond Subocârmuirea Plaiului despre Buzău, 53/1834).

62 T.C.W. Blanning, *Joseph II* (London, 2013), 64; On diplomatic ritual, see also: Christine Vogel, 'The Caftan and the Sword: Dress and Diplomacy in Ottoman–French Relations Around 1700', in Claudia Ulbrich and Richard Wittmann (eds.), *Fashioning the Self in Transcultural Settings: The Uses and Significance of Dress in Self-Narratives* (Würzburg: 2015), 25–45.

63 For the Ottoman protocol of hand-kissing, see Palmira Brummett, 'A Kiss is Just a Kiss: Rituals of Submission along the East-West Divide', in Matthew Birchwood and Matthew Dimmock (eds.), *Cultural Encounters between East and West, 1453–1699* (Cambridge: 2005), 107–131.

64 HHStA, Türkei, II/77, f. 11, 60.

65 Văcărescu, *Istoria Othomanicească*, 136.

Impressed by the rhetoric of the Wallachian boyar, but also as a consequence of the information with which he had been provided[66]—he is known to have had a 'mania for gathering detailed information about all manner of social phenomena'[67]—Emperor Joseph II promised that he would not receive the young Ipsilanti princes into his service: 'I promise you upon my imperial word that neither in my lands nor in my service will I keep them, and I will certainly return them to Turkey, only that I must first bring them here, to ensure that they have a pleasant stay, without worries.'[68] In other words, the good manners specific to diplomatic ceremonial must be respected to the end, and the right to hospitality remains a principle that cannot be stepped over.

Being a Boyar: Luxury, Civility, and Prestige

Travelling across empires, entering into contact with different forms of civilization, dealing skilfully with languages and people, Ianache Văcărescu is a key figure for the understanding of peripheries. Wallachia and Moldavia were 'contact zones', to borrow the term used by Mary Louise Pratt, where, for more than a century, three great empires, Ottoman, Habsburg, and Russian, had met.[69] The meetings between the three cultures are reflected in personal memoirs, which try to define identity and alterity in relation to the other.[70] The local elite is the bearer of this 'cultural mix'. Although common features often unite the narrators and their characters, these seem to get lost when the test of civility is set out as an inexorable criterion. In many cases, the writers of travel narratives do not understand the way of being of these boyars, even if it fascinates or intrigues them, and thus they categorize them as 'barbarian'. Even those who have spent many years among them, occupying official positions, are repelled and criticize certain customs or behaviours, which are always entered in the balance of alterity. Consuls, ambassadors, diplomats, missionaries, or simple travellers are the guests of the courts and mansions of the boyars, which they

66 Ianache Văcărescu writes: 'He asked me many questions, about Tsarigrad (Constantinople), about Wallachia, about customs and other things,' Ibid., 136.

67 Judson, *Habsburg Empire*, 55.

68 Văcărescu, *Istoria Othomanicească*, 136.

69 Mary Louise Pratt, *Imperial Eyes: Travel Writing and Transculturation* (New York: 1992), 4.

70 For this topic, see Larry Wolff, *Inventing Eastern Europe: The Map of Civilization on the Mind of the Enlightenment* (Stanford, CA: 1994); and Maria Todorova, *Imagining the Balkans* (Oxford: 1997).

then describe in their eager quest for *turqueries*.[71] Good manners as a form of social distinction and self-fashioning were very much in vogue in central and northern Europe. For the Wallachian boyars, the model of good behaviour was inspired by the manners and conduct displayed by the princes at court. These were adapted according to the context and the guests: 'Greek', 'Turkish', and 'Ottoman' in the company of Ottoman envoys and Wallachian office-holders, 'French' in the company of 'western travellers.'

In his book devoted to the Ottoman Empire, Ianache Văcărescu often uses the term *ypolipsis* (and never *politíe*), to describe the behaviour of others and to speak about himself. His readings were diverse and in various languages,[72] but when it came to good manners, and above all conduct, although he had read *Il giovane istruito*,[73] he preferred the Greek word *ypolipsis* (*ὑπόληψις*). The significance of the term *ypolipsis* was connected to the place one occupied in society, to the social classifications made by others, to the way one was seen by others, and to a certain status displayed and promoted. For Văcărescu, *ypolipsis* represented a public recognition of his learning and wisdom. The individual with *ypolipsis* is the one who shows himself, by his accumulation of knowledge and learning, to have wisdom. True learning is that which brings wisdom, and together they lead to respect, prestige, and fame. Prestige is recognized by measures capable of ensuring 'the well-being of all.'[74] This *ypolipsis* may be quickly lost if the individual does not strive always to retain people's respect. This is what he is speaking of when he seeks the help of Emperor Joseph II to recover the sons of Prince Ipsilanti, and the term is clothed in the same sense when he uses it to characterize others. Consider what he says about Alexandru Mavrocordat, Dragoman of the Porte, whom he describes as 'a man of a subtle and lively spirit', with immortal *ypolipsis*, obtained by virtue of 'noteworthy service to the Empire',[75] or Selim Pasha, *muhafíz* of Nikopol, who is 'learned and wise'.[76] Ianache Văcărescu presents himself as the foremost boyar of Wallachia,

---

71 See Alexander Bevilacqua and Helen Pfeifer, 'Turquerie: Culture in Motion, 1650–1750', *Past and Present* 221 (2013), 75–118.

72 Văcărescu frequently borrowed Greek, Italian, French, Turkish, or German terms to convey notions without an equivalent in Romanian.

73 The reference is to the work of the Italian author Geminiano Gaetti, *Il giovane istruito ne'dogmi cattolici: nella verità della religione cristiana e sua morale* (Venice, 1749). *Serdar* Anton Manuil composed a Greek translation, published in 1794 and dedicated to *Spătar* Ianache Văcărescu (Cârstoiu, *Văcărescu*, 227).

74 Văcărescu, *Istoria Othomanicească*, 94.

75 Văcărescu, *Istoria Othomanicească*, 77–78.

76 Văcărescu, *Istoria Othomanicească*, 149. Of Selim he writes that he was from Nikopol, and that he had been *kapicibaşi* and *ayan*, in recognition of which he received 'three tails' from the sultan and command of the citadels of Nikopol and Kula.

a man of great *ypolipsis*, worthy to be ruler of the principality.[77] Those around him, 'Greeks' or 'Turks' like himself, describe him in the same terms. 'You have heard of the wealthy Vakarescolo, the Croesus of Boyars,' says Iordache Condilo admiringly,[78] while Prince Alexandru Moruzi, elevating Văcărescu to the office of grand *ban*, recognizes him as 'the foremost noble boyar [...] capable and with good *ypolipsis*.' Moruzi held this opinion despite having every reason to hate the 'worthy' and 'faithful' boyar, given the rumours that Văcărescu was Princess Zoe Moruzi's lover: the prince heard the populace singing daily under his window of their illicit and 'fiery passion'.[79]

The high office-holder Ianache Văcărescu gave particular attention to the body that was seen, to appearances, and to the education of the mind. At a certain point in his memoirs, he wonders which it is better to have, 'a jar of good fortune or a drop of intelligence,' and he answers: 'A splash of intelligence I want, rather than good fortune.'[80] And so he would be all his life, educating his mind with diverse reading and writing and taking care of his body. Nevertheless, the education of the mind and the care of the body did not turn him into a *giovane istruito* such as the ambassadors, princes, and chancellors—in a word, the 'Europeans'—considered themselves to be. Consider the following eye-witness account by the Swiss Franz Joseph Sulzer, one of the secretaries of Prince Alexandru Ipsilanti and an Austrian agent in Wallachia, who knew the elite at the princely court at close quarters. Invited to a ball held there in 1778, he describes the atmosphere as follows:

> At the table of the Prince of Wallachia, the Grand Ban Dudescu wanted to honour the name day of the Prince, which was celebrated then, with an unusual toast. Perhaps he had drunk too much. He stood up as the foremost boyar in the land, according to custom, together with the Metropolitan, and the whole table stood up after them; he uttered his toast, tasted a little from the great toasting

77 Văcărescu, *Istoria Othomanicească*, 103. Drace-Francis, *Making*, 63, also points out Văcărescu's eagerness to underline his social distinction when he signed his books as a *dikaiophylax* of the Great Eastern Church. Similarly high levels of self-esteem can be found among the Ottoman diplomats discussed by Denis Klein, 'The Sultan's Envoys Speak: The Ego in 18th Century Ottoman Sefâretnâmes on Russia', in Ralf Elger and Yavuz Köse (eds.), *Many Ways of Speaking About Self: Middle Eastern Ego-Documents in Arabic, Persian and Turkish (14th–20th Century)* (Wiesbaden: 2010), 89–103.

78 Iordache Condilo was the brother-in-law of the Phanariot prince Nicolae Mavrogheni (1786–1790) and a diplomatic agent. He appears as a character in the novel *Anastasius* by Thomas Hope (London: 1819), II, 293.

79 See the document of April 30, 1795, in Urechia, *Istoria românilor*, vol. 5, 306–307.

80 Văcărescu, *Istoria Othomanicească*, 118.

> cup, and poured the rest of the cup in the face of the Grand Vornic Filipescu, so that the wine flowed over his beard and over his fur, down to the ground.[81]

For Sulzer, with his Jesuit education and experience of the discipline of an Austrian infantry regiment, the toast is nothing but 'the playful fancy of a drunkard'.[82] The unusual toast was, however, a local custom, which is also recorded elsewhere. For example, in the collection *Îndreptări moraliceşti tinerilor foarte folositoare* (Moral guidelines very useful to the young), Dimitrie Ţichindeal notes and condemns such behaviour: 'abandon the foolish and vulgar custom that some observe towards their friends and their beloved wife, that the wine that they cannot drink from the glass they pour on the clothes of those who cannot drink it. This is great foolishness and vulgarity.'[83] At another ball, also at the princely court, Sulzer is scandalized by the sight of elegant ladies eating with their fingers from a common dish, eagerly devouring the food 'without forks'.[84] Nor does he have a better opinion about our Văcărescu: among the exiles in Braşov in 1774, he witnessed a truly revolting scene: 'At the official ball of the commandant of Braşov, the grand *vistier* [i.e. Ianache Văcărescu] got so drunk that he threw up in the ballroom all that he had consumed.'[85] Sulzer notes the excesses of this boyar class, whom he does not like much and among whom he did not manage to integrate himself, although he spent more than eleven years in Wallachia.

All the same, it must be observed that the term *ypolipsis* does not completely correspond to the term *politíe* (civility) as it was expressed in Romanian at the time.[86] Civility includes a 'code of refined manners, the practices of polite behaviour'.[87] From Erasmus onwards, via Antoine de Courtin, Jean-Batiste La Salle, and Louis-Marin Henriquez, practices were constructed that regulated the behaviour of the individual in society: 'legitimate behaviours' necessary for common life and the promotion of decency. All these treatises were directed principally at the education of children, and their use in schools was

81 Sulzer, *Geschichte des transalpinischen Daciens*, III, 335. See also *Călători străini*, X/I, 473

82 Sulzer, *Geschichte*.

83 Dimitrie Ţichindeal, *Îndreptări moraliceşti tinerilor foarte folositoare* (Moral guidelines very useful to the young) (Buda: 1813), 62. Dimitrie Ţichindeal (1775–1818) was a Romanian teacher and priest from the Banat who translated or wrote many manuals of savoir-vivre.

84 Sulzer, *Geschichte*, III, 334.

85 Sulzer, *Geschichte*. See also the episodes analyzed by Dariusz Kołodziejczyk, 'Semiotics of Behavior in Early Modern Diplomacy: Polish Embassies in Istanbul and Bahçesaray', *Journal of Early Modern History* 7, 3–4 (2003), 245–256.

86 *Politíe* comes from *polis* and adds the modern sense of 'polite.'

87 Roger Chartier, *Lecturi şi cititori în Franţa Vechiului Regim* (Bucharest: 1997), 57–59.

recommended, as civility was incorporated among the Christian virtues.[88] A 'virtue of society', civility has the role of making connections between people pleasant.[89] *Politíe* (civility) and *ypolipsis* are expressed by the same references to honour, prestige, and respect but without covering exactly the same meaning. Ianache Văcărescu was mainly interested in social distinction, inscribing himself in a logic of prestige, by working on appearances.[90] Vestimentary opulence and 'subtle spirit' (brilliant and educated intelligence) provided him with the respect and self-esteem that were indispensable for dominating the political stage.

Far from Vienna: Working on an 'Ottoman History'

While waiting for his sons, who had gone off to discover Europe, Alexandru Ipsilanti resigned his mandate for fear of losing his head. As the boys did not stop in Vienna, instead making a short trip through Italy before embarking for Constantinople, there was nothing their father could do but pay the massive debts they had left behind them.[91]

As for Ianache Văcărescu, he remained faithful to the Ottoman Empire but not to the new prince, Nicolae Mavrogheni (1786–1790). Mavrogheni's appointment to the Wallachian throne constituted for Văcărescu an opportunity to express his admiration for the Phanariot network and his allegiance to it: '[Mavrogheni] was not a man who had grown up in the Phanar, so that he would have known the rules of the Phanar, or those of the Sublime Porte.' Moreover, a good candidate for the Wallachian throne should be familiar with the 'custom of the land' and possess the linguistic skills necessary for interacting with multiple centres of power. Mavrogheni, however, was ignorant of the customs, 'he spoke neither Greek nor Turkish,' and 'was even unable to master Romanian throughout his life.'[92] Hence, Văcărescu despised him for his lack of education and for the fact that he did not belong to the Phanariot elite, being a

88 Ibid., 79.

89 Ibid., 81.

90 Norbert Elias, *La société de cour* (Paris: 1985), 115.

91 Emperor Joseph II respected the promise he had made to the Wallachian office-holder. The young Constantin and Dimitrie Ipsilanti were well received at the court of Vienna, but they were urged to return home. See the relevant diplomatic correspondence in HHStA, Türkei, II/77, ff. 152–155. Hurmuzaki, *Documente*, vol. 7, 333–334, 361–363, 377–378, 441–442; and 9, 124.

92 Văcărescu, *Istoria Othomanicească*, 142. Philliou writes that Mavrogheni knew Greek, Turkish, and Italian. He came from a family from Paros that was well represented in the ranks of office-holders in the Ottoman Empire. Philliou, *Biography of an Empire*, 44–47.

mere ship's captain—in other words, 'a man foolish in his behaviour, his thinking, and his feelings.'[93]

Văcărescu was not alone, however, in expressing dissatisfaction with Mavrogheni. Other boyars could identify with his bitter criticism of the Phanariot prince. In fact, the boyars' contempt for the Phanariots appears in all its splendour during the reign of Nicolae Mavrogheni. They deserted him one by one. Michael Merkelius, the Austrian envoy to Bucharest, describes in one of his reports to Chancellor Kaunitz the arrest of the grand *ban* Pană Filipescu, who was lifted from his home in the middle of the night on 22 January 1788, taken in a carriage guarded by six Arnauts as far as the Danube, and there handed over to the Turks. The boyars had interceded, asking that the *ban* be forgiven, as he was far too old to endure the cold and the rigours of exile, but Mavrogheni would not be moved and refused to pardon the 'ugly' words that Filipescu had uttered about the Phanariots.[94] Before long, other boyars too shared the grand *ban*'s fate, and were sent into a sort of forced exile, at Nikopol (Ottoman Niğbolu) and then on Rhodes. Among them were Nicolae and Emanuel Brâncoveanu, Scarlat and Costache Ghica, Ianache Moruzi, Dumitrașco Racoviță, and Manolache Crețulescu.[95] Ianache Văcărescu refused to follow Mavrogheni and his strategies in the war of 1787–1790, and ended up going into exile in Nikopol.[96] It was there, in 1788, that he began work on what would become his *History of the Most Puissant Ottoman Emperors*.

In writing his *Ottoman History*, Ianache Văcărescu placed himself on the side of the empire that had helped him in his social ascent. As was mentioned at the beginning of this chapter, Ianache firmly believed that the Ottoman Empire had the economic and political resources to survive. Without offering a comprehensive analysis of the work, as this has already been ably done by others,[97] I shall use the autobiographical information it offers to situate Ianache Văcărescu in the regional political context of the second half of the eighteenth century. By analysing the personal and professional network into which Ianache Văcărescu introduced himself, we may understand the interpretation he offers of his status and duties within the Phanariot—and implicitly Ottoman—administrative system.

93 Văcărescu, *Istoria Othomanicească*, 142.

94 Hurmuzaki, *Documente*, XIX, 25 January 1788, 387.

95 Fotino, *Istoria Generală a Daciei*, 175.

96 HHStA Moldau-Walachei I/26, f. 74–75, March 10, 1791.

97 For the most recent presentation, see Radu G. Păun, *Ianache Văcărescu*, in David Thomas and John Chesworth (eds.), *Christian–Muslim Relations. A Bibliographical History*, vol. 14. *Central and Eastern Europe (1700–1800)* (Leiden: 2020), 364–381.

Ianache takes advantage of the opportunities provide by regional conflicts to highlight his qualities and to offer his services. His self-promotion can be traced through each of the actions described in his history. As noted in the previous chapter, Ianache Văcărescu made use of the gathering of the boyars to approve the intervention of Russia in Wallachia in 1769 as a pretext for his flight to Brașov:

> I proceeded through the foothills of Buzău with letters to the boyars, commanding them to come to Bucharest. And going through the foothills of Săcuiani I arrived at Cerași, where I took my wife and my mother and a child that I had and crossed into Transylvania, to Brașov, by the Buzău lazaretto, together with as many boyars as were there; and immediately I informed my father-in-law, Iacovache, who was with the Turkish army at Babadagî.[98]

Both he and the Brâncoveanus wrote to Chancellor Kaunitz, asking for a loan of money but also in order to introduce themselves. Summoned by the grand vizier and advised by his father-in-law, Iacovaki Rizo, Văcărescu returned in 1772 from Brașov to Craiova, where both the prince appointed and recognized by the Turks (Emanoil Giani Ruset) and the grand vizier were, in order to put himself at the service of the Porte. In his letter to Kaunitz, Văcărescu includes information about the network of which he was a part, mentioning his participation in the peace negotiations at Focșani, summoned by Osman Efendi and the grand vizier, Muhsinzade Mehmet Pasha, but also the fact that he had met the grand vizier, who praised him for his conduct.[99] However, in order to reach Focșani, Ianache Văcărescu needed a passport, since, coming from the Habsburg Empire as an Ottoman subject, he had to pass through an area occupied by the Russian army. Văcărescu writes that Osman Efendi, being desirous—he uses the Hellenism *periergos* (περίεργος)—of knowing and finding out information from different sources, invited him to Focșani, asking the Austrian envoy Johann Amadeus von Thugut to obtain a passport for him so that he could travel.[100] In addition to the representatives of the two empires, Osman Efendi and Aleksei Mikhailovich Obreskov, representatives of the great powers with an interest in developments in the region had also come to Focșani.[101] According to Văcărescu, Internuncio Thugut should have requested his passport from the Russian representative in the Principalities, Pyotr Rumyantsev; however, whether for the sake of convenience or for some

98 Văcărescu, *Istoria Othomanicească*, 105.
99 HHStA Moldau-Walachei I/26/Vaccaresculi, f. 39–40, 19 April 1773.
100 Văcărescu, *Istoria Othomanicească*, 111.
101 Urechia, 'Istoria evenimentelor', 408–409.

other unknown reason, he had obtained a passport from the military commandant of Transylvania, with the following notification: 'This boyar of the Ottoman Empire, who is going to Focșani, under imperial protection, being summoned as an envoy to the congress, is to pass in peace.'[102] I referred in the previous chapter to the passport issued by the imperial representatives for Emanuel Brâncoveanu, signed apparently by Empress Maria Theresa herself, and the failure of the document to have any effect in the Russian camp. Much the same happened in Ianache Văcărescu's case. He quickly realized that 'this passport was not sufficient,' and hoped that Thugut had also written to Field Marshal Rumyantsev about his arrival. His hopes proved in vain: on his arrival at Focșani, 'close to the congress,' Văcărescu was stopped by the Russian army because he 'did not have the field marshal's passport,' and was left in the open, 'under the sun,' to wait for eighteen days.[103] He writes that his protector, Osman Efendi, was very upset, 'going into a rage' and forcing Thugut to do what he should have done from the start. Indeed, Osman Efendi was well-known for his violent outbursts and strange behaviour.[104] While he waited for the situation to be resolved, Văcărescu wrote directly to Rumyantsev, masterfully drawing attention to the different layers of his identity: an Ottoman subject, under temporary Habsburg protection, a prisoner, in time of armistice, of the Russians, solely because 'he had kept as was his duty his faithfulness to the masters that God had ordained for him.'[105] We do not know whether it was this letter or the intervention of Internuncio Thugut that contributed to the resolution of the situation. What is certain is that three days later, Văcărescu was allowed to move on and was received with 'liubov' (love) by Osman Efendi.[106] When the negotiations broke down and Osman Efendi withdrew to Shumen, Văcărescu followed his patron. At Shumen, he had occasion to renew acquaintance with the grand vizier, who received him 'very well', thus providing him with an occasion to present the grievances of the boyars in Brașov, and also to be charged with 'certain services for the Porte' in Wallachia. Armed with 'an imperial ferman to all the viziers beyond the shores of the Danube,' Văcărescu travelled in safety along the Shumen–Ruse–Nikopol–Vidin–Mehadia–Brașov route.[107] We do not know what mission he had received from the grand vizier,

102 Văcărescu, *Istoria Othomanicească*, 112.

103 Văcărescu also suspected that the boyars in the Russian camp, particularly the Cantacuzinos, had contributed to the blocking of his access to the Ottoman camp. Ibid., 112.

104 Aksan, *An Ottoman Statesman*, 158.

105 Văcărescu, *Istoria Othomanicească*, 113.

106 Văcărescu, *Istoria Othomanicească*, 113.

107 Văcărescu, *Istoria Othomanicească*, 113–114.

but we do know the Ottoman network that supported him and that he cultivated assiduously, both through his parents-in-law and in person. He did not get to the peace negotiations in Bucharest, but he narrates the events, introducing Sultan Abdülhamid (who succeeded to the throne following the death of the 'wise' Mustafa III), Ahmed Resmi 'who had all power with the emperor', Melek Mehmet Pasha, Sahib Giray, Devlet Giray, and all the Russian actors in the war.[108] The appointment of a new prince of Wallachia proved another opportunity to promote himself and enter further into the network.[109] From Brașov, Văcărescu did not return to Bucharest together with the other boyars, as he had been instructed to do by 'imperial command',[110] but headed to Silistra, in order to join the princely suite: 'As I went through the country, I passed by Silistra, where I found Seit Hasan Pasha Stanchioiulâul serascher [Rusçuklu Hasan Paşa], a vizier full of goodness and a lover of good deeds, and he received me with much love and gave me five *mektup*s (official letters): to the vizier, to the kahya bey, to the reis efendi, to the yazıcı efendi, and to the prince of Wallachia.[111]

With the five official letters, Ianache Văcărescu, for the third time, as he writes, took the road to 'Tsarigrad'. He was making this journey because he wanted to return to Bucharest not as an ordinary boyar who had hidden for fear of the war in the citadel of Brașov, but as one whose merits had to be recognized and rewarded. His return in the suite of the new prince was the best strategy. In Istanbul, he was received with goodwill—he uses the Hellenism *evmenie* (*εὐμένεια*)—by the grand vizier, the reisülküttab, and others who had recognized his merits, who offered him 'a *ferman* showing his faithful services to the Porte,' and with permission (*musaadea*) he returned in the suite of Prince Alexandru Ipsilanti who appointed him to the office of grand *vistier*.[112]

From this moment on, Văcărescu's career and prestige knew no bounds. Even if the Ottoman Empire had lost the war, his network had won the game. His rivals, the Cantacuzinos, had taken refuge in Russia, leaving the field open, while the Brâncoveanus, returned from exile, needed time to remake their alliances. When Nicolae Caragea became prince (1782–1783), Văcărescu

108 Girays had a special position, coming from the dynasty ruling the Crimean Khanate that Russia was in the process of annexing. See on this Denise Klein (ed.), *The Crimean Khanate Between East and West (15th–18th Century)* (Wiesbaden: 2012).

109 On 15 September 1774, Alexandru Ipsilanti was appointed prince of Wallachia.

110 See Abdülhamid I's *ferman* of 5/14 November 1774, in which he asks the inhabitants to return to their homes, assuring them that they will be 'completely forgiven' and that the pre-war situation will be restored. *Documente turceşti*, III, 2–4.

111 Văcărescu, *Istoria Othomanicească*, 119.

112 Văcărescu, *Istoria Othomanicească*, 122.

received the office of grand *spătar* and married the prince's youngest daughter.[113] Under Prince Mihai Suţu (1783–1786), he took up again the office of grand *vistier*, and played his part in preparations for the war that threatened on the imperial frontiers.[114] Not even the appointment of Nicolae Mavrogheni shook his position as a powerful and influential boyar with extensive connections in the Ottoman Empire. On the contrary, while Mavrogheni kept him in office and consulted him regarding various political issues and the path to follow in the new Russian–Austrian–Turkish war that had broken out in the region, Văcărescu had such contempt for the prince that he requested his recall to Istanbul.[115]

Mavrogheni did not count for much in the eyes of the other Phanariot families either. They did not consider him one of themselves, referring him to as 'the peasant from the archipelago' and doing all they could to prevent his appointment to the Wallachian throne. 'All the great Greek families, despite the hatred that always divides them, have united to prevent a peasant from the archipelago from taking from them a position that they regard as their birthright and have clubbed together to convince the whole Divan of Mavrogheni's incapability,' wrote French ambassador Choiseul in his report to Vergennes of 27 January 1786.[116] Ianache Văcărescu was the new prince's confidential advisor

---

113 Văcărescu, *Istoria Othomanicească*, 137. Through this marriage, Văcărescu entered one of the most powerful Phanariot networks. His brothers-in-law held the offices of grand dragoman and dragoman of the imperial fleet; others became princes of Moldavia and Wallachia; he became related to the Moruzi, Ghica, Mavrocordat, and Callimachi families. See Rizo-Rangabé, *Livre d'or*, 37–39.

114 Văcărescu, *Istoria Othomanicească*, 141. He writes about the mission he was given to gather army provisions on the Danube border, to prepare bridges, and even to build a ship: 'We arranged to build in Wallachia a naval ship as we had already done in '76.' See in this connection the *ferman* of Sultan Abdülhamid I of 19/28 February 1787, in which he asks for the galley that was being built at Galaţi to be finished and sent. *Documente turceşti*, II, 106–107.

115 'What shall I say of his deeds and works, for I am ashamed to take note of them? So I leave them to those who write the annals of the princes.' Văcărescu, *Istoria Othomanicească*, 143. Dionisie Fotino describes Mavrogheni as 'bizarre', 'eccentric', and with 'strange behaviour', as examples of which he mentions presenting his dreams at meetings of the divan and making his horse Talambaşa a boyar, with the rank of *serdar*. Fotino, *Istoria Generală a Daciei*, 175. Dionisie the Ecclesiarch also recounts the prince's eccentricities, including going through the city on inspection disguised as a priest and conferring boyar status on whoever he caught, giving them kaftans of plain cloth and demanding money from them. Dionisie Eclisiarhul, *Scrieri alese. Hronograf*, 23–26, 38.

116 'Toutes les grandes familles grecques, malgré la haine qui les divise toujours, se réunirent pour empêcher un paysan de l'archipel de leur enlever une place qu'elles regardent comme leur patrimoine et se cotisèrent pour convaincre toute le Divan de l'incapacité de Mavroyeni.' Hurmuzaki, *Documente*, I/2, 37. Regarding Mavrogheni, see also Théodore

for a time, but he distanced himself and criticized him severely for his desire to become 'seraskier'. To achieve this ambition, Mavrogheni devised 'crazy' plans. I shall present only one of the episodes narrated by Ianache Văcărescu, still a closer adviser in his capacity as grand *vistier*:

> I myself have seen him write a *takrir* [report] to the Porte declaring not only that the Germans have no alliance with the Russians, but he said that they are also enemies. He himself showed me this *takrir* when he was writing it. I asked him, 'And what enmity to they have?' He answered that the Germans do not want to give the title of empress to the empress of Russia. What a ridiculous answer, readers![117]

The exiling of boyars, or of members of boyar families (wife, son, father) was one of the methods used to extort 'ransom' money, if they wished to return to Wallachia.[118] Following the prince's refusal to let him go to Istanbul, where the family of his wife, Ecaterina Caragea, were, Văcărescu chose to join the exiled boyars in Nikopol. The protection he requested from the Ottoman Empire gradually turned into captivity, as the situation in Wallachia developed and relations between Mavrogheni and his boyars deteriorated.[119]

The life of an exile always depends on political circumstances, but above all on social and political connections with the local authorities. In the previous chapter, I presented the experience of the Brâncoveanus in the world of

---

Blancard, *Les Mavroyéni. Essai d'étude additionnelle à l'histoire moderne de la Grèce, de la Turquie et de la Roumanie* (Paris: 1893); Sophia Laiou, 'Between Pious Generosity and Faithful Service to the Ottoman State: The *Vakıf* of Nikolaos Mavroghenis, End of the Eighteenth Century', *Turkish Historical Review*, 6 (2015), 151–174.

117 Văcărescu, *Istoria Othomanicească*, 146.

118 Văcărescu, *Istoria Othomanicească*, 149. Mavrogheni took advantage of an order of the sultan, who required that in wartime the prince should send his family to Istanbul to be 'protected', but also to prove his devotion. Together with the princely family, the principal boyars of the country with their families were also required as a guarantee. Such a *ferman* was issued on 25 August/3 September 1787 for the prince of Moldavia, Alexandru Ipsilanti. See also the complaint of the Wallachian boyars to Nicolae Mavrogheni in which they expressed their agreement to leave for Nikopol as the sultan's *ferman* of 1/13 October 1788 required. *Documente turceşti*, II, 179, 204–205.

119 On 26 March 1788, Nicolae Mavrogheni issued a sort of 'travel letter' in which he requested the Ottoman authorities on the other side of the Danube to support the journey of the boyars 'sent to the region of Nikopol'. The document names Emanuel Brâncoveanu, Dumitraşco Racoviţă, Manolache Creţulescu, and Costache Ghica, accompanied by their wives and children, forty-one servants, and a doctor assisted by with five helpers, together with a large number of carriages. It recommends that they be treated as 'guests' and asks 'that they not be troubled with the demand for *cizye* or on other pretexts' and that they enjoy 'guarding and protection'. *Documente turceşti*, II, 293.

Transylvania, their dependence on a patron and their struggle for survival in everyday life. Văcărescu describes in his *History* another aspect of exile: the boyars exiled in the Ottoman empire were refugees because of the war, but they were also hostages, used as a sort of currency of exchange both by Mavrogheni and by the vizier. The fate of the refugees depended on the outcome of the war. At first everything looked relatively good, and Văcărescu used his personal contacts to ensure his safety. At Nikopol he had friendly relations with the local notable Selim Pasha, who, 'holding him in great affection' and being a 'learned' man, ensured his and the other boyars' access to the necessities of life. When Selim Pasha was sent to Bender, however, the refugees found themselves transformed into hostages: 'We were shut in, for we were not free to go anywhere, and lacking in what was necessary,' writes Văcărescu. He observes how the status of the hostages changed during their period of captivity according to the personal relations they had with the Ottoman authorities. The status of hostage was displeasing to him, especially as he had in all circumstances behaved as a good and faithful Ottoman subject, with 'merits at the Devlet' and faithful service proven by '*fermans* and many orders to demonstrate.'[120]

Making use of his connections and his linguistic and rhetorical abilities, Văcărescu drafted an *arz* (petition) to the sultan on behalf of the boyars in which he magnified his faithful services to the Porte and requested easier conditions of exile in Edirne. He listed his rights as an Ottoman subject, using diplomatic language and invoking international treaties, and enumerated his faithful service to the Empire, and implicitly to the sultan. When Mavrogheni found out about the boyars' *arz*, he accused them of conspiracy and succeeded in having them sent to Rhodes.[121] Their salvation was determined by an unexpected event: the death of Sultan Abdülhamid I. Văcărescu thus experienced exile in a number of Ottoman centres: Nikopol, Târnovo, Edirne, and Rhodes. Other boyars were detained at Meteora, Mount Athos, Vidin, Silistra, or other regional centres of the Empire. Their conditions of captivity varied: some were sold as slaves and had to spend vast sums of money to regain their freedom; others were held hostage only for the duration of the war and released with the signing of the peace treaty.[122]

In response to numerous requests from opponents of Mavrogheni, Abdülhamid's successor, Sultan Selim III, ensured the release of the boyars:

120 Văcărescu, *Istoria Othomanicească*, 153.

121 Văcărescu, *Istoria Othomanicească*, 154.

122 On prisoners and their treatment, see Smiley, *From Slaves to Prisoners of War*.

> The most merciful emperor, taking cognizance of our condition and that we are on Rhodes and our families in Târnovo, gave command to the most elevated Mustar Pasha, the *kaymakam*,[123] to write to the army, to the vizier, to make us an *itlak* [order of release] without fail.

The Filipescu boyars, who had been banished for two years to Meteora, were also released by an *itlak*.[124] It was in February 1790 that the Wallachian boyars received their *itlak* and set out for Târnovo, where their families were, before settling for a time at Edirne.[125] Material lack, daily fear, and the unfavourable surroundings had had a negative effect on the families, and the weaker among them had not survived. 'We had come from Rhodes to Arvanitochori,[126] by Târnovo,[127] and we had found our families in a poor state, especially I myself, who of four children whom I had left with my lady wife when I went to Rhodes, found only one,' writes Văcărescu.[128]

There was pain at the loss of dear ones in all the families of those banished, but there was little time for mourning: no sooner had Văcărescu arrived in Edirne than he was summoned by an *emirname* of the grand vizier Hasan Pasha to be of service to the Porte: 'So at once leaving my wife and a small child that I had at Odriiu (Edirne), taking my eldest son I left with the *menzil* [courier] and went to Ruse.'[129] Along with Văcărescu, by Sultan Selim III's *ferman*, another eight boyars were summoned 'for certain questions and answers.'[130]

---

123 The *kaymakam* at that time was Sılahdar Mustafa Pasha.

124 Văcărescu, *Istoria Othomanicească*, 157.

125 See the *ferman* of Sultan Selim III of Văcărescu, *Istoria Othomanicească* 21/31 August 1790 by which he requires the kadı and bostancı of Edirne to help the Wallachian boyars to move there to the village of Arnavud 'so that their families and children may live in peace.' The *ferman* also mentioned the fact that the boyars 'had carried out the tasks they had received,' and 'had made efforts to strengthen the conviction of the High Devlet and to please the padishah.' Likewise, they had proved 'honour and devotion' as valuable signs of 'their submission as non-Muslim subjects'. See also the other two *fermans* issued in succession by which the local authorities were required to ensure peace and protection for the boyars. *Documente turceşti*, II, 312–315.

126 Arvanitochori is also known as Arbanasi, Arnavud. Arbanasi is nect to Veliko Turnovo.

127 Probably today's Veliko Turnovo, but there are several places called Turnovo in the Balkans.

128 Văcărescu, *Istoria Othomanicească*, 153.

129 Văcărescu writes with pride that the order is preserved in the family archives as an important document: 'which *mektub* is kept in care with much honour in the archives of my house.' Similarly, he received from the vizier Hasan Pasha 'two *emirname*s of introduction with much praise. Which too are guarded among the letters of my house with much veneration.' Văcărescu, *Istoria Othomanicească*, 153–154, 167.

130 *Documente turceşti*, II, 311, 23 July/1 August 1790.

At Rusçuk (Ruse), in the tent of the grand vizier Hasan Pasha and surrounded by *kahya* Feyzulla Efendi, *defterdar* Raik Ali Efendi, and *reisülküttab* Berrî Abdullah Efendi, Văcărescu decided Mavrogheni's fate: 'These three ministers arrived and the vizier told them to sit down; he commanded me also to sit down and told me to say before these *rical*s what I had said to his Excellency. And I told them again.'

He told them of the irreconcilable difference between the boyars and the prince, of the exodus of part of the population across the Danube for fear of the prince's extortions, of the forced 'kaftan-granting' [elevation to boyar rank] of peasants for money, and much more.[131] Hasan Pasha made use of these accusations, set down on paper by Văcărescu and sent to the sultan, to call for the elimination of Mavrogheni.[132] When the latter's head fell, Văcărescu returned to centre stage:

> And the vizier summoned me and sent me to the *leylek çadırı*[133] with his highness's *caftangiu*[134] to see his head. And when I returned, he commanded me to write to Bucharest to the boyars a letter saying that at His Excellency's command and to show them the justice of the most puissant emperor, having found out about the deeds of Mavrogheni that he had done in Wallachia, he had given him his reward. And according to the command I immediately informed them, and they all rejoiced.[135]

Ianache Văcărescu behaved like a high Ottoman official, even if he was without portfolio. The Ottoman office-bearers, from the vizier to pashas and *ayan*s, treated him as such, outlining his duties[136] and rewarding him for carrying them out with the orders of recognition of merit (*émr-namé*s and *mehtup*s), and with praise, protection, and affection. In the winter of 1791–1792, when he withdrew to Edirne to spend time with his family, he wrote:

---

131 See also the *ferman* of Sultan Selim III of 19/28 October 1791 by which he requires prince Mihai Suţu to annul all boyar titles accorded by Nicolae Mavrogheni in the course of his reign, 1786–1790. *Documente turceşti*, III, 14–15.

132 On the killing of Mavrogheni, see Fotino, *Istoria Generală a Daciei*, 179–180; Philliou, *Biography of an Empire*, 44–47.

133 The *leylek çadırı* was a tent in the Ottoman camp which was used for executions, close to the commanders quarters

134 'Kaftan bearer', the keeper of the princely wardrobe.

135 Văcărescu, *Istoria Othomanicească*, 167.

136 He was appointed by Hasan Pasha as a sort of administrator of Wallachia, with the mission of ensuring the provisioning of the Ottoman forces by encouraging the peasants and merchants along the Danube to sell their produce direct to the army. At the same time, he also served in the role of judge for litigation among the inhabitants of the Danube border. Văcărescu, *Istoria Othomanicească*, 161–162.

> I passed the winter in great honour for I was much loved also by Mola Efendi[137] and by the *bostancıbaşı*,[138] by the janissary agha,[139] and by the *kaymakam* pasha himself, Izzet Mehmed Pasha, who had come to Edirne and with whom I dined most evenings.[140]

The removal of Hasan Pasha from the office of vizier did not affect Văcărescu, as he had managed to make himself indispensable through his knowledge about the region, his connections in Wallachia, the prestige he enjoyed among the boyars, and above all the efficiency with which he managed to carry out the duties assigned to him in wartime. The new vizier, Koca Yusuf Pasha entrusted him with various missions in Wallachia, aimed at supporting the Ottoman army: building bridges over rivers and ensuring provisions.[141]

Văcărescu succeeded in building very strong regional connections, binding himself in clientelary relations with the *ayan*s along the Danube.[142] His matrimonial alliances helped him to establish important connections in various power centres, but the maintenance of these was also very much due to his linguistic and diplomatic abilities. He made use of all sorts of situations to interact with others, presenting himself in a natural manner, regardless of the setting or the interlocutor, be it Emperor Joseph II, Grand Vizier Hasan Pasha, or Field Marshal Pyotr Rumyantsev. For Văcărescu, the intensity of a relationship was expressed through the emotions it generated: Osman Efendi was a close acquaintance who received him every time with affection (*liubov*); things stood similarly in his relations with Seyyid Hasan Pasha, who protected him with 'much love' (*multă dragoste*): in Istanbul, however, he was received only with goodwill (*evmenie, musaadea*). At Adrianople he was very much loved, while the grand vizier Usuf Pasha treated him with great honour.

*

137 Possibly to be identified with Mekki Mehmed Efendi, who served in the post of *şeyhülislam* from March 1791 until June 1792.

138 The position of *bostancıbaşı* (chief of gardeners) was held at the time by Osman Ağa.

139 In the winter of 1791–1792, the position of Janissary Agha was held by Arapzade Ahmed Agha (October 1791–25 June 1792).

140 Văcărescu, *Istoria Othomanicească*, 168.

141 Ibid., 169–170.

142 On the importance of these regional power centres, see Ali Yaycioğlu, 'Provincial Powerholders and the Empire in the Late Ottoman World', in Christine Woodhead (ed.), *The Ottoman World* (London: 2012), 436–452.

Văcărescu's memoirs contain important information about the role of mediator that he assumed in various social, political, religious, and linguistic contexts.[143] In writing about and serving the Ottoman Empire,[144] he was one of those intermediaries who participated in the production and dissemination of a literature about the Ottomans in Europe. The knowledge he accumulated came from his interactions with scholars from the three empires on the borders of Wallachia. His manuscript (together with numerous reports) responded to an already existing curiosity about all that came out of the Ottoman Empire. At the same time, Văcărescu modelled his education and career according to the requirements of the Ottoman imperial system, adopting 'the service and culture of the Phanariots.'[145] In its turn, the Phanariot elite integrated him into its own networks by means of matrimonial alliances and employed him for numerous diplomatic and political missions.

143 See also the chronicle of events in Wallachia narrated (in Greek) by another boyar close to Văcărescu, *Ban* Mihai Cantacuzino, who in 1778, after several attempts by his brother Pârvu Cantacuzino to become prince, chose to leave for Russia. Mihai Cantacuzino, *Genealogia Cantacuzinilor*, edition by Nicolae Iorga (Bucharest: 1902).

144 In his view, the mission to bring back Ipsilanti's sons was 'a service rendered to the [Ottoman] Empire'. Văcărescu, *Istoria Othomanicească*, 127.

145 Philliou, *Biography of an Empire*, 39.

PART III

Seeking a Home: People and Destinies in Southeastern Europe

CHAPTER 5

Ottomans, Serbs, Bulgarians, Greeks, Wallachians, Moldavians: Subjects, Protégés, and Their Journeys Through the Empires

We know little about Neaga, the wife of the merchant Ionașco, although her portrait by the painter Constantin Lecca is well known to connoisseurs of nineteenth-century Romanian art. It is said of Neaga and her husband that they amassed countless riches in the expectation that they would have legitimate heirs to enjoy them. But these hoped-for heirs never materialized, so Ionașco and Neaga invested their entire fortune in erecting places of worship, schools, and hospitals. In the church that they founded in Slatina, their portraits were painted in the pronaos, as was customary, around the end of the eighteenth century. It was from here that the painter Lecca would later give them new life and a place in the art of his time. In her portrait, Neaga wears ten strings of pearls around her neck, together with four strings of red coral and the omnipresent necklace of gold coins. From the same gold coins, she has had a pair of jangling earrings made, which emphasize her beauty. Her dress seems to be made of yellow silk, perhaps the material known as *ghermeșut*, and is bound at the waist with a belt fastened with gold clasps. A long jerkin (*tivilichie*) of atlas silk lined with mink completes her wardrobe.

Her husband, the merchant Ionaşcu, is simply dressed in the typical garb of the Balkan merchants who traded in grain on both sides of the Danube. He wears a yellow silk *anteri* fastened at the neck with three buttons and bound at the waist with a striped sash, under a white jacket (*fermene*) of which only the outline and the pearl serving as a button can be seen. Over this, he wears a long coat (*cüppe*) of blue felt trimmed with marten fur.[1]

On his gravestone, Ionașcu added to his name the designation *osmanlâu* (Ottoman). He was also known among his fellow merchants as Sârbul the *mazil* (petty boyar without an office), indicating that he had among his ancestors a Serb or a Bulgarian who had settled and married in the plains of Oltenia. I find the complexity of this merchant's identity particularly interesting: Ottoman, or rather Ottoman subject, Serb, Orthodox Christian, bound to the

1 For the churches founded by Ionaşcu the merchant and Neaga, see George Poboran, *Istoria oraşului Slatina* (Slatina: 1908).

Fig. 4
Constantin Lecca – Neaga, the wife of Ionaşcu *cupeţu*, 1840–1845, Art Museum of Braşov.

Fig. 5
Constantin Lecca – Ionaşcu *cupeţu* (merchant), 1840–1845, National Museum of Art, Bucharest.

lands of Oltenia by his founding of schools and hospitals. Virginia Aksan offers a complex definition, according to which to be identified as *osmanlı*, someone should be 'a sincere Muslim, educated in the Ottoman imperial culture, dedicated to the perpetuation of religion and state as embodied in the sultan, and a member of the select group which protected the revenue-generating classes and promulgated the official ideology'.[2] The definition is far too circumscribed for an Orthodox Christian Danube merchant who claimed the label of *osmanlı* through his involvement in trade with the Ottomans across the river Danube. However the designation affirms the status of Ottoman subject, an 'essential element' for merchants pursuing their commercial strategies between the Ottoman Empire, the southeast European spaces, and the Mediterranean.[3]

Ionașcu and Neaga settled where their business prospered, bought estates and built manors, established themselves as residents of Oltenia, and paid their taxes according to the register of the incorporation of merchants to which they belonged. Their foundations copied a model established by Christian merchants from the Balkans who wished in this way to show thanks to God for divine assistance in the thriving of their trading activities.[4] At the same time, they testify to the strong bonds that they had managed to forge with the local community, which was the beneficiary of such places of worship and social assistance.

Mobility and ethnic and religious diversity make southeastern Europe a fertile ground for research into identity and cultural syncretism. As Brubaker writes, 'self-identification and the identification of the other are fundamentally linked to situations and contexts.'[5] Along the same lines, Eric Dursteler argues that 'early modern identity was fluid and instrumental.' People worked with this flexibility, which gave them the possibility of defining and redefining

2 Aksan, *An Ottoman Statesman*, xi–xii. See also Maurits H. van den Boogert, 'Resurrecting *Homo Ottomanicus*: The Constants and Variables of Ottoman Identity', *Journal of Ottoman Studies*, XLIV (2014), 9–20.

3 Mathieu Grenet, '"Grecs de nation", sujets ottomans: experience diasporique et entre-deux identitaires, v. 1770–v. 1830', in Jocelyne Dakhlia and Wolfgang Kaiser (eds.), *Les musulmans dans l'histoire de l'Europe*. T. 2. *Passages et contacts en Méditerranée* (Paris: 2013), 326.

4 Lidia Cotovanu, '"Qu'on prie pour moi là-bas et ici". Donation religieuse et patriotism local dans le monde othodoxe (XVIe–XVIIe siècles)', in Radu G. Păun (ed.), *Histoire, mémoire et devotion. Regards croisés sur la construction des identities dans le monde orthodoxe aux époques byzantine et post-byzantyne* (Seyssel: 2016), 207–255; Mihai-Cristian Amăriuţei, Lidia Cotovanu, Ovidiu-Victor Olar, 'Phanariot Donations to the Mega Spileon Monastery (18th Century)', *Annales Universitatis Apulensis. Series Historica*, XVIII/1 (2014), 219–250; Petronel Zahariuc, '"Au milieu de l'étranger". Deux documents de donation pour le monastère de Lipnic de Bulgarie', in Snezhana Rakova, Gheorghe Lazăr (eds.), *Au Nord et au Sud du Danube. Dynamiques politiques, sociales et religieuses dans le passé* (Brăila: 2018). 153–166.

5 Rogers Brubaker, 'Au-delà de l' «identité»', *Actes de la Recherche en Sciences Sociales*, no. 139, 4 (2001), 66; See also Roger Brubaker, Frederick Cooper, 'Beyond "identity"', *Theory and Society*, 29 (2000), 1–47.

themselves according to the context.[6] Nevertheless, as Dimitrie Cantemir writes, there are certain criteria for describing the others. He makes use of two of them: nation (here in the sense of place of birth and belonging to a certain territory) and religion. For some historians, religion is 'a primary element of individual and group identity', an essential key in the construction of identity.[7] We may recall that in the Ottoman Empire, people were classified according to their religion and grouped in confessional communities, *millets*.[8] As social and above all political changes transformed the region, language turned from a means of communication and differentiation into another instrument for the definition of national identities.[9] To these three criteria may be added others that serve to fashion regional, confessional, and linguistic belonging: costume, culinary traditions, local practices, and the sharing of a common historical past.[10] In the pages that follow, I shall try to demonstrate that self-identification is part of a dynamic process, one that is adaptable according to context, opportunities, and immediate needs. I shall show that, although religion is considered a key element in the process of identification, in certain situations it may become an instrument of manoeuvre adaptable to the local context.[11]

Who Are 'The Subjects of the Prince'?

Princely charters (*hrisoave*) are always addressed to imagined subjects, identified generically as 'the subjects of the prince' (*supuşii domniei*). At the moment when the charter was issued, these subjects shared the same territory, paid taxes to the princely treasury, appealed to the princely law courts, prayed for the prince and his family in church, and could feel that they belonged to a community. The abolition of the army by Constantin Mavrocordat did not imply that subjects had been relieved of all military obligations, especially in the case of the boyars, who in return for these duties were exempt from taxes and enjoyed other privileges. In various circumstances, the prince would appeal to

6 Eric Dursteler, 'Identity and Coexistence in the Eastern Mediterranean, ca. 1600', *New Perspectives on Turkey*, 18 (1998), 114.

7 Dursteler, *Venetians in Constantinople*, 13.

8 Elizabeth A. Zachariadou, 'Co-Existence and Religion', *Archivum Ottomanicum* 15 (1997), 119–129; Benjamin Braude and Bernard Lewis (eds.), *Christians and Jews in the Ottoman Empire. The Functioning of a Plural Society* (New York and London: 1982).

9 Zanou, *Transnational Patriotism*, 2; See also Peter Mackridge, *Language and National Identity in Greece, 1766–1976* (Oxford: 2009).

10 Dursteler, *Venetians in Constantinople*, 18.

11 Grenet, *La fabrique communautaire*, 219–220.

his subjects for military assistance, which was considered an obligation, either by direct participation in war, or in the form of indirect participation by building fortifications or bridges or ensuring provisions for the Ottoman army. All these obligations helped to establish a close bond between the prince and his subjects, offering the sense of belonging to a community. Ordinary folk in the most isolated hamlet could feed on the image of the good and wise ruler whose duty it was to protect them in exchange for the taxes they paid.[12]

In their petitions addressed to the prince, the population constructed a very close relationship with the sovereign imagined as a master, while the subject was no more than a 'slave' (*rob*). Analysing the relation between the tsar and his subjects in Russia, Valerie Kivelson argues that 'Muscovites articulated their claims on the state through litigation or through other means of invoking the protection of legal norms and processes.'[13] Thus, legal institutions and norms are important reference points in identifying the criteria for belonging to a society. In the eighteenth century, this formula of subjecthood, inserted at the end of a petition, was part of a well-aimed rhetoric. Reading between the lines of the petition, it is clear that the 'slave' raises himself up as a subject free to demand his rights by virtue of his payment of taxes: 'I am a man with tax [obligations] and it is not right that I should perish through judgements.' The subject underlines the importance of the time that is so precious in order to cultivate his crops and to pay his tax to the prince, but equally the prince must find the time and the mercy to protect him. The contractual relationship that exists between the apex and the base of the pyramid is evident: the subject pays the tax and enjoys the prince's protection. Of course belonging to a community involves other aspects too: confessional, linguistic, relational, bonds of kinship and affinity. In this part, I shall focus on foreigners belonging to various occupational categories whose destinies brought them to Moldavia and Wallachia. What process of identification did a foreigner go through in order to be accepted? How did they negotiate their belonging to a community? As 'identity' is such an 'ambiguous' concept,[14] I shall try to observe the process of identification operated by individuals in relation to their own criteria for analysing what they are. At the same time, I shall try to pick out the criteria of

12 See, in this connection, Constanţa Vintilă-Ghiţulescu, 'Legal Process and the Meanings of Justice (dreptate) in Eighteenth Century Romania', in *Crime, Histoire & Sociétés/ Crime, History & Societies*, 23, 2 (2019), 5–27.

13 Valerie Kivelson, 'Muscovite "Citizenship": Rights without Freedom', *Journal of Modern History*, 74 (2002), 468.

14 Brubaker, 'Au-delà de l' «identité»', 66.

identification and categorization used by institutional agencies in defining a foreigner as 'assimilated' or not.[15]

The judicial archives of Moldavia and Wallachia testify to a very dynamic trans-border mobility throughout the eighteenth century and the first half of the nineteenth. The people recorded by these archives moved with ease between empires, bearing with them information, tastes, and novelties, transporting what wealth they had in backpacks and carts, desperately seeking security, stability, a future. Wandering in search of a 'home', some settled in the Principalities, eager to start a family, to build a fortune, to find a lineage. However, the success of a trajectory in life depends on the context, on the individual, and above all on the connections necessary for one to anchor oneself in a not always friendly environment. Of course, the courts, by their very nature, tended to record the failure of such attempts, when people were unable to achieve their desired goal and set out on a new journey, towards a new destination. But their records are the living mirror of an acute need to become socially integrated, to model an identity, and to seek a safe 'homeland'. These archives are complemented by personal or family records—property documents, testaments, dowry contracts, litigation over inheritance—which provide us with details about those who managed to settle, at least for a time. Taken together, they help us to characterize people based on the information offered to the authorities by the individuals themselves or by those who had dealings with them.

Seeking a Patron on the Danube Frontier

The migration was not all in one direction, from the Ottoman Empire to the Principalities, or from there to the Habsburg territories or Venice. Orthodox Christians from Wallachia and Moldavia also went to seek their fortune in the Ottoman Empire. Mobility might be collective or individual. It was often provoked by conflicts in the region when the population fled to save their lives and what little they owned. After each war, imperial *fermans* encouraged people to return to their houses and estates, granting collective pardons, privileges, and periods of tax exemption.[16] The Phanariot princes too were urged to busy

15 Ibid., 75.

16 *Documente turceşti*, II, 5–6, the *ferman* of 7/16 September 1775.

themselves with the repopulation and economic recovery of their countries in order to ensure the payment of tribute to the Porte.[17]

Whole groups of peasants migrated south of the Danube in hope of lighter taxes. Indeed, the phenomenon of peasant families migrating between empires is documented along all borders. This seasonal migration was encouraged by the need for labour in agriculture and the reduced level of a population decimated by the wars in the region and by frequent outbreaks of plague.[18] In these conditions, explicit competition arose between boyars with properties along the borders and the provincial elites (*ayans*) and military notables of the three surrounding empires, both for the extension of their properties and, above all, for labour force.[19] For example, along the Danube frontier, the development of large livestock farms (*çiftliks*) stimulated mobility and increased the power of the *ayans*.[20] Boyars and *ayans* alike offered privileges and advantages to attract workers to their lands. The most capable of the peasants were hired in supervising posts, especially once they had proven their abilities and above all their loyalty.

The Brâncoveanu boyars held large estates in the south of Wallachia, with their main residence being in the village of Brâncoveni in Olt county.[21] The grandson of the prince decapitated in Istanbul, named like his grandfather Constantin, became the rightful heir to the latter's moveable and immoveable goods. Marica Brâncoveanu, his grandmother, went to considerable effort to have the right of succession of this sole male survivor of the lineage recognized,

---

17 Ibid. 8–9, *Ferman* of 20/29 May 1776 commanding 'that the old *re'aya*s of Wallachia, who have scattered, be picked up, by the intervention of the prince, from wherever they may be and in whoever's villages and huts and farms they may be found and be brought back and settled there.'

18 For these episodes and the sultan's repeated interventions, see Damian Panaitescu, 'The Ottoman Empire and the Preservation of Wallachia's Fiscal Potential (1730–1774)', *Revista Economică*, 66/6 (2014), 56–76.

19 For economic change in the region, see Fikret Adanir, 'Tradition and Rural Change in Southeastern Europe During Ottoman Rule', in Daniel Chirot (ed.) *The Origins of Backwardness in Eastern Europe* (Berkeley–Los Angeles: 1989), 131–176. For the border with Russia, see Ştefania Costache, 'The Ottoman-Russian-Habsburg Information Networks and the Negotiation of Ottoman Affairs on the Danube (1800–1820s)', *Revista Istorică*, XXVI, 3–4 (2015), 249–280.

20 Halil İnalcik, 'The Emergence of Big Farms, Çiftliks: State, Landlords and Tenants', in Jean-Louis Bacqué-Grammont, Paul Dumont (eds.), *Contributions à l'histoire économique et sociale de l'Empire ottoman* (Louvain: 1983), 105–126, Gilles Veinstein, 'On the Çiftlik Debate', in Çağlar Keyder, Faruk Tabak (eds.), *Landholding and Commercial Agriculture in the Middle East* (Albany, NY: 1991), 35–53.

21 Iolanda Ţighiliu, 'Domeniul lui Constantin Brâncoveanu', in Paul Cernovodeanu, Florin Constantiniu (eds.), *Constantin Brâncoveanu* (Bucharest: 1989), 123–138.

and for him to come into possession of his inheritance.[22] Gradually Constantin Brâncoveanu built up a property empire in Oltenia and along the Danube. His wealth and his belonging to one of the most well-known boyar families facilitated his access to important administrative functions: grand *comis* (1730–1731, 1733–1734, 1739), grand *stolnic* (1732–1733, 1734, 1735), grand *logofăt* (1748–1752, 1755, 1756, 1758–1761), grand *vornic* (1753), grand *spătar* (1753–1754, 1755), and grand *ban* (23 July 1757–30 May 1758).[23] His fame spread beyond the Danube, enabling him to form connections with the provincial elite of Rumelia. 'To his excellency my honourable and able friend, the boyar Brâncoveanu, who is one of the well-known boyars of Wallachia': so he is addressed around 1750 by the *kehaya* Mehmed. Mehmed was writing to him in the name of the military commander (*muhafiz*) of the citadel of Vidin, to request protection and assistance for two merchants who had to bring goods quickly from Bucharest.[24] From the documents issued in this period, it would appear that the Brâncoveanus, father and sons, maintained amicable relations both with the kadı of Giurgiu (Yergöğü) and with his counterpart in Ruse (Rusçuk). Thus it was that a certain Ștefan (Istefan in the Ottoman documents) 'the Latin' from the Old Mosque district of Ruse came to cross the Danube and enter the service of the boyar Constantin Brâncoveanu.[25] Soon after, having proven himself useful and won the boyar's trust, Ștefan was leased the estate of Brâncoveni. With Brâncoveanu's approval, Ștefan established a flourishing business, trading on both sides of the Danube and becoming well-known among the townsfolk and garrison of Vidin. As the *ferman* of Sultan Mustafa III of 11/20 January 1758 puts it: 'Being a trustworthy man and renowned, he held estates in Wallachia, in the vicinity of Vidin, and had close connections with all the inhabitants of Vidin, taking something from them and giving them something else in exchange.'[26] Though his place of origin is unknown, Ștefan the Latin was probably a Catholic

22 See the document of 17 June 1717 published in Nicolae Iorga (ed.), *Studii şi documente cu privire la istoria românilor* (Bucharest: 1907), vol. XIV, 331–333.

23 Rădulescu, *Sfatul domnesc*, 116, 119, 128, 295, 316, 321.

24 Documente turceşti, I, 261–262.

25 Ştefan the Latin probably belonged to one of the Catholic families who managed to escape from the town of Chiprovtsi, which was home to one of the largest Catholic communities in the Balkans, at the end of the seventeenth century. The town's revolt against Ottoman rule in the autumn of 1688 ended in failure, leading to the flight of the population to other towns along the Danube, in Wallachia and the Banat. Those who did not manage to flee were captured, and the city was pillaged and destroyed. See Dzeni Ivanova, 'Ottoman Subjects, Habsburg Allies: The Reaya of the Chiprovtsi Region (Northwestern Bulgaria) on the Front Line, 1688–1690', in Colin Heywood, Ivan Parvev (eds.), *The Treaties of Karlowitz (1699): Antecedents, Course and Consequences* (Leiden: 2019), 110–130.

26 *Documente turceşti*, I, 269.

who had come and settled in the Old Mosque district of Ruse, where his family were: his wife Lotissa and their four minor children, Matei, Anton, Maria, and Isaveta. His business activities were inspired by those around him, who for years had been trying their luck on one side or the other of the great river.[27]

As Virginia Aksan has shown, the Danube frontier always constituted a problem. Even if, in theory, Muslims were not allowed to build houses or buy land in Wallachia or Moldavia, many did so. At the same time, a series of raids took place across the Danube; Oltenian villages, as far as Craiova, were pillaged whenever the opportunity arose. The event analysed in these pages took place a few years before the enquiry carried out by an Ottoman commission regarding the complaints of princes, boyars, and locals who were discontented at the depredations of outlaws and janissaries, and at the abuses of the Muslims settled from Orșova to Craiova, who imposed unfair charges and prices and illegally took possession of the locals' estates and shops. In 1759, Girid Ahmed was sent to restore order and to pacify the population.[28] The case of Ștefan the Latin helps us to take the pulse of the region, showing the collaboration between Muslims and non-Muslims in the development of business and the appeal to Ottoman institutions for mediation, but also the inherent raids of outlaws. At the same time, it brings to light the power and influence acquired by the provincial elites, who attracted numerous clients seeking both protection and leverage for their own businesses.[29] As Sophia Laiou has argued, the economic changes of the eighteenth century were profitable for a considerable number of non-Muslim Ottoman subjects, who were able to accumulate wealth that differentiated them not only from the other members of their communities but also from members of the Muslim community.[30]

It is in this context that Ștefan pursued his activity, doing business not only with the Christian locals, but also with the janissaries and other mercenaries in the region. Some of them are recorded as being *ağa*s in Vidin: El-Hacı-Memed of the 30th *bölük* (company), El-hacı-Mustafa of the 64th regiment,

27 In this connection, see Rossitsa Gradeva, 'War and Peace Along the Danube: Vidin at the End of the Seventeenth Century', *Oriente Moderno*, 20, 81 (2001), 149–175.

28 Virginia Aksan, 'Whose territory and whose peasants? Ottoman boundaries on the Danube in the 1760s', in Frederick F. Anscombe (ed.), *The Ottoman Balkans 1750–1830* (Princeton, NJ: 2006), 61–86.

29 For a mathematical analysis of the social networks created by the *ayans*, see Nilüfer Alkan Günay, 'A Study of Social Network Analysis: The Âyan of Bursa in the Late 18th Century', *Journal of Gazi Academic*, 5/10 (2012), 30–49.

30 Sophia Laiou, 'Patronage Networks in the Aegean Sea, End of the 18th—Beginning of the 19th Century', in Marinos Sariyannis (ed.), *New Trends in Ottoman Studies* (Rethymno: 2014), 413.

Molla Mustafa of the 15th, and Fazlî-beşe of the 31st.[31] These men lent Ștefan the sum of 3,300 kuruşlar, counting both on the trust arising from the business activities they had been involved in together and, even more, on his renown through 'all parts of Vidin.' At the same time, Ștefan had managed to put himself under the protection of a patron who was powerful, rich, influential, and feared by those round about. Across the Danube, it was said that Brâncoveanu was 'wealthy and possessed riches and villages,' and that he was 'one of the oppressors of that country, so much so that it is in no way possible to stand up to the aforementioned man in the aforementioned land.'[32] In accumulating a considerable fortune, extending his network among the Danube *ayan*s, and obtaining power and influence, Brâncoveanu was himself behaving just like an *ayan*, as Deena Sadat and Ali Yaycioğlu have argued, in analysing the behaviour of the Christian notables of the Empire.[33]

When Ștefan was found dead one day on the Brâncoveni estate, a series of abuses and networks of protection and power came to light. We do not know how wealthy Ștefan the Latin was, but rumour had it that he had extensive lands, ox carts, livestock, and bags of money. It was this presumed fortune, apparently kept at Brâncoveni, where he had his dwelling place as a lease-holder, that prompted his family to make a petition to the kadı of Ruse, requesting the right of inheritance. In her petition of 7 September 1757, Ștefan's wife accused none other than his landlord and patron, the boyar Constantin Brâncoveanu, of killing her husband in order to take possession of his immense wealth.[34] The same accusation recurs in the petition of the four *aga*s who had lent Ștefan money: 'the abovementioned Brancovan-oğlu Konstantin, of Wallachia, where the aforementioned Ștefan the Latin was present as leaseholder (*mültezim*) coveting the aforementioned's wealth, had the aforementioned killed, in his own village, with musket shot and took and laid his hands on all the wealth that he owned, and also his money and the wealth coming from his estates.'[35] The case was judged in several phases, according to Sharia law, by Kadı Ibrahim at Ruse and in the presence of Kadı Ilyas of Giurgiu. The investigation at the scene of

31 On the involvement of the janissaries in the exploitation of the peasants and estates across the Danube, see Aysel Yıldız, İrfan Kokdaş, 'Peasantry in a Well-protected Domain: Wallachian Peasantry and Muslim *Çiftlik/Kışlaks* under the Ottoman Rule', *Journal of Balkan and Near Eastern Studies*, 22, 1 (2018), 175–190.

32 Documente turceşti, I, 269.

33 Deena Sadat, 'Rumeli Ayanlari: The Eighteenth Century', *Journal of Modern History*, 44, 3 (1972), 350; Ali Yaycioğlu, *Partners of the Empire: The Crisis of the Ottoman Order in the Age of Revolutions* (Stanford: 2016), 149.

34 *Documente turceşti*, I, 266.

35 *Documente turceşti*, I, 269.

the crime established that 'the non-Muslim subject Ștefan' had been killed by outlaws, who were very numerous in the area, and that Lotissa could not claim the 'blood-price' from the boyar given that the outlaws had not been caught.[36] Brâncoveanu, represented by an estate manager named Polizu, proved generous, and gave the family 250 *kuruşlar*, thus taking the heat out of the conflict.[37] Ștefan the Latin was an Ottoman subject, but not a subject of the Phanariot prince of Wallachia. He had been under the protection and in the service of the Brâncoveanu family, but his extended family continued to live in Ruse, where he paid the *cizye* and other taxes to the Empire. For this reason, the case was brought from the start before the local Ottoman authorities, even though the murder had taken place in Wallachia.

The rumour of a huge fortune amassed by Ștefan the Latin and seized by the boyar Brâncoveanu continued to circulate, however, and led the four janissaries of Vidin mentioned above to request the recovery of Ștefan's debts through a *ferman* of Sultan Mustafa III.[38] In fact the trial served to enhance the renown of the Brancoveanus as rich and powerful boyars under whose protecting wing a client could make a living. Among those who sought their protection was one Ahmed bin Halil of Ruse. He asked the *cămăraș* Manolache (Emanuel) Brâncoveanu to take him under his protection and to give him the office of *beşliagă* (from the Turkish *beşli ağası*, captain of the princely couriers).[39] To hasten matters, Ahmed offered the boyar by way of incentive 'twenty-five shining gold pieces and twenty-three *kuruşlar*, together with a package of twenty-six *ocas* of high-quality tobacco.'[40]

Ten years later, the fortune amassed by Ștefan the Latin from the Brâncoveanu estates was still haunting the members of his family. Thus it was that one of his sons, Mano (Matei) reopened the suit and sought his father's inheritance from Constantin Brâncoveanu's son Nicolae, whom he accused of having in fact been the murderer. In his petition, he writes that the fortune amassed was made up of 'sixteen thousand one hundred *kuruşlar*, two thousand one

36 This customary practice was also present in Wallachia, under the name of 'redemption of the throat' (*răscumpărarea gâtului*), and involved the reconciliation of the parties by the payment of a sum of money to pay for the life of the person who had been killed.

37 *Documente turceşti*, I, 266–269. The certificate was reinforced on 19 November 1757 by the new *kadı* of Ruse, Abdulkerim.

38 See the *ferman* of 11/20 January 1758 by which Prince Constantin Mavrocordat is required to oblige the boyar Constantin Brâncoveanu to pay the dept or to send him before the *kadı* of Rahova. *Documente turceşti*, I, 268–270.

39 Manolache Brâncoveanu was grand *cămăraş* in 1762. See Rădulescu, *op. cit.*, 660.

40 *Documente turceşti*, I, 276–277, 16 September 1762. Ten years later, Ahmed bin Halil was still waiting either to receive the post of *beşleagă* or to be given his 'gift' back (Ibid., I, 305–306, 18 May 1768–6 May 1769).

hundred sheep, and four hundred and sixty horses and four carriages and two gold rings,' plus a further forty bags of *kuruşlar* borrowed for the purposes of trade.[41] That Ștefan the Latin did indeed amass a very considerable fortune from his activity as a tenant farmer and merchant is perfectly plausible. On the basis of the documents supplied by the Ottoman commission of 1760, Aysel Yıldız and İrfan Kokdaş have shown how fertile the region between the Danube and Craiova, Caracal, and Teleorman was, and how advantageous for raising livestock and for the (sometimes illicit) development of intensive animal farms.'[42] Indeed, the colossal wealth of the Brâncoveanu family was based on the raising and selling of cattle.

But let us return to the trial. Nicolae Brâncoveanu was brought before the kadı of Giurgiu, the same Ilyas who had judged the case ten years previously. The kadı confirmed the previous judgement on the basis of Muslim witnesses brought to Ruse and of the certificates issued earlier.[43] That the trial was reopened shows in the first place that an existing judgement had no authority, but it also highlights the differences of status between non-Muslim Ottoman subjects depending on their residence in the Ottoman Empire itself or in the autonomous vassal provinces.[44] At the same time, as we shall see in other cases of litigation between Christians and Muslims, the document underlines the inferior status of non-Muslim Ottoman subjects, who could not testify as witnesses in a case where one of the parties was a Muslim.[45]

A House Here, Kin Over There: Multiple Belongings

The mere fact of settling in a city or town did not automatically turn a foreigner into a subject. The cities of Moldavia and Wallachia did not enjoy the autonomy necessary for the establishment of a juridical framework capable of creating a class of burghers by defining the attributes of their inhabitants and granting them rights. Cities were directly subordinated to the prince, administered via the princely office-holders, to whom they were sometimes

41 *Documente turceşti*, I, 306–307, 3/12 September 1768.

42 Aysel Yıldıx, İrfan Kokdaş, *op. cit.*, 178–180.

43 Documente turceşti, I, 307–308, 11 November 1768.

44 Nándor Erik Kovács, 'The Legal Status of the Danubian Principalities in the 17th Century as Reflected in the Şikayet Defteris', *Güney-Doğu Avrupa Araştırmaları Dergisi*, 1 (2014), 11.

45 Baki Tezcan notes that religion was an important factor in social distinction throughout the eighteenth century, resulting in a 'second-class status' for non-Muslim subjects. Baki Tezcan, *The Second Ottoman Empire. Political and Social Transformation in the Early Modern World* (Cambridge: 2010), 235–237.

even concessioned.[46] As such, we find little sign of a 'juridical reality' managing the presence of foreigners by granting them rights and institutionalizing those rights.[47] Likewise, the absence of urban statutes regulating residence and access to the resources of the city makes it necessary to base any hypotheses on the analysis of individual cases.

First, the foreigner was recorded in the treasury register as a payer of the tax owed by any foreigner who carried out activity in the country, which was established according to the nature of the activity. The next step consisted of buying a house to live in, a necessary requirement in order to establish residence. Immoveable patrimony was protected by the right of pre-emption (*protimisis*).[48] For example, in 1773, Zaharia the Greek, a 'foreign man', bought a house in Iași from Maria Ghirgicăi, after being assured that there were no heirs who might lay claim to it. Having become the owner, Zaharia busied himself with repairing and enlarging the house, investing the sum of 45 lei. In the autumn of 1775, Ambreni, Maria's daughter, returned from Constantinople, where she had been 'abroad' for a time, and contested the sale, requesting 'her right to exercise pre-emption to recover the house from Zaharia.' Ambreni had every right to make this claim to the house, 'it being the parental home,' especially as it had been sold without her knowledge. Zaharia seems to have depended on the support of his neighbours to be able to keep the house and his place in the community. However, on the day of the trial none of them turned up to confirm that Zaharia had looked into the situation and had made enquiries as to whether there were any heirs. Instead the court sent a *vornic de poartă* (a judge of minor cases), the *pivnicer* Toader, to evaluate the repairs and convert Zaharia's investment into money. It cannot be said that Zaharia the Greek's efforts came to nothing, as with the money he received he tried again elsewhere, in a different neighbourhood.[49] Property owning was a first step towards establishing residence, just as the length of time spent in a community might be another indicator of one's desire to settle there.

Important information also comes to us from the content of testaments, which show, as Simona Cerutti has demonstrated in her analysis focused on the foreigner, that belonging may be multiple.[50] Integration in the host country did not mean breaking connections with one's place of origin, one's family,

46 Simion Câlţia, *Aşezări urbane sau rurale? Oraşele din Ţara Românească de la sfârşitul secolului al 17-lea la începutul secolului al 19-lea* (Bucharest: 2011).

47 Do Paço, 'Extranéité et lien social', 126.

48 Valentin Al. Georgescu, *Preemţiunea în istoria dreptului românesc. Dreptul de protimisis în Ţara Românească şi Moldova* (Bucharest: 1965).

49 *Documente Iaşi*, VII, 27 October 1775, 183–184.

50 Simona Cerutti, *Étrangers*.

kindred, or hometown. The best example of this is Cernea Popovici, who, on 1 December 1823, drew up his testament, relating in detail his wanderings in search of a home.[51] Born into a modest family in Philippopolis (Ottoman Filibe, today Plovdiv in Bulgaria), Cernea decided at the age of eighteen, after his parents' death, to leave his hometown to escape poverty: 'not to go to ruin in my country, Philippopolis, remaining only in a parental home that was left to us three siblings [...] making myself a foreigner I went to Anadol (Anatolia), to Arvanitea (Albania), to Rumele (Rumelia), and to many other places in the Turkish Land.'[52] Mobility was not yet regulated and tamed at the end of the eighteenth century,[53] especially on the peripheries of empires, where political instability was very pronounced. It is true that some princes tried to regulate the mobility of foreigners, charging officials in border areas with identifying, recording, and reporting them to the political authorities. However in the absence of effective political stability, the regulation process was renewed with each successive reign and failed to become a long-term administrative and policing measure capable of protecting the population from foreign wrongdoers or from the abuses of Turkish merchants and soldiers at the borders.[54] In spite of this instability, we may observe, as I have already shown in this chapter, an intense social life along the Wallachian–Ottoman border: what Mariusz Kaczka terms 'frontier society'.[55] In other words, the inhabitants of the border zone did what they could to forge peaceful social relations and to profit from the advantages of the region for the development of their own economic activities.

Cernea Popovici carried his goods and his life with him as he sought his fortune through the Ottoman Empire. Of Serbian birth and Orthodox faith, Cernea was an Ottoman subject and devoted his life to trade. When he had amassed considerable wealth, after his experience of mobility through many Ottoman towns, he decided to settle in Wallachia. The Serbian merchant

51 BAR, MS 614, f. 120r-126r; The testament has been published by Gheorghe Lazăr: 'Un testament şi o poveste de viaţă: Cazul negustorului Cernea Popovici', in Cristian Luca, Claudiu Neagoe, Marius Păduraru (eds.), *Miscellanea, historica in honorem Professoris Marcel-Dumitru Ciucă septuagenarii* (Brăila: 2013), 597–624.

52 BAR, MS 614, f. 125.

53 Cerutti, *Étrangers*, 21.

54 See the numerous documents issued by Constantin Mavrocordat in an attempt to regulate the conflicts generated by foreigners on the 'margin'. To this end, the prince made sure of the help of the Ottoman officials in Moldavia, whose collaboration he requested. *Condica lui Mavrocordat*, ed. Cornel Istrate (Iaşi: 2008), III, 9–17.

55 Mariusz Wieław Kaczka, 'The Gentry of the Polish–Ottoman Borderlands: The case of the Moldavian-Polish Family of Turkuł/Turculeţ', *Acta Poloniae Historica*, 104 (2011), 149.

justified his settling in Wallachia in terms of the success of his business activities.[56] For years he had wandered the Empire, increasing his wealth and probably taking stock of the advantages and disadvantages of each place that might potentially be a 'home'[57]. In his case, it was not the 'Ottoman yoke' that led him to cross the Danube, but simply the economic advantages. As we shall see, he had friendly relations with Christians and Muslims alike, both south and north of the Danube. For a time, he returned to his 'homeland' of Philippopolis, and he maintained connections with his relations: he was not a refugee, but simply a Christian in search of a home.[58] We do not, unfortunately, know at what point Cernea received local rights and acquired the status of princely subject. The assimilation process has its 'ambiguities and frictions', as Wolfgang Kaiser puts it, moving forward tacitly on the basis of *ius domicilii* and the passage of time.[59] Our candidate had considerable property in the south of Wallachia, belonged to the majority Orthodox confession, and was a merchant, which meant that he travelled with his goods. It is not very clear from his testament how he came into possession of his estates, given that, especially in the countryside, property was protected by the right of *protimisis*. However this right could be evaded at any time, by donations, by forming a bond of blood-brotherhood, by the purchase of monastic land, or by mortgage loans.[60] One of these procedures must have been resorted to by Cernea Popovici, who had no wish to marry or to have heirs ('I did not have it in my plans to marry'). The wealth he amassed from his trading activity he invested in estates purchased in Teleorman county: the villages of Zmârdioasa, Găuriciu, Cervenia, and Răteasca. From the moment he bought the estates, Cernea Popovici began the process of integrating himself in the rural society of the county, collaborating closely not only with the local community, but also with the political authorities. Cernea proved to be an able landowner, concerning himself with the good administration of his estates, but also a good master to the peasants

56 BAR, MS 614, f. 125.

57 As recent research has shown, Filibe was an important trade center in this period. See Andreas Lyberatos, 'From Stratum Culture to National Culture: Integration Processes and National Resignification in 19th century Plovdiv', *Balkanologie. Revue d'études pluridisciplinaires*, XIII, 1–2 (2011), 1–24; Andreas Lyberatos, "Men of the Sultan: The Beglik Sheep tax Collection System and the Rise of Bulgarian National Bourgeoisie in Nineteenth-Century Plovdiv", *Turkish Historical Review*, 1 (2010), 55–85.

58 In this connection see also Mathieu Grenet, '"Grecs de nation", sujets ottomans', 316.

59 Kaiser, 'Extranéités urbaines', 78.

60 It was in this way that he gained possession of the Răteasca estate in Teleorman county. The owner had borrowed a large sum of money against the property deeds of the estate. As he was unable to pay back the loan with interest at the appointed time, he lost the estate to his creditor, a certain Cernea Popovici. BAR, MS 614, f. 121.

who worked his fields. In order to live comfortably ('for the peace of my life with plenty') and as befitted his social status, he build a house with 'rooms of brick in the earth', barns, kitchen, and bakehouse, all of brick, he repaired the mill, cleared the fields, planted orchards (120,000 trees), expanded the vineyards, and looked after the hayfields. All this was done with the help of the peasants of Zmârdioasa, whom he advised and urged to do the same on their patches of land. As I have already pointed out, depopulation was a pressing issue in the region, and the labour shortage was often compensated for by the colonization of whole groups, encouraged to leave their 'homeland' by the offer of privileges. Cernea implemented such a colonization policy on his estates, at his own initiative but with the approval of the prince. Acting on the prince's approval, but also in the interests of the 'good use and adornment of his estate,' Cernea brought 'eighty-two families of Serbs from the Turkish Land,' and settled them on his lands in Teleorman, thus forming the small village of Găuriciu, close to his own manor house. He obtained a princely decree (*hrisov*) giving them a considerable tax reduction, with just a single annual payment required. He also took charge of building the village, digging wells, planting orchards, clearing the space 'for the use and ease of the families,' and offering food and assistance to the newcomers. Colonization with families of Serbs and Vlachs brought from the 'Turkish Land' also took place at Cervenia.[61] Cernea Popovici's success in obtaining privileges for his Serb co-nationals is evidence of his collaboration with the political authorities, and supports the hypothesis that he was already a princely subject. We do not know when exactly the colonization of the region by Serbs brought from the Ottoman Empire took place, but it was probably after the outbreak of plague that wiped out a large part of the population.[62] Prince Ioan Caragea (1812–1818) encouraged this policy of colonization, especially after the Russian–Ottoman war (1806–1812) and the plague that followed.[63] The pressing need for revenue, and thus implicitly for tax-paying subjects, called for extreme measures: the placing of guards along the Danube border who were to let 'no taxable inhabitant nor any of the old

61 'Serbs' was often used also for Bulgarian colonists from Rumelia.

62 In 1823, Cernea Popovici provides a rather vague indication of the time: 'the colonies that I have recently established on my estate of Găurici and my estate of Cerveniia'. See BAR, MS 614, f. 122).

63 On 14 November 1814, 114 families of Serbs from Transylvania who had settled in Dolj county in Wallachia complained to prince Caragea that his *ispravnic* (administrator) of foreigners was not taking account of their privileges, namely exemption from taxes for a period of eight months. ANIC, Administrative Vechi, ds. 2152d/1814, f. 128; the *logofăt* Iane brought several families of *ungureni* (Transylvanians) to his estate in Fântânile, Saac county, promising them eight months tax exemption. See ANIC, Fond Administrative Vechi, ds. 2198/1818, f. 33, 45v, 20 April 1818.

Serbs, who came before the war' cross to the other side, in other words into the Ottoman Empire. Meanwhile, Cernea Popovici did his best to create the most propitious environment possible for his colonists, so that they would put down roots and become useful to him in the exploitation of his estates.[64]

As his wealth increased, the Serbian merchant built a further two brick houses, at Găuriciu and Zimnicea, and fitted them out with all that was necessary. Architecturally they belonged to a type specific to the Ottoman Empire and the world of southeastern Europe: the kula.[65] As his estates were in a frontier zone, populated by outlaws, brigands, and soldiers, Cernea had in his possession Turkish muskets, English pistols, and a silver sword. It was for the same reason that he adapted his home to a specific building type that would give protection in case of armed raids. Two Serbs, Gheorghe from Dervet and Neculce from Kanzalıc (today Stara Zagora, Bulgaria), were his faithful servants, ready to assist him day and night. In an area subject to frequent invasions, the memory was kept alive of the violent raids of Osman Pasvantoğlu's men, the incursions of Alexandru Ipsilanti's Etairists, the rising of Tudor Vladimirescu's pandours, and the frequent interventions of the Ottoman army.[66] As a witness to these aggressions, Cernea Popovici adapted to the dangers, fortifying his houses, arming himself, and ensuring the safety of his valuable belongings. Important documents—the title deeds of his estates and the registers of debts that he had to recover or to repay (26,000 lei loaned out in Wallachia and 9,000 lei borrowed)—were deposited in an 'iron chest' stored safely in Bucharest, 'in

64 On the competition between empires for human resources, see Benjamin Landais, 'Enregistrer l'ethnicité au XVIIIe siècle: L'identification des migrants ottomans à la frontière habsbourgeoise', *Revue d'Histoire Moderne & Contemporaine*, 66/4 (2019), 89–120.

65 'My house in Zimnicea made by me, in the form of a kula, with a two-room cottage surrounded by a yard and with a stable and a large barn'. BAR, MS 614, f. 121. On this architectural form, specific to the region, see Maurice Cerasi, 'The Formation of Ottoman House Type: A Comparative Study in Interaction with Neighboring Culture', *Muqarnas*, 15 (1998), 116–156; Tchavdar Marinov, 'The "Balkan House": Interpretations and Symbolic Appropriations of the Ottoman-Era Vernacular Architecture in the Balkans', in Roumen Daskalov, Tchavdar Marinov, Diana Mischkiva and Alexander Vezenkov (eds.), *Entangled Histories of the Balkans*, vol. 4. *Concepts, Approaches and (Self-) Representations* (Leiden: 2017), 440–593.

66 Rossitsa Gradeva, 'Osman Pazvantoğlu of Vidin: Between Old and New', *Interdisciplinary Journal of Middle Eastern Studies* (2005), 115–161; Sophia Laiou, 'Entre les insurgés reaya et les indisciplinés ayan: la révolution grecque et la réaction de l'Etat ottoman', in Marios Hadjianastasis (ed.), *Frontiers of the Ottoman Imagination. Studies in Honour of Rhoads Murphey* (Leiden: 2015), 213–228; Andrei Oţetea, *Tudor Vladimirescu şi revoluţia de la 1821* (Bucharest: 1971).

the vault at Mr Ianachi Naum's under the house of Mr Iona.' Clothes, bedding, and various items of silverware he also kept in chests, but in Ruse.'[67]

As both a princely subject and an Ottoman subject, Cernea Popovici built for himself a cross-border network of friends and business associates linking Teleorman to Istanbul, Ruse, and Bucharest. Of some, he says only that they were his friends, as in the case of the 'merchant friends' in Bucharest who warned him about the fraud committed in his name by a nephew; others he mentions by name, such as the grand *clucer* Nicolae Trăsnea, whom he designated as his heir, and Velișco, the kaymakam (interim governor) of Ruse, in whose care he left many of the chests containing his wealth. To these friends, Cernea Popovici entrusted his life, his wealth, and the memory of his name. Although he had kept in contact with family members still living in Philippopolis—a brother and a sister—and helped them whenever he could, they tried to trick him and even to poison him in order to get possession of his wealth sooner. It was this that led him to leave his entire wealth and indeed to entrust the commemoration of his soul to a friend: Nicolae Trăsnea.[68] When this friend declined, however, on the grounds that the task was too difficult, Popovici was left to die alone, leaving his vast wealth to fall inevitably into the hands of his relatives in Philippopolis.[69] The wealth of foreigners who died without heirs went by rights to their relatives and not into the Phanariot prince's treasury, as was the practice elsewhere.[70] For thirty years, relatives, no matter how distant their relationship, could claim the deceased's goods if they could prove a family connection.[71] No matter much how he tried to keep his relatives at a distance, the absence of direct heirs forced Cernea Popovici to fall back on his family roots.

From the information he offers and from his actions, he would appear to belong to the Serbian nation, but when he defines himself it is as 'an Ottoman subject'. He was also a princely subject by virtue of his services to the community and his close collaboration in the colonization process, in which he proved himself useful and to have an interest in his new homeland. The Greek signature on the document shows that he had become Hellenized through his

67 BAR, MS 614, f. 122–123.

68 In Popovici's testament, Trăsnea is recalled with much affection: 'my chosen, most good and excellent heir', 'a wise person, honest and God-fearing', to whom he was bound by a long friendship. BAR, MS 614, ff. 120r-v.

69 BAR, MS 614, f. 142v, 24 April 1826.

70 Cerutti, *Étrangers*, 35. Sahlins, *Unnaturally French*.

71 *Îndreptarea Legii (1652)* (Bucharest: 1962), 274–278. Valentin Al. Georgescu, *Bizanţul şi instituţiile româneşti până la mijlocul secolului al XVIII-lea* (Bucharest: 1980), 228.

profession: commerce.[72] Indeed the use of the Greek language was part of the cultural baggage of the southeast European Christian elite.[73] In fact, Cernea Popovici built for himself a small Serbian community, which he looked after, obtaining for them fiscal privileges, local rights, and the right to practise their faith freely. For this population, he erected churches in three of his villages. Contrary to the general pattern of the period, Popovici did not rise to boyar status by purchasing an administrative office[74]; rather he preferred to remain in the ranks of the merchant class and to collaborate with the local notables on the Danube by way of a system of patronage, maintaining close connections in both Muslim and Christian worlds.[75] As a bachelor, Cernea Popovici excluded family from this network, relying on bonds of friendship and clientelary relations.[76] However he was an exception; the majority of commercial networks were based on the extended family, because business involved a considerable measure of trust and loyalty.[77]

It should also be noted that the vast wealth that he managed to accumulate was invested, as his death approached, in the building of churches, or simply in Christian charity, forgiving all his debtors and cancelling all their debts, including the money and provisions borrowed over the years by the peasants on his estates and the 26,000 lei owed by his business associates. His charitable works served to consolidate his prestige in his country of adoption, but also among his Serbian co-nationals. His behaviour was common and specific to the southeast European Orthodox elite, which displayed its generosity by visible charitable actions with profound social significance: Gypsy slaves were

72 Philliou, *Biography of an Empire*, 15–16.

73 Victor Roudometof, 'From *Rum Millet* to Greek Nation: Enlightenment, Secularization, and National Identity in Ottoman Balkan Society, 1453–1821', *Journal of Modern Greek Studies* 16 (1998), 14.

74 Lazăr, *Les marchands*, 233–293.

75 On the system of patronage in the Ottoman Empire, see Palmira Brummett, 'Placing the Ottomans in the Mediterranean World: The Question of Notables and Households', *Journal of Ottoman Studies*, XXXVI (2010), 75–91; Elena Frangakis-Syrett, 'Networks of Friendship, Networks of Kinship: Eighteenth-Century Levant Merchants', *Eurasian Studies*, 1, 2 (2002), 184–205; Metin Ibrahim Kunt, 'Ethnic Regional (*Cins*) Solidarity in the Seventeenth-Century Ottoman Establishment', *International Journal of Middle East Studies*, 5, 3 (1974), 233–239.

76 Laiou shows that in the Ottoman world, 'the patronage system was closely connected with the "household" organization,' with kinship relations being dominant. Laiou, 'Patronage Networks in the Aegean Sea', 414.

77 Olga Katsiardi-Hering, 'Christian and Jewish Ottoman Subjects: Family, Inheritance and Commercial Networks between East and West (17th–18th C.)', in Simonetta Cavaciocchi (ed.), *The Economic Role of the Family in the European Economy from the 13th to the 18th Centuries* (Florence: 2009), 413.

freed and household servants were generously recompensed. In the absence of heirs, generosity was the only instrument by which one's memory might be perpetuated, as one's name was preserved for a time among the beneficiaries of charity, moved by gratitude to light a commemorative candle. Cernea Popovici's weakness lay precisely in his lack of heirs in whose hands to place his estate, his affection, his memory, his future.

One Individual, Different Subjecthoods: *Sudiți* and Protégés

With the end of the eighteenth century, the intervention of the state in the definition and identification of foreigners began to make itself felt. It started to become of the most important agents in naming, identifying, categorizing, and stating who was what. The necessity of economic development in a region lacking professional categories meant that there was an interest in attracting foreigners. The absence of a middle class has been much discussed in Romanian historiography.[78] In fact the phenomenon is a general characteristic of southeastern Europe and the Ottoman Empire, where the bourgeoisie, as it is generally termed, only began to take shape or to become visible in the nineteenth century.[79] For this reason, the princes encouraged master craftsmen to come to the Principalities, either to practise their trades or to open manufactories that would be of use to everyone.[80] Their contribution to the economic and cultural

78 Ştefan Zeletin, *Burghezia română. Originile şi rolul ei istoric* [1925] (Bucharest: 1997); Alexandru-Florin Platon, *Geneza burgheziei în Principatele Române (a doua jumătate a secolului al XVIII-lea—prima jumătate a secolului al XIX-lea). Preliminariile unei istorii* (Iaşi: 1997); Petronel Zahariuc, 'Sugestii genealogice pentru o cercetare a începuturilor burgheziei române', *Revista de Istorie Socială*, IV–VII (2005), 26–36.

79 Edhem Eldem, '(A Quest for) the Bourgeoisie of Istanbul: Identities, roles and conflicts', in Ulrike Freitag, Nora Lafi (eds.), *Urban Governance Under the Ottomans Between Cosmopolitanism and Conflict* (London: 2014), 159–186; Edhem Eldem, 'Un bourgeois d'Istanbul au milieu du XIXe siècle: Le livre de raison de Mehmed Cemal Bey, 1855–1864', in Nathalie Clayer, Erdal Kaynar (eds.), *Penser, agir et vivre dans l'Empire ottoman et en Turquie: Etudes réunies pour François Georgeon* (Paris, Leuwen: 2013), 372–406; Fatma Müge Göçek, *Rise of the Bourgeoisie, Demise of Empire: Ottoman Westernization and Social Change* (Oxford, New York: 1996).

80 See in this connection the efforts of Prince Ioan Callimachi to support the settlement of Protestant German craftsmen at Filipeni, around a felt manufactory (1 July 1759). The privileges of these craftsmen, which included the right to freely practice their faith, were reinforced by Grigore Callimachi, only for Grigore Ghica III to consider that there would be better conditions for the development of the manufactory at Chipereşti, which he bought, and to transport the German craftsmen to the new manufactory, which was named Filipenii Noi (23 August 1766). See Mihai-Răzvan Ungureanu, and Petronel

development of urban life was recognized by the granting of tax exemptions. For example, on 3 September 1772, at the height of the Russian–Ottoman war, when Moldavia was under Russian military occupation, the Italian Petru Mați (Pietro Mazzi) bought the glass and paper workshops at Hârlău from the Jew Hegel Marcovici. Marcovici had set these up during the reign of Grigore Callimachi (1767–1769), from whom he had obtained privileges and tax exemptions on 30 March 1768. (These were later reinforced by Field Marshal Pyotr Rumyantsev on 1 April 1771.) Petru Mați had been one of the foreign master craftsmen brought in to establish the manufactories. Marcovici's reasons for selling them to his employee are not stated.

However, the document recording the sale is essential evidence for the insertion of a foreigner into the administrative fabric of the state. Petru Mați was a skilled master craftsman who had to be kept. For this reason, the boyars of the Divan and Field Marshal Rumyantsev transferred to him the privileges previous enjoyed by 'the Jew' (*jidovul*) Hegel Marcovici: exemption 'from all taxes and demands of the Divan'. He was also granted the right to bring in 'sixty foreigners', qualified master craftsmen to work in the paper and glass manufactories. As the foreigners he brought were exempt from taxation, the Italian was obliged to register them at the Treasury, including them in a process of identification (name, origin, appearance) to distinguish them from the tax-paying population round about. According to the document: 'these foreign men whom he will bring from elsewhere, as soon as they come he is to bring before the grand *vistier* to investigate them. And it being proven that they are foreign, after the recording of their names, which he will give to the Treasury, they will be given certificates with their features so as to be known from the other inhabitants of the country.' As long as they are employees of the manufactories, 'they will not be troubled in any way': in other words, they would not pay taxes. However if they left this privileged condition, they would come into the category of ordinary foreign residents (*rândul străinilor*) and would be subject to taxation.[81] The certificate is thus an official document containing the identification details necessary for a foreigner to enjoy the privilege of tax exemption.

Zahariuc, *Documente privitoare la începuturile coloniei protestante din Moldova*, in Ovidiu Cristea, Petronel Zahariuc, and Gheorghe Lazăr (eds.), *Aut viam inveniam aut faciam. In honorem Ştefan Andreescu* (Iaşi: 2012), 451–466.

81 BAR, Fond Documente Istorice, CCCC/23. Before the arrival of the foreign craftsmen, Pietro Mazzi received thirty men (classed as *liude*: tax-paying subjects) who helped him in the glass manufactory and were given exemption from tax. Vezi BAR, Fond Documente Istorice, III/17, 4 September 1773.

A further step in the recognition and registration of foreigners and the regulation of their status took place in the context of the construction of the category of *sudiți*. The establishment of consulates in Iași and Bucharest created new centres of power and influence. The new Russian consulate had barely opened before it was attracting the Wallachian elite, boyars and wealthy merchants alike, like a magnet. Writing to Chancellor Kaunitz, Internuncio Herbert von Rathkeal enviously described the atmosphere in the house of the Russian consul, Sergei Lazarevich Laskarev. The consul 'enjoyed such great favour in Bucharest that his house was much frequented by the boyars, he gave grand assemblies twice a week, and he involved himself in protections and intrigues.'[82] 'Protection' was the key word that attracted Christian Ottoman subjects, implying not just fiscal privileges but the right to elude princely justice and to benefit from a favourable judgement through the intermediary of the consul-patron.

Russia, Austria, Prussia, France, and Britain appointed consuls to Iași and Bucharest to protect their subjects,[83] but also accepted under their jurisdiction not only non-Muslim Ottoman subjects and foreigners who did not have consular representation in the Principalities, but also locals. The provisions of the capitulations were now extended to cover foreign subjects (*sudiți*) in the Principalities. In the late eighteenth century, litigation between *sudiți* and *re'aya*s was judged by the justice departments of Wallachia and Moldavia, but the nineteenth century brought the imposition of consular jurisdiction as a parallel institution privileging the *sudiți* as a distinct social category. By their interventions before the princes or the Porte, the consuls managed to obtain privileges for their subjects; likewise they strove to ensure consular assistance in case of litigation, and to firmly impose respect for their rights.[84] In this context, some inhabitants of the Principalities, native or foreign, purchased the right to be 'protected', attracted by the privileges it involved. In the absence of regular income, consuls encouraged this practice in their countries of residence, and sold 'patents of protection'.[85] The consuls were copying the model of the Ottoman Empire, where ambassadors and consuls had been granted

---

82 '[...] jouissait d'une si grande faveur à Bukarest que sa maison était très fréquentée par des bojars, qu'il donnait de grandes assemblées deux fois par semaine, qu'il se mêlait de protections et d'intrigues.' See HHStA, Türkei, II/77, f. 415–419, 10 September 1782, Herbert Rathkeal to Wenzel Anton von Kaunitz.

83 On the official mission of the first consuls, Russian and Austrian, see Hurmuzaki, *Documente,* VII, 125, 380, 390–391, 405; XIX/1, 22, 25, 111–112, 116, 155–162, 187.

84 Mărieş, *Supuşii străini,* 37.

85 Ioan C. Filitti, 'România faţă de capitulaţiile Turciei', *Analele Academiei Române. Memoriile Secţiunii Istorice,* t. XXXVIII (1915–1916), 128–135.

the right to employ non-Muslim Ottoman subjects, offering them protection by means of *berats*.[86] The founding of the Chancellery of Foreign Affairs (*Logofeţia Străinilor Pricini*) thus came as a necessary step towards countering the growing power of the consulates and of their protégés in relation to natives and the power of the princes.[87] As I mentioned in the Introduction, there is not yet agreement among historians with regard to the founding of the two Chancelleries (in Moldavia and in Wallachia), but their activity is increasingly well documented for the nineteenth century.

The increase in the number of *sudiți* led to the intervention of the Porte, which demanded the exclusion from the protected category of those already resident in the Principalities.[88] To this end, on 27 January 1813, Prince Ioan Caragea ordered the grand *vistier* to draw up a register listing the 'genuine' *sudiți*, while *re'ayas* who had purchased patents of protection were to be returned to the ranks of taxpayers:

> Honourable and faithful boyar of My Highness, you, grand *vistier*, since the Most High Devlet [the Porte] has been informed that in this country a great abuse is being carried on with the making of *sudiți* by the consulates of foreign courts that are here, in this connection we have been sent a Most High Imperial *ferman* comprising and commanding the order that is to be applied from now on for *sudiți*, namely: as many as may be inhabitants of the country from their ancestors or may be subjects of the Most Puissant Empire and, having their dwelling elsewhere, happen to come to this country for some temporary matter of their business [...] to be subject to tax, remaining again [subjects] of the Most Puissant Empire and to follow the old rule.[89]

The command was to be sent to local *ispravnic*s, whose mission was to make an inventory of all those who were or had 'made themselves' *sudiți*, confiscating their patents and returning them to the list of taxpayers.[90] These measures must be analysed in the economic and social context of the moment:

86 In the Ottoman Empire, Christian subjects who were under the protection of the European powers enjoyed commercial privileges and tax reductions. In this connection, see Bernard Lewis, 'Berātlı', *Encyclopaedia of Islam*, (Leiden: 1990–1991), vol. I, 1171; van den Boogert, *The Capitulations*, 63–72.

87 See the example of the first Prussian consul in Bucharest, Ernest Frederic König, who had as his interpreters the Greeks Frangopulo and Sandu Panaiotti (ANIC, Microfilme RDG, Rola 46, c. 72–74, 30 November 1784, Iaşi and c. 150–151, 6 July 1788).

88 Indeed, the Porte opposed the appointments of the first consuls precisely because of their status as Ottoman subjects, as was the case of Ignatius Stefan Raicevich and Constantin Stamati. See Part I, chapter 1.

89 V.A. Urechia, 'Justiţia sub Ioan Caragea', *Analele Academiei Române. Memoriile Secţiei Istorice*, 2d ser., t. XX (1897–1898), 288–291.

90 Ibid.

the Russian–Ottoman war (1806–1812) and the plague epidemic. The Ottoman Empire, and implicitly also the Principalities, had a pressing need for human resources to restore their treasuries. Making a register of these resources was one of the priority measures of the reign of Ioan Caragea, especially after the great boyars in the Divan informed him in May 1814 that 'the total of the Treasury's fiscal units has come to be very much reduced,' and that consequently it was difficult to cover the country's expenses.[91] To find out the extent of the country's taxable human resources, Caragea resorted to a fiscal census of the population of Wallachia. The project involved counting all the inhabitants of the principality, rigorously noting each social category with the privileges and exemptions that it enjoyed. Among these categories were foreigners and *sudiți* in towns and villages. It is clear from his order that the register requested in 1813 had not yet been compiled.[92]

Making a register of the population made heavy demands on the princely authorities in general and on the officials charged with carrying out the count in particular. What is of interest to us here is the recording of the *sudiți*. The following example is provided by the *vornicie* of Bucharest (the department which collected taxes and judged various court cases in the city). The official Petre Nenciulescu writes to the grand *vistier*:

> I draw to your attention that the *vornicie* has no register of French *sudiți* and could not make a register without a princely command. Second, I humbly beg that it be explained to me which patents are to be gathered, that is, only from those who are good French *sudiți* or also from the others who previously were French *sudiți* and now have become English *sudiți*, because these too, after they have in their hands French patents also have English patents.[93]

The confusion was sustained by the multiple games of self-fashioning advanced by foreigners and natives alike according to their interests and profiting from the authority vacuum created by the competition between the consulates and the princely administration. The fiscal census of the population, now termed by Caragea the 'settlement' (*așezământ*), showed the difficult of knowing one's subjects in the absence of functional institutions and functionaries capable of handling such a task. The abuses committed by the officials were numerous, and equally the unwillingness of the population to be recorded was evident.[94]

---

91 BAR, MS 357, f. 51–55v, 28 May 1814. The fiscal units (*lude*) referred to were groupings of one or more families, treated together for tax calculation purposes.

92 BAR, MS 357, f. 64–67, 69–70, 70v–72, 1 August 1814.

93 ANIC, Fond Adminstrative Vechi, ds. 2152c/1814, f. 116, 8 September 1814.

94 See the examples mentioned in the petitions addressed to the princely chancellery and the solutions proposed, all in September 1814: ANIC, Fond Administrative Vechi,

On 27 September 1814, the register counted 1,723 *sudiți* in Bucharest, specifically '956 Russian, 694 German and 73 French'. The officials noted that 'most were men married to local women, with houses and outbuildings, some acquired as dowry, others bought by themselves and are in good condition.'[95] All the same, the officials were faced with a major problem: they did not know the criteria by which they were to establish who were the 'real' *sudiți*, so they asked the Treasury for guidance. 'May we be sent the register, so we can pick out the *good sudiți* from the others,' writes Grand *Vornic* Iordache Văcărescu.[96] I shall not insist here on the privileges of the *sudiți* or on the political disputes between princes and consulates regarding jurisdiction over these foreigners. What is of interest here is the manner in which the status of *sudit* was used in the process of identification and obtaining social or fiscal advantages.

As word spread that the fiscal burden on *sudiți* and foreign settlers in village colonies was much lighter, some townspeople and villagers purchased patents and refused to continue paying taxes, while others fled to the colonies and declared themselves 'foreign'.[97] Some were defended by the consuls who issued the patents, while others were defended by landowners who needed labour. A process of collective identification was thus triggered which involved the local and central authorities, the consulates, and the village and town population, each having its own specific interests: the political authorities were interested in avoiding the creation of precedents and in recovering their taxpayers; the consular agencies were interested in enhancing their power and increasing the number of their subjects; and the subjects did not want to pay taxes. The situation led to inter-communal conflicts and the intervention of the authorities to restore peace and impose some degree of order.[98]

Under the capitulations, foreign subjects, the *sudiți*, did not have the right to own immoveable property in the host country.[99] The investigations carried out by the authorities showed, however, that many of them had permanent

---

ds. 2373/1812, f. 16, 19, 26–31v; Fond Administrative Vechi, ds. 2152c/1814, f. 3, 24v, 27, 30, 33–39v.

95 Fond Administrative Vechi, ds. 2152c/1814, f. 3, 24v, 27, 30, 33–39v.

96 ANIC, Fond Administrative Vechi, ds. 2152c/1814, f. 208.

97 ANIC, Fond Administrative Vechi, ds. 2204/1818, f. 79, 94v, 22 June 1818.

98 Among other examples, see the document of 30 June 1818 where it is noted that many taxpayers in Ilfov and Dâmbovița counties 'have become Kaiserly and Kingly *sudiți*, and by virtue of the patents they have, this sort of people can no longer pay tax.' ANIC, Fond Administrative Vechi, ds. 2198/1818, f. 80, 95v, 129, 142v.

99 Ignatius Mouradgea d'Ohsson, *Tableau general de l'Empire ottoman*, III/2 (Paris: 1820), 448.

residence in the Principalities, with houses and land, families and kin.[100] The reports of these investigations point with precision to important indicators in defining the boundary separating *sudiți* from 'locals': foreigners who settled in Moldavia or Wallachia could not be considered *sudiți* if they lived 'in this country with their own houses, buying also outbuildings and making plantations and other appurtenances.'[101] The report of the great boyars to Prince Alexandru Suţu bases itself on the provisions of the 'sacred capitulations', which establish that 'a *sudit* who is placed under some foreign protection is not free to have outbuildings and appurtenances on the land of the country.' Possession of properties, their administration, and economic and social concern for the growth of one's income were privileges restricted to the 'local'; consequently, the *sudit*, and also his protector, knowing 'the sacred treaties' ('*sfintele tractaturi*'), had assumed a social transformation: 'wishing to obtain such possessions and uses on the land of the country that belong to the locals, he can no longer be considered a *sudit*, but is a local and as a local is obliged to answer to the country with his duty.'[102]

The point of view expressed by the leading boyars and put in practice by the prince did not correspond to the expectations of the Austrian consulate, which had requested protection for its subjects. Such disputes were relatively numerous in the first half of the nineteenth century. Some princes appealed to the Porte to mediate and indeed to intervene by charging the European powers to respect the true provisions of the capitulations,[103] but at other times the disputes were settled more directly in the street, as Hugot, agent of the French consulate, reports:

---

100 'For some time now, many of the young men of the guilds, namely exempted peasants, servants, priests, deacons, even sons of taxpayers and taxpayers themselves, finding the occasion, have become *sudiți*, declaring themselves foreign, and they are born and raised here, good inhabitants of this county,' writes Constantin Caragea, the *ispravnic* of Muşcel, on 11 June 1818, presenting his conflict with the leader of the *sudiți* in the town of Câmpulung, who had taken under his protective wing all those who had declared themselves to be *sudiți*. ANIC, Fond Administrative Vechi, ds. 2198/1818, f. 64, 79v.

101 Note the similarity with the assimilation of foreigners who settled in the Ottoman Empire and proceeded to buy properties and cultivate them. See van den Boogert, *Capitulations*, 30–31.

102 Muzeul Judeţean de Istorie şi Arheologie, Prahova, Mapa 3/ II, Ţara Românească, no. 1650, doc. 32, II, file 131, 27 July 1819.

103 See the complaint addressed by Ioan Sandu Sturza to the sultan, in which he alleges that 'the *sudiți*, wrongfully protected by the consulates, live as they please' Nicolae Iorga, 'Plângerea lui Ioan Sandu Sturza Vodă împotriva sudiţilor din Moldova', *Analele Academiei Române. Memoriile Secţiunii Istorice*, t. XXXV (1912–1913), 4–6.

> Some Austrian subjects, found in the evening in the street, were beaten a few days ago by the Moldavian Guard. Two days later, the Moldavian Guard was beaten by Austrian subjects whom it had attacked without reason when they were returning from their work. Tranquillity is now completely re-established. Despite the cessation of the Austrian Agent's relations with the local authorities, the department of foreign affairs receives the Austrian, Russian, and English subjects who present themselves, and judges their trials with the subjects of the principality.

He proceeds to give details on the diplomatic conflict between the prince and the diplomatic representation of the Habsburg Empire.[104]

As I shall show in the following chapters, taking as examples Dumitrache Merișescu and Iorgu Hartulari, the population continued to purchase *sudit* patents, using the protective umbrella of consular power to further their own interests by changing their political status. The patents could only be sold by consuls, and only to Christians. The phenomenon grew so chaotic and expansive that at a certain point it became hard to control. Just as princes sold ranks, so consuls sold patents to whoever wished to buy.[105] Ridiculous situations sometimes arose, like that of the British subject Costea Papadopulos in Saac county:

> I was at first *re'aya*, but this autumn, the honoured Consulate of the Britons being at Vălenii de Munte, Saac county, on the urging of some or other of my friends, *sudiți* of the consulate, deluding myself, I too obtained a patent to count myself an English *sudit*. And, later, I see that this patent is of no use to me, because I am here with my family in this land and a subject under the protection of the honoured Treasury from the beginning.[106]

A Greek judging by his name, settled in Wallachia with a family, properties, and wealth, Costea Papadopulos thought it would do no harm to have a subject's

104 'Quelques sujets autrichiens, trouvés le soir dans la rue, ont été, il y a quelques jours battus par la Garde Moldave. Deux jours après, la Garde Moldave a été battue par de sujets autrichiens qu'elle avait attaqués sans raisons lorsqu'ils revenaient de leur travail. La tranquillité est maintenant tout à fait rétablie. Malgré la cessation des rapports de M. l'Agent d'Autriche avec les autorités locales, le département des affaires étrangères reçoit les sujets Autrichiens, Russe et Anglais qui se présentent, et juge leurs procès avec les sujets de la principauté.' Hurmuzachi, *Documente*, XVII, 39, 2/13 December 1824, Iaşi.

105 I have written elsewhere about the devaluing of boyar ranks by princes selling them in order to increase their income. The number of boyars grew so much that it gave rise to the saying 'pitarii ca măgarii' ('*pitar*s as [common as] donkeys). See Constanţa Vintilă-Ghiţulescu, *Evgheniţi, ciocoi, mojici. Despre obrazele primei modernităţi româneşti (1750–1860)* (Bucharest: 2013).

106 ANIC, Vornicia Treburilor Dinlăuntru, ds. 73/133. F. 5–7, 16 February 1834.

patent too, if others had.[107] Indeed he invokes this patent in a trial that he had with another British subject, Hristodor Kaloian, and his heirs. As in this case the status of *re'aya* would have been more useful to him, Papadopulos wrote to the Department of the Ministry of Internal Affairs (*Departamentul Vornicia Treburilor Dinlăuntru*) requesting support in recovering his former identity.[108] Unfortunately, we do not know how much the status of 'British protégé' cost him. In Moldavia, in the same period, a merchant could buy a patent for 2–3 ducats from the Austrian consul or 5 gold pieces from the French vice-consul in Galați.[109]

The fabrication of an identity was not guided according to the criteria of the present day, but drew on specific sources connected to a social, political, and cultural context. The status of *sudit* was for some an opportunity that they would access whenever they needed it. 'The *sudiți* relying on their status as sudit' ('*Rezemându-se în puterea sudiţii*') is an expression we find in some documents, when certain individuals take advantage of their status as foreign subjects to avoid respecting the norms of the country in which they live.[110] Others changed their religious confession along with their subjecthood. Avram Berman was a Jew, a foreigner settled in Bucharest. The process of his integration in the local community is best described by his wife, 'Haela the Jewess', who offers the following information necessary for the process of identification:

> I being at the age for marriage [and living] at my parents', and one Avram Berman the Jew, Prussian *sudit* repeatedly asking for me to take me as his wife, my parents did not want to give me to him, for the reason that he was a foreigner, unknown and then recently arrived here. And later, my parents trusting in the testimony of the Prussian consul (under whose protection the abovementioned was) and the attestations that we saw in his hands about the schools where he had studied, and that he had knowledge of several foreign languages, and likewise the trade of doctor, for all that he had no wealth but my parents considering him of good behaviour, they were deceived into giving me to him as his wife, about five months ago, the Prussian consul too being present at the wedding.'

---

107 Van den Boogert shows that in the eighteenth century, protection became 'a commodity'. Van der Boogert, *The Capitulations*, 76.

108 Ibid.

109 Mărieş, *Supuşii străini*, 132. Some of the consuls in Iaşi and Bucharest made considerable fortunes for themselves from the sale of such patents. In his report, Antoine-François Andréossy, ambassador of France to Istanbul, writes that the wealth of the Russian consul in Bucharest might be as much as 300,000 piastres. Hurmuzaki, *Documente*, I_2, 739, 4 January 1813, Pera. On the price of the patents offered by ambassadors to their protégés in the Ottoman Empire, see also van den Boogert, *The Capitulations*, 80–84.

110 See the case of Haralambie, the owner of a club ('*clup*') in Bucharest and a British subject, who established his own rules with no regard for the local urban regulations. ANIC, Departamentul Spătăriei, ds. 829/1815, 1 December 1815.

Avram Berman was a foreigner trying to integrate himself very quickly in the local community by marriage. The protection of the Prussian consul, Baron Louis Kreuchely-Schwerdtberg, was essential in his case, intervening before 'Maer the Jew', and recommending Avram Berman as a good prospective son-in-law.[111] After five months, however, Avram Berman left his wife and his home. Having set out in search of him, Maer discovered his son-in-law's multiple tricks with his identity: now he had presented himself as Jewish, at other times variously Orthodox, Catholic, again Jewish, again Orthodox, again Catholic, 'holding to no law' (*'neţinându-se de nici o lege'*). One's religious confession was an important element in the process of identification, but also an essential lever in becoming anchored in a community. A change of religion ('and again he turned to other laws' (*'şi iarăşi s-au întors în alte legi'*) was not well regarded by the community, who considered it tantamount to an act of betrayal.

Avram Berman's identity games did not stop here: Haela and her father took their case to the office of the Jewish haham, to the Chancellery of Foreign Affairs, and to the Prussian consulate. Each institution added another element to the identification of Doctor Avram Berman. The Prussian consulate continued to protect him, to represent him, and to keep his belongings and documents safe when he was out of town. When asked, the consulate sent to the Chancellery, by way of its representative the *vechil*[112] Sotir Floronulo, an appeal signed not by Avram Berman but by Iosef Leopold Berman (sometimes written 'Bermann') in which he affirms 'that no enacted law code commands him to give an act of separation according to the decision of the hahams' (*'că nici o legiuită pravilă nu-i poruncește ca să dea carte de despărțeniie după hotărârea hahamilor'*). In refusing to recognize the ruling of the Jewish court, which had decreed his separation from his wife Haela and the return of her dowry, Berman was, in fact, refusing to recognize the authority of the community to which he belonged. This is not to say that he had much more respect for the rules of the host country that had received him: he did not turn up in court, but left the city and sent his *vechil* with applications for compensation 'for time lost' in court hearings that had caused considerable prejudice to his image. One of the criteria for integration and assimilation is respect for the norms of one's country of adoption. Shortly after, he changed his mind, probably on the advice of the Prussian consul, and addressed a complaint to Prince Grigore Dimitrie Ghica (1822–1828), asking to be heard. He was supported by the consul, who wrote

111 For Baron Louis Kreuchely-Schwerdtberg, consul in Bucharest, see ANIC, Microfilme RDG, Rola 46, c. 352–356, 26 June 1830, Berlin.

112 An overseer, sometime empowered to represent his employer in litigation (from the Turkish *vekil*).

to the prince in this connection.[113] Two years later, the *sudit* Joseph Leopold Berman again benefitted from the assistance and protection of the consulate, which tried to protect its subjects in wartime. When he was arrested by Russian troops and sent to Bessarabia during the Russian–Ottoman war of 1828–1829, the consulate intervened for his release.[114]

Ahmet, Ahmet, and Ahmet: Ottomans and Christians

The foreigners listed by Dimitrie Cantemir as living in Moldavia also included Ottoman Turks. Relations between Christians and Muslims did not always find expression in violence and abuses. They may have been separated by religion, but, especially in border zones, there was frequent collaboration and interaction between the two ethnic groups. As merchants and money-lenders, the Turks did business with the local population, trying to survive, to build themselves a home and a future.[115] One of the Muslims who tried to make a living on the Moldavian border was Ahmet 'who was previously called Murtaza'. Ahmet Murtaza was a distinctive figure who wandered Moldavia in search of patrons and business. A licensed honey-merchant (Tk. *balğy*), he went from village to village buying honey for the Ottoman Empire. He was just one among many Ottoman merchants who enjoyed the privilege of having first option on certain products that were needed to feed Istanbul.[116] Alongside the honey trade, Ahmet Murtaza also dealt in money-lending, providing loans to whoever needed them, but focusing particularly on those with resources, in other words, the great boyars. His honey-trading and money-lending activities helped him to enter the network of great boyar families such as Neculce and Racoviță.[117] Thus it was that he became close to *hatman* Dumitraşco Racoviţă,

113 ANIC, Departamentul Spătăriei, ds. 1267/1827, f.1r-4v, 3 May 1827, 16 June 1827, 10 August 1827, 30 September 1827.

114 ANIC, Microfilme RDG, Rola 46, c. 394–397, 17 June 1829, Berlin; c. 407–409, 22 December 1830, The report of Consul Kreuchely.

115 See also Gheorghe Lazăr, 'Marchands Ottomans en Valachie (XVIIe–XVIIIe siècles)', in Faruk Bilici, Ionel Cândea, Anca Popescu (eds.), *Enjeux Politiques, Economiques et Militaires en Mer Noire (XIVe–XIXe siècles). Etudes à la Mémoire de Mihai Guboglu* (Brăila: 2007), 291–314.

116 See the *ferman* of Sultan Mustafa III commanding that essential products be sold to Ottoman merchants and not 'enemy' merchants. *Documente turceşti*, vol. I, 21/30 June 1774, 278–279.

117 On this subject, see also Michał Wasiucionek, 'Ethnic Solidarity in the Wider Ottoman Empire Revisited: "cins" and Local Political Elites in 17th Century Moldavia and Wallachia', in Marinos Sariyannis (ed.), *New Trends in Ottoman Studies* (Rethymno: 2014), 232–245.

the brother of the prince of Moldavia, Mihai Racoviţă (1716–1726), to whom he made numerous loans of money. The money was lent at interest, based on contracts, on a series of occasions in 1726 and 1727.[118] When Dumitraşco Racoviţă plotted against Prince Grigore Ghica (1726–1734) in hope of bringing his brother back to the throne, Ahmet Murtaza joined him. The plot failed, and in the autumn of 1727, Dumitraşco Racoviţă took refuge among the Tatars of Budjak to escape punishment.[119] From there, he proceeded to Istanbul to save his head, with Ahmet Murtaza as his guide and adviser. Ahmet helped him to cross the Danube and to reach Babadag, where he hid him in his brother's house for several days. To reach Istanbul, where Dumitraşco's brother, Mihai Racoviţă, was, who he hoped would help him, Dumitraşco and Ahmet joined up with a group of *celepi* (livestock-merchants) on their way to the capital (most likely changing their clothes for the latter's garb). When they were close to Istanbul (at the village of Küçük Köy), Dumitraşco sent Ahmet as an emissary to his brother, but Mihai Racoviţă refused to receive him or indeed to get involved in any way, for fear of losing his head. Left helpless, Dumitraşco Racoviţă put himself in the hands of Ahmet Murtaza, who did what he could to conceal him, travelling again among the *celepi* in order to cross imperial territory without being caught. As they wandered through Dobrogea, their contemporary Ion Neculce writes, Dumitraşco Racoviţă took shelter in the home of a Turk in Silistra.[120] It was not long, however, before he was denounced by the Turk, captured, and imprisoned. Murtaza, 'his guide on all his journeys', did not escape unpunished: 'The prince brought the Turk Murtaza too and judged him in the Divan, with the Divan-Efendi present together with many Turkish merchants settled in Iaşi', writes the chronicler. Having been 'whipped on the soles of his feet' as an example to others, Murtaza was imprisoned, and later, on the sultan's orders, banished across the Danube.[121]

But Ahmet Murtaza's story does not end here. Time passes, rulers change, people die, and some things are forgotten. So it was that he returned to Moldavia,

---

118 BAR, Fond Documente Istorice, CLXI/132. See also Mihai Racoviţă-Cehan, *Familia Racoviţă-Cehan. Fişe nominale şi fotografii* (Bucharest: 1942), 32.

119 Dumitraşco Racoviţă had alongside him his son-in-law, Iordache Costache. For the conspiracy of the two and the capture of Dumitraşco Racoviţă see Grigore Ghica's letter to Chrysanthos Notaras, patriarch of Jerusalem. As I have shown in the previous chapter, family solidarities were set in motion when a member was in danger. On this occasion, Nicolae Mavrocordat, not only Dumitraşco's cousin but also prince of Wallachia, wrote to Patriarch Notaras, an important figure respected by all political factions, seeking his assistance. The patriarch's intervention led to the boyar's being pardoned. Both letters are published in Hurmuzaki, *Documente*, XIV/2, 971–972, 19 May 1728.

120 Neculce, *Letopiseţul Ţării Moldovei*, 704.

121 *Cronica Ghiculeştilor*, 269, 283, 287.

and indeed to Iași, and renewed his trading and money-lending activities. In 1737, he was serving as *vechil*[122] for two Muslim merchants, the brothers Ismail and Mahmud. In this capacity, he was sent by his employers to recover a debt from the grand *vornic* Ion Neculce. At this point, we discover that Neculce had had commercial relations with the brothers ('the *vornic* having much business with my master, hagi Ismail, and with his brother Mahmud'), to whom he had offered the agricultural produce they were looking for: honey, butter, hides, large livestock. The deal had gone well, but the Russian–Ottoman war of 1711, followed by Neculce's exile until 1720, had interrupted their relations for a time. Mahmud had recovered part of the debt by forcibly taking 'some honey and some beehives' from the *vornic*'s estates. He had then left for Anatolia, leaving Ahmet with the task of recovering part of the remaining debt. Years had passed and for a long time their paths had not crossed: Neculce had wandered in Russia, waiting for the sultan's pardon, Ismail had left for Mecca, while his brother Mahmud had wandered in Anatolia. It was only on 18 May 1737 that they met again, each adding to their process of identification the experience accumulated on their travels through the empires. For Neculce this had meant Muscovy and then the office of grand *vornic*. Ismail had become a *hajji*, and Mahmud had acquired wealth and possibly some education, enough for him to call himself *çelebi*. Their understanding was authenticated with four signet seals in smoke and the Turkish signatures of the protagonists.[123] From his signature, we know that Ahmet also called himself *çelebi*: probably the experience of exile had helped him to raise his financial and social status. This gave him the courage to produce the contracts recording his loans to Dumitraşco Racoviţă and to seek their repayment. In the meantime, Dumitraşco Racoviţă himself had died intestate, leaving an uncertain inheritance and three sons (Radu, Dumitraşco, and Ion), who dissociated themselves from their father's past, including his debts.[124] Radu Racoviţă declared that the four contracts recorded a 'hereditary debt' ('*datorie părințească*') which would have to be recovered from his mother and brothers, who had all settled in Wallachia. He had already paid heavily due to the 'danger' ('*primejdia*') into which his father's actions had pushed him: 'On the flight of his parents, the prince [Grigore Ghica] sent [men] to arrest him, he being in the country, in his house, and not being in any way associated with his father in his actions, and as he escaped from the hands of those sent, they took from him what they found in his house, everything,

122 Vechil, from Turkish vekil, administrater of an estate or household; a sort of lawyer who had the right to represent his master's in justice.

123 BAR, Fond Documente Istorice, CXX/114.

124 *Documente Iaşi*, V, 300–303, <1746 June 28, Iaşi>.

inside and out, to the value of 60 bags and more of money.'[125] Radu Racoviță is here recalling the year 1727, when his father had made an alliance with Aadil Giray against Grigore Ghica, encouraging Tatar rebellions and incursions into Moldavia.[126] Radu considered that there was no reason why he should also be held responsible, given that he was already separated from the 'parental home' ('*casa părintească*'), married and an office-holder, while his mother, Ilinca Cantacuzino, and his brothers, Dumitraşco and Ion, had followed the 'traitor' to Budjak and then on his journeys for survival through the empire. The *hatman*'s treachery had brought repercussion on the whole Racoviţă family: their wealth had been confiscated, the *hatman* himself had died shortly after his release from imprisonment, his younger sons had taken refuge in Wallachia, and his wife Ilinca Cantacuzino had had to sell their houses and vineyards in Iași and Huși to Grigore Ghica in order to cover part of the damage caused by the Tatars in Moldavia. Ahmet Murtaza was not so much interested in the dramas of the Racoviţă family, however, as in recovering his debt, which was a considerable one. It was more than twenty years since the contract for the first loan had been signed, and the family had recovered both socially and economically. Radu Racoviţă had managed to obtain the prince's pardon, to recover part of the confiscated goods, and to have a relatively distinguished career as an office-holder.[127] The other two sons, Dumitraşco and Ion, had also managed to advance in administrative office and by marriage and inheritance they had amassed substantial wealth. In court, the Racoviţă brothers threw the debt onto one another, forcing Ahmet (and his companion Ahmet Chiosea, another creditor of the boyar Racoviţă) to go now to Iași, now to Bucharest, starting trials both in Moldavia and in Wallachia. In the end, Ahmet had to travel to Istanbul and request (probably buy) from Patriarch Neophytus a letter of anathema against the Racoviță family in order to establish the truth about their fortune.[128]

Through the intervention of the prince, Ioan Mavrocordat (1744–1747), Murtaza received in lieu of the money owed two estates, which Radu Racoviță, having risen to the office of grand *vornic*, later bought back from him, thus effectively repaying the debt. On 18 August 1747, Ahmet was identified as

125 *Documente Iaşi*, V, 300–303, <1746 June 28, Iaşi>.

126 Named Adel Gherei sultan in the document. He is Aadal Giray, kalga of the khan Mengi II Giray. On his rebellion see Gilles Veinstein, 'Les tatars de Crimée et la seconde election de Stanislas Leszczynski', *Cahiers du monde russe et sovietique*, 11 (1), 1970, 24–92.

127 See the document of 12 August 1747 by which Grigore Ghica grants to Radu Racoviţă, grand *vornic* of Ţara de Sus (the 'Upper Land') the houses and vineyards in Iaşi and Huşi that had been confiscated from his father. *Documente Iaşi*, V, 321–322.

128 *Documente Iaşi*, V, 304–305, 18 July 1746.

'Ahmet aga Buiucli, merchant from here in Iași'.[129] It is not known what became of him after that date. Given the nature of the sources, it is far from surprising that we should lose track of him on his journeys between Iași, Silistra, and Istanbul. Moreover, Ahmet is such a common name that the researcher has to distinguish between various possible figures whose 'tracks' could match those of the Ottoman Murtaza.[130]

Ahmet, Mehmet, and Osman were the most common names associated with Turks in the Principalities. In the absence of other criteria of identification, the researcher's ability to follow trails and construct working hypotheses is very much a matter of luck. For example, in the same period, another Turkish merchant named Ahmet was also travelling around Moldavia, but his fate was a tragic one. His story offers us precious information about the need for collaboration between Christians and Ottomans in a time when the two groups had common interests. In this case, fear of the sultan's punishment led to a local reconciliation, and recourse to the imperial Divan was avoided. So what happened?

In the spring of 1745, there was a conflict between a group of Turks and a group of Moldavian peasants in the village of Ţigăneşti, in the region of Tecuci. The four Turks, one of whom was Ahmet Pirpiriul (Tk. *pırpırı* = weak, poor), were guarding the vineyards and casks of the surrounding inns. They thus made up a sort of patrol, which regularly went along the same roads, as the grand *armaș* Iordache Mavrodin[131] wrote in his report to the princely administration:

> Now on the day of Easter, here in Tecuci, in a village, namely Ţigănești, a tragedy has taken place, for the peasants being drunk, a Turk came, namely Ahmet Pirpiriu, who also in previous years had frequently passed by those villages around Ţigănești, guarding the vineyards and the melons.

Both parties were drunk, the document tells us. The meeting on a day of such importance for Orthodox Christians was sufficient to trigger the dispute (*pricina*). The peasants jumped on Ahmet and disarmed him: 'They took his musket from his hand and his pistols and beat him'. Ahmet fled in terror, as did his three comrades. The conflict seemed to be over: the peasants returned to their

129 *Documente Iaşi*, V, 323–324.

130 Carlo Ginzburg and Carlo Poni, 'La micro-histoire', *Le débat*, n° 17, 1981, 133–136.

131 Iordache Mavrodi(n) arrived in Moldavia together with Ianachi Mavrocordat (1743–1747), and then served the latter's brother, Constantin Mavrocordat. See *Cronica Ghiculeştilor*, 585. In 1755, Iordache Mavrodi(n) is later recorded as grand *paharnic*. *Documente Iaşi*, V, 613–614, 12 October 1755.

drinking and the frightened Turks withdrew. However, Ahmet had the misfortune to bump into an old woman, with tragic consequences:

> The Turk escaping from the hands of the peasants took flight, and in his flight he knocked into an old woman, and the old woman fell down and started to scream, and the peasants thinking that he was beating the old woman, some of the peasants rose and pursued the Turk. And when they pursued him to the banks of the Bârlad, the Turk jumped into the Bârlad for fear and was drowned.

His three comrades (the word used is *ioldaș*, from the Turkish *yoldaș*) looked for him and found his body in the waters of the River Bârlad. This was the starting point of a series of petty negotiations and complicities in the attempt to reach a solution that would avoid any repercussions. The grand *armaș* seems very scared: 'I took all possible steps to assuage the dispute' ('*m-am sălit în tot chipul pentru a potoli pricina*'), he writes. First, he bought the silence of Ahmet's three Turkish comrades: 'And I settled with the Turks for them not to say that he drowned because of the peasants, but to say that he drowned being drunk'. Then he asked them to put down on paper a credible *story* that would throw all responsibility onto the dead man. The testimony is written by Ismail aga of Brăila and goes as follows:

> I have given this letter of mine into the hands of the villagers of Ţigănești so that it may be known that I, Ismail, having a comrade, namely: Ahmet from Ruse, bachelor. That he getting drunk at a tavern, he proceeded towards his lodgings, in the village of Săsăștii, and wanting to cross the Bârlad by a footbridge he fell from the footbridge into the Bârlad and drowned. And I hearing from a man that he had seen him falling into the Bârlad and he had drowned, I asked the villagers of Ţigănești to jump, to search for him in the water, to get him out. And many people jumped and got him out of the water, and they buried him on the banks of the Bârlad.

This distortion of the truth was apparently not sufficient to avoid an imperial enquiry, which appears to have brought to light the local complicities of Muslim and non-Muslim subjects. Ismail aga diminishes the subject Ahmet as much as he can: 'I testify upon my soul that that comrade of mine [...] was completely poor, not a penny did he have, being a drunkard'. Ismail was backed up by his Turkish comrades, Ahmet, son of Boșnici of Brăila, Abdula[h] of Fiștok, Mustafa hagi beșleaga of Tecuci, and Ismail of Galați. The testimony is accompanied by five signatures, two of them simply handwritten and followed by signet seals in smoke, while the other three are confirmed with finger prints.[132]

132 BAR, Fond Documente Istorice, CCLXXX/79, 15 April 1745.

The villagers of Ţigăneşti had to pay no less than 100 lei to obtain the testimony that absolved them of guilt. So said the grand *armaş*, sending the document to the prince of Moldavia, Ioan Mavrocordat, and asking him to obtain for them an *ilam* from the kadı of Brăila.[133] Three weeks later, the kadı of Brăila, Molla Mehmed, issued the *hoget* (Tk. *hüccet*) requested by the *pârcălab* (governor) of Tecuci, Iordache Mavrodin, in which he reiterates the story of poor Ahmet the Turk, drowned in the waters of the Bârlad. The tale has acquired new details, however, both in the outlining of the character and in the shaping of the fiction. According to the *hoget*, Ahmed was a merchant from Ruse, who was in the region of Bârlad for purposes of trade, and fell 'by chance' into the river, which was bursting its banks due to heavy rain. His body, pulled onto the banks, was examined by his three comrades, who reported that: 'he had no marks of any kind of a wound on his body and that he had simply drowned.'[134] The *hoget* also provides elements for the identification of the Muslims who are listed differently in the document issued in Moldavia. The witnesses are: Abdullah beşe bin Mehmed, of Shumen; Ahmet aga bin Ali, of Brăila; Ismail beşe, of Ruse; Halil beşa bin Ibrahim; and Matarcı-zade Osman aga.[135]

The rearrangement of the story reminds me of Natalie Zemon Davis's excellent study of *Fiction in the Archives* and the protagonists of the tales that she analyses.[136] Most likely, the kadı of Brăila received a substantial gift together with the documents and the request to issue an *ilam*. The three texts use the same information, but shape it differently, providing or omitting details and changing the order of events according to the recipient.[137] Ismail aga of Brăila shows an astonishing capacity for transforming the narration into a 'credible fiction' by manipulating language, reinterpreting facts, and reordering action. Of course, I am starting from the hypothesis that Ismail was the author of the testimony, and thus that he knew the Moldavian language and Cyrillic script. Even the kadı participates in the rewriting of the narration, enhancing the credibility of the fiction with a detail that is not to be found in the other accounts: the Bârlad overflowing. April is indeed a month characterized by heavy rain, which might indeed have resulted in the river bursting its banks.

*

133 BAR, Fond Documente Istorice, CCLXXX/80, 21 April 1745.

134 *Documente turceşti*, I, 252–253, 12 May 1745.

135 *Documente turceşti*, I, 252–253, 12 May 1745.

136 Natalie Zemon Davis, *Fiction in the Archives: Pardon Tales and Their Tellers in Sixteenth-Century France* (Stanford, CA: 1987).

137 Davis, *Fiction*, 3.

In this chapter, I have tried to sketch some portraits of foreigners interested in building a home and a career in southeastern Europe. These figures belong to the 'little people', with none of the family, social, and political interconnections that underpinned the careers constructed by the Phanariots, by the high office-holders, or by the *ayan*s of the Danube border. Writing about those who held power in the provincial areas of the Ottoman Empire, Ali Yaycioğlu shows the levers on which they relied in order to maintain their wealth and status and transmit them to the next generation. 'A large household community' depended on 'dozens, even hundreds of servants; household officers, [...] armed units, [...] clients or allied groups of the central household from lesser families in the locality or broader regional setting.'[138] Ștefan the Latin, Cernea Popovici, and Ahmet Murtaza occupied the position of clients in a wide transborder network of which they tried to take advantage. The positions they occupied did not offer them the visibility of their patrons or the strength to impose themselves. All the same, they moved within quite well outlined groups in which ethnicity, confession, or social status could be made or unmade depending on political circumstances and above all on the solidarities of common interests. Their mobility from one region to another played its part not only in the circulation of information and objects, but also in the mediation of a certain type of religious and social acceptance. However, cohabitation also implies multiple tensions, often generated by confessional differences. People adapted to times and institutions, skilfully using them for day-to-day survival. 'Protection' is one of the best examples that permits us to observe adaptability to the political and social changes of a period.

138 Yaycioğlu, *Provincial Power-Holders*, 441.

CHAPTER 6

Dimitrie Foti Merişescu and His Journey

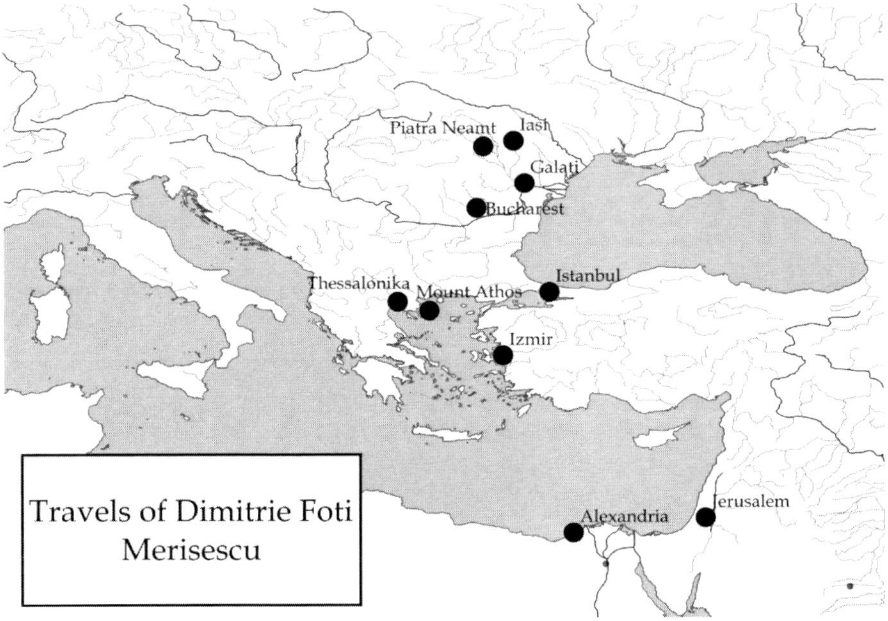

Map 3 Travels of Dimitrie Foti Merişescu cc. 1817–1820. Made by Michał Wasiucionek.

'One day, I sat after reading the tragedies of Orestes[1] and of Erotocritos[2] and I wondered. I resolved that I too should make a history of the things that had happened to me.' Pie-maker, shoemaker, and later cup-bearer (*paharnic*),[3] Dimitrie Foti Merişescu (Mirişescu), a young petty boyar born in 1797 in Colentina and brought up in the Biserica cu Sfinţi (Church with Saints) quarter of Bucharest, decided to write about the adventures of his life. His memoir, presented in thirty-six leaves of manuscript, written in Romanian in the

1 Voltaire's play *Oreste*, translated into Romanian by Alecu Beldiman under the title *Tragodia lui Orest*, published in Buda in 1820.

2 The poem *Erotocritos* by Vincenzo Cornaro had significant circulation and echoes in Romanian culture. See the most recent edition prepared by Eugenia Dima, *Poemul Erotocrit a lui Vincenzo Cornaro în cultura română. Versiunea lui Alecu Văcărescu* (Iaşi: 2014).

3 A minor official rank open to members of the boyar class.

transitional alphabet,[4] but with some dialogue in Greek and Bulgarian, is striking for its humour, its irony, and above all the unusual stories it contains.

On the last page of the manuscript, the author writes: '20 September 1817. Dimitrie Merişescu, 20 years of age. Dălhăuţi.' The inscription might lead us to assume that the text was composed around then, especially as the events narrated are close in time to 1817, but the handwriting points rather towards the middle of the nineteenth century, a period characterized by such literary products. Merişescu's manuscript is unusual, and may be a re-transcription of his initial notes, as in places the writing has been corrected with a chemical pencil or amended with interventions above the line.[5]

This chapter concentrates on the value of memoirs for knowledge and interpretation of identification, belonging, and allegiance. Dumitrache gives us a good example of how the literature of the time could impress someone so much that he sat down at his writing desk to recount his own day-to-day life. Orestes, Erotocritos, and perhaps also Telemachus helped him to put his everyday experiences into a literary form, encouraging him to give them meaning, to rewrite his past as a narrative, perhaps with the thought that his memoir would be read by someone. His narrative is no more than a backward look on a life spent in the vicinity of the 'great ones' of the time and ending somewhere on the margins of anonymity. Following the thread of the story, I have tried to supplement the picture with other documents of the period (private archives, images, other memoirs), focusing on the way in which Dimitrie (also referred to as Dumitrache and Tache in the journal and in the documents) Merişescu constructs an identity for himself, making use of clothes, consumption, education, and manners.

Two circumstances made possible the appearance of a journal like that of Dumitrache Merişescu: the enhanced valuing of education and the birth of a new literary genre. The enhanced valuing of education as a form of social advancement took place around the turn of the century, enabling a considerable number of petty boyars, merchants, and artisans to emerge from collective anonymity. The rise of the memoir, a literary genre that had been almost nonexistent in Wallachia and Moldavia before 1800, coincided with investment in

4 The transition from the Cyrillic to the Roman alphabet for Romanian involved a long period (1840–1860) when the letters of the two were mingled.

5 The manuscript is preserved in the Central National Historical Archives in Bucharest (Fond Manuscrise, no. 1773), and bears the title *Viaţa lui Dimitrie Foti Mirişescu de la Colentina, scrisă de el însuşi la 1817* (The life of Dimitrie Foti Mirişescu from Colentina, written by himself in 1817). For a critical edition see Dimitrie Foti Merişescu, *Tinereţile unui ciocoiaş. Viaţa lui Dimitrie Foti Merişescu de la Colentina scrisă de el însuşi la 1817*, ed. by Constanţa Vintilă-Ghiţulescu (Bucharest: 2019).

education and gave anonymous individuals the courage they needed to believe that their memories would be of use to someone, someday.[6]

Dumitrache Merişescu is a 'little man' who writes his memoir and leaves notes about his time. But, as I have pointed out, the first half of the nineteenth century saw the birth of a literary movement favourable to memoirs, and which encouraged Teodor Vârnav, Elena Hartulari, Ioan Solomon, and Scarlat Dăscălescu to write theirs.[7] All these authors belonged to the so-called 'middle class', in other words, the social category including merchants, petty boyars, and the holders of minor administrative positions.

It is his style that differentiates Dumitrache Merişescu from all the others, because he recounts his memories in a heroic manner, considering his deeds to be worthy of a veritable epic. His writing is nonetheless simple and direct, laced with verses and popular songs that were in circulation at the time.[8]

Such ego-documents appear here and there in the Ottoman and Balkan worlds. They constitute inestimable testimonies for the historical reconstruction of processes of identification and representation of a population caught between various regional origins and linguistic, political, and social borders.[9] Dumitrache Merişescu and his 'history' might be part of a wider trend flowing across the Ottoman world, linking him to figures such as Osman-Aga of Temeşvar,[10] Hanna Dyâb,[11] and Markos Antonios Katsaitis.[12] The trend continued through the nineteenth century, as literature flourished and others wrote about their lives and experiences.

---

6 Note in this connection the importance of memoirs in England and France and the enthusiasm generated around such writers as Menetra, Rétif de la Bretonne, and Samuel Pepys. For the Ottoman Empire, Dana Sajdi has brought the genre back into discussion with her recent book *The Barber of Damascus: Nouveau Literacy in the Eighteenth-Century Ottoman Levant* (Stanford, CA: 2013).

7 See Teodor Vârnav, *Istoria vieţii mele. Autobiografie din 1845* (Iaşi: 2016); Ioan Solomon, *Amintirile colonelului Ioan Solomon*, [first edition 1862] (Vălenii de Munte: 1910); Nicolae Iorga, 'Un cugetător politic moldovean de la jumătatea secolului al XIX-lea: Ştefan Scarlat Dăscălescu', *Analele Academiei Române, Memoriile Secţiei Istorice*, XIII/I (1932), 1–60.

8 For this type of writing in the Ottoman Empire and the relation between ordinary people beginning to write and the birth of a literary genre, see also Dana Sajdi, 'A Room of His Own: The 'History' of the Barber of Damascus (fl. 1762)', *MIT Electronic Journal of Middle East Studies, Crossing Boundaries: New Perspectives on the Middle East*, 3 (2003), 19–35.

9 See Fatma Müge Göçek, *East Encounters West: France and the Ottoman Empire in the Eighteenth Century* (New York:1987); Bekim Agai, Olcay Akyıldız, Caspar Hillebrand (eds.), *Venturing Beyond Borders—Reflections on Genre, Function and Boundaries in Middle Eastern Travel Writing* (Würzburg: 2013).

10 See Frédérick Hitzel, *Prisonnier des infidèles. Un soldat ottoman dans l'Empire des Habsbourg* (Arles: Sindbad-Actes Sud, 1998).

11 See Hanna Dyâb, *D'Alep à Paris. Les pérégrinations d'un jeune Syrien au temps de Louis XIV*, translated by Paule Fahmé, Bernard Heyberger, Jérôme Lentin (Arles: 2015).

12 See Katsaitis, 'Călătorie', 391–494.

Education

The young Dumitrache was educated at the church school of the Biserica cu Sfinţi quarter in Bucharest, where he lived and learned from others. This education reflects a world of linguistic diversity: Dumitrache speaks and understands Romanian, Greek, Bulgarian, and Turkish. His memoir is written in a vernacular Romanian, which would appear to be a kind of 'Balkan' or 'Phanariot' variant, into which are mixed words and expressions borrowed mostly just as he heard them. Even though he could speak Greek, the Greek dialogues in his memoirs are transliterated using the same Romanian transitional alphabet; he rarely writes using Greek script. He may also have been a pupil at the Princely Academy of Saint Sava in Bucharest. A boy named Merişanu is listed in 1812 among the pupils there. His classmates would have included a string of Greeks and Bulgarians who had come to receive an education in the Greek language in Bucharest.[13] Having attended the Academy might be an explanation both for his linguistic knowledge and for his reading.[14] On the other hand, given his tendency to boast, would Dumitrache Merişescu not have taken care to make at least a passing mention of his time at this prestigious institution?

Erotocritos and Orestes are two prominent characters in the Romanian popular literature of the end of the eighteenth and the beginning of the nineteenth centuries, influencing local behaviours and tastes, as well as inspiring poets and minstrels. It was also possible to read of Telemachus and his educational journeys: Fénelon circulated in manuscript, translated and copied countless times in various miscellanies.[15] And Dimitrie Merişescu underlines the role played by his reading in leading him to write down on paper adventures

13 Paschalis M. Kitromilides, *The Enlightenment as Social Criticism: Iosipos Moisiodax and Greek Culture in the Eighteenth Century* (Princeton, NJ: 1992).

14 Camariano-Cioran, *Academiile Domneşti*, 281. The Merişanu recorded in 1812 at the Princely Academy in Bucharest could be our Dumitrache, who is able to speak Greek and some Bulgarian. However he could also be another member of one of the two families—Merişescu and Merişanu—, which were relatively numerous at the time.

15 BAR, Fond Manuscrise, MS 342, which contains *Întâmplările lui Telemah, fiul lui Odisefsu* (The adventures of Telemachus, son of Odysseus). Constandin Stănescu writes that he began his transcription of the journeys of Telemachus on 20 June 1772 and finished on 2 August 1772, 'at the urging of and with all expenses paid by' the grand *paharnic* Iordache Darie, at the time *ispravnic* of the land of Neamţ. Another note shows the changing ownership of this miscellany, which on 15 October 1778 came into the possession of protopresbyter Enache of Târgul Ocna and his son Ioniţă (BAR, Fond Manuscrise, MS 343, f. 2v and f. 106.v). Similar notes can be found on other manuscripts of the tales of Telemachus, offering information about the forms of reading in Romanian society before the spread of printing. For the importance of such annotations in studying the self, see Konrad Petrovszky, 'Marginal Notes in South Slavic Written Culture. Between Practising Memory and Accounting for the Self', *Cahiers du monde russe*, 58 (2017), 483–502. The first printed

that he considers equally (or almost equally) spectacular and worthy of being remembered. But this reading came later, when he had already returned from his travels and had made his home in Moldavia, trying to find a purpose in his own life.

Who is Dimitrie Merişescu

The life and career of this Dimitrie Foti Merişescu may be reconstructed with difficulty, after extensive research in the archives of Wallachia and Moldavia. Some details are divulged in his 'history': 'I was born in the year 1797, baptized by Ioan Hagi Moscu.[16] My father traded in cattle. In the autumn, he slaughtered them at the shambles in Colentina. He was known as *Cupar*[17] Foti Merişescu.' We also learn that he had an uncle, *Paharnic* Manolache; several brothers, Anastasie, Ioan, and Niţu; several sisters, one of whom was called Păuna; and a series of other uncles, aunts, and cousins of both sexes. In the autumn of 1814, when he starts his story, his mother had died and his father had remarried and was on his estate of Dălhăuţa, near Focşani, where he owned a vineyard. Manolache the *paharnic* and *epistat* (superintendent) of meat supplies for the city of Bucharest[18] seems to have been a man of some wealth, as, according to the manuscript, he had 'a threshing mill with hammers in his garden with the wheel turned by the water of the Dâmboviţa.' Working in the cattle trade, the family of Foti Merişescu were in close clientelary and commercial relations with Ioan Hagi-Moscu. This connection leads me to think that Foti and Manolache had come from south of the Danube, from somewhere in the region of Epirus. They had probably arrived sometime in the 1780s, when Ioan Hagi-Moscu first appears in the records in connection with trading deals. They seem to have become acclimatized very quickly, marrying and integrating in the local petty boyar class by buying the boyar titles of *cupar* and *paharnic*. Who is Dumitrache Merişescu? The answer would tell us about an entire category marked by high social mobility and a capacity to adapt according to the changing context. All I can say for now is that our hero, born in Bucharest of Epirot parents, bears the identity of his religious confession: Orthodox Christian.

translation into Romanian (from Italian) of the *Adventures of Telemachus* appeared in 1818, through the efforts of Petru Maior in Buda.

16 In other words, Ioan Hagi Moscu was his godfather.

17 Assistant to a *paharnic*. *Cupar* and *paharnic* were two lesser boyar ranks of little importance. Entry into the boyar class brought with it privileges, including access to official posts in the administrative apparatus and exemption from certain taxes.

18 Urechia, *Istoria romanilor*, XI, 259, 350, 396.

The Context of the Narrative

In the first three decades of the nineteenth century, Moldavia and Wallachia experienced two major occupations that were of great importance for their history, contributing to the dissolution of the old political system and the promotion by a new generation of a new institutional structure. The simple people, the populace, the mob were far from the effervescence of political ideas, but rather experienced the occupations with emotion and with collective fears. Here is how Tache Merişescu describes the entry of the Russian army in 1806, as he recalls it, having been around ten years old at the time:

> In the autumn of 1806, the Muscovites came. There were also Turks in Bucharest, at Radu Vodă [monastery] in the tower were Arnauts and Oltenians[19] (why I do not know). There was great fear in Bucharest, for the Turks were with the Turkish pasha of Giurgiu. I remember that women with yokes frightened the Turks. They said they fled without saddles and without harness, but we children and the bigger ones among us, we went out by the Street of the Outside Market, just where the Moşilor Market is held. The Muscovites came by the Colentina road. They were in a long line, and it seemed to us that the end would reach as far as Pantelimon. There were Cossacks with long lances, there were dragoons. It seemed to us that they had two heads, they had swords in their broad hands, and on the ground there was a great stream in green coats, up to the horses' heads. And they fired the guns one by one as the line went on to Pantelimon, but something more beautiful had never been heard before … and they beat their drums, the Cossacks sang, the dragoons with trumpets and the chasseurs, slowly, the whole line. Perhaps the whole of Bucharest had come out into the fields, to watch. It was almost night when they entered the city. We boys all went along to the music of the dragoons because they came into Bucharest. We heard the officers: '*na prava, na leva, cistka.*'[20]

The people of Bucharest were impressed by the great parade put on by the Russian army, which was to linger on Wallachian and Moldavian territory for over six years, imposing rules, values, and ways of thinking, often by force. Only the French threat, with Napoleon's advance towards Moscow, forced the Russians to make peace with the Ottoman Empire and to leave Moldavia and Wallachia in great haste, as Dumitrache Merişescu writes:

---

19 Arnauts, originally Albanian mercenaries, formed the princely guard. The Oltenians referred to here are *panduri*, mercenaries recruited from among the population of Oltenia.

20 More correctly: *Na pravo. Na levo. Za chest'!* (Left, right! For honour!).

> In 1812, I watched the *beyzade*[21] Dumitrache Moruzu playing *cirid*[22] with the Turks called *mürahas*, and Generals Kameski and Sovorofu who drowned at Râmnicu-Sărat … The Russians were returning to go into battle against the French. The women went with them as far as Colentina. Some women were hiding under the bridge. We boys yelled and called to them: 'To Colentina, Plumbuita, to the soldiers.'[23]

And so the high Turkish, Greek, and Russian officials spent their time playing *cirid* on the waste ground, waiting for Napoleon. And when he came closer, their differences became easier to resolve. The wars in Europe, and especially the fronts opened up by Napoleon, were of interest to everyone. If the deacon Ioan Dobrescu in the Batiştei district of Bucharest could afford to curse the French emperor under his breath, categorizing him as 'the bad part' (a play on '*bon part*', 'Bonaparte'),[24] politicians paid good money for any sort of intelligence that would offer them more or less accurate information about the progress of events. For example, in 1812, *The bulletins of the French army regarding the conduct of military operations on the Russian front*, printed in Wilna (Vilnius), a city which by the date of the seventh bulletin (16 July 1812) was in the possession of the French army, arrived in Bucharest.[25]

When Tsar Alexander I and Sultan Mahmud II arrived at a peace agreement, the president of the Divans Vasilii I. Krasno-Milashevich[26] asked the metropolitans to have bells rung, to summon Christians to church, and to offer prayers of thanks for the end of the war.[27] The same day, 10 July 1812, coincidentally or not, a certain Bishop Gherasim wrote to a priest in Bolintin, near Bucharest, to hold a service of blessing in his church, which had been 'polluted by the pagans'.[28] After six years of Russian occupation, the army that had been received with fear, but also with some hope of salvation from the hands of the 'pagan' Turks, was now itself seen as belonging on the side of those without any law. It may be added that all those mentioned by Dumitrache Merişescu in

21 Beyzade, from Turkish, son of a prince.

22 A Turkish game, played on horseback and involving throwing and catching a stick like a lance.

23 The Russian soldiers were billeted in the Plumbuita Monastery, in Colentina.

24 Ilie Corfus, ed. 'Cronica meşteşugarului Ioan Dobrescu (1802–1830)', *Studii si articole de istorie*, VIII (1966), 341.

25 BAR, Fond Documente Istorice, DCII/172, 173, 175, 176, 177.

26 Moldavia and Wallachia were headed by a president of the two Divans, directly appointed by the Tsar.

27 BAR, Fond Documente Istorice, MCCXLII/262, 10 July 1812.

28 BAR, Fond Documente Istorice, CMXXII/22.

the passage cited above died tragically in the turmoil of the wars: the Russian general Arkadi Suvorov drowned in April 1811, during the crossing of the River Râmnicul Sărat, and his fellow general Nikolai Mikhailovich Kamensky succumbed to fever, also in April 1811, in Odessa, while the *beyzade* Dimitrie Moruzi, grand dragoman and negotiator of the Peace of Bucharest, was hanged at Schumla (Shumen) by Ahmed Pasha's janissaries, on the orders of the sultan, for his lack of diplomatic ability in the peace negotiations.[29]

In the Shadow of Ioan Hagi Moscu

Dumitrache Merişescu is no more than a minor character in a world of major figures dominating commercial, political, and diplomatic relations. From this position in the background, like a veritable puppet-master, Dumitrache brings into his narrative important personalities of his time: Ioan Hagi Moscu, Grigore Brâncoveanu, Grigore Băleanu, Ioan Caragea, Costa Foru, Dimitrie Moruzi, Alexandru Suţu, Manouk Bey,[30] and Iancu Jianu all made their mark on the period.[31] His life proceeds in the shadows of history, changing direction according to the destinies of the great. As has already been mentioned, his father was a 'Greek' or a Vlach from the Balkan peninsula, who, together with his two brothers, came to Bucharest in the wake of the merchant Ioan Hagi Moscu, originally from Salonica.[32] In fact, the careers and wealth of the Foti Merişescu brothers flourished (or withered) under the protection of this merchant, who became a high office-holder and later a significant figure in Balkan and southeast European diplomacy.

29 Dimitrie Moruzi was the son of Constantin Moruzi, Prince of Moldavia (1777–1782), and brother of Alexandru Moruzi, Prince of Moldavia (1792–1793, 1802–1806, 1806–1807) and of Wallachia (1793–1796, 1799–1801). On his activity see Marinescu, *Etude généalogique sur la famille Moruzi*, 62–69. The episode is also narrated by the Greek historian Dionisie Fotino, *Istoria Generală a Daciei*, 225. Hurmuzaki, *Documente*, I_2, 738, the report of Antoine-François Andréossy to the duke of Bassano, 25 December 1812, Constantinople, including news of Moruzi's death and the confiscation of his wealth: 'lorsque le Grand Visir donna l'ordre de sa mort, il dit: 'Allez couper la tête à ce traître qui était vendu à la Russie'.

30 Manouk Bey was a very active and rich Armenian merchant. He built the Manouk Inn in Bucharest, still standing, where the peace accord was signed on 16/28 May 1812. See Ştefania Costache, 'From Ruscuk to Bessarabia: Manuk Bey and the Career of an Ottoman-Russian Middleman at the Beginning of the 19th Century', *Cihannüma*, III/1 (2017), 23–43.

31 Iancu Jianu was a famous brigand (*haiduc*) and boyar from the region of Oltenia.

32 Limona, *Negustorii 'greci'*, 308.

Fig. 6
Anonymous – Grand *ban* Grigore Brâncoveanu (1764–1832), 1830–1832, National Museum of Art, Bucharest.

Right from the beginning, Dumitrache Merişescu makes it clear that he was baptized by Ioan Hagi Moscu, while a few pages later he adds the equally precious information that Anastasie, another brother, 'stayed with his godfather and relation Hagi Moscu, also in Bucharest.' It was in the autumn of 1814. At that date, Ioan Hagi Moscu was a notable personality in the political life of Wallachia, being in the entourage of Prince Ioan Caragea and temporarily occupying the office of grand *vistier*.[33]

Ioan Hagi Moscu was an important supplier of information to the Habsburg Empire, and also of hay to the Austrian army. For this reason he was twice involved in litigation on financial and diplomatic matters with the court in Vienna.[34] In the Austrian reports, Ioan Hagi Moscu, agent and banker in Vienna for Prince Nicolae Mavrogheni (1786–1790), is portrayed in dark colours

33 On 3 July 1813, Ioan Hagi Moscu was appointed grand *vistier* and *epistat* of the Epitropy of Announcements. Two months later, he was 'ex' grand *vistier*, but *nazir* of the Office of Streets, in other words, he occupied an equally important position from a financial point of view. In November 1813, he obtained the post of 'grand *vornic* of the city', and in June 1814, he was again *epistat*, this time of the salt mines. (See Urechia, *Istoria românilor*, X/1, 231, 541, 833, 1040).

34 See Limona, *Negustorii 'greci'*, 311–331.

as a '*parfait canaille*', driven only by '*point d'argent*'.[35] On 23 December 1810, the French Consul in Bucharest, Ledoux, writes: 'Hagi Moscu, un des principaux boyards de la Valachie, le plus éclairé et le plus considéré [...] est très-dévoué à la France'.[36] Count Louis Alexandre Andrault de Langeron, general of the Russian army of occupation, confirmed the habit of the merchant Hagi Moscu of selling information both to France and to the Ottoman Empire, after he managed to intercept Ledoux's letters. 'I had long considered him a traitor,' writes Langeron, expressing his desire to arrest him and interrogate him 'severely' to find out not only 'the secret of his understanding with the Turks and with the French,' but also the name of the person who was informing him regarding the Russian army. According to Langeron, General Kutuzov, the commander of the Russian army, had not had the courage to take such a measure, 'for fear of somehow offending Napoleon,' and when General Kamenski dared to arrest him, 'he found nothing,' and had to apologize.[37]

Two levels of clientelary relations may be traced here, and their value may be measured in terms of the 'gifts' that passed among the members of each group.[38] What Ioan Hagi Moscu offered was important, costly, inestimable, but not at all visible: information. Navigating with ease through empires, thanks to his commercial activity, proficient in the languages of the nations, Ioan Hagi Moscu sold, together with fashion and luxury, the latest news from the empire of Vienna or from the Ottoman seas. I have insisted on this figure because he helps us to understand the expeditions and wanderings of his godson and protégé Dumitrache Merişescu through the world of the well-born. A first characteristic of this group is the solidarity that is manifested in material and clientelary support. Even if he does not say so explicitly in his memoirs, Dumitrache often talks of interventions in his favour by those who have the same 'mobile identity': Epirots, Greeks, Serbs, Orthodox Christians, always on the move.

---

35 Blancard, *Les Mavroyéni*, 768.

36 Urechia, *Istoria românilor*, X/1, 5.

37 *Călători străini despre țările române în secolul al XIX-lea*, vol. I, 349.

38 For example, a curious transaction in 1815 proves the value of the services offered in the context of these clientelary relationships. On 17 February 1815, Ioan Hagi Moscu sold to Princess Ralu Caragea the estate of Conţeşti in Dâmboviţa county, with a stone boyar house, a walled courtyard, a barn, a wooden church, a mill, and alehouses, for the sum of 115,000 thalers. A few months later, on 1 August 1815, Princess Ralu Caragea sold the same estate of Conţeşti in Dâmboviţa county back to him, but for 162,500 groschen (ANIC, Fond Documente Munteneşti, CLIII/ 14, 15, 16, 17).

Journeys Through the Deeper Reaches of a Country

We know little today about the deeper reaches of the world of the past, about the journeys and shared destinies that are lost in the broader history of a country. Dumitrache Merişescu raises the curtain and allows us to penetrate what we may call the banality and promiscuity of daily life. He proves to be an 'outsider' discovering with curiosity the world that he meets. His memoirs are constructed as a travel journal,[39] penetrating through various temporal and social layers, through diverse worlds linked by confessional solidarity and clientelary networks.

Dumitrache's journeys all start from an apparently convivial meeting that ends badly one autumn day in the open air at Filaret in Bucharest: 'One autumn day, we made a decision together. We bought a loaf from Babicu and roast meat from Furnu, and autumn garlic. We went over to Filaret, and we were eating, and drinking must.' The bitter grape must goes quickly to the heads of the seventeen-year-olds, who start fighting. After hitting one of his friends on the head with a brick and seeing the blood flowing, Dumitrache takes fright and flees into the unknown, throwing himself, in fact, into an adventure. Heads hanging in a noose, hands, noses, and ears cut off, corpses left in full view: these are the images that pursue him, that feed his fears and hasten his steps:

> No one chased me, but it seemed to me that they would catch me and take me to Prince Caragea and put me on the stake, because often on Saturdays they put thieves on the stake. I watched and I took fright; on Saturdays, too, in the prison, they cut off the hands of some of the guilty people with a cleaver, they cut off the noses and ears of others; with their hands tied behind them, they could only shake their heads.

Such images imprint themselves in the mind of the traveller, and settle in the memory of an adolescent, setting out on the journey of life. In the same period, Teodor Vârnav, on his arrival in Bucharest, reports: 'The first thing that filled me with amazement when I arrived on the edge of Bucharest was this: two people impaled alive on stakes, and likewise another hanged by the neck.'[40] This eye-witness report is from May 1813, when the young Teodor Vârnav arrived in Bucharest as a child of twelve to be entrusted for his education to the merchant Constandin Lada. Internal documents confirm the intransigence of the

39 On the definition of this literary genre, see Alex Drace-Francis, 'Towards a Natural History of East European Travel Writing', in Wendy Bracewell and Alex Drace-Francis (ed.), *Under Eastern eyes. A Comparative Introduction to East European Travel Writing on Europe* (Budapest: 2008), 1–26.

40 Vârnav, *Istoria*, 34.

system of justice set in motion by the administrative ability of the Phanariot prince Ioan Caragea, and all the more severe in the circumstances of a plague epidemic.

Fig. 7
Pavel Đjurković (1772–1830) – Portrait of Caragea Vodă (Wallachia, 1812–1818), [1824], National Museum of Art, Bucharest.

By jumping over fences and bypassing the alleys of the city, Tache arrives in the fields, beside the Bulgarian carts that were then gradually departing after feeding the people of Bucharest with their vegetables. Slowly but surely we enter another reality that is relatively little documented: that of the Bulgarian vegetable traders brought by the Russians during the occupation of 1806–1812. While some of them made their base in Cioplea-Dudeşti, others were scattered among the villages around the capital, with the intention of supplying the city with fresh vegetables.[41] Later, Prince Ioan Caragea renewed their privileges, encouraging them to settle, to build homes, to send their children to school, to learn Romanian, to build churches. It was the children of these Bulgarians that were among Tache's classmates at school. From them he received turnips and learned Bulgarian: 'The boys of the Bulgarians were at school. They gave us turnips when they came to school. We asked: "What do you call such and such?" And they told us all [the words], and we showed them the slate because they were wooden-headed.'

41 For the Russian policy of colonization in this period, see Andrew Robarts, 'Imperial confrontation or regional cooperation?: Bulgarian migration and Ottoman-Russian relations in the Black Sea region, 1768–1830s', *Turkish Historical Review*, 3/2 (2012), 149–167.

After all sorts of wanderings among the 'ugly' villages of the south, 'without gardens or trees,' as he writes, he manages to slip into the porch of a Bulgarian house in Olteniţa. His first encounter, his first Platonic love, his first insertion into the Bulgarian minority introduces us into the routine of everyday life. It is an opportunity for the author to delve into introspection and above all to explore a definition of the 'self'. It is the first time that these adolescent analyses who he is in relation to those he meets and how he relates to them. The 'Bulgarians', and notably the women of the community, enable to him to narrate his own identity.

The son of a small merchant turned boyar, Tache speaks from the perspective of a 'petty *logofăt*',[42] thus superior from a social point of view, but also from the perspective of the 'outsider' in a different hierarchical position from the Bulgarian vegetable sellers, simple people who eat millet polenta with their fingers (and whom, on top of that, he considers to be 'wooden-headed'). Such a socially constructed distance is accentuated by the veneer of education that our protagonist has received. Everything differentiates him from those around him. In the first place, he is distinguished by his clothing. Costume is central to the affirmation of one's identity, for the maintenance of social pride and the statement of social distinctions, obvious to a hierarchal society. Tache Merişescu asserts his pre-eminence with the help of his clothes on every possible occasion. And such occasions are numerous in the course of his travels. Describing the wonder and curiosity of the Bulgarian women who surround him one early October morning, in the village of Olteniţa, he writes:

> They all kept looking at me to see what I was. I was dressed in a cotton *anteri*[43] with a felt sash, I was wearing a red *çaksır*,[44] my tall boots were from Tsarigrad, yellow, I had a fez and a cap like a Cossack one and I always wore my *fermene*.[45] It also had a little bit of wire embroidery on it, and I tied a white neckerchief around my neck.

Next, he stands out through a control of the body, which shows the acquisition of norms for eating at table, integrating the use of the knife and the fork, something quite unknown to peasants, and even to market traders and petty boyars:

> Păunica prepared polenta. It was made from millet. She turned it out on the table and cut it in pieces. She also poured the milk that was in the cream dishes. She put cows' cheese too. She said to me: 'Eat up, dearie.' I answered that I had

42 The term denotes a clerk in a chancellery, but was also a minor boyar title.

43 Long, sleeved robe.

44 Wide trousers.

45 Short jacket worn over the *anteri*.

> eaten the bread [*azima*] from the string. I tried the polenta and I could hear it. I wanted to eat, but it really made a grinding noise between my teeth. She put it in milk. She said it was good that way. I tasted it with a wooden spoon, but it stuck to my mouth, as I wasn't used either to millet polenta or to a wooden spoon. At home and in everyone's home there were tin spoons and plates also of tin, ladles and large and small bowls, also of tin. At Easter and Christmas they brought out silver onto the table. There were also porcelain plates, but they weren't used about the house.

The extract highlights two different worlds: the young petty boyar from the urban world of Bucharest, dressed cleanly and according to the boyar fashion, with carefully studied manners and for whom millet polenta smells of poverty, of provincialism, of vulgarity (in the older sense of pertaining to the masses, to the common people).[46]

These two elements, clothes and good manners, characteristic of a certain social stratum, recur in the narrative and are amplified when the author comes into the presence of people who are his superiors from a social point of view.

Journeys Into the Feminine Universe and the Mysteries of Love

His stay in the village of Olteniţa, with its largely Bulgarian population, is his first initiation into the feminine universe and the mysteries of love.[47] Dumitrache Merişescu, the seventeen-year-old adolescent, penetrates the world of flirtation through the intermediary of play: blind-man's-buff and the *corăbiască* (a slow dance in which the dancers join hands in a circle). These games are his first initiation into the mysteries of love. Although he claims, as does Eufrosin Poteca in his memoirs,[48] to have had experience with girls through his sisters

46 A series of rules of good behaviour circulated in the period, addressed principally to the middle category in society, as Anton Pann argues, probably influenced by Dimitrie Ţichindeal or Dositej Obradović. Until discovering this journal, I had not found any information about their impact on society. We know only that *Şcoala Moralului* (The school of morals), reworked by Anton Pann, went through numerous editions, the first being printed in 1830. (See Vintilă-Ghiţulescu, *Patimă şi desfătare*, 123–170.) It remains likely that the rules of good behaviour in the booklets reworked by Dimitrie Ţichindeal after Dositej Obradović were read and assimilated. For Dositej Obradović, see Wladimir Fischer, *Dositej Obradović and the Ambivalence of Enlightement*, in Harald Heppener and Eva Posch (eds.). *Encounters in Europe's Southeast. The Habsburg Empire and the Orthodox World in the Eighteenth and Nineteenth Centuries* (Bochum: 2012), 217–230.

47 Similar episodes occur in the memoirs of Osman-Aga of Temesvar. See, Hitzel, *Prisonnier des infidèles*, 81–82.

48 Eufrosin Poteca was a monk who studied in Paris and Pisa in the years 1826–1828. For a time he taught philosophy at the Princely Academy in Bucharest, before ending up as

and cousins, embraces, caresses, risqué talk, and sexual allusions scare him, excite him, and arouse him, so that 'Platonic love' turns to 'fire'. This 'Platonic love', as he characterizes it, contains a considerable dose of fear, due to loss in translation and in the assimilation and processing of information. The girls speak to each other in Bulgarian, and when one of them, 'a plump[49] girl', comes out with: 'We'll have to work on this lad before he understands us,'[50] the young man finds all his senses reactivated: 'I fell silent for fear after what the Bulgarian girl had said.' Without giving away the fact that he understands Bulgarian, Dumitrache joins in the game, while the girls make risqué jokes at his expense—'Hey, where did you find him, sister? Give him to me!' They ask him for money, stare constantly at him, tear him to pieces with their words and threaten him—'Guard the lad, girls, because our Bulgarian men have a devilish temper.' The 'fire' turns into a terrifying blaze when the girls start to sing: 'Hurry, Iană, to the clearing / Let's dig up a plant / The poppy plant / To give it to the man / For him to go to the devil.'

Over and above these scenes of passing flirtation, Dumitrache describes the bucolic love he experiences at the side of the peasant woman Păuna among the haystacks and grapes of autumn, with nowhere to go.

Love in a Time of Plague

The events of Dumitrache Merişescu's narrative take place in the years of the terrible plague, whose arrival coincided with that of the Phanariot prince Ioan Caragea. While another contemporary observer, Ioan Dobrescu, described the ravages of the plague that descended over Wallachia, and especially over Bucharest, as a punishment for the sinful Christians who had come to be 'worse than the pagans', taking delight in Voltaire and the French language,[51] Tache described it from the perspective of a wandering adolescent:

> I left the village [of Olteniţa], but not by the road, because there was a guard because of the plague. There was smoke and rubbish around the houses. If by chance someone lost something on the road, no one would take it, and there weren't even thieves. On the one hand fear of falling ill, and on the other the severity of Prince Caragea: the stake, the gallows, cutting off of hands, cutting

archimandrite of the Motru monastery. His memoirs are constructed around his condition as a monk who often finds it impossible to overcome his passions. See Eufrosin Poteca, *Scrieri filosofice*, ed. Adrian Michiduţă (Craiova: 2008), 106.

49 The Romanian word (*dolfană*) also has connotations of prosperity.

50 In Dumitrache Merişescu's rendering of the Bulgarian: 'Ima malcu da rabota a da icdim.'

51 'Cronica meşteşugarului Ioan Dobrescu', 341.

> off of nose and ears, nailing of ears, even for petty boyars. I saw even the *sameş*[52] of Craiova displayed at the gate of the courtyard. They had dressed him in boyar clothes [but] he was only in his indoor slippers and condemned for fraud.[53]

The fear was recurrent and any 'sign' turned into a hysteria, which moreover was fed by the images encountered in the visible zones of the community. Another episode shows us how fragile was the stability of this world and what terror could be induced by any kind of epidemic:

> On Friday morning the overseer left me in the house. There was a bottle of raki, there was salmon and roe. He ate and said that he hadn't got ill. I took the bottle, I drank the raki. I ate the roe too; as I was unaccustomed, I got dizzy. I started to vomit. The Gypsy went upstairs and said that I was stricken. There was a great uproar. They heard that I was at home and that perhaps I had taken ill. There was fear in the whole courtyard. The boyar, in the end, prepared his horses and went to the court. He was the *vistiernic*.[54] He ordered the gates to be kept shut and a Gypsy at the gate. The overseer did not enter the house.

The episode takes place in the house of the great boyar Grigore Băleanu, where Dumitrache Merişescu, godson, client, and protégé of the grand *vistier* Ioan Hagi Moscu, had become a houseboy, responsible for the cage of canaries. The unruly servant helps himself to the bottle of raki, to the roe and salmon, while the household overseer is not around; 'unaccustomed', as he puts it by way of excuse, he vomits, and scares everyone around him. The alarm is given, the gates of the mansion are locked, the 'stricken' person is isolated, the servants and the ladies of the house wait, petrified, on the lookout 'like mice' to see if it is time to flee. Only Dumitrache, once recovered, resumes his walk along the veranda 'to see what had happened.'

---

52 Tax collector.

53 A reversal of the usual custom: condemned boyars normally had first to be deprived of their rank and dressed in humble peasant clothes before the sentence was carried out. Vodă Caragea lets the condemned man's rank remain visible, thus reinforcing the message that even a boyar is subject to punishment if he commits a crime.

54 Dumitrache Merişescu misidentified Grigore Băleanu's office: he was actually grand *vornic* (justice minister), not *vistiernic* (treasurer). Christine Philliou describes him as a boyar of Armenian origin (Philliou, *Biography of an Empire*, 17). In fact, the Băleanu family took its name from the village of Băleni in Dâmboviţa county, the principle residence of the lineage. In the seventeenth century, when family names became stabilized, the boyars of Băleni turned their place of residence into a name, as in the cases of other boyar families. For example, the Brâncoveanu family, who are also mentioned in this study, took their name from the village of Brâncoveni in Olt county. For details on the Băleanu family see Ştefan Andreescu, 'Familia boierilor Băleni', in Mihai Dimitrie Sturdza, *Familiile boiereşti din Moldova şi Ţara Românească. Enciclopedie istorică, genealogică şi biografică* (Bucharest: 2004), I, 224–230.

Fig. 8
Votive portrait of Grand *ban* Grigore Băleanu (+ 1842), Church of St. John the Baptist, Băleni village, Dâmboviţa county. Photograph by Marius Păduraru.

The Băleanus were one of the most important boyar families of the period. Grigore Băleanu held the office of grand *vornic*, and was constantly in the company of Prince Caragea.[55] Madame Băleanu[56] spent her time with Lady Caragea, keeping her company in the quiet of their country house in Băneasa. In the presence of the prince, these boyars, high office-holders, were obliged, for reasons of prestige, to display a degree of luxury at least equal to that displayed by the ruler and his court. Dumitrache Merişescu enters into the world of this noble boyar; he is accepted within the intimacy of the private quarters because he carries with him the name of his protector Ioan Hagi Moscu. Moreover, Dumitrache finds another protector in the person of the nanny, Kyra Fotini, a 'Greek' and a 'Tsarigrad woman' as he describes her—in other words, another important link in the network that connects those with this type of 'mobile identity'.

Here, the young merchant's son has the occasion to undergo a new initiation into the mysteries of love, which he will then describe under the influence of *Erotocritos*. The stage set this time is quite different: the mansion in

55 Grigore Băleanu held the office of grand *vornic* (and sometimes grand *logofăt*) throughout the reign of Ioan vodă Caragea (Urechia, *op. cit.*, 10/1, 35, 42, 262, 308, 432).

56 Maria Brâncoveanu, the daughter of Emanoil (read Emanuel) Brâncoveanu and Zoe Sturdza, married to Grigore Băleanu.

the centre of the city houses a young lady, 'beautiful as the wick of a candle', as he says when he meets her for the first time. But before entering upon the mysteries of love, it is only right to offer some information about the young lady who lets herself be courted by an ordinary adolescent, far below her in the social hierarchy.

Zoe Băleanu's destiny was that of many of the daughters of great boyars, important playing pieces in matrimonial strategies directed by the heads of their families. Married in 1811–1812 to *beyzade* Matei Ghica, son of the *ban* Costache Ghica, Zoe was quickly deserted by her husband. Suffering from tuberculosis, young Matei set out in search of health, following his father, who was in the service of the Ottoman Empire, now to Vienna, now to Istanbul. After waiting for three years, Zoe Băleanu, accompanied by her grandmother, Zoe Brâncoveanu, applied for and, after many petitions and hearings, obtained a separation.[57] The divorce trial was a very curious one: her application was rejected in the first instance by Prince Caragea, who 'ripped up' the metropolitan's report, but was approved several weeks later. The British consul in Bucharest, William Wilkinson, stated that it was only a divorce of convenience because the girl's father, Grigore Băleanu, had found a better match: 'Her father, who was the chief instigator of her sudden resolution, had negotiated the second marriage, because it suited his own interests.'[58] This assertion by Wilkinson, who was shocked by the libertinage of the Romanians, comes in support of the narrative of young Dumitrache Merişescu.

Nanny Fotini pulls all the strings of this story played out in great secret, behind locked doors and under cover of darkness.[59] Under various pretexts, Dumitrache is called to keep the young lady company, although the boyar Băleanu had fired him after his first day of work, categorizing him as a 'bungler'. While every morning he leaves by the garden gate, hidden from the gaze of others, into the light of day, nanny Fotini strives to find various roles in which to bring him back to the mansion: nephew, passing Leipzig merchant, servant from the palace. Any hesitation on the part of the young man results in his

57 The divorce proceedings took place between 15 May and 2 June 1815, the application being signed by Zoe Băleanu and her grandmother, Zoe Brâncoveanu. If we start from the hypothesis that Dumitrache Merişescu indeed spent some time in the house of grand *vornic* Grigore Băleanu in the company of the latter's daughter, then this must have taken place not in October 1814, but in October 1815, when she was divorced and free. (Urechia, *op. cit.*, 10/2, 259–262).

58 Wilkinson, *An Account of the Principalities of Wallachia and Moldavia*, 148–149.

59 Here nanny Fotini departs considerably from the model of the nurse Frusina in *Erotocritos*, who is very close to the principal character Aretusa (Dima, *Poemul Erotocrit*, 7–25).

being severely berated by the nanny with: '*Ghiezi, gide, pusti*!'—in other words he is told that he must be a sodomite not to like such a beautiful young lady.[60]

The evenings are whiled away in games of cards for kisses or blind-man's-buff, sweetened by pastries and various conserves, triggered by the darkness, ending under the covers:

> The boyar stayed for dinner at court. The mistress had been at Băneasa with Lady Caragea for about four days. Evening came. I kissed the nanny's hands and asked what I was to do. She said: '*Sopa, pidi mu*.'[61] She showed me which way to go, *is to anangeo*.[62] She lit lights all around. In our room it was dark. The young lady found me even in the dark … We started playing, playing … I had got the hang of it like a bear at the honey trough. The nanny came with candles. She said: '*Ti kanite esis?*'[63] As an answer we burst out laughing. The nanny pretended she didn't understand. She said: '*Pinases*.'[64] I answered: '*Den pino*.'[65] '*Katalava. Esi, kori, pinases*.'[66] She answered: '*Okhi*.'[67] We got back to our games. I was about the same age as the young lady. 'Come into the yard.' She didn't know where I was because she asked me: '*Pu tha kimithisis?*'[68] I shook my head. '*Kathise edo eos avrion ki avrion si orminevo*.'[69] I answered with silence. Miss Zoiţa said: '*Nene, ela na se filiso*.'[70] She came and she kissed her. The nanny said to me: 'Why don't you kiss her?' I took her hands and I kissed them. The nanny had things to do outside. She came and went. It was late, but I didn't feel it, I didn't think of anything. She gave me the young lady's indoor slippers, we ate pastries and laughed. The nanny went outside and opening the door she said: '*Ela agligora!*'[71] As she went out I heard her locking the door with a key from outside. I went to bed with my clothes on because I was in a trap. Thinking, I fell asleep.
>
> It was late when nanny Fotini came. The candle was running out. She woke me and said to me: '*Plai su kala, enia su*.'[72] I kept quiet and undressed, but the covers were not for the likes of me, because my feet were unwashed and my

60 Gr.: 'Gehazi, goat, sodomite!' Gehazi is a Biblical character who becomes a leper (2 Kings 5: 20–27). His name was often invoked in formulaic curses. '*Pusti*' was a current term of invective directed at a man, its primary sense being that of 'sodomite'. The translations of the Greek dialogue were made by Dr. Lidia Cotovanu, and Professor Peter Mackridge contributed further suggestions; I take this opportunity to thank both for their kind assistance.

61 'Quiet, my dear!'

62 'For a necessity' (in other words, to relieve himself).

63 'What are you (plural) doing?'

64 'Are you (singular) hungry?'

65 'I'm not hungry.'

66 'I understand. Are you hungry, girl?'

67 'No.'

68 'Where will you sleep?'

69 'Stay here till tomorrow and tomorrow I'll direct you.'

70 'Nanny, come and let me kiss you.'

71 'Come on quickly!'

72 'Take care and behave yourself.'

stockings torn. I said [to myself]: '*Nene katarisi ta chorapia! Ti khali ekhon.*'[73] I heard: '*Enoia sou, pidi mu.*'[74] I thought that Kyra Fotini was going to bed too, because the quilt was of cotton with long pillows and three small ones. I crossed myself and got into bed. She took the candle; she went and locked the door from outside. Late. In the dark, the nanny came and she got under the covers. For a moment I thought that it was Kyra Fotini. '*To khava su, nene Taki.*'[75] It was morning when we heard the door opening. When we saw the nanny we pulled the quilt over our heads, but Kyra Fotini said: '*Sikothite, agligora!*'[76] Zoiţica left. She was in a dressing gown. I pulled on my *çaksır*, I got my boots onto my feet. She invited me to leave by the garden gate and to come in by the [main] gate, to go straight to the overseer. If he asked me, to say I was coming from home: 'I'll be there too, so you don't make a fool of yourself.'

I went out, she locked the little gate. It wasn't yet fully day. I went round to come in at the [main] gate. I didn't meet anyone I knew. The gate was half unlocked, because the butler had gone to the market. I went straight to the overseer. Kyra Fotini was waiting. Since I had just come, I bid good morning.[77] I kissed the hand of Kyra Fotini. She said: '*Pou ise pidi mu apo[p]se? Thios iti porni?*'[78]

While he spends his nights by the side of Zoe Băleanu, during the day Dumitrache wanders the alleys of Bucharest, meeting friends, eating pies (*bogaci*, from the Turkish *poğaça*) and rolls (*simiţi*, from the Turkish *simit*), frequenting the house of a famous courtesan, Marghioala, going to the service at the Metropolitan Cathedral on Saint Demetrius's day, bathing in the public baths, going on various errands for the young lady, dropping in at home only to change his shirt.

A Princely Wedding

Young Dumitrache's job for one day as a houseboy provides the reader with the opportunity to enter the house of a great boyar with a position at the princely court. It is an eyewitness report from inside, laying bare the foundations of the sumptuous lives of the nobility, lost on the paths of obligatory wastefulness. The early years of the nineteenth century saw the decline of some important

73 'Nanny, wash the stockings. They're pitiful.'

74 'No worry, my dear.'

75 'You weren't thinking, Mr Tache.'

76 'Get up (plural), quickly!

77 In the original, 'Am calimeritu', making a Romanian verb from the Greek '*kalimera*', 'Good morning'.

78 'Where are you, my dear, this evening? An uncle or a whore?' Prof. Mackridge considers the Greek 'Thios iti porni' to be 'extremely problematic'. He suggests: 'Uncle/divine or prostitute'.

boyar families, who met their end in the defiant aura of appearances, and the emergence of new lineages founded upon the lucrative hedonism of money. The occasion of a wedding was used to highlight the prestige of the family by way of luxury. The planned marriage between the daughter of the grand *vornic* Grigore Băleanu and one of the numerous *beyzade*s in the entourage of Prince Caragea—perhaps even one of the prince's own sons—provides us with an opportunity to observe close-up the fever of purchases that were indeed significant from a financial point of view.

The 'supplier' of the Băleanu family was Constantin Costa Foru, a 'Leipzig merchant' with an important place in the luxury market of Bucharest.[79] We may imagine him arriving at the mansion in Băneasa accompanied by his journeymen Gheorghe Furculiţă and Dumitrache Merişescu, with a cart loaded with boxes. With quill and inkwell hanging from his belt, with his ledger prepared for the entry of goods bought on credit, for the addition of more and more merchandise, the desired lace and other trimmings, with his carriage (*braşoveancă*)[80] ready to dash back to the shop for unexpected requests, Costa Foru skilfully directs the transaction … The picture is inspired by the account offered by Tache Merişescu, journeyman for a day:

> They all went to the shop and began to choose stuff: lace, trimmings, and so on. I watched. They loaded us up with boxes and packages. We went home and they placed them in a carriage sent from Băneasa. We made a big parcel and climbed into the carriage. We carried the boxes into a salon. They announced us and Kyra Fotini came out with Mistress Zoiţa […] They chose, they put aside. They said to bring such and such too.

Costa Foru, following the instructions of the future bride and of nanny Fotini, returns to his shop to bring even more goods. Dumitrache, turned into a Leipzig merchant in a day, for the day, continues his account: 'He filled the salon with merchandise. A large number of ladies came out; it might have been a fair. They chose; they bargained. I, the Leipzig merchant, moved boxes with

---

79 He was a Greek, referred to as a 'Leipzig merchant' (*lipscan*) because of his economic connections with the German town. On material culture and circulation of goods see Suraiya Faroqhi, 'Moving Goods Around, and Ottomanists too: Surveying Research on the Transfer of Material Goods in the Ottoman Empire', *Turcica*, 32 (2000), pp. 435–466; Donald Quataert (ed.), *Consumption Studies and the Ottoman Empire, 1550–1922. An Introduction* (New York: 2000); Suraiya Faroqhi, 'The Material Culture of Global Connections: A Report on Current Research', *Turcica*, 41 (2009), 403–431.

80 A large covered carriage made in Braşov.

and without purpose. Only Gheorghe Furculiţă could stop me, because he was senior in the shop.'

Judging by ledgers of merchandise and ladies' correspondence, the fashion was relatively mixed in the autumn of 1814. The predilection was for French style, as regards the form of garments, combined with a preference for precious oriental fabrics. In the salon of the Băleanu house in Băneasa, the boxes that the Leipzig merchant Costa Foru unpacked contained shawls and Lahore headscarfs (one alone cost around 600 Groschen),[81] lace, Holland linen, satins, English cloth, *kondura*s (shoes) and *çaksır*s, brocade and damask, earrings with rubies and emeralds, diamond rings, floral brooches and aigrettes, clasps and slippers, bonnets and ribbons, *anteri*s embroidered with wire, *fermene*s trimmed with ermine, *ibrişim* thread, kerchiefs, sashes, fezzes and shalwars. Merchandise brought from India, Damascus, Moscow, Livorno, Vienna, Paris, London, and Venice decked the bride from the banks of the Dâmboviţa. Luxury was the bridge connecting merchants, princes and boyars, kings, chancellors, emperors, and viziers. The petty artisans worked from dawn to dusk in their various workshops in order to satisfy customers on a daily basis.

We do not know how Zoe Băleanu looked as a bride when, in the Advent fast of 1815, she was married to *beyzade* Dimitri Caragea. Dumitrache Merişescu simply notes: 'The wedding was splendid. The prince himself with the princess were their godparents.'

For the poor Leipzig merchant, the young lady's wedding meant only 'bitterness'. Intruding into the intimacy of the Băleanu family's mansion, Tache Merişescu had made so bold as to believe in the phantasms of *Erotocritos*, falling 'head over heels' in love with the young mistress Zoe Băleanu. '*Zoi mu*', '*pidimu*', 'beautiful as the wick of a candle', the poor adolescent never comes to the end of his compliments addressed to the young lady who accepts him in her company only 'because she was bored of being shut indoors.' And then, when for reasons of policy she has to marry, she has no backward glance to spare for the young man who had kept her company at night, kissing her hands, pampering her, caressing her, singing to her now in Greek, now in Bulgarian, giving her lace trimmings and many, many 'tearful sighs'.

81 See the correspondence between two 'Greek' merchants concerning the sale of these shawls in Bucharest and Moscow (ANIC, Fond Documente Munteneşti, LXXVII/7, 9/17 December 1813).

On the Road to Tsarigrad

When Mistress Zoe and Dimitri Caragea have to leave for Tsarigrad, where he is to occupy the post of *capuchehaia* (diplomatic representative of the prince of Wallachia), Dumitrache Merişescu has a place in their suite. Thanks to the intervention of nanny Fotini, Dumitrache is appointed page (*yedecli*) in the *beyzade*'s court. For all the goodwill shown by the merchant Costa Foru, the adolescent is considered far too old to start an apprenticeship. His new job makes the boy arrogant and full of himself beyond all limits: 'I went about like a spinning top; I went in and out without a care. I was unstoppable, of course, as the *beyzade*'s page.' And when he receives his livery too, he becomes full of himself to the point of paroxysm:

> The head tailor of the palace came. He made me two suits of clothes, two page's caftans and a *cüppe*[82] and *biniş*,[83] shoes with *meşti*.[84] He brought two *donlucs*[85] to tie round my head. When I was dressed, I was full of myself. [...] He also gave me the *hanjar*[86] of a big boss. Hey, Dimitri. That's what he called me. It seemed to me that I was as grand as the *beyzade*.

His arrogance lasts until the cold of the Christmas fast. Under pressure from the Porte, Prince Caragea sends this *beyzade*, his son or close relative, away to Constantinople, where he is to be *capuchehaia* and guarantor, as was the usual practice:

> With a suite of Arnauts, we set out with the *beyzade*'s carriage. They were all mountain ponies. Arnauts before and behind. Boyars and the *Vodă*, with beating of drums and with their suite, took us out on the Mogoşoaia Road. We were in a cart, sitting in disorder. It was in the Christmas fast. There was a cover over us. We threw ourselves into the bottom of the cart. After escorting us as far as Colentina, the *beyzade* went on faster.

The journey to Tsarigrad was made along the post roads, in convoy, or by other well-known roads in order to avoid highway robbery, which was prevalent in the period. Moreover, the plague was still lurking, and quarantine obligatory.[87] And so Tache bumps along in post carts, keeping Kyra Fotini, the native of

---

82 long felt jacket.

83 sleeveless mantle.

84 leather slippers for indoor wear.

85 cotton cloths.

86 dagger.

87 On the plague and the sanitary measures in the Otoman Empire see Daniel Panzac, 'Politique sanitaire et fixation des frontiers: l'exemple ottoman (XVIIIe–XIXe siècles)',

Tsarigrad, company, passing through Brăila, Măcin, and Hârşova, met by pashas, smoked and aired so as not to take the plague back to where it came from. At Hârşova, the young mistress feels more and more ill, so 'the lady came to bring her medicine.' Since her state of health worsens, or perhaps as the consequence of a political plan carefully laid by Prince Caragea, so as not to leave his children in the hands of the Turks, the young mistress and the *beyzade* return to Bucharest. However, the convoy, 'with Turkish guarantees,' goes on to Varna and Mesembria (Nesebar), and from there they are loaded onto boats and escorted to Caragea's houses in Therapia, to the recurrent and prolonged sighs of Kyra Fotini, who repeats fearfully: 'Ah, my dear, my dear, whatever anyone says, what do we care?'

Fotini's worries are only too real in an Empire in which suspicion and fear occupy a central place. Those generally known by the name of 'Phanariots' have the most vulnerable position, living in grandeur or squalor, always in fear of losing their own and their families' heads. Nikolaos Soutzos, another *beyzade*, attentive to expectations and diplomatic games in Arnavutköy, on the shores of the Bosphorus, notes: 'God only knows how much caution was needed even about children's amusements in the harsh and bloody time of the reign of Sultan Mahmud.' He then tells how, while improvising a dance in the dark and without music, he was seen by the *bostangi-başa* (chief of police), who was passing by sea, and summoned to the chancellery of the police in Istanbul. Or how young Aleco Vlahuţi came to lose his head because he was seen in the window of a house in Therapia with a shawl wound around his head, not knowing that turbans had just been banned.[88] The research conducted by Matthew Elliot and Maurits H. van den Boogert[89] backs up what Nikolaos Soutzos observes with regard to the codes of dress and behaviour that were obligatory in the Ottoman Empire and especially in Istanbul. An additional factor was the insecure status of these Phanariots, who were made use of and rapidly eliminated as soon as a question mark arose concerning their loyalty.[90] There were moments when Prince Caragea's prospects hung in the

Turcica, 31 (1999), 87–108. See also Daniel Panzac, *La peste dans l'Empire ottoman, 1700–1859* (Louvain: 1985).

88 Nicolas Soutzo, *Mémoires du Prince Nicolas Soutzo*, 55–59.

89 Elliot, 'Dress Codes in the Ottoman Empire', 103–123; Maurits H. van den Boogert, 'Intermediaries par excellence? Ottoman Dragomans in the Eighteenth Century', in Bernard Heyberger, Chantal Verdeil (eds.), *Hommes de l'entre-deux. Parcours individuals et portraits de groupe sur la frontier de la Méditerranée (XVIe–XXe siècle)*, (Paris: 2009), 95–114.

90 On this topic see Philliou, *Biography of an Empire*, 18–21.

balance, and these can be glimpsed in Merişescu's memoirs, when fears turn into rumours that smother the truth.

Kyra Fotini has experience of princes and sultans, but Dumitrache is far too young to sigh or to be paralysed by fear. Under the protection of his *yedecli*'s clothing, and 'not guarded by anyone,' as he writes, he slips through the alleyways of the city. One day, he meets a Serbian cloth merchant whom he knows from Bucharest, who advises him to leave Therapia as 'envoys have been sent to Bucharest because the prince has not paid the tribute for five years and the Turks will slaughter you.' The information scares the young *yedecli*, and if until then he has sometimes sighed in expectation of seeing the young mistress, the prospect of his head being cut off prompts him to give up love for more practical concerns.

The Sümbüllü Khan (*Zumbul han*) was where Christian merchants from southeastern Europe, merchants from the Principalities, and 'Braşov merchants' stayed.[91] As presented by Merişescu, the khan appears to be a veritable fortification, which closes its gates during the night. The rooms have 'two rows of beds' one on top of the other, so that the resident has to 'climb up stairs' in order to get into bed. The rent is not too high, and for this reason 'many merchants stay there' and all the rooms are occupied. Another important reason is that it is largely inhabited by 'German *sudiţi*', protégés of the Habsburg Empire or of Prussia, who benefitted from the intervention of these two consulates in the interests of the safety of their merchants. Indeed, the Serbian merchant who helps Tache is just such a 'German *sudit*'. He advises him to quickly change his clothes and to obtain documents in order to be able to survive in Istanbul.[92] Shutting himself inside the khan for fear, Tache emerges only when he has changed his appearance: 'he made me German clothes, he bought me a hat and gave me a German passport, to show to the Turks if they asked me.'

What sort of identity did Dumitrache Merişescu buy for himself? What did this 'German passport' look like? Dumitrache does not offer any kind of information, but we may note his transition from the status of *homo ottomanicus*

---

91 On this khan see Sophia Laiou, 'The Ottoman Greek 'Merchants of Europa' at the beginning of the 19th century', in Evangelina Balta, Georgios Salakidis, Theoharis Stavrides (eds.), *Festschrift in Honor of Ioannis P. Theocharides. Studies on the Ottoman Empire and Turkey* (Istanbul: 2014), 327.

92 See the measures taken by Sultan Selim III regarding the security of city, after the Ayasofya Mosque incident, on 17 December 1791. For more details see Betül Başaran, *Selim III, Social Control and Policing in Istanbul at the End of the Eighteenth Century. Between Crisis and Order* (Leiden: 2014), 2–3.

to that of 'German',[93] in other words, 'Frank'.[94] Moreover, Dumitrache never pronounces the names of those he encounters. What name does this Serbian merchant bear? And what of the uncle whom he will meet a few pages further on? Or the other members of the group of merchants 'hidden' in the Sümbüllü Khan? Who were they? What languages did they speak? How did they manage to understand each other? Was there a common language specific to merchants? These are questions that remain unanswered as we read the narrative of Dumitrache Merişescu.

With his new appearance, Dumitrache steps out on a new journey through the passages of the Bezisten in search of cheap merchandise, gaping as often as not at what he saw, following and helping the merchant in order to repay his 'debt': 'Wherever he went, I [went] with him too and carried a box containing silk thread, woven silk, and whatever he bought for Bucharest.' In the evening, after the gates of the khan had shut and the night watchmen had set out on their rounds, the merchants would gather in a coffee-house to pick up useful information, watch the *karagözlük*,[95] take coffee and tobacco, and forget the worries of their journeys. The coffee-house was, together with the inn, one of the most important places of socialization, where information, gossip, and rumours spread and were shared. Here Dumitrache finds out that Prince Caragea has 'fled to the German land of Beci [Vienna],' that the suite and baggage of the *capuchehaia* from 'Bogdania'[96] have been taken by the vizier, and that the young page has been declared missing and is being searched for. In the coffee-house they tell jokes, they make comments, they pass on stories. Here, one of the merchants has a laugh at the expense of the 'pretty' page taken by the Turks to be their 'boy'. And the merchant adds: 'Damned be the Turks!' Given the widespread folklore around the theme of Turks' being sodomites, it

93 The term *neamţ* (German) was used generically for someone with European habits or clothing.

94 For the definition of what an Ottoman subject was considered to be, see Maurits H. van den Boogert, 'Resurrecting *Homo Ottomanicus*: The Constants and Variables of Ottoman Identity', *Journal of Ottoman Studies*, XLIV (2014), 9–10. See also Yeşil, 'How to be(come) an Ottoman', 123–139.

95 The *karagözlük* (Romanianized as 'Caraghioslâc', from Turkish *karagöz*) was much enjoyed in Wallachia too. It was performed as shadow theatre at the princely court and in great boyar households, but, together with the *maskaralık*, it was equally appreciated by the common people, and was performed as a puppet show in the open air in alleyways or at fairs. Because of its obscene language, the *karagözlük* was frequently banned in the early nineteenth century (See Contanţa Vintilă-Ghiţulescu, *Patimă şi desfătare*, 384–385). For the popularity of the shadow theatre in the Ottoman Empire, see Sajdi, *The Barber of Damascus*, 162–165.

96 The name of Moldavia in the Turkish documents.

is not difficult for poor Dumitrache to imagine himself caught in the embrace of a janissary and to take fear: 'I kept quiet and listened.'[97]

'Turks' is a generic name, as Palmira Brummett shows in her study of travel narratives.[98] Dumitrache does not stop to offer details, but merely expresses succinctly what other travellers say about the 'Turks'. The 'Turks' encountered by Dumitrache are aggressive and capricious (*belâlı*), ferocious, 'accursed', sodomites.[99] Thus he categorizes a group without pausing to consider individuals, whom he avoids. Indeed, interaction between the two worlds was almost nonexistent: Tache observes from a distance the watch (*kulluk*) crossing the city, the 'capricious' janissaries ready to start a fight, the crowds in the alleyways, but he never approaches, out of fear, out of lack of knowledge.[100]

However, the coffee-house is also the crossroads where different travellers' journeys intersect with one another. Being a place of meeting and socializing, one day the coffee-house brings together Tache and one of his uncles, a brother who had remained in the Ottoman Empire while Foti sought his fortune beyond the Danube. And so a new adventure begins, and a new identity is proposed: 'The next day, I crossed to Pera, to the monastery administrator (*díkios*), and he got for me a passport as a German *sudit*.' His apprenticeship in the cotton trade now begins. For a year and a half, he travels to well-known and less well-known places, from Smyrna to Venice, from Ostrov to Salonica, from Mount Athos to Jerusalem, with boxes containing cotton, lining material, *castambol, alaca*, and silk thread. The adventure ends in Alexandria, when his uncle dies unexpectedly of the plague, leaving a ship loaded with stacks of cotton and a helpless nephew in the hands of the consulate. The consulate intervenes by virtue of the right it held over its subjects, the *sudiți*, and confiscates the entire cargo, giving Tache seven hundred lei and sending him to Galaţi on board the galleon Altar Saneli. He disembarks in the Moldavian port after being away for almost two years, with a knapsack containing prayer beads, musk, rose butter, Turkish delight, and Indian carobs. It is September 20, 1817.

97 Iordache Golescu (1768–1848) frequently refers in his plays to this practice. It is probably a legend arising from fear of the Turks, who were both in both ethnic and confessional terms 'other'. (Golescu, *Scrieri alese*, 31, 32, 308).

98 Palmira Brummett, 'You Say "Classical", I Say "Imperial", Let's Call the Whole Thing Off: Empire, Individual, and Encounter in Travel Narratives of the Ottoman Empire', *The Journal of Ottoman Studies*, XLIV (2014), 21–44.

99 See also Ambroise Firmin Didot, *Notes d'un voyage fait dans le Levant en 1816 et 1817* (Paris: 1821).

100 Eldem, *Foreigners on the Threshold of Felicity*, 114–131.

The last sentence of the memoir is a sort of profession of faith: 'Consequently I believe in stories.' In other words, if all these things happened to me, a mere mortal, then all stories ought to contain a grain of truth.

Post-Journey Destinies

Except that the adventures of Dumitrache Merişescu do not end here: Dumitrache Merişescu wrote down only a part of his life experiences in the manuscript. It is possible that there are other manuscripts that I have not yet found. In the absence of a sufficiently informative catalogue, research in the Romanian archives is largely a matter of luck and perseverance. As soon as I began to read the memoirs of this young man, I embarked on a search for any other traces of him that might remain in the archives. More adventurous than practical-minded, Dumitrache drifted between Galaţi and Focşani, working as a *cavaf*, in other words, making and selling cheap shoes. Later, he connected himself to the *beyzade*s Alecu and Iorga Sturza (1822), just when their father Ioniţă Sandu Sturza became prince of Moldavia (1822–1828). For a time he was *becer* at the princely court: an official position involving supervision of the palace kitchen. Prince Ioniţă Sandu Sturza raised him to the rank of *paharnic*, and at the same time offered him the hand of a young girl from the princess's entourage.[101] The rank did not bring him any great wealth. Most likely *paharnic* Dumitrache Merişescu was not as good at exploiting the privileges that his rank offered as he had been at adventurously pushing himself into various clientelary networks. In 1829, Dumitache is reported in the *vidomostia* (catalogue) of the boyars of Moldavia to be poor, without an estate, living in Târgul Petrii (today's Piatra Neamţ).[102] However, later, in the middle of the nineteenth century, *paharnic* Dumitrache Merişescu appears to have been a wealthy local boyar with close connections to the educated Moldavian elite.[103]

Nor did Zoe Băleanu have a very happy destiny, although at least she was never to experience poverty. Her marriage to *beyzade* Dimitri Caragea lasted till 1818, when Prince Ioan Caragea took refuge in Pisa, accompanied by a numerous suite of clients and *beyzades*, after first taking care to see that his

101 Constantin Sion, *Arhondologia Moldovei* (Bucharest: 1973), 167–168. He was married with Smaranda Manoliu having as 'god-parents' the princely family following a local custom. See V.A. Urechia, *Din tainele vieţei. Amintiri contimporane (1840–1882)* (Iaşi: 2014), 4, 14, 27.

102 Alexandru V. Perietzianu-Buzău, 'Vidomostie de boierii Moldovei aflaţi în ţară la 1829 (II)', *Arhiva Genealogică*, 1–2 (1994), 277.

103 Urechia, *Din tainele vieţii*, 27; See also ANIC, Fond Achiziţii Noi, MMCCCXLVII/1, 10 October 1856.

accumulated wealth was stowed in safety, mainly in banks in western Europe. The princely flight must have come as a heavy blow to the grand *vornic* Grigore Băleanu, but he got over it quickly, and found for his daughter perhaps the best match available: Ştefan Hagi Moscu, the son of the rich boyar, merchant, and banker Ioan Hagi Moscu.

*

As Maurits H. van den Boogert has asserted, 'the complex nature of Homo Ottomanicus' contains several constants and a series of variables.[104] I enumerate them here in order to see whether Dumitrache Merişescu could be admitted to the 'species' of *homo ottomanicus*, together with the other candidates analysed both by van den Boogert and in the volume dedicated to this subject coordinated by Meropi Anastassiadou and Bernard Heyberger.[105] Born in the Ottoman Empire, of Orthodox Christian parents, Dumitrache was an Ottoman subject, and it was as such that he set out on the roads of the Empire. As part of the social group of merchants, Dumitrache spoke Romanian, Bulgarian, Greek, and Turkish, an essential ability for any merchant in the exercise of his occupation. Similarly, he was very well integrated both in urban and wider Balkan commercial networks, which facilitated his access to information and connections. In other words, he may be considered a true *homo ottomanicus*. But if in retrospect, Dumitrache Merişescu speaks of himself as being a 'Christian', born in Bucharest, of Christian parents, payers of taxes to the Phanariot prince Caragea, and thus to the Grand Signor, others attribute more precise identities to him. For example, ten years later, in the catalogue compiled by the Moldavian authorities (1829), Dumitrache is recorded as the son of 'Fotachi Merişescu the Greek'.[106] In the middle of the nineteenth century, his Balkan origins had not yet been lost sight of, despite his integration in the network of the local Moldavian boyar class. Constantin Sion writes in his 1856 registry of the boyars of Moldavia, that Dumitrache is a 'Bulgarian shoemaker' who has 'settled in Moldavia with the help of the Sturza family.'[107]

---

104 Van den Boogert, *Resurrecting Homo Ottomanicus*, 18.

105 Van den Boogert, *Resurrecting Homo Ottomanicus*, 16–17; See also Meropi Anastassiadou, Bernard Heyberger (eds.), *Figures anonymes, figures d'élite: Pour une anatomie de l'Homo ottomanicus*, (Istanbul: 1999).

106 See A.V. Perietzianu-Buzău, 'Vidomostie de boierii', 277.

107 Sion, *Arhondologia Moldovei*, 167–168.

Dumitrache Merişescu's destiny is, however, much closer to that of the figures studied by Christine Philliou—Dionisyos Photeinos or Stephanos Vogorides, for example—without, of course, attaining their degree of visibility. Belonging to a family of southeast European merchants who had taken refuge for various reasons in Wallachia, Merişescu may be numbered among those 'entering the service and culture of phanariots.'[108] Dumitrache began his career under the protective wing of his patron, Ioan Hagi Moscu. When this patron was no longer there, he tried to find a place in another clientelary network under the patronage of another influential family: Sturza. His entire career in the administration of Wallachia or Moldavia was connected to the progress through time of his chosen patrons, and he advanced or fell behind along with them.

108 Philliou, *Biography of an Empire*, 39.

PART IV

Women, Consumption, and Patronage

CHAPTER 7

Women and Their Well-Being

In spite of the international explosion of gender studies, many aspects of the history of women in southeastern Europe still remain relatively unexplored. The freedom of movement resulting from the fall of the communist regimes has allowed researchers to integrate themes of international and interdisciplinary research into their field, taking advantage of hitherto unpublished archive material and the curiosity of a public eager to know its past. However, research in this area still has much to offer, and rich archival material awaits researchers to decipher it, read it, interpret it, and use it in the sort of analysis that is very necessary for an understanding of local societies. In this chapter, I shall deal principally with women whose traces are to be found in the archives of Wallachia and Moldavia. While it might be imagined that these archives would contain only information relating specifically to these two Ottoman provinces, a careful analysis brings to light the ethnic and religious diversity of a population that wandered through the empires, leaving documentary traces that enable a reconstruction of the past.

With the help of unpublished documents, I propose in this part to examine the active role of women in political networks and in trans-imperial mobility. Studying women and their networks helps us to understand better not only the circulation of people, ideas, and knowledge between empires, but also inter-regional integration through matrimonial alliances or political sociability. Before analysing their active role in the construction of intercultural networks, I shall turn first to the relation between women and wealth in order to shed light on their economic and social position, an important instrument in appreciating women's agency. What sort of goods could women own? How was their well-being defined? Who contributed to this well-being, and how? What sort of sources speak of women's goods? These are the questions that I shall try to answer in the first part, by examining local and regional sources, but also through corroboration with other studies dedicated to the economic situation of women. This part also looks at the social life and sociability experienced by women through consumption and travel. It shows how women and their relationships structured the social and political life of a household, underlining how female friendships contributed to the advancement of a political career, the upkeep of networks, and the establishment and maintenance of useful connections.

Women and Their Goods

Women of a certain class most often came into possession of certain goods upon their marriage. This was the crucial moment when a woman left the parental home with part of her inheritance in the form of a dowry. In the following pages, I shall analyse the way in which Wallachian and Moldavian society engaged in the construction of norms designed to protect these feminine goods within the marriage, protecting them from being absorbed by the husband's expenses or debts. Likewise, I shall examine how women looked after (or failed to look after) these goods, trying to transmit them to the next generation by way of their testaments. In the first part, I shall focus on dowry documents and the steps taken to make the dowry secure, and in the second, I shall turn my attention to the rights of women to dispose of their goods by way of consumption.

Marriage was an important political game, but also an economic investment for any man, supporting a career and building a future. Through marriage, the outsider had direct access to a family's patrimony because of the dowry received. A marriage would be negotiated between the two parties orally, without the element of a written contract as such. However, some of the 'contractual aspects' of a marriage may be recovered from dowry documents, when these are not limited to a mere inventory. In addition to listing the moveable and immoveable goods offered, the dowry document may give details about the couple, the moment of its drafting, witnesses, and other clauses that had been negotiated. The concept of 'contract' was first introduced by the Calimah Code of 1817. Marriage contracts (*alcătuiri căsătoreşti* or *tocmeli căsătoreşti*) decided 'the rights and obligations between those persons who have married or who wish to marry, with regard to their wealth.'[1] Such a contract should include: 'the dowry, the *exoprică* (property belonging to the wife and administered solely by her), the counter-dowry, the *theoritri* (gifts on the wedding day), and other gifts.' But the same law code provided that this agreement did not necessarily have to be made in writing, but could also be a verbal contract, on condition that it was made before at least three witnesses 'worthy of trust'.[2] Thus, in the absence of the institution and person of the notary, the social and economic utility of dowry lists led the authorities and society in general to establish norms around these documents that substituted for marriage contracts. It should be added that in a largely illiterate society, orality played an important role in all forms of negotiation. Access to education was relatively

1 *Codul Calimah (1817)* (Bucharest: 1958), 555.

2 *Codul Calimah (1817)*, 557–559.

limited. It is true that there were Academies in Iași and Bucharest, staffed by teachers from southeastern Europe, some of them true scholars. However, this type of education was insufficient, offering nothing to whole categories of the population, including women. The situation seems to have been somewhat improved by the beginning of the nineteenth century, when private teachers were becoming more numerous, and some girls were starting to be included in a system of education. Nevertheless, a woman could draw up a dowry document only in the absence of her husband, when she took over his powers and responsibilities regarding the raising, educating, and marrying of their offspring. I would add that many of the people I am writing about in these pages were educated, and had a good knowledge of reading and writing, including Greek and sometimes the languages of European diplomacy—Italian or French. This was not the rule for society as a whole, however, and the norms that developed around dowry documents highlight the importance of priests and clerks as intermediaries between orality and a cult of the written word.[3]

The dowry document, according to the articles of the Wallachian law code of 1780, developed into a complete form, imposing: the obligatory signature of the son-in-law, the valuation of the objects in the trousseau, drafting in duplicate—the original remaining with the owner, while a copy was to be transcribed in the register of a nearby monastery—, the obligation on brothers to endow their sisters, and the status of the husband in relation to the dowry.[4] The effects become visible from the beginning of the nineteenth century. It was now no longer sufficient for the document to be drafted by the priest who performed the religious ceremony of betrothal and read in front of the witnesses. There was a shift of authority from the circle of the family—immediate family, other relatives, friends, neighbours—towards a 'public institution': the document was now read, authenticated, and registered by a special department.[5]

At the end of the eighteenth century, the great number of divorce proceedings, in which the restitution of the dowry was insistently sought, led to another measure: the valuation of each object in the dowry list.[6] Thus, the document

---

3 Alex Drace-Francis's detailed analysis shows that the education of the population of Wallachia and Moldavia was quite precarious and remained so throughout the nineteenth century. The urban elite and the boyars preferred to send their offspring to the private schools that appeared particularly from the 1830s onwards and to study in great European centres. Drace-Francis, *The Making of Modern Romanian Culture*, 42–44, 102, 112.

4 *Pravilniceasca Condică (1780)* (Bucharest: 1957), 94. See also the document issued by Nicolae Mavrogheni (1786–1790) that puts into practice the article of the law, requiring that dowry contracts be copied into a special register, on which occasion they were checked and authenticated. ANIC, Fond Manuscrise MS 17, f. 7, 3 May 1786.

5 ANIC, Fond Achiziţii Noi, CCCI/9, 2 May 1830.

6 Antim Ivrireanul, *Opere. Didahii* (Bucharest: 1996), 354, *Pravilniceasca Condică*, 92–94.

no longer merely passed through the hands of the priest who drew it up, but went also to the master of the merchants' guild for everything to be valued as precisely as possible and assigned its 'correct' price, regardless of whether the item in question was a house, a string of pearls, or a simple ploughshare, and even if a dress was worn, a blanket past its best, or a pan missing its lid. A new column appeared on the left of the document, where the values of the items were given in the currency of the time (*taleri, bani*).

But what was the social function of the dowry list? In what processes and stages of life was it involved that it received so much attention from those around? What information could it offer contemporaries, and what can it tell the researchers of today about the mechanism by which a social system functioned? Whatever its form, the dowry list provides details about the social and economic position of the woman and her family in a community. It sets down in writing the woman's rights over a certain type of mobile goods and properties and establishes her place both in the system of succession and in relation to her husband's wealth.[7] These clauses transform the dowry list from a mere inventory into an indispensable document with important social and economic implications, one that might be invoked and utilized in any divorce trial, and in various family conflicts and disputes over property. Theoretically, the dowry provided the woman with economic autonomy, offering her protection whatever might happen. However, this autonomy must be understood in the context of a period in which the distance between norm and practice was considerable; even if, according to the law, the dowry was supposed to accompany the woman in all stages of her life, in practice, a number of social and political circumstances made it hard to for this to be achieved. Likewise, the situation varied from one social category to another, indeed from one woman to another, according to her ability to keep and defend her belongings.[8]

I seek to demonstrate that women should be seen not as a silent and obedient majority, but as important social actors in the construction of family networks and matrimonial strategies. A careful analysis of the documents shows

7 This subject has been much debated both in Romanian and in foreign historiography. I mention here only a few relevant works: Constanţa Vintilă-Ghiţulescu, *În şalvari şi cu işlic. Biserică, sexualitate, căsătorie şi divorţ în Ţara Românească a secolului al XVIII-lea* (Bucharest: 2011), 135–171; Angela Jianu, 'Women, Dowries and Patrimonial Law in Old Regime Romania, c. 1750–1830', *Journal of Family History*, 34/2 (2009), 189–205; Violeta Barbu, 'De la comunitatea patrimonială la comunitatea de destin: zestrea în Ţara Românească în secolul al XVII-lea', în *De la comunitate la societate. Studii de istoria familiei din Ţara Românească sub Vechiul Regim* (Bucharest: 2007), 19–93; Elena Bedreag, 'Church Endowments and Family Inheritance in 18th-Century Moldavia', *Romanian Journal of Population Studies*, vol XIV, 1 (2020), 5–18.

8 BAR, Fond Documente Istorice, CXCVII/71, 23, 15 June 1756.

a complex situation with regard to the connection between women and the wealth that the political authorities were trying to keep for them.[9] Women were not static objects[10]: they often appear in the court records defending or demanding their rights (of which they were aware, few as they might be), just as they appear as vectors of the change and promotion of certain fashions through the purchases they made, the adoption of certain manners as a result of their reading, and the advancement of their families and wider kinship network by assimilating education or political strategies.[11]

The dowry document included women in the inheritance of patrimony, but also excluded them. According to the written law code (*pravilă*), upon marriage, a Wallachian woman left her father's house with a dowry.[12] This did not remove her from the sharing of the patrimony, as the dowry was to be added to the other goods in the estate, which was then shared out.[13] In the case of Moldavia, it has been argued that women participated on an equal basis in the transmission of patrimony,[14] though more recent studies have tended to nuance this hypothesis, demonstrating that in fact, even if women received properties and lands, these never included what was considered to be the nucleus of the family patrimony.[15] On the other hand, the customary system in both Moldavia and Wallachia excluded women who had received a dowry

9 BAR, Fond Documente Istorice, DCCXCVI/128, 20 January 1817.

10 Maria Bucur, 'To Have and to Hold: Gender Regimes and Property Rights in the Romanian Principalities before World War I', *European History Quarterly*, 48/4 (2018), 601–628.

11 See also Evdoxios Doxiadis, 'Women, Wealth, and the State in Greece (1750–1860)', in Evguenia Davidova (ed.), *Wealth in the Ottoman and Post-Ottoman Balkans. A Socio-Economic History* (London: 2016), 9–29.

12 The system of the dowry, as part of the paternal inheritance, occurs frequently in other regions too. See Bernard Derouet, 'Transmettre la terre. Origines et inflexions récentes d'une problématique de la différence', *Histoire et sociétés rurales*, n° 2, 1994, 33–67; The Special Issue 'Femmes, dot et patrimoine', *Clio. Histoire, femmes et sociétés*, 7 (1998).

13 *Îndreptarea legii (1652)* (Bucharest: 1962), 271–272.

14 Most of these studies are based more on the analysis of the law codes than on an examination of the documents. George Fotino, *Contribution à l'étude des origines de l'ancien droit coutumier roumain. Un chapitre de l'histoire de la propriété au moyen âge* (Paris: 1926); Alexandru Gonţa, 'Femeia şi drepturile ei de moştenire în Moldova după obiceiul pământului', *Anuarul Institutului de Istorie şi Arheologie "A.D. Xenopol" Iaşi*, XVII, 1980, 597–602; Gheorghe Cronţ, *Instituţii medievale româneşti*, (Bucharest : 1969), 31–80. For a more recent study see Maria Magdalena Székely, 'Structuri de familie în societatea medievală moldovenească', *Arhiva Genealogică*, IV (IX) 1–2, 1997, 59–117.

15 See in this connection Petronel Zahariuc, 'Despre o casă de pe Uliţa Mare şi despre o poveste cu drepturile femeii din Moldova (prima jumătate a secolului al XVIII-lea)', *Ioan Neculce. Buletinul Muzeului Municipal 'Regina Maria'*, I (2019), 29–50.

from the succession.[16] These provisions of the customary system were later adopted in the law codes of 1780 and 1817.[17]

The status of the dowry and of a woman's patrimony was very clearly specified both by law and by custom. The husband enjoyed only the usufruct of these 'riches', but could not alienate anything without his wife's agreement. Governed by the same Byzantine tradition as in Greece,[18] Moldavian and Wallachian legislation accorded the right to compensation for part of the dowry that had been dispersed or used by the husband for his own purposes. For example, Smaranda Merișescu sought from her husband, Dimitrie Merişescu, the protagonist of the previous chapter, compensation for goods from her dowry that had been used to cover household expenses. By a document dated 6 November 1834, Dimitrie Merișescu offered her a considerable part of his vineyards and estates in Târgul Pietrei, both as compensation for the dowry consumed and as a 'guarantee' to ensure her well-being in the event of his unexpected death.[19]

The study of a considerable number of dowry documents—around two thousand, from both Moldavia and Wallachia—has shown the importance of the dowry in the realization of a marriage. Over and above norms and customs, the wishes of the father played an essential role in constituting a dowry, as is shown in the repetition of a formula: 'out of all that I had, out of all this I have given her' (*din toate câte am avut, din toate i-am dat*). Following this formula, a daughter received her dowry according to the wishes of her father and taking account of the social status of the future son-in-law. As in other regions of the Ottoman Empire, marriage was an obligation.[20] Thus the majority of women married, on which occasion they received a considerable share of the family's wealth by way of dowry documents. For this reason, I have insisted on the legal framework governing the drawing up of these documents, which are an important source for studying the well-being of women in the past.

From the examples mentioned in previous chapters it may easily be observed that the 'Greek' favourites in the entourage of the Princes looked towards marriage alliances with wealthy and prestigious boyar families. Over and above the

---

16 Marcel Emerit, 'La femme en Valachie pouvait-elle hériter?', *Revue historique du Sud-Est européen*, t. IV, 1–3 (1927), 38–46; Marcel Emerit, 'A propos du droit des femmes à l'héritage en Valachie', *Revue historique du Sud-Est européen* , V, 1–3 (1928), 32–33.

17 M.I. Peretz, *Privilegiul masculinităţii în Pravilniceasca Condică Ipsilanti şi în Legiuirea Caragea* (Bucharest: 1905).

18 See, for comparison, the situation in Greece in Doxiadis, 'Women, Wealth, and the State in Greece', 11.

19 BAR, Fond Documente Istorice, MDXLI/13.

20 Doxiadis, 'Women, Wealth, and the State in Greece', 10.

dowry, they were interested in entering a network that could ensure that they would retain their powerful position even after the deposition of the current prince. As Pierre Bourdieu has suggested, belonging to a solid network played an essential role in the creation of symbolic capital.[21]

The dowry constituted an equally important stake for the local elite: boyars, prosperous merchants, or craftsmen would sit down at the table to negotiate not only a patrimony but also a social status. On these negotiations depended on the status of the married woman, whose destiny was prefigured in the networks and relations developed by the two families. Conscious of the role they played not only from an economic but also from a social point of view, women affirmed and emphasized their participation in the construction of a fortune or of a social position. When they came before the courts of justice, women showed that they knew not only their rights, but also the legal options available to help them to resolve a conflict. Just as men crossed confessional and legal frontiers in order to appeal to the Ottoman courts, so women set out to seek justice, hoping that the Ottoman authorities would be less influenced by local power relations. The example of Zoe Dudescu is eloquent in this connection. After the death of her husband, Matei Cantacuzino, Zoe opened a lawsuit against her brother, the grand *vistiernic* Nicolae Dudescu, one of the most powerful and influential boyars in the political arena. She claimed part of the immense patrimony that had been inherited only by her brother.[22] Considering that she had no chance of success in a country where her brother could influence any judge, Zoe went to Istanbul to appeal to the sultan.[23] In fact, this practice can be seen frequently among Ottoman Christian women, who would appeal to Muslim courts, considering that Islamic law was often more to their advantage.[24]

The law court was an 'arena', as Fariba Zarinebaf puts it, where many family disputes were put on show, offering us the possibility of discovering both the economic situation of women and the abilities they used to defend their

---

21 Pierre Bourdieu, 'Le Capital Social', *Actes de la Recherche en Sciences Sociales*, 31 (1980), 2–3.

22 BAR, Fond Documente Istorice, XIII/103, 104, August 1768.

23 Cantacuzino, *Genealogia*, 287–289.

24 Sophia Laiou, 'Christian Women in an Ottoman World: Interpersonal and Family Cases Brought Before the Shari'a Courts During the Seventeenth and Eighteenth Centuries. (Cases Involving the Greek Community)', in Irvin Cemil Schick (ed.), *Women in the Ottoman Balkans. Gender, Culture and History* (London: 2007), 243–271; Rossitsa Gradeva, 'A kadı Court in the Balkans: Sofia in the Seventeenth and Early Eighteenth Centuries', in Christine Woodhead (ed.), *The Ottoman World* (London: 2012), 57–71; Eugenia Kermeli, 'Marriage and Divorce of Christians and New Muslims in Early Modern Ottoman Empire: Crete 1645–1670', *Oriente Moderno*, 93 (2013), 527–546.

goods and to demand their rights.[25] Putting together the various studies on the women of southeastern Europe and their well-being, we may observe that they were active players in the economy of the region, owning land and other immoveable property, buying and selling, ordering various goods, founding places of worship, borrowing and lending. Fariba Zarinebaf has dealt with a number of these roles in her study of the place of women in the urban economy of Istanbul,[26] Evdoxios Doxiadis has shed lights on the relation between Greek women, their wealth, and the evolution of the legal framework,[27] and Evguenia Davidova has analysed the economic agency of women in Bulgarian merchant networks.[28] In the following pages, I shall examine the place of women in matrimonial strategies through the prism of their social status and the economic value of the dowries they received.

The Matrimonial Policies of the Phanariots

Marriage was an important instrument both in social ascent and in the construction of transborder networks. In the previous chapters, I have insisted especially on the foreigners who built their careers and made their homes in the Principalities, without saying much about marriage and matrimonial policies. The archives preserve an impressive number of documents regarding inter-ethnic marriages that took place in the Principalities during the period I am dealing with. In most cases, the parties were Orthodox: Greeks, Bulgarians, Serbs, Vlachs, or Russians. But there is also information in the archives about Jews, Armenians, Turks, French or Germans who converted to the Orthodox faith in order to get married.

The dowry and access to a network of local solidarity constituted the principal objectives for a foreigner adopting such a matrimonial policy. As a favourite of the prince, a foreigner could obtain an important office that provided an income. However this favour lasted only as long as the patron's reign, usually three years but sometimes less. When the patron was removed from

25 Fariba Zarinebaf, 'From mahalle (neighborhood) to the market and the courts: women, credit, and property in eighteenth-century Istanbul', Jutta Gisela Sperling and Shona Kelly Wray (eds.), *Gender, property, and law in Jewish, Christian, and Muslim communities in the wider Mediterranean, 1300–1800* (London and New York: 2009), 231.

26 Zarinebaf, 'Women, credit, and property', 224–237.

27 Evdoxios Doxiadis, *The Shackles of Modernity: Women, Property, and the transition from the Ottoman Empire to the Greek State* (Cambridge – London: 2011).

28 Evguenia Davidova, *Balkan Transitions to Modernity and Nation-States Through the Eyes of Three Generations of Merchants (1780–1890s)* (Leiden: 2012), 101–129.

power, access to resources was limited or interrupted. Marriage and entry into the local network constituted effective strategies that could help a foreigner to remain connected not only to economic, but also to social and political resources. I should add that some of the princes themselves consolidated their connections with the local boyar class by means of marriage, thus offering a powerful example to others.[29]

On the other side, boyars, merchants, craftsmen, and other townsmen had various objectives when they accepted a foreigner as son-in-law and included him in the family and its patrimony. By agreeing to his daughter's marriage with a favourite in the entourage of the prince, a boyar was extending his network and at the same time positioning himself in the close circle of power.[30]At this social level, matters of power can frequently be seen to have played a part in the choice of a partner. A great boyar would seek the blessing of the prince for the marriages of his children and sometimes would choose him to be their sponsor. At the same time, it may be observed that, when it was in his interests, a prince would intervene in the choices made by his subjects, to the point of forcing a boyar or boyaress to accept a matrimonial alliance. The chronicles and documents in the archives of boyar families record such cases, where the will of the prince became an incontestable command.

Prince Nicolae Mavrocordat (January–November 1716 and 1719–1730) constructed matrimonial strategies aimed at facilitating long-term access to power. In the second part of this book, I referred to Iordache Ruset, considered one of the most powerful and influential boyars in Moldavia, and how Mavrocordat took the opportunity to remove him from the political game, fearing that through his matrimonial alliances and especially his kinship with Mihai Racoviță, Ruset posed a threat to his throne. Instead of having Ruset beheaded, as some of his rivals among the high office-holders were demanding, he made him an ally. When he returned to the throne of Wallachia, Nicolae Mavrocordat was accompanied by one of Iordache Ruset's sons, for whom he mediated a marriage to Ancuța Filipescu, who came from an important boyar family and brought a substantial dowry: 'This favour his highness did [...] to Ioniță Ruset, the son of the *vornic* Iordache of Moldavia, who being in Tsarigrad, his highness came here into the country, and in this year (1716)

29 On social mobility by means of marriage, see Radu G. Păun, 'Some Remarks about the Historical Origins of the "Phanariot Phenomenon"', in Gelina Harlaftis and Radu G. Păun (eds.), *Greeks in Romania in the Nineteenth Century* (Athens: 2013), 47–94.

30 I have already discussed above the striking example of the marriages of Ianache Văcărescu. See chapter 4.

officiated his marriage, giving him Ancuța, one of the daughters of the *stolnic* Matei Filipescu, favouring him with a princely edict exempting him from taxes.'[31]

Coming closer to the native boyars through marriage helped the Phanariots to consolidate loyalties and to construct an internal power network. In his long reign in Wallachia, Nicolae Mavrocordat mediated many other marriages, cementing relations with the local boyars and ensuring the fidelity of his Greek favourites.[32] Matrimonial strategies became the most readily available instrument for entering a community and obtaining local rights and access to estates, houses, shops, and Gypsy slaves. Not every such alliance was crowned with success, however. The foreigner embodied a significant dose of alterity, in which insecurity and lack of trust were essential elements. To defend itself from unknown foreigners, society developed a series of protective instruments: some written, others oral. The archives have preserved 'certificates of guarantee' (*zapise de chezăşie*) in which a would-be bridegroom asked his business partners to write about his behaviour, his wealth, and his family in far-off lands.[33] In most cases, however, marriages between locals and foreigners were entered into on the basis of word-of-mouth recommendation. In other words, the community supplied the information that the parents needed to decide on the prospects of a marriage. Any marriage negotiation was preceded by at least a minimal enquiry, which would become more thorough when the prospect of failure was on the horizon. Petitions addressed to the prince speak of the breakdown of such alliances, in which the abandoning of the wife was often accompanied by the scattering of the dowry.[34] This must be the background to the drafting of the decree issued by Prince Ștefan Racoviță (1763–1764) in

31 *Istoriile domnilor Țării Româneşti de Radu Popescu vornicul*, ed. Constantin Grecescu (Bucharest: 1963), 268–269.

32 Among the examples recounted by *Ban* Mihai Cantacuzino may be mentioned the marriages of Constantin Ramadan, first to Maria Cantacuzino (d. 1731) and then to Maria Creţulescu, both belonging to rich and influential boyar families. In both situations, Nicolae Mavrocordat intervened. See Cantacuzino, *Genealogia*, 359. See also Mariana Lazăr, 'Spre lumea "de dincolo", trecând împreună prin lumea pământeană. Marele vornic Iordache Creţulescu şi soţia sa, domniţa Safta Brâncoveanu', in Mircea Ciubotaru, Lucian-Valeriu Lefter (eds.), *Mihai Dim. Sturdza la 80 de ani. Omagiu* (Iaşi: 2014), 799–822.

33 Suraiya Faroqhi has shown that recourse to such guarantees was a common practice in the Ottoman Empire, especially for 'outsiders' who wanted to settle in a locality. Vezi Suraiya Faroqhi, *Artisans of Empire. Crafts and Craftspeople Under the Ottomans* (London: 2009), 144–145.

34 In this context, the petitioners mention their suspicion regarding the introduction of foreigners into the family network. Increasing mobility and the appearance of a growing number of foreigners thus led to a rise in distrust among the population.

Wallachia on 3 July 1764. The first part of the document presents itself as an analysis of the phenomenon and at the same time a justification of the necessity of the measures that are to be taken. There are references to the diverse ethnic origins of the newcomers—Greeks, Albanians, Serbs—who are divided into two categories: 'men of respectability and of known kin' (*oameni mai de cinste şi cu neamul ştiut*) and 'others of low quality and unknown' (*alţii proşti şi neştiuţi*). The real problem is posed by the latter, who are further divided between 'those with a trade' and 'those with no trade' (*cei cu meşteşug* [...] *cei fără meşteşug*). Those arriving in Wallachia include some who have committed reprobable acts in their countries of origin and have had to flee to escape punishment. Enriching themselves by various methods, some less than honest, these foreigners purchase administrative posts with ease. Then, to be completely assimilated, they marry the daughters of boyars, sometimes taking their names, and thus entering 'the ranks of the office-holding boyars' (*în rîndul boierilor cu dregătorie*). Some of the boyars behind this document consider this to be unfair competition, claiming that the newcomers 'dishonour' (*necinstesc*) the positions that they have purchased in this way 'and the race of boyars is denigrated' (*iar neamul boierilor pămînteni se ocărăşte*). This practice is blamed for all the 'evils' (*relele*) and damage that the country has suffered, as some of the 'natives' (*pământeni*) have been contaminated in their ways by the example of the 'intruders' (*intruși*). In order to control mobility, Ştefan Racoviţă decided to forbid marriage between the daughters of local families and foreigners, on pain of the banishment of the couple from the country and the confiscation of their wealth by the prince; parents, sponsors, and priests were to be punished if they did not respect this decision. Those already married were tolerated only if they were prepared to remain 'at the rank of boyarship where they are' (*la starea boieriei ce să află*) and did not wish 'to raise themselves to a higher level' (*a se înălţa la altă treaptă mai mare*).

The document was requested by a part of the boyar class who found themselves threatened by increasing and uncontrolled mobility. Even if its subject is the mobile population, whether merchants or craftsmen, who have set out in search of a 'home', it focuses on the favourites in the entourage of the Phanariots. Owing to their position, these individuals occupied profitable offices, which enabled them to penetrate the local boyar class by means of marriage, and they would remain after the prince's departure, becoming part of a local network.[35] The decree was applied only when it was in the prince's

35 On this dissension, see Gheorghe Brătianu, *Sfatul domnesc şi adunarea stărilor în principatele române* (Bucharest: 1995), 185–193. The document may also be understood in the

interest.[36] After the deposition of Ștefan Racoviță, the law, like other similar legislation, fell into disuse.

The princes continued to impose their own matrimonial strategies. I referred in a previous chapter to the saga of the Brâncoveanu brothers, who went into self-imposed exile on their estates in Transylvania to escape the violence of the Russian–Ottoman war of 1768–1774. At the time, Nicolae Brâncoveanu was married to Maria, daughter of Ştefan Văcărescu. During those years in exile, she bore him a son, Constantin, who died soon after. When the war was over, Nicolae returned to Wallachia and divorced her.[37] I have not yet found the papers of the divorce proceedings; in their absence, I can only presume that the motive was his desire to have progeny, which was apparently not possible with Maria Văcărescu.[38] Around 1776, Nicolae married Safta Fălcoianu, who was herself divorced from Grigore Băleanu. The marriage did not last long, however, as Prince Ipsilanti needed an important pawn within the local boyar class. The prince thus accused Nicolae Brâncoveanu of having remarried without having a certificate of separation from the metropolitan, as was the custom of the country, and annulled his second marriage, only, shortly afterwards, to offer him the hand of Elena Moruzi, first cousin of his own wife, Caterina Moruzi.[39] Once again, Mihai Cantacuzino astutely grasps Prince Ipsilanti's policy: 'This was the occasion to marry him to a relative of his; and indeed he was sponsor at his marriage to Elenița, widow of the *aga* Ioniţă Guliano, who was Moruzi's daughter and first cousin of Prince Alexandru's lady.'[40]

The document and the examples given here might suggest that the local elite was opposed to such 'misalliances'. However, the matrimonial strategies of the late eighteenth century and even more the early nineteenth, when

context created by Constantin Mavorcordat's social reforms, which had given a new form to the boyar class, linking their status to the holding of administrative office.

36 Urechia, *Istoria românilor*, II, 147–148.

37 Regarding divorce in Wallachia, see: Constanţa Vintilă-Ghiţulescu, 'Autour du divorce: disputes et réconciliations au tribunal (Valachie, 1750–1830)', *Annales de Démographie Historique*, 2 (2009), 77–99; Constanţa Vintilă-Ghiţulescu, 'Usage des corps/ usage des mots au tribunal. Conflits et réconciliations dans la société roumaine (1750–1830)', in Claude Gauvard, Alessandro Stella (eds.), *Couples en justice, IVe–XIXe siècle*, (Paris: 2013), 197–213.

38 On 19 September 1797, Maria Văcărescu drew up her testament, noting among other things the dowry that she had recovered from the house of her former husband, the *ban* Nicolae Brâncoveanu. See BAR, Fond Documente Istorice, MLXXXVI/34, Fond Manuscrise MS 611, ff. 35r–37v.

39 On the family relation between the two women, see Marinescu, *Etude généalogique*, 36, 42.

40 Cantacuzino, *Genealogia*, 349.

the presence of the Russian army became a constant factor, show the interest of the elite in attracting protection or consolidating networks by means of marriage. Many boyars' daughters became pawns in alliances with Russian officers, and left, with their dowries, for Russia.[41] Others directed Moldavian and Wallachian political life from the shadows, either as the wives of Russian generals or as their lovers. The first to write about the roles assumed by these women and their involvement in decision-making in the political arena was General Louis Alexandre Andrault de Langeron. Present in the Principalities during the 1806–1812 Russian military occupation, General Langeron left memoirs that are useful for an understanding of the networks and alliance policies developed by boyars and Phanariots alike in order to gain access to resources and power.[42] Another episode, portrayed in his memoirs by Colonel Grigore Lăcusteanu, unfolded under the government of General Pavel Kiselyov, when once again the women of Moldavian and Wallachian high society entered the foreground of the political arena through their involvement in influencing political decisions.[43]

Women and Luxury Consumption

The value of the dowry depended on the social category to which the bride belonged. It was a means by which objects and other goods circulated, making it a good indicator for the material culture in a particular period, for the tastes and styles that were in fashion. An analysis of dowry documents shows that dowries were made up of estates, livestock, houses, shops, mills, vineyards, beehives, Gypsy slaves, the bride's trousseau, and money.[44] In addition there were wedding presents, received at various stages in the nuptial ceremony: gifts before the wedding, 'Monday gifts' (*daruri de luni*) given by the bridegroom after the wedding, and gifts from wedding guests. To the dowry and gifts might be added a series of other donations or parts of the woman's inheritance

41 Paul Cernovodeanu, 'Strategii matrimoniale ruse în societatea românească din perioada regulamentară', *Arhiva Genealogică*, IV (IX), 3–4 (1997), 243–252.

42 Hurmuzaki, *Documente*, I/3, 216–370.

43 Grigore Lăcusteanu, *Amintirile colonelului Lăcusteanu*, ed. Radu Crutzescu (Bucharest: 1935), 75–79.

44 Nicoleta Roman, 'Dowry Contracts, Women's Objects and the Circulation of Goods in Mid-Nineteenth Century Romanian Families. The Case of Oltenia', *Revista Istorică*, XXIX, 1–2 (2018), 105–139; Nicoleta Roman, 'Starting a married life: women and goods in the mid-nineteenth-century Romanian towns of Pitești and Câmpulung', in Annette Caroline Cremer (ed.), *Gender, Law and Material Culture. Immobile Property and Mobile Goods in Early Modern Europe* (London: 2020), 239–263.

received by her from her family. To what extent did she have all these at her disposal? Did women truly participate in luxury consumption? Were they consumers? Were they 'customers' of the merchants and shops of the period? How might this consumption and the role of women in the accumulation of goods and objects be documented?

The trousseau was part of the dowry, and was listed in the order of the items that were placed in the dowry chest: jewellery; the set of clothes (*rânduiala hainelor*: dresses, blouses, *anteris*, stockings, capes, jackets, shoes); the set of bedding (*rânduiala aşternutului*: sheets, pillows, blankets, carpets, quilts, mattresses, icons, incense burners, mirrors, prayer ropes); and the table set (*rânduiala mesei*: towels, table napkins, table cloth, sets of spoons, knives, forks, teaspoons, coffee cups, saucers for conserves, dishes, trays, jugs, basins, large and small cauldrons, trivets, brass and silver candlesticks, icons, mirrors). All these items belonged by right and in fact to the woman, and should ease her integration into her new home, her new kindred. The gifts offered to parents-in-law and to brothers- and sisters-in-law constituted another stage in the acceptance of the bride and her winning the goodwill of her 'adoptive' family. The composition of the trousseau pointed to femininity, with the items listed following a certain model.[45] However, information is scarce when it comes to the woman's role in assembling her trousseau. We may suppose that the mother dealt with the procurement from the market of items of clothing or of fashionable textiles and embroidery, whether the daughter was interested in cashmere shawls or silk fabrics, in satin slippers and diamond earrings, in capes of velvet embroidered with silver thread and shalwars, in headscarves and Indian fabrics, expensive and prestigious.[46] This interest is documented in purchase lists. It is not yet clear whether the items were for home consumption or to make up dowries. However, testaments permit us to observe how mothers redirected towards their daughters considerable quantities of jewellery and textiles that had made up part of their own trousseaus. They were an important instrument by which women could dispose of their belongings as

45 The dowry list follows a standard model, in which the goods were listed beginning with objects in the bride's trousseau and continuing with houses, estates, animals, and Gypsy families. The same model is found in Poland too. See Andrzej Pośpiech 'Majątek osobisty szlachcica w świetle wielkopolskich pośmiertnych inwentarzy ruchomości z XVII w.', *Kwartalnik Historii Kultury Materialnej* 29/4 (1981), 465. My thanks to Michał Wasiucionek for this information and for translating the text.

46 On the Ottoman elite's appetite for expensive Indian textiles and cashmere shawls, see Faroqhi, *op. cit.*, 175.

they pleased.[47] Moreover, women were frequently named as executors of their husbands' estates, testifying to a peaceful life together and to a high degree of confidence in their ability both to manage a patrimony and to divide it among the heirs according to all the customs of the family.[48]

Over the last few decades, a series of studies have addressed the woman's status within a marriage, trying to trace the relation between consumption and well-being.[49] 'Marriage is linked to well-being in various ways,' states the introduction to the volume *The Transmission of Well-Being*. The authors point out the change in status that took place with marriage, which allowed a woman access to *well-being*. Even if marriage did not offer rights, statuses, and roles equal to those of her husband, it ensured that the woman had material and emotional support.[50] As Maria Bucur points out, there is a difference between 'having' and 'holding' the right to enjoy the goods and properties received by way of dowry or acquired during her marriage.[51] Nevertheless, the rights of these women must always be analysed in the context of the period and according to the material provided by the historical sources. For south-eastern Europe, there are as yet no serial studies, only various investigations into specific aspects.[52] For this reason, I shall limit myself here to nuanced hypotheses regarding the relation between women and consumption, avoiding labels or pronouncements that belong more to our contemporary world than to a society in which social and gender inequalities were part of a social,

47 In recent years, testaments have attracted increasing interest on the part of researchers. This has led to the publication of a considerable number of testaments.

48 See Daniel H. Kaiser's study, in which he considers that testaments are a good instrument for observing the improvement of women's status in relation to property and inheritance rights. Daniel H. Kaiser, 'Gender, Property, and Testamentary Behavior: Eighteenth-Century Moscow Wills', *Harvard Ukrainian Studies* 28, 1–4 (2006), 161–170.

49 Anna Bellavitis, Beatrice Zucca Micheletto (eds.), *Gender, Law and Economic Well-Being in Europe from the Fifteenth to the Nineteenth Century. North Versus South?* (Abington: 2018).

50 Margarida Durães, Antoinette Fauve-Chamoux, Llorenç Ferrer, Jan Kok (eds.), *The Transmission of Well-Being: Gendered Marriage Strategies and Inheritance Systems in Europe (17th–20th) Centuries* (Bern–Berlin–Bruxelles–Frankfurt am Main–New York–Oxford–Vienna: 2009), 6.

51 Bucur, 'To Have and to Hold'.

52 Maria N. Todorova, *Balkan Family Structure and the European Pattern. Demographic Developments in Ottoman Bulgaria* (Budapest, New York: 2006); Haris Exertzoglou, 'The Cultural Uses of Consumption: Negotiating Class, Gender, and Nation in the Ottoman Urban Centers during the 19th Century', *International Journal of Middle East Studies* 35 (2003), 77–101; Rossitsa Gradeva, 'On "Frenk" Objects in Everyday Life in Ottoman Balkans: the case of Sofia, Mid-17th–mid-18th Centuries', in Siomnetta Cavaciocchi (ed.), *Europe's Economic Relations with the Islamic World 13th–18th Centuries* (Florence: 2007), 769–799.

political, and religious structure.[53] Women participated in the consumption and circulation of goods by way of the dowries they received, but also through their involvement in the procurement of items that were necessary or merely fashionable. Likewise, the documents testify to the inclusion of the wife in the administration of common wealth, taking an active part in decisions concerning the management of the household. My hypotheses, of course, consider the following: the woman's role within the household is intrinsically linked to the marital relationship, to the kinship group from which she came, and to the dowry she brought to her new home. Thus, wealth and the marital relationship construct a feminine status within the home. An equally important element may be added: the woman's ability to sustain and impose this status. In this book, I refer to many women of the upper stratum of society, such as Zoița Brâncoveanu, Ecaterina Caragea, and Elena Hartulari, who played an active role in their husbands' political activity.[54] These women are certainly not representative of the majority, but nor should it be considered that they represent only a small minority. Admittedly, however, their voices are only heard due to a father or husband who encouraged and supported their participation in the construction of a household, of a wider kinship identity.

At the same time, with the help of correspondence, we may observe the active involvement of women in the consumption of objects, clothes, and various fashionable foodstuffs.[55] This role is better documented from the second half of the eighteenth century, especially for the upper social strata. In other words, with more and more documents being discovered in family archives, historians are better able to trace the contribution of women to the circulation of goods and objects through lists of purchases and letters. Furthermore, the fact of drawing up a list presupposes a certain level of education—enough not only to draft a letter but also to give one access to catalogues, fashion albums, travel, and knowledge.[56] Phanariot women provided the essential model in the launch of a taste for education and consumption. As members of an

53 Bucur, *op. cit.*, 601–628.

54 For another example, see Constanţa Vintilă-Ghiţulescu, '"Curls and Forelocks": Romanian Women's Emancipation in Consumption and Fashion, 1780–1850', in Constanţa Vintilă-Ghiţulescu (ed.), *Women, Consumption, and the Circulation of Ideas in South-Eastern Europe, 17th–19th Centuries* (Leiden: 2017), 124–150; Anastasia Falierou, 'European Fashion, Consumption Patterns, and Intercommunal Relations in 19th-Century Ottoman Istanbul', ibid., 150–168; Nicoleta Roman, 'Women in Merchant Families, Women in Trade in Mid-19th Century Romanian Countries' in ibid., 169–199.

55 On the relation between women and consumption see Leora Auslander, 'Culture matérielle, histoire du genre et des sexualités', *Clio. Histoire des femmes*, 40 (2014), 171–195.

56 See also Anastasia Falierou, 'Urban Transformation of the Mytilenian Bourgeoisie: The Case of the Kourtzis Family', *Revista Istorică*, XXIX, 1–2 (2018), 141–161.

educated elite, they brought from the Phanar to Bucharest or Iași not only a taste for cashmere shawls or satin slippers, but also a certain inclination for reading Greek and French literature, for theatre, music, and travel. These women travelled frequently between Bucharest, Iași, Brusa, Edirne, Rhodes, Izmir and other places in the Ottoman Empire, accompanying their husbands to positions of power or into exile.[57] In addition to journeys of this type, which were in a sense part of ordinary life, there was travel undertaken as part of one's education or to spas in various areas of Europe.[58] The women of southeastern Europe travelled less, however, than those of central or western Europe,[59] and fewer of them have left accounts of their travels and impressions of the world they discovered. As Evguenia Davidova argues, 'physical mobility' may be seen as a 'form of consumerism', offering women 'novel ways of constructing gender and class identity.'[60] Through travel, women encountered objects, lifestyles, and tastes that influenced their way of behaving or thinking.

In the summer of 1813, Elena Glogoveanu set out for Vienna, accompanied by her minor daughter (Maria, known by the pet name Masinca) and two servant women. The daughter of the *ban* Costache Ghica and Maria Cantacuzino, Elena (or Elenco, to use the Greek diminutive) had married Nicolae Glogoveanu, who at the time held the office of *ispravnic* (prefect) of Mehedinți county. Her journey followed the pattern of the time: from Cerneți, then the county town of Mehedinți, she left by diligence for Vienna, via Buda, a journey of about twelve days. Elena suffered from 'chest' trouble, and was seeking health in Vienna, where her father had been settled for some time.[61] Her

57 See the example of the Dudescu family (wife Maria Cantemir, son Nicolae and daughter Zoe) who went into exile in Mytilene, accompanying the grand *ban* Constantin Dudescu: Cantacuzino, *Genealogia*, 131. See also the correspondence between different branches of the Manu family exiled to Zila after 1821 and those who remained in Bucharest. The letters are preserved in a fonds—*Documente Istorice*—of the Library of the Romanian Academy.

58 See the project 'The European Spa as a Transnational Public Space and Social Metaphor': https://www.theeuropeanspa.eu/team/index.html.

59 Wendy Bracewell, Alex Drace-Francis, (eds.), *Balkan Departures. Travel Writing from Southeastern Europe* (New York: 2009); Wendy Bracewell (ed.), *Orientations. An Anthology of East European Travel Writing, ca. 1550–2000* (Budapest: 2009); Matei Cazacu, *Des Femmes sur les routes de l'Orient. Le voyage à Constantinople au XVIIIe–XIXe siècles* (Genève: 1999).

60 Evguenia Davidova, 'Women Travellers as Consumers: Adoption of Modern Ideas and Practices in 19th Southeast Europe', in Constanţa Vintilă-Ghiţulescu (ed.), *Women, Consumption and the Circulation of Ideas in South-Eastern Europe, 17th–19th Century* (Leiden: 2018), 201.

61 Constantin Ghica was kept under supervision, and it had been proposed that he be expelled from Vienna, accused of spreading false rumours about an imminent war. With him was the merchant (become Russian counsellor) Grigore Cariboglu. The latter was

correspondence with relatives, friends, and her family at home in Wallachia helps us to study the impact that this journey had on her, and later on her children and even her husband. In the first part of her time in Vienna, Elena Glogoveanu stayed in her father's house. Being ill, probably with tuberculosis, she interacted in the first place with relatives and with a number of friends and acquaintances: Hristodulos Ghirlakidis, Nicolae Cutcudache and his wife Ecaterina, Elena Fălcoianu. Belonging to the same cultural and linguistic space united them: they were Orthodox Christians, they spoke Greek, and they were bound to the Ottoman Empire by family connections and ethnic roots. In that period, Vienna was considered a cosmopolitan city, where members of different ethnic groups developed common practices.[62] According to Gontier de Paifal, in Vienna in 1800, no fewer than fifteen languages were spoken: 'allemand, latin, français, italien, grec, hongrois, bohémois, polonais, flamand, wallach [Romanian], turc, illyrique, croatique, windique, ruthénique.'[63] The city attracted and was frequented by many Orthodox merchants, who got rich from trade with the Habsburg Empire, but also by Moldavian or Wallachian boyars and by all who were interested in professional and intellectual training.

Hristodulos Ghirlakidis was a Greek merchant who had enriched himself from trade between the Ottoman and Habsburg Empires, via Wallachia. He had then settled in Vienna, where, with the help of his money, he had obtained subjecthood and the title of baron, adapting his identity to the new social and political context under the name of Kirlian, baron of Langenfeld.

Before settling in Vienna, 'Kir Nicola' had been a Vlach merchant, born in the region of Pindus or Epirus, who busied himself with trade in hides, living sometimes in the Ottoman Empire, sometimes in Wallachia, and sometimes in the Habsburg Empire. When he had amassed some wealth, he had married Ecaterina, with whom he had five children, and then decided to settle in Vienna, becoming an Austrian subject with his home at no. 557 Fischhofstraße. He continued to trade in hides, but now through his agents, and became 'one of the most experienced in this branch of commerce.'[64]

Elena Glogoveanu's banker. ANIC, Microfilme Austria, Rola 99, c. 586–602, 620–626, 11 March 1817, 24 June 1817, 10 July 1817.

62 Françoise Knopper, 'Le cosmopolitisme viennois', *Dix-Huitième Siècle*, 25 (1993), 129–151; David Do Paço, 'A case of urban integration: Vienna's port area and the Ottoman merchants in the eighteenth century', *Urban History*, 48, 3 (2020), 1–19.

63 Gontier de Paifal, *Nouveau Guide de Vienne pour les étrangers et les nationaux* (1800), cited by Knopper, *op. cit.*, 131.

64 See the letter of Hristodulos Ghirlakidis, baron de Langenfeld to Nicolae Glogoveanu, Vienna 16/28 June 1814, published in *Arhivele Olteniei*, XV (1936), 391–395.

Because of the precarious state of her health, Elena Glogoveanu seldom frequented Viennese society and even more rarely participated in the sociability of the salons. She was, however, visited by those closest to her, and above all by doctors. These included her regular doctor, one Iosif Lantz, together with Doctors Frank, Krasin, Malfatti, and Nord, who were considered 'the emperor's most renowned physicians'.[65] However, while Elena herself might not be active because of her illness, her daughter Masinca, who seems to have shone for intelligence and beauty, was led through the salons of the Viennese elite and even introduced at the imperial court: 'Your, and my, beloved Masincuța is in good health and from day to day grows in body and in mind. The whole imperial family know her and the emperor himself. She is an angel,' writes Baron Lagenfeld in his letter to her father, Nicolae Glogoveanu.[66]

Correspondence was one of Elena's daily pastimes. She wrote to her husband, relatives, and friends, telling them about her state of health and that of those around her, about everyday life in the Austrian capital, about fashion and education. Written in French, Greek, or Romanian (using the Cyrillic alphabet), Elena Glogoveanu's letters reflect her multilingualism.[67] She had benefitted from a select education thanks to the interest of her father, who had paid for private teachers of Greek and French.[68] Contemporary accounts testify to the inclination of women towards acquiring knowledge of foreign languages, which they then used with considerable pleasure and effectiveness.[69]

Elena found life in Vienna very expensive, according to her complaints in a letter of 21 September 1813 to her husband, Nicolae Glogoveanu. Her money went on doctors and medicines, and on meals, servants, firewood, clothes,

---

65 *Arhivele Olteniei*, XV (1936), 391–395.

66 *Arhivele Olteniei*, XV (1936), 391–395.

67 On the importance of the French language and the appetite for culture, see also the analysis proposed by Michelle Lamarche Marrese regarding the Russian nobility and 'westernisation'. She shows that Peter the Great's reforms were slow to take effect, especially among the elite. The use of French and the enthusiasm for European culture and luxury, visible especially in the first half of the nineteenth century, did not lead to a rejection of 'native tradition'. Michelle Lamarche Marrese, '"The Poetics of Everyday Behavior" Revisited: Lotman, Gender, and the Evolution of Russian Noble Identity', *Kritika: Exploration in Russian and Eurasian History* 11, 4 (2010), 701–739.

68 On 19 March 1804, the French teacher Bonnet Pavillon and Constantin Ghica went to court over unpaid fees. Urechia, *Istoria românilor*, vol. 8, 456–467. See also Drace-Francis, *Making*, 49.

69 Auguste Marie Blathasard Charles Pelletier comte de Lagarde, *Voyage de Moscou à Vienne par Kiew, Odessa, Constantinople, Bucharest et Hermanstadt, ou Lettres adressées à Jules Griffith, par le comte de Lagarde* (Paris: Strasbourg: 1824), 321–322, 324.

and other items intended to maintain a rank, a social status.[70] With Maria Hangerli, she exchanges impressions about lace, jewellery, or cotton and silk thread for embroidery (*tire-iplik*)[71]; with Alexandru Villara she discusses carriages and the plague that was then haunting Bucharest.[72] Over and above her concern for comfort in daily life and her financial adaptation to the demands of Vienna, Elenco is interested in the education of her daughter Masinca and her son Costache. With this in view, she asks her husband to send Costache to her in Vienna to study.[73] Sadly she did not live to see her son arriving in Vienna, as she died on 5/17 May 1814. Masinca, however, remained in Vienna, with her grandfather, to complete her education.[74]

Also in Vienna was Elena Glogoveanu's cousin Elena Fălcoianu, who lived close to the Landstraße with her French servant Zonnette. A rather unpleasant incident gave birth to a rich dossier concerning Elena Glogoveanu and her daughter's period of residence in Vienna. On Holy Monday 1814, Elena Fălcoianu robbed her cousin, stealing jewellery, shawls, and money. The Viennese police, who were called to deal with the case, compiled an inventory of the jewellery and other items stolen. The incident hastened the death of Elena Glogoveanu. The theft and the boyaress's death led to Theodor (also known as Tudor) Vladimirescu being sent to Vienna to take charge of recovering the stolen items and to bring the remaining possessions and the minor daughter back to Cerneți.[75] The expensive dresses, the cashmere shawls, the jewellery of gold and precious stones were inventoried, and the lists were sent to Elena's husband for confirmation. Pragmatically, Theodor proposed that his master should sell the expensive dresses because 'fashions change from day to day' (*modele se schimbă în toate zilele*), the only certainty being money, which

70 BAR, Fond Documente Istorice, CCCXXX/192. She is not alone in complaining of the 'expensive living' in the European capitals. In the same period, the boyar Iancu Balş wrote about how expensive it was to live in Vienna (BAR, Fond Documente Istorice, MCLXXIX/188, 13 July 1812), while another boyar complained about the cost of living in Geneva (BAR, Fond Documente istorice, DCCCXXVI/120, 9 January 1829).

71 BAR, Fond Documente Istorice, CCCXXX/205, 206, the two letters of 10 January 1814.

72 Bar, Fond Documente Istorice, CCCXXX/193, letter (in Greek) from Alexandru Villara, 28 November 1813. For Elena Glogoveanu's undated reply, in which she tells him that she will attend to the purchase of the carriage as soon as she is given more details, see Nicolae Iorga (ed.), 'Scrisori inedite ale lui Tudor Vladimirescu din anii 1814–1815', *Analele Academiei Române. Memoriile Secţiunii Istorice*, XXXVII (1914), 147–148.

73 BAR, Fond Documente Istorice, CCCXXX/192.

74 Iorga, 'Scrisori inedite', 136, 28 December 1814, Pesta.

75 On this episode, see Emil Vârtosu, *Mărturii noi din viaţa lui Tudor Vladimirescu* (Bucharest: 1941); Andrei Oţetea, *Tudor Vladimirescu şi mişcarea eteristă în ţările româneşti, 1821–1822* (Bucharest: 1945), 103–108.

should be allowed to circulate and to bring profit.[76] At the same time, Theodor described in detail little Masinca's preparations for her return home. As winter was approaching, he took care to buy her suitable clothes: 'for Mistress Masinca, I have made clothes for the road.'[77] He also enquired about the easiest way to travel from Vienna to Cerneți, thus enabling us to learn about time, comfort, and means of transport: 'I have fitted out the young lady with winter clothes and I have paid a good fee for a carriage from Vienna to Orșova 480 florints in which people travel as if in a stove [... in] which the girl can come better than in summer. I have also spoken to the doctors and they have told me that by this means children can go anywhere, both winter and summer.'[78]

Lists of purchases show very clearly the active role played by women in the circulation of goods and objects along the roads of the empires. Most of them they addressed directly to the merchants, describing in detail the items that they wanted, sending or requesting samples, asking for the 'painting' (*zugrăveala*) of fashionable items so that they could be ordered, demanding a refund when they were not pleased with the goods received, making deals and incurring debts.[79] The effervescence of consumption may be observed in their husbands too, ordering on behalf of their wives, daughters, or mothers, or for themselves, striving to preserve and uphold the social status of the household and of the family.[80] Even in the case presented above, the recently widowed Nicolae Glogoveanu took advantage of his estate manager's presence in Vienna to ask him to buy a carriage, muskets, remedies, and healing balsams.[81] In the mid-nineteenth century, the expenses of the Oteteleșanu household in Bucharest show very clearly that it was the wife, Safta Oteteleșanu, who took charge of domestic consumption, instructing the household manager (*vechilul*

76 Iorga, 'Scrisori inedite', 127, 18 June 1814, Viena.

77 Iorga, 'Scrisori inedite', 135, 25 November 1814, Vienna. See also the letter of 15 March 1815 containing a list of expenses incurred in Vienna for the upkeep of Masinca and of the servants, and for the progress of the trial. Iorga, 'Scrisori inedite', 141–145.

78 Iorga, 'Scrisori inedite', 136, 28 December 1814, Pesta.

79 Nicolae Iorga (ed.), *Scrisori de boieri şi negustori olteni şi munteni către casa de negoţ sibiiană Hagi Popp* (Bucharest: 1906).

80 Leora Auslander, 'The Gendering of Consumer Practices in Nineteenth-Century France', in Victoria DeGrazia, Ellen Furlough (eds.), *The Sex of Things: Gender and Consumption in Historical Perspective* (California: 1996), 83.

81 Iorga, 'Scrisori inedite', 137, 140, where Theodor Vladimirescu writes to him that he has bought 'boxes of balsams' at 350 florints, which were highly praised and much sought-after in Vienna.

casei) what to buy and from where, administering not only the kitchen and everyone's wardrobe, but also donations and her husband's journeys.[82]

The relation between consumption, women, and cultural changes is, however, a particularly complex one. It must be traced over a considerable number of years for us to grasp its development and the assimilation of changes. Many technological transformations took place in the nineteenth century, contributing to faster and easier mobility, to the diffusion of the press, and thus of information, to the development of a taste for travel and spas, to the circulation of a literature of consumption. All these instruments played their part in the spread of ideas, tastes, and products coming from the West. All the same, as Haris Exertzoglou has shown, 'consumption' is 'discursively construed, negotiated, and appropriated by different groups within a specific historical context.'[83] Exertzoglou concentrates his analysis on the Orthodox and Greek-speaking 'middle class' of Istanbul and Smyrna, which took advantage of the reforms in the Ottoman Empire to develop commercial and financial relations with European economies and to construct 'modern professions.'[84] In Wallachia and Moldavia, this middle level emerged with considerable difficulty, and the archives show that the principal consumers of goods and commodities remained the wealthy boyars.

The premises of social changes took shape only with the Organic Regulations, which outlined the reform of the two principalities and established the need for qualified personnel able to implement the desiderata of the modern state.

The appearance and spread of 'national' gazettes favoured the circulation of information about new fashions, new tastes, and new ideas. A glance at the content of these gazettes shows the relatively easy path taken by goods and products from the 'West' into the homes of boyars, merchants, doctors, teachers, and functionaries in the urban environment. The need for qualified people opened the door for a long series of professions to take Moldavia, Wallachia, Serbia, and Greece by storm, offering their services as gardeners, valets, teachers (of dance, music, piano, foreign languages, or painting), engineers, architects, and doctors. The education of women became a preoccupation of

---

82 BAR, Fond Manuscrise Ms 893 and 894. For an analysis of these manuscripts, see Constanţa Vintilă-Ghiţulescu, *Patimă şi desfătare*, 38–65. For domestic consumption as the woman's responsibility, see Davidova, *op. cit*, 306; Carol E. Harrison, *The Bourgeois Citizen in Nineteenth-Century France. Gender, Sociability, and the Uses of Emulation* (Oxford: 1999), 13.

83 Haris Exertzoglou 'The Cultural Uses of Consumption: Negotiating Class, Gender, and Nation in the Ottoman Urban Centers during the 19th Century', *International Journal of Middle East Studies* 35 (2003), 77.

84 Exertzoglou 'The Cultural Uses of Consumption, 78.

Fig. 9 Miklós Barabás (1810-1898) – View of Bucharest, 1832, Private Collection.

wealthy families, stimulated by the opening of private schools, and also by the possibility of sending their daughters to study in institutions in Vienna, Geneva, or Paris.[85] The years 1830–1850 were marked by all this effervescence, as will be seen in the following chapter, though reflected not so much in Elena Hartulari's own education as in that of her daughter.

So far, I have talked about the importance of women in achieving matrimonial alliances. Their family networks and dowries were points of attraction for foreigners who aspired to high offices in the princely council. However, I have examined only their position as passive actors both in the process of putting together a dowry and in the choice of a husband and implicitly the construction of a matrimonial strategy. An unmarried woman, under the authority of

85 The case of Maria Bogdan is an interesting one. Married to Teodor Balş, who became grand *hatman* of Moldavia, Maria is known for her 'affair' with Pushkin in 1821–1822 during his exile in Bessarabia. Euphrosine Dvoicenco, 'I. Puškin et les Balsch à Kišinev', *Revue des Etudes Slaves*, 18/1–2 (1938), 73–75. An intelligent woman and a good French-speaker, Maria often set out alone on journeys through Europe, on the pretext of caring for her health. Her prolonged and expensive absences led her husband to write to the Metropolitan of Moldavia, requesting his help to bring her home. Her itinerary—Cernăuţi (Chernivtsi), L'viv, Baden, Italy—may be reconstructed from her correspondence with relatives. See the document of 15 July 1842, Iaşi, published in Sturdza, *Familiile boiereşti din Moldova şi Ţara Românească* I, 295.

her father (or of her elder brothers) was in a position of inferiority, but her status changed with marriage. Let us now look at what became of women on their own who either had not married or were widowed. I shall examine the way in which these single women managed to dispose of their belongings, making use of the legal instruments provided by the social and political context.

The Countesses: Seeking a Destiny

In 1718, Oltenia, the western part of Wallachia, came under Austrian rule following the peace treaty of Passarowitz. In the course of the next twenty-one years, this new territory of the crown underwent a process of reform aimed at transforming it into an efficiently administered province by co-opting the local boyar class.[86] Among the boyars who remained in Oltenia was Ioan Bălăceanu, the descendant of an important boyar family which took its name from the village of Balaci in Teleorman county. His father, Constantin Bălăceanu, had served the Holy Roman Empire and had died in 1690, during the wars between the Ottoman Empire and the Holy League; Emperor Leopold had conferred on him the title of count (German, *Graf*; Hungarian, *gróf*), and had then raised him to the rank of general of the Austrian armies in the Principalities.[87] His mother, Maria, was the daughter of Prince Șerban Cantacuzino (1678–1688) and went on to spend the last years of her life in the Dintr-un-lemn Monastery under the monastic name Magdalina.[88] Prince Constantin Brâncoveanu (1688–1714), being in the Ottoman camp, confiscated Count Bălăceanu's wealth for treason (*hiclenie*) and demolished his house in Bucharest as a punishment for his treachery.[89] The count's son, Ioan Bălăceanu, born in these troubled times, continued the policy established by his father, by virtue of his descent and of his title as a 'Count of the Empire'. Thus it is that we find him in Oltenia, collaborating with the Habsburg Monarchy in the administration of the province. In Craiova, the provincial capital, he married Ilinca Brezoianu. 'Grof' Bălăceanu, as he is known in the documents of the period, managed to recover the wealth that had been confiscated and to extend his property. However, his marriage brought him three daughters—Smaranda, Maria, and Elena (who sometimes

86 For this period see Şerban Papacostea, *Oltenia sub stăpânire austriacă, 1718–1739* (Bucharest: 1998).

87 Radu Greceanu, *Istoria domniei lui Constantin Basarab Brâncoveanu Voievod (1688–174)*, ed. Autora Ilieş, (Bucharest: 1970), 78.

88 Nicolae Iorga (ed.), *Studii şi documente cu privire la istoria românilor* (Bucharest: 1906), XVI, 77.

89 Stoicescu, *Dicţionar*, 113–114.

appears in documents as Ilinca)—and no son to help him construct matrimonial alliances or strategic networks.

The new Russian–Ottoman war of 1735–1739 and the invasion of Oltenia by Turkish forces caught him unprepared. Away from home to administer his estates, he was captured by the Ottoman army at Lotru[90] in March 1738 and killed: 'being ill, he died at the hands of the pagans, who caught up with him at Lotru,' it is recalled in a donation document issued by his daughters. It is also recorded that his wife, Ilinca, sent men 'to gather his bones from the road and take them to bury them in the Holy Monastery of Cozia, in the great church.'[91] Shortly afterwards, the widowed Ilinca with her three daughters crossed the mountains into Transylvania and took refuge in Sibiu, from where they begged the emperor to help them, in memory of the sacrifices and loyalty of the Bălăceanu lineage. In this context, Smaranda, Maria, and Elena were taken under the protective wing of Emperor Charles VI and sent to the court of Vienna to serve as ladies in waiting to the emperor's daughter, Maria Theresa. The fate of these daughters, left orphans, is of interest here as a large number of documents are preserved that record their struggles to recover the wealth and renown of their family and a social status within a society of ranks.[92]

The story of the Bălăceanu sisters is an extremely interesting one and revealing for the relation between woman, celibacy, well-being, and social status. Furthermore, as recent research has shown, women were important agents in the construction of trans-imperial diplomatic and cultural networks.[93] Circulating with ease between Vienna, Bucharest, and Sibiu, crossing paths with Ottoman, Austrian, or French diplomatic representatives, writing a multilingual correspondence (German, Latin, Italian), the Bălăceanu sisters participated actively in the production and circulation of information and in the maintenance of networks through using and negotiating their position in order to obtain influence, favours, and privileges. Their period in Vienna is known from relatively frequent mentions in Wallachian internal documents and from the diplomatic correspondence of the Austrian representatives in

90 River in Vâlcea county.

91 ANIC, Fond Manuscrise, Ms 213, f. 14, 3 February 1743; published by Nicolae Iorga in *Studii şi documente privitoare la istoria românilor* (Bucharest: 1901), vol. III, 60–62. In the document, the sisters sign with the rank they held, 'Smaranda grofina Bălăceanu, Maria Comitessa Bălăceanu, Ilinca comitessa Bălăceanu'.

92 Their mother, Ilinca Brezoianu, died shortly after in Sibiu. On the Bălăceanus, see also Paul Cernovodeanu, 'Cronici de familie: Bălăcenii', in Sturdza, *Familiile boiereşti*, I, 176–185.

93 Do Paço, 'Women in Diplomacy', 1–23; Kühnel, '"Minister-like cleverness', 130–146.

Istanbul.[94] Maria Bălăceanu's return to Wallachia, probably around 1744–1748, launched her struggle to recover the family's immense wealth, first that of her grandfather, Constantin Bălăceanu, and then that of her father, Ioan *grof* Bălăceanu. Maria was to have a hard fight, bearing on her shoulders not only her descent from the Bălăceanu and Cantacuzino lineages and imperial protection, but also the treachery and alienation of her grandfather and father. The sisters' taking refuge in Sibiu in 1738–1739 and their subsequent entry into the service of Maria Theresa were judged by the political authorities in Wallachia to be an alienation (*înstrăinare*). The written law provided that the wealth of one who 'alienates himself' (*să va înstrăina*) would be at the disposal of the prince (*pe seama domniei*). The prince had the right of usufruct, 'to manage it and to take what yield there may be' (*să o cârmuiască şi să ia roada ce va fi*). The return of 'alienated' persons entitled them to reclaim their estates.[95] As was the case for male heirs, women too had the right to reclaim their parents' wealth within thirty years.[96] Proud of the lineage to which she belonged, Maria Bălăceanu embarked on a veritable crusade to recover the wealth dispersed by the Phanariot princes and swallowed up by other members of the lineage. Her grandfather's skull, which had apparently lain for more than a year in the Bălăceanu property in Bucharest, accompanied her on all her travels.[97] Her relatives did not offer her protection and solidarity, as might have been expected; on the contrary, they shared the lands and buildings among themselves and refused to return to her the documents that would have eased the process of restoring her paternal patrimony.[98]

In June 1752, Grigore Ghica gifted some estates in Teleorman county that had belonged to the Bălăceanus to St. Panteleimon's Monastery, on which occasion he reiterated the motives behind the confiscation in order to justify once more the appropriation of the lands of a treacherous (*hiclean*) boyar. After introducing the well-known story of Constantin Bălăceanu, the chancellery *logofăt*

94 To date, I have not succeeded in finding them in the inventory compiled by Irene Kubiska-Scharl and Michael Pölzl, *Die Karrieren des Wiener Hofpersonals, 1711–1765, eine Darstellung anhan der Hofkalender und Hofparteienprotokolle* (Vienna: 2013). Because of the current pandemic, research in the Vienna archives has not been possible.

95 *Indreptarea legii*, chapter 296, article 14, 282; *Cartea Românească de Invăţătură*, chapter 1& 14, 56.

96 Valentin Al. Georgescu, *Bizanţul şi instituţiile româneşti până la mijlocul secolului al XVIII-lea* (Bucharest: 1980), 228.

97 According to Neculce, the head of Constantin Bălăceanu was brought from Zărneşti, where he had been killed in battle, and allowed to hang for a year in the middle of his courtyard. See Neculce, *Letopiseţul Ţării Moldovei*, 327.

98 George Potra (ed.), *Documente privitoare la istoria oraşului Bucureşti (1594–1821)* (Bucharest: 1961), 602–604, 10 April 1797, 603.

turned to that of his son, the *grof* Ioan, who although he could have chosen not to follow in his father's footsteps, 'did not want to bow his head and to come to his land and his country, but stayed there a subject, under the support and shelter of the foreign emperor.'[99] The document informs us that the *grof*'s daughters returned to Wallachia in the reign of Constantin Mavrocordat (1744–1748), who had mercy on them, 'they being daughters of boyar kin and bereft of their parents' (*fiind fete de neam boieresc şi sărace de părinţi*) and restored all their estates to them.[100] But instead of showing gratitude, the document continues, the daughters 'rose and went again to the German land.' (In fact, while Maria and Elena returned to the imperial court in Vienna, Smaranda married Manoil Manu, son of Apostol Manu, the master of the merchants' guild of Bucharest.[101]) This 'desertion' must be put down to fear following the change of reign. Constantin Mavrocordat was replaced on the Wallachian throne in April 1748 by Grigore Ghica, who confiscated the wealth of the Bălăceanu sisters again. From Vienna, the sisters sought the help of the Internuncio Heinrich Christoph Freiherr von Penkler. The Austrian diplomat was in the best possible position to intervene and mediate the restoration of the Bălăceanu fortune. Based in Istanbul, as representative of the Habsburg emperor, he knew the Phanariots very well. On 22 and 30 October 1748, von Penkler wrote to Prince Grigore Ghica about the two 'Palagiani' orphans, requesting the restoration of their former properties.[102] In support of this decision, von Penkler invoked article 8 of the capitulations and the peace treaty signed between the two powers, which had regulated this issue.[103] He announced that he had intervened before the 'Shining Porte' (*la Fulgida Porta*) for a second *ferman* and granting of forgiveness, emphasizing that the Ottoman ministers had assured him of

99 Alexandru G. Gălăşescu, *Eforia spitalelor civile din Bucuresci* (Bucharest: 1900), 206.

100 Ibid., 207. On 29 July 1748, the two Bălăceanu sisters were in Sibiu. One of them was to go to Bucharest, and the other to Braşov to recover a debt. With this in view, Baron von Platz asked the city of Braşov to help them. They are not specifically named, but merely referred to as 'zweyen Graf-Balacsanichen Fräulen'. See Hurmuzaki, *Documente*, XV/2, 1679–1680.

101 Cantacuzino, *Genealogia*, 258. Manoil Manu died in 1740, and after the death of their son, Manolache (in 1749), Smaranda chose to become a nun under the name Samaria. She died in 1795. Her sisters too lived long lives. Maria died in 1797 and Elena in 1804.

102 On the activity of Heinrich Cristoph Freiherr von Penckler, see Rudolf Agstner, '"Mithin sind auch alle Gesandtschafts-Acten verbrannt": Vom Teutschen Palais zum Trinitarier-Kloster. Zur Geschichte der k.k. Internuntiatur bei der Hohen Pforte, 1730–1799', in Elmar Samsinger (ed.), *Österreich in Istanbul III. K. (u.) K. Präsenz im Osmanischen Reich* (Vienna: 2018), 82–113.

103 The reference is to the Treaty of Belgrade, 21 August 1739. See Aksan, *Ottoman Wars*, 83–128.

full support. The internuncio further wrote that he was acting on instructions from the imperial court and that he must make sure of a satisfactory conclusion.[104] In this connection, von Penkler wrote to Empress Maria Theresa, offering her information about the case of the Bălăceanu daughters.[105] His letters show how anchored the sisters were in the society of Vienna, from where they were trying, by appealing to networks and connections, to resolve the issue of their property. Writing letters to powerful and influential people was a common practice in the period. It was a useful instrument for all those who sought protection, fiscal privileges, or recognition on the part of others.[106] Writing about themselves, the Bălăceanu sisters adopted different roles and identities, constructed according to whom they were addressing.

Grigore Ghica was not impressed by von Penkler's interventions or by his invocation of the capitulations and the peace treaty. Princely forgiveness was dependent on display of loyalty: while Smaranda was forgiven, Maria and Elena were harshly criticized, accused of betraying their country and their faith (by converting to Catholicism) in order to make themselves a family and a destiny in a foreign land. As yet I have not found any document attesting to the two sisters' conversion to Catholicism or confirming their marriage to 'foreigners from the German Land' (*oameni străini din Ţara Nemţească*). These accusations in Grigore Ghica's document justify the description of them as 'treacherous and hostile to their country' (*haine şi vrăjmaşe patriei lor*), thus entitling the prince to confiscate their wealth and their estates again. We may note that the loyalty of women is considered as important as the loyalty of men. At no point do Grigore Ghica and his divan, made up of the great boyars of Wallachia (some of them related to the sisters under accusation), judge the two women's decisions through the prism of their inferiority. Women are considered responsible for their decisions just as much as men are: 'According to law and justice, and also to the written codes [*pravile*], I command, that of persons treacherous and hostile to their country, who have left their land, alienating themselves; the shares, whether of estates or of vineyards [...] belonging to those two daughters being taken into princely possession, I as prince have granted and dedicated to St. Panteleimon.' Smaranda's estates did not come into this category. Her marriage and her having settled in Bucharest with her husband were taken as indicating her faith and loyalty to the political authorities.[107] It should be

104 Hurmuzaki, *Documente*, VI, 604–605.

105 Hurmuzaki, *Documente*, VI, 606–607, 31 October 1748.

106 Paul D. McLean, *The Art of the Network. Strategic Interaction and Patronage in Renaissance Florence* (London: 2007), 4.

107 Gălăşescu, *Eforia spitalelor*, 207. The document was reconfirmed by Prince Matei Ghica on 1 February 1753 and Prince Scarlat Ghica on 9 July 1759, (Ibid., 237–260, 231).

mentioned that her husband's father, the 'Greek' merchant Manu Apostol, was the second generation of his family in Wallachia and had managed to amass considerable wealth in the service of Prince Constantin Brâncoveanu.[108] Their marriage might seem a sort of 'misalliance', in view of the social pride affirmed by Smaranda when she referred to herself as 'Manda comitissa Balacsánka'.[109] However, Manoil Manu had inherited from his father the title of baron of the Holy Roman Empire, which must have gone some way towards cancelling the social difference between them.[110] Moreover, both belonged to the same network that linked Wallachia to Brașov and the Viennese chancellery.[111] It is possible that the members of this network had planned the alliance, bringing the two orphans together. The same network continued to bombard the Porte with requests for the 'poor orphans' to be forgiven and their property restored. After von Penkler left Istanbul, the new internuncio, von Schwachheim, took over his mission regarding the wealth of the Bălăceanu sisters. It was he who managed to obtain a *ferman* giving the sisters the right to return to Wallachia and to receive their confiscated wealth.[112]

The countesses, as they are known in documents, tried to find their destinies travelling between Habsburg and Ottoman realms. Several conclusions may be drawn from a reading of the documents they have left us (testaments, letters of donation, dowry contracts, conflicts over property, records of the purchase or sale of estates, petitions to the Viennese court). In the first place, we may note the mobility of the two women—Maria and Elena—who crossed borders and travelled the roads of the empires, making use of their dual identity: countesses and ladies-in-waiting to Maria Theresa, but also Wallachian boyaresses. We find them in Bucharest, Brașov, Sibiu, and Vienna in various periods between 1738 and 1797, equipped with travel papers or passports, invoking now imperial

---

108 Gheorghe Lazăr, 'In umbra puterii. Negustori "prieteni ai domniei" şi destinul lor (Ţara Românească, secolul al XVII-lea)', in Ovidiu Cristea, Gheorghe Lazăr (eds.), *Vocaţia istoriei. Prinos Profesorului Şerban Papacostea* (Brăila: 2008), 605–634.

109 On 7 January 1741, 'Manda comitissa Balacsánka' was at Scăieni and opened a law suit against Cristophoro Voicul of Braşov, from whom she had some debts to recover. Hurmuzaki, *Documente*, XV/2, 1672.

110 On 24 May 1713, in Luxemburg, Charles VI, conferred the title of noble of the Holy Roman Empire on Manu Apostol, as a reward for his loyalty and faithful service. See Constantin Giurescu, Nicolae Dobrescu (eds.), *Documente şi regeste privitoare la Constantin Brâncoveanu* (Bucharest: 1907), 242–244.

111 On the removal from power of his protector, Constantin Brâncoveanu, Apostol Manu had taken refuge in Transylvania. Here he entered the service of the Holy Roman Empire, which entrusted him with the mission of finding the wealth of Prince Brâncoveanu, which was rumoured to be immense. Lazăr, 'In umbra puterii', 632.

112 Hurmuzaki, *Documente*, VII, 1876, 20 June 1761, 24–25.

protection, now that of the Phanariot princes.[113] In these documents, they sign their names in different ways, as Elena Bălăceanu and Maria Bălăceanu or with identities adapted to the situation: Helena von Balatschan, Helena Gräfin von Beleciann, Maria Gräfin von Belacian, Maria comitissa Balacsánka, Smaranda comitissa Balacsánka.

In Vienna, Maria and Elena received payment for their service. Maria reproached her sister that while she was fighting in Wallachia to recover the estates, Elena was living in comfort with her pay at the Viennese court: 'my share of the pay she took from the German empire, as long as she was there. And I here, in a time of war, got nothing from the income of the estates.' She thus requested that from certain parts of the estates, Elena should receive nothing, because 'she did not grow up here in this country to know what the estate is.'[114] The pay they received cannot have been very high, and nor were the positions they held among the empress's servants. Furthermore, as Katrin Keller has shown, a 'court maiden' had to follow a certain trajectory in her career and to demonstrate her loyalty and her competence in administrative matters. A lady-in-waiting also needed a network of family and connections if she was to advance.[115] The Bălăceanu sisters were alone in a competitive environment where advancement was very difficult. The court of Vienna was a 'central arena for decision-making', leading to bitter competition.[116] Lacking connections and unable to make themselves useful, the Bălăceanu sisters could not penetrate an environment with its own rules and solidarities.[117] The positions they had received were honorary, a reward for their father's and especially their grandfather's loyalty, and gave them the right to be at court only on certain occasions.[118]

113 On 2 March 1754, the three countesses were together in Bucharest. See George Potra (ed.), *Documente privitoare la istoria oraşului Bucureşti (1634–1800)* (Bucharest: 1982), 200–201.

114 BAR, Ms 611, ff. 12v-13r; 18r-21r. Maria Bălăceanu drew up two documents: a letter of donation to her adoptive son, and her testament. Both have been preserved in several copies and were published form another fonds by Potra (ed.), *Documente privitoare la istoria oraşului Bucureşti (1594–1821)*, 602–604, 13 March 1797, 10 April 1797.

115 Katrin Keller, 'Ladies-in-Waiting at the Imperial Court of Vienna from 1550 to 1700: Structures, Responsibilities and Carrier Patterns', in Nadine Akkerman, Birgit Houben (eds.), *The Politics of Female Households: Ladies-in-waiting across Early Modern Europe* (Leiden: 2013), 94–95.

116 Jeroen Duindam, *Vienna and Versailles: The Courts of Europe's Dynastic Rivals, 1550–1780* (Cambridge: 2003), 223.

117 See also Katrin Keller, *Hofdamen. Amtsträgerinnen im Wiener Hofstaat des 17. Jahrhunderts* (Vienna: 2005).

118 On the organization of the court, see Jeroen Duindam, 'Versailles, Vienna, and Beyond: Changing Views of Household and Government in Early Modern Europe', in Jeroen Duindam, Tülay Artan, Metin Kunt (eds.), *Royal Courts in Dynastic States and Empires. A Global Perspective* (Leiden: 2011), 401–432.

It was probably this that, at a certain point, made them assign different roles to themselves, as Maria returned to Wallachia to recover their estates and social status, while Elena, younger and perhaps the most able of the three to handle the duties of a lady-in-waiting, continued her career in Vienna and lived either in Brașov or Sibiu, on the territories of the Habsburg Monarchy. At the urging of her sister, Elena addressed numerous petitions to the imperial court. On 24 October 1784, she wrote from Sibiu to General Frederick von Preiss, asking him to write to Vienna for pressure to be put on the prince of Wallachia regarding the restoration of the confiscated wealth.[119] The letters continued in the years that followed: Elena, or 'Helene von Balatschanischen' wrote to Stefan Raicevich, the Austrian agent in Bucharest, to General Michael von Ritter Fabri, and to General Joseph Anton Franz Mittrowsky von Mittrowitz, asking for their intervention before the Wallachian prince, pensions, and assistance.[120] From a supplication addressed to the Austrian agency in Sibiu on 21 April 1793, it emerges that Elena Bălăceanu had been living in Bucharest for two years, and that an imperial pension that she had been lifting from the customs office in Brașov had now been stopped. The new regulations specified that only those who had properties on the territories of the crown could receive pensions; consequently, the countess's pension would be paid only if she returned within the Empire.[121]

Second, the letters testify to the ability and perseverance with which Maria Bălăceanu pursued lawsuit after lawsuit to add another small portion of an estate to the patrimony. Here we may note the inferiority that Maria assumes in relation to her male relatives in the Bălăceanu kindred. 'We being unable to go to court with everyone, not being male' (*Neputând a ne judeca cu lumea, nefiind parte bărbătească*), Maria writes, the best parts of the estates remained under the control of the Bălăceanu kindred. Nevertheless, she opened and won numerous lawsuits against those who had unfairly acquired estates, houses, mills, forests, or fishponds that she considered were rightfully hers.[122]

---

119 Iorga, *Studii*, III, 62.

120 Iorga, *Studii*, III, 62–65, documents of 20 October 1784 and 10 August 1785.

121 Iorga, *Studii*, III, 64. Generalul Joseph Anton Franz Mittrowsky sought the advice of the imperial court as how to proceed in the case of the countess, who no longer lived in Brașov. On the new legislation concerning foreign subjects see Judson, *The Habsburg Empire*, 77.

122 The documents are numerous and present the three sisters in their patrimonial disputes with the others. See the documents published by Potra, *Documente București (1594–1821)*, 512, 535, 539–540, 546, 557, 575, 590; idem, *Documente București (1634–1800)*, 201, 202, 206, 389, 390, 391, 433, 411, 465, 468.

Third, the countesses' loneliness is striking. Their journeys through empires in search of a destiny did not help them to put down roots anywhere. Smaranda, widowed and childless, chose to become a nun. Maria, taking refuge in Brașov during the Russian–Ottoman war of 1768–1774, decided to adopt a child. She returned with him to Wallachia; the boy, 'German' and probably Catholic, was baptized into the Orthodox faith and raised according to all the rites and traditions of the Bălăceanu lineage. Only that, even after twenty-seven years, Petre had not become a Bălăceanu. His adoptive mother added a new element of gender differentiation, present in the period, which was to the advantage of men and the disadvantage of women: the exclusion of women from political life.[123] Her words 'and I, not being male to have been able to help him with some posts and earnings' (*şi eu, nefiind parte bărbătească ca să-l fi putut ajutora cu nescarevaşi slujbe şi câştiguri*)[124] show the impossibility of achieving a connection with the social and political network that would have introduced her adoptive son onto the political stage. We know that boyars' sons began their political ascent with the position of *postelnic*, from which they advanced in the hierarchy with the support of their family networks. Participation in political life implied not only entry into a network, but also benefits and fiscal privileges.[125] Maria Bălăceanu tried to compensate for this lack by giving her adoptive son a fortune, which would ensure his means of existence but not his participation in political life. In 1797, Petre was around thirty years old, but had no administrative office. The Bălăceanu kindred had not accepted him into the lineage, and had tried to take control of the estates left by *grof* Ioan. In her testament, the adoptive mother gave her son her house in Bucharest (in the Sfânta Vineri district) and a number of estates, but not the right to take the family name.[126] Although he had gone over to the Orthodox faith and had been brought up by Maria, Petre still retained the alterity of the foreigner, reiterated both in her letters of donation and in her testament. More than that, the adoptive mother's donation seems to have been made more out concern for her soul than out of duty towards a son, being justified as follows: 'that he

123 The situation is similar for other regions of Europe. See, in this connection, Feci, 'Mobilité, droits et citoyenneté des femmes', 47–72.

124 Potra, *Documente Bucureşti (1594–1821)*, 602.

125 Many boyaresses claimed and received fiscal privileges, especially when they were widowed and took over both the patrimony and the administration of the house. See ANIC, Administrative vechi, ds. 2152c/1814, f. 132, 12 September 1814 and Administrative vechi, ds. 2203/1818, f. 513, 530v, 16 June 1818.

126 See Andreea-Roxana Iancu, 'Adopter ou nourrir un enfant en Valachie, XVIIIe–XIXe siècles: norme et pratique. Etude de cas', *Méditerranées*, 37 (2004), 237–277.

too remains contented, and not curse me with his children to weigh down my soul for taking him away from his people and even more from his country.'[127]

Elena Bălăceanu let herself be led in all this patrimonial adventure by her sister, Maria. Following her example, she adopted a girl, whom she christened Maria, and then arranged her marriage and provided her dowry. The dowry contract is rich in jewellery and other household objects, but does not include estates, vineyards, houses, or Gypsy slaves: all these were swallowed up by the kindred.[128] The composition of the dowry contract is typical for the region, with clothes and jewellery of Ottoman influence, showing no trace of Elena's German and Viennese education. Or perhaps we should not look here for Viennese influence on the countess's lifestyle. In Wallachia, she behaved like other boyaresses, and resorted to the internal market to assemble a dowry. After Maria's death (probably soon after she drew up her testament, around May 1797), Elena appears hesitant and unprotected. Maria's testament is clearly formulated, aimed at providing for those close to her—her adoptive son and her sister Elena—and keeping the relatives at a distance. Among these were one Costache Bălăceanu and one Ioniță Bălăceanu, cousins who would speculate on Maria's death, urging Elena not to respect the clauses of her testament. Thus, Elena wrote a testament by which she left her entire wealth to her cousin Costache Bălăceanu. Shortly after, she realized that Costache's actions had been motivated only by 'his own interest [...] tricking her' (*enteresul dumnealui* [...] *înşelând-o*) and she reconfirmed the authority of Maria's testament as an expression of her last wishes which must be scrupulously respected.[129]

The countesses' mobility was something uncommon, which did not apply to all women in the period. Of course, many boyaresses accompanied their husbands into exile, sharing their fate. However, the Bălăceanu sisters were forced by circumstances to cut their own path, travelling in spaces with different social, economic, and legal systems. Thus they came to know and to work with different systems of law, applying to the right institutions and individuals to obtain the results they sought in a certain matter, and manoeuvring the trans-imperial networks that could help them to obtain privileges, and protection.

The women I have considered in this chapter do not have the 'pan-European' visibility enjoyed by, for example, Lady Mary Wortley Montagu or Dora d'Istria, whose activities have been thoroughly researched.[130] Much of the

127 Potra, *Documente Bucureşti (1594–1821)*, 603.

128 BAR, MS 611, f. 8r-8v, 8 February 1797.

129 BAR, MS 611, 21r, 3 August 1801.

130 The bibliography is extensive. I cite only Cynthia Lowenthal, *Lady Mary Wortley Montagu and the Eighteenth-Century Familiar Letter* (Athens, GA and London: 2010); Angela Jianu, 'Dora d'Istria: un dar făcut Europei', in Violeta Barbu, Maria-Magdalena Székely,

documentation about them remains scattered through the archives in Bucharest, Iaşi, Vienna, Paris, Moscow, and Istanbul.

In the following chapter, I shall turn my attention to Elena Hartulari, in whose case I have managed to assemble hundreds of documents, in addition to her memoirs. With their help, I shall attempt to reconstruct the everyday life of a woman of the early nineteenth century and the role played by a wife in the social ascent of a foreign husband in Moldavian society. As David Do Paço has argued, women cannot be seen solely through the prism of their traditional roles as wives, mothers, sisters, or daughters.[131] The following case study, focused on Elena Hartulari, will examine the role of women as unofficial agents in the structuring of a network and in the maintenance of a day-to-day sociability that was a necessary support for the political, economic, and social plans of a family. They were their husbands' partners in accessing economic and political resources, often through their own relations of clientelism or friendship.

Kinga S. Tüdős, Angela Jianu, *Grădina Rozelor. Femei din Moldova, Ţara Românească şi Transilvania* (*sec. XVII–XIX*) (Bucharest: 2015), 331–339.

131 Do Paço, 'Women in Diplomacy', 5.

CHAPTER 8

Women and Their Role in a Network: A Wife and Her Husband's Career: The Hartulari Family

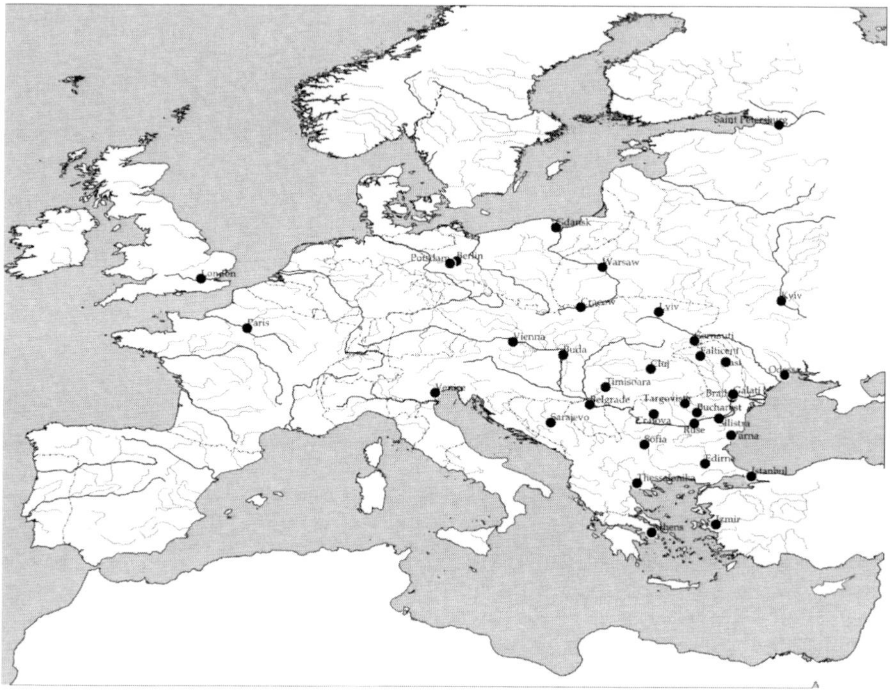

Map 4 Map of Eastern Europe cc. 1850. Made by Michał Wasiucionek.

Feeling the approach of old age, hounded by her own children in interminable court cases, weary after a difficult marriage to an unfaithful husband, Elena Hartulari (née Plitos) made up her mind to write her memoirs, setting down on paper the unhappy course of her life. By the testament of her husband, Iorgu Hartulari, who died in 1849, Elena was his executor and inherited his entire estate. Their three children were displeased at their father's decision, and joined together to contest, by various methods, including in court, their mother's right to administer the family inheritance. After numerous conflicts, Elena gave up the patrimony to her children and withdrew to live alone on one of the family's estates, with only a few servants to care for her in her old age. It was here that she began to write her memoirs, addressing them expressly to her children, who were to learn and understand the role that she, Elena Hartulari,

© CONSTANŢA VINTILĂ, 2022 | DOI:10.30965/9783657704873_009

had played in the amassing of a huge fortune and the building of a social status. Her memoirs were not addressed to a wider public, but were to be read only by her children, so that they might realize how mistaken they had been in judging their mother. Written on lined paper and bound in a pink folder, Elena's memoirs were published in the early twentieth century as a sort of feuilleton novel by their discoverer, the historian Gheorghe Ghibănescu, under the title *Istoria vieţii mele de la anul 1801* (The story of my life from the year 1801 [sic]).[1] Scattered through various issues of the journal, Elena Hartulari's memoirs failed to attract much interest either from literary scholars or from historians.[2] The pages published by Gheorghe Ghibănescu made no claim to be a critical edition, and they contain numerous errors of transcription.

Elena Hartulari: Education

Elena Hartulari was born in Iaşi in 1810 into the Plitos (Pletosu) family of petty boyars. Her father, Grigore Plitos, owned estates close to Iași and was in the service of the Sturza boyar family.[3] His career and his wealth were closely connected to the Sturzas, whose client and protégé he remained all his life. Born and raised in the house of the boyar Grigore Sturza, Grigore Plitos became an indispensable administrator of his patron's house and property. For his services, in addition to a salary, Grigore received boyar titles, help whenever he needed it, and various other benefits.[4] This type of patron–client relation is a classic one, and was the basis on which many fortunes and careers were built in early modern Moldavia.

At the age of fifteen, Elena married Iorgu Hartulari, a poor young Greek and a second cousin of hers. His father, Manolache Hartulari, had arrived in

1 Elena Hartulari, "Istoria vieţii mele de la anul 1801", ed. by Gheorghe Ghibănescu, *Convorbiri Literare* 5–8 (1926), 729–745; 9–10 (1926), 841–855; 11–12 (1926), 915–926; 9–11 (1927): 291–312; 3–4 (1928): 69–78; 5–8 (1928), 301–308.

2 See Angela Jianu, 'Elena Hartulari's Story: The Presentation of the Emotional Self', in Faruk Bilici, Ionel Candea, and Anca Popescu (eds), *Enjeux économiques, politiques et militaires en Mer Noire, XIVe–XXIe siècles—Etudes à la mémoire de Mihail Guboglu* (Brăila: 2007), 429–449.

3 Constantin Sion says that he was a peasant from the vicinity of Iaşi, who on entering the boyar class Hellenized his name from Pletosu (the name means 'long haired') to Plitos. (Sion, *Arhondologia Moldovei*, 220). The practice was a current one throughout the Balkans, as Christine Philliou shows, the most conclusive example being the one that she analyses, namely Stephanos Vogorides. See Philliou, *Biography of an Empire*.

4 Gheorghe Platon, Alexandru-Florin Platon, *Boierimea din Moldova în secolul al XIX-lea. Context european, evoluţia socială şi politică (Date statistice şi observaţii istorice)* (Bucharest: 1995).

Moldavia at the beginning of the nineteenth century and settled in Târgul Ocna, where he knew the Greek hegumen of the monastery. He later summoned his wife and children and other family members to join him and tried to become 'naturalized' through the purchase of estates and noble titles.[5]

The story of Elena Hartulari is the mirror of a Moldavian society caught in the grip of changes that it was barely able to assimilate and work with. Her education reflects this period of transition, and her writing is sprinkled with Moldavianisms, Hellenisms, and Gallicisms. What sort of education, then, did Elena Plitos receive before she became Hartulari? In her memoirs, Elena writes that from the age of seven she was busy with 'the study of Greek and Moldavian.'[6] In 1817, Greek was still the language of the elite, the language spoken in boyar salons, the language of correspondence, the language of cultural experiences. She completed her education at home with the help of some of those private tutors who were an important presence in the Moldavian world of the early nineteenth century. Elena's parents took care to pay a number of private teachers who could offer her an elementary knowledge of reading and writing, rather than insisting on the sort of 'feminine' education followed in other parts of Europe. Indeed, feminine education was not yet among the concerns of Moldavian society. It was only in the 1830s that Moldavia and Wallachia became very attractive to a series of foreign entrepreneurs who opened private schools for girls. Such *pensionnats* were expensive and elitist, however, and in any case, they came rather late for Elena Hartulari.[7] Even if she was not *pensionnat*-educated herself, Elena Hartulari cared about the education of her children, and took steps to send them to private schools in Iaşi, Czernowitz in Habsburg Bukovina, and later Paris. In so doing, she came in contact with the owners of these schools: some she visited, and with others she became friends. This was the case of Charles Tissot, who had come to Moldavia to open a private school for boys. His *pensionnat* began its activity in Iași in September 1834. Later he taught French grammar at the Academia Mihăileană, the most prestigious higher education institution in Moldavia.[8] He also served as secretary to Elena's protector, Prince Mihail Sturdza,[9] and it was through this connection that he found his way into the Hartulari family's social circle. He

5 Sion, *Arhondologia Moldovei*, 302.

6 SJAN, Iaşi, Colecţia Gh. Ghibănescu, MS 164, f. 1r.

7 Dan Dumitru Iacob, 'Copii de boieri la pension. Educaţia în familia postelnicului Iancu Costache-Negel (1838–1861)', in Cătălina Mihalache, Leonidas Rados (eds), *Educaţia publică şi condiţionările sale (secolele XIX–XX)* (Iaşi: 2015), 145–196.

8 See Vasile A. Urechia, *Istoria şcoalelor de la 1800 la 1864* (Bucharest: 1901), vol. 4, 388, 417.

9 See Simion-Alexandru Gavriş, *Viaţa şi opiniile prinţului Grigore Mihail Sturdza, 1821–1901* (Iaşi: 2015), 34.

and his wife became close friends of Elena's, and were constant guests at her residence in Fălticeni. With their help, she improved her knowledge of French.

Apart from the sufferings that she mentions on every page, Elena Hartulari had an active social life as daughter, mother, wife, lady of the house, friend, neighbour, and petitioner. Her activities place her in the ranks of the feminine 'bourgeois' elite of the nineteenth century. Her memoirs help us to reconstruct the relations between the status of women and their social identity through the intermediary of consumption and sociability. In this chapter, I shall try to analyse Elena Hartulari's memoirs with regard to four aspects: the linguistic experience of love; women and social networks; sociability and consumption; consumption and knowledge.

The Linguistic Experience of Love

From the beginning of her narration, Elena Hartulari commits herself to what Philippe Lejeune terms an 'autobiographical pact', promising to recount her life in 'the spirit of truth.'[10] In telling the story of her life, Elena Hartulari represents herself, placing herself in the centre of her narration, trying to gain the pity, admiration, and goodwill of her children. Thus her memoirs are constructed in such a way as to accentuate the sufferings, hardships, and unhappiness she has experienced in the course of a life entirely dedicated to her husband and children.

In 1824, Elena was fourteen and living with her parents in Iași. She had her own room and maidservant. Her father had succeeded in rebuilding his fortune after the revolutionary upheaval of 1821 and was able to provide his daughter with a life relatively free from cares. Grigore Plitos dreamed of a good marriage for Elena within the local Moldavian elite, a marriage that would bring her material stability and a good position in the social hierarchy and would provide the family with another connection in the social network of Iași. Iorgu Hartulari was an outsider—his origins were in the region of Epirus. He was poor, and on top of that he was an inveterate card player. No father would have wished for a son-in-law like Iorgu, with no past or present, followed by a numerous family—parents, brothers, and sisters, all poor, arriving on Moldavian soil to seek their fortune.

Iorgu Hartulari played the card of the perseverant lover with an excellent command of words, gestures, and the art of *galanterie*.[11] A young man of twenty,

10 Philippe Lejeune, *Le Pacte autobiographique* (Paris: 1975), 14.

11 Erving Goffman, *L'arrangement des sexes* (Paris: 2002).

he staged all the art of seduction, declaiming poems, promising eternal love, swearing oaths, entering by the window when he was put out by the door.[12] After seven months of more or less pretend resistance, Elena gave in: 'He went down at my feet, telling me to do what I wanted with him, for he was my lover, he was going to be my husband, with whom I was to live happily.'[13] There followed a prolonged period of hidden courtship because of the somewhat fierce opposition of the girl's parents, given the youth's utter poverty and above all his passion for games of chance. However, parental opposition did nothing to dampen the erotic passion expressed in visits organized with her sister's complicity, fiery declarations, hand-holding, and voluptuous embraces.

> Over the course of a year and two months there followed a daily correspondence between us; every day two notes, one [to each] from the other, with the purest words of love, and sometime every week we would meet at my sister's and in our own home,[14]

notes Elena in her memoirs. When the young man threatens to shoot himself if they do not run away together, Elena writes to him:

> It is I who have declared to you my love and my faith till my end; do you now want me to leave my poor parents in tears and suffering for your love?! Know now that you are all my future happiness; repay me with unfeigned love and with pity; I am yours till the grave.[15]

And he replies:

> I come, please, my dear, at the hour you have decided for me and be sure that I will be the most faithful and the most suffering for you, innocent being and so strong in your words, which will remain in my memory until my end, witnessing to [good] behaviour and innocence, which with great nobility you wear upon yourself. I am yours and you mine and no one is capable of preventing us. Your slave until the grave.[16]

The amorous correspondence and the adventures that follow, the flight of the two lovers, their capture by a posse of guards, the young man's imprisonment,

12 Arlette Farge shows that the art of seduction takes on different forms 'according to the social level at which partners are found'. Arlette Farge, 'Jeu des esprits et des corps au XVIIIe siècle', in Cecile Dauphin, Arlette Farge (eds.) *Séduction et société. Approches historiques* (Paris: 2001), 72.

13 SJAN, Iaşi, Colecţia Gh. Ghibănescu, MS 164, f. 2r.

14 SJAN, Iaşi, Colecţia Gh. Ghibănescu, MS 164, f. 2v.

15 SJAN, Iaşi, Colecţia Gh. Ghibănescu, MS 164, f. 3r.

16 Ibid., f. 5r.

his letters from prison, *billets-doux*, often signed with blood 'from his finger', seem inspired by a popular literature in circulation at the time.[17] Elena, for her part, had a whole arsenal of protector saints, miracle-working icons and prayers to guide her, protect her, and help her at every step. Let me take one episode as an example:

> … an idea came to my parents that my mother and my sister and I should go to the Metropolitan Church [in Iași], where there was a miracle-working icon of the Mother of the Lord, to say prayers for my peace. When we entered the church, the first person to be seen before the icon [was] the young man saying prayers, and the priest mentioning the name of my parents, that their hearts might turn towards him; where my mother also heard these words. And when he had read the prayer he turned to go. Then he caught sight of my family, which startled him, confused as to what apparition this might be, or the miracle of the Mother of the Lord; and he sat down on a pew till we too finished our prayers.[18]

After this episode, thought/seen/felt to be a miracle by all involved, the couple received the blessing of Elena's parents. Of course, the 'miracle' had been preceded by the young man's (and his family's) appeal to Metropolitan Veniamin Costachi, to Grigore Plitos's confessor, and to Grigore Sturza and other leading boyars of the day, which hastened the enactment of the divine will.[19]

From the scenes above let us try to understand the connection between book consumption and learning. Elena and Iorgu were consumers of a Greek literature, both being good speakers of the language.[20] Phanariot literature had turned some into poets, others merely into imitators and inveterate dreamers.[21] In the Moldavia of the early nineteenth century, Iași was home to quite an effervescent literary scene, developed around Greek lyric. Costache Conachi, Costache Negri, Alecu Beldiman, and Gheorghe Asachi composed

---

17 Alex Drace-Francis, *The Making of Modern Romanian Culture*, 114–124.

18 SJAN, Iaşi, Colecţia Gh. Ghibănescu, MS 164, f. 4r–4v.

19 Elena and Iorgu were second cousins. Metropolitan Veniamin gave them his blessing, considering that this degree of kinship was not an impediment to their marriage. SJAN, Iaşi, Colecţia Gh. Ghibănescu, MS 164, f. 2r.

20 Andrei Pippidi, 'Lecturile unui boier muntean acum un veac: Ioan Manu', *Revista de Istorie şi Teorie Literară*, XX, 1 (1971), 105–119.

21 For a pertinent and interesting analysis of this Phanariot literature, see Peter Mackridge, 'Some Greek Literary Representations of Greek Life and Language in the Late Eighteenth Century', in *Revista de Istorie şi Teorie Literară*, X, 1–4 (2016), 171–195; Peter Mackridge, *Enlightenment or Entertainment? The Intolerable Lightness of Phanariot Literature, 1750–1800*, consulted at https://www.academia.edu/41212631/Enlightenment_or_entertainment_The_intolerable_lightness_of_Phanariot_literature_1750–_1800 [1 February 2020]; Yannis Xourias, 'L'européanisation fictive des Phanariotes', *Cahiers balkaniques* [Online], Special issue, 2015, published online 27 January 2016, [accessed 9 March 2020].

verses full of erotic feeling, which then circulated through the intermediary of itinerant bands. Gheorghe Asachi, for example, also translated and wrote plays. Plays staged by troupes of amateur actors may have been another source of inspiration for the two lovers. The Greek theatre, promoted especially by the elite, found propitious ground on which to develop in the Wallachian and Moldavian capitals in the early nineteenth century.[22] By 1827, the theatre had already advanced beyond the stage of amateur performances in boyar salons, and troupes of professional actors were performing in Italian, French, and German.[23]

Elena's contemporary, Dimitrie Foti Merişescu, expresses, right from the start of his own memoirs, his admiration for the novels *Erotocritos* and *Oreste*. It was reading these, in Romanian translation, that gave him the urge to start writing himself.[24] Elena Hartulari, on the other hand, has left no indications as to what she read. The vocabulary she uses, however, leads me to believe that her daily reading consisted of 'light' French novels. Many of the French words were adapted and introduced into everyday speech: *emabl* (*aimable*), *rezonarisit* (*raisonné*), *dezida* (a word used frequently: *decider*), *demuazela* (*demoiselle*), *rezon* (*raison*), *fraparisi* (*frapper*), *suvenir* (*souvenir*), *noblesă* (*noblesse*), *furioază* (*furieuse*), *estaziată* (*extasiée*), *galantă* (*galante*), *riscarisi* (*risquer*). They were already part of an everyday vocabulary filling in gaps in the Moldavian language, especially when it came to the expression of feelings. As such, the influence of the sentimental literature typical of the period can be clearly seen both in the epistolary style of the two lovers and in the vocabulary they use. It may be mentioned that Elena Hartulari's memoirs capture very well the changes that the Moldavian language was undergoing as it 'modernized' together with the birth of the young modern state. Greek vocabulary is not yet completely abandoned, however, but is sprinkled through the memoirs wherever events, situations, or even sentiments may be better expressed in Greek.

The day after their marriage, the 'ecstasy of love' came up against everyday routine: 'I told my husband to send [someone] to buy us two loaves. He answered that he had no money. We took coffee still with that pleasure,'[25]

22 Chrysothemis Stamatopoulou-Vasilakou, 'Greek Theater in Southeastern Europe and the Eastern Mediterranean from 1810 to 1961', *Journal of Modern Greek Studies* 25 (2007), 267–284.

23 For the repertoire and translation of various plays, see Paul Cornea, *Originile romantismului românesc* (Bucharest: 2008).

24 See Part III, Chapter 6 of this book.

25 SJAN, Iaşi, Colecţia Gh. Ghibănescu, MS 164, f. 6v.

Elena consoles herself. Two months later, they were assailed by his numerous creditors:

> After two months my husband's creditors started to come, to whom he owed 3,000 lei, and after a week they imposed administration on him for him to pay, and he had nothing from which to pay. I asked my father and he told me he had nothing, that as I had liked it ... to bear it! I asked my sister to lend to us, and she said she had nothing, knowing that if they gave to me I had nothing from which to pay them back.[26]

How Iorgu Hartulari was to emerge from poverty and debt, alongside an 'ugly' wife, we shall now examine.

Women and Social Networks

Fălticeni, in northern Moldavia, was the market town in which the Hartulari couple decided to build their residence. The Hartulari house grew as Iorgu worked his way into a network that ensured access to jobs, contacts, and influence. His marriage to Elena Plitos was his first step in penetrating a powerful network that he was to succeed in making his own. Constantin Sion, a contemporary boyar, would later write in his *Arhondologia Moldovei* (Book of the nobility of Moldavia) that this was the aim of the marriage, Elena being ugly (*slută*) but very well positioned socially.[27] Elena talked about this aspect, trying to make sure that her future husband would not later hold her physical appearance against her:

> Consider well that this is to be a bond for our lives, firstly that I have no wealth, secondly that I have no beauty or learning other than my language as a Romanian and the Greek language. For these [reasons], consider well, lest there come a time that you hold them against me or are unfaithful to me, which would break me down utterly.[28]

No likeness of Elena Hartulari survives, although she lived till 1860, well into the age of portrait painting and photography. However Iorgu Hartulari's behaviour tends to support the hypothesis formulated by Constantin Sion. Poor and a foreigner, but 'handsome and witty', on his arrival in the town of Iași, Iorgu clung to Elena like a lifebelt, offering her, as I have shown in the first part, a

26 Ibid., f. 7v.
27 Sion, *Arhondologia Moldovei*, 302.
28 SJAN, Iaşi, Colecţia Gh. Ghibănescu, MS 164, f. 6r.

restless and unsettling love. He would later cheat on her at every opportunity, however, either with passing dalliances or with long-term relationships. But that is not our concern here.

What sort of connections? What sort of patronage? Through his marriage, Iorgu Hartulari acquired the social connections of his wife and father-in-law. Career advancement was facilitated in the first place by spiritual affinity: Mihail Sturdza, who had been Elena's godfather at her baptism, was now sponsor at their wedding: 'at the right time, behold, a surprise from our protector [Grigore Sturza], urging his son Mihail Sturdza, by whom I was baptized, to come and marry us: where indeed he came with his son Dimitrie, the year 1827 June 10.'

By this gesture, the Hartulari couple were brought under the patronage of the Sturdzas, further strengthening existing connections. Grigore Plitos was already the right-hand man of Grigore Sturza, Mihail Sturdza's father. Iorgu Hartulari was now officially introduced into the powerful network of the Sturdza kindred. Indeed, a contemporary witness records how 'Iorgu, a fine cunning robber ... through the influence of his father-in-law (Grigore Plitos)' was appointed customs officer in the frontier town of Suceava and later, enjoying the protection of his godfather (Mihail Sturdza), who in the meantime had become prince of Moldavia, began to become wealthy by leasing the lands of monasteries.[29] With Mihail Sturdza's ascent to the throne in 1834, Grigore Plitos was appointed princely adjutant, charged with administering the princely palace in Iași.[30] The preservation of an impressive number of documents about the activity of Iorgu Hartulari helps us to understand how a 'new man' (a foreigner) could work his way into the fabric of his country of adoption and succeed in amassing impressive wealth and an enviable social position.

Iorgu Hartulari set out with three pieces of silver to his name, and advanced by making intelligent use of his wife's connections and dowry.[31] His various activities may be summed up as follows: he held offices in the state administrative apparatus, he attended to his estates, and he embarked on 'speculations'. The offices and the 'speculations' were closely linked. The higher he advanced in the administration, the more access he had to information, protection, and a reputation that could help him in his business ventures. Before dealing with the activities that Elena termed 'speculations' (*speculații*), I shall endeavour to sketch a portrait of Iorgu as he emerges from his wife's memoirs and from

29 Sion, *Arhondologia Moldovei*, 302.

30 SJAN, Iaşi, Fond Documente Moldovenesti, XIII/88. Grigore Plitos held this position for two years, till 10 August 1836, when at his own request he was replaced by Costache Tomazichi.

31 SJAN, Iaşi, Colecţia Gh. Ghibănescu, MS 164, f. 50v.

the surviving documents. Iorgu Hartulari brought flair, skill, and intelligence to the development of any business venture; he gave no thought to moral considerations, and he calculated the prospects well. His career developed in a period when there was an acute need for 'bureaucrats'.[32] Iorgu could write well in Moldavian and in Greek; moreover he had the ability to explain rules and regulations clearly. The Russian administration needed such men to put the Organic Regulation into application. Through his patron, Grigore Sturza, he came to be part of the administration in Moldavia, where he was used, first by General Pyotr Zheltukhin and later by General Pavel Kiselyov, in the implementation of the new rules and rewarded with ranks and promotions in the administrative hierarchy.[33]

Once accepted into the network, Iorgu was well able to feign subservience towards his patrons, Grigore Sturza and Mihail Sturdza. The acceptance of a 'minimum of voluntary compliance', as Max Weber remarks, involves an 'interest', whether that interest is material, affective, or 'ideal'.[34] And this docility may be based on 'purely opportunistic grounds, or [...] reasons of material self-interest.'[35] Iorgu asked his patrons' advice before embarking upon a business venture, talking to them about the opportunities offered by particular investments, with the result that his 'compliance' and competence made him someone to be trusted. In their turn, his patrons offered him their trust, involving him in the solution of various economic and personal problems or in the management of public business that could bring them personal gain. He speculated on any connection that could bring him an advantage, worked hard, and followed closely every negotiation or business deal. As Elena testifies, Iorgu was 'exact' in all his accounting and kept a careful record of the income and expenditure of his estates.[36] Already from the middle of the eighteenth century, Moldavian boyars had begun to keep ledgers of income and expenditure for their estates. Copying the model of the Russian nobility, they took an interest in calculating the wealth at their disposal and investing it in the best possible exploitation of their lands.[37] The ledgers were maintained by

32 Max Weber, *Bureaucracy*, in Malcom Watters (ed.), *Modernity: Critical Concepts in Sociology*, vol. III, *Modern Systems* (London, New York:1999), 351–367.

33 SJAN, Iaşi, Colecţia Gh. Ghibănescu, MS 164, f. 9v-10r.

34 Max Weber, *Economy and Society: An Outline of Interpretive Sociology*. (Berkeley: 1978), 212–213.

35 Ibid., 214.

36 SJAN, Iaşi, Colecţia Gh. Ghibănescu, MS 164, f. 15r–16r.

37 Elena Korchmina, *The Practice of Personal Finance and the Problem of Debt among the Noble Elite in Eighteenth-Century Russia*, in Andreas Schönle, Andrei Zorin, and Alexei Evstratov (eds.), *The Europeanized Elite in Russia, 1762–1825. Public Role and Subjective Self* (Illinois: 2016), 116–135.

estate managers, who were then checked on by their masters.[38] At first, Iorgu was far too poor to be able to afford to employ an estate manager, so he kept the accounts himself.[39] Even when he became very rich, he trusted no one and still preferred to keep personal control of his business affairs.

Iorgu's rapid rise to wealth would have been impossible without advancement in the hierarchy of ranks, together with the effective holding of administrative offices. In 1835, he was raised to the rank of *căminar* (the official responsible for collecting the tax on alcoholic drinks and wax) and appointed a member (*cilen*) of the court of justice of Suceava county; before the year was out, he moved on to the civil position of *ispravnic* (prefect) of the same territory and the military rank of *serdar* (commander); he subsequently managed to attain membership of the *protipendadă* (the elite category of great boyars), receiving the rank of *agă* (chief of police), *spătar* and later, in 1847, that of *postelnic*.[40] Along with the posts and ranks he received came influence, privileges, and power. Iorgu was a good speaker of Greek, Hungarian, German, and Moldavian, and expanded his connections beyond the borders of the principality, succeeding in establishing good relations with the Patriarchates of Constantinople and Jerusalem. Once he had begun to create his own network and to make his fortune, Iorgu Hartulari considered that the time had come to part with Elena. In 1835 he threw his wife out of the house and requested a separation. However, Iorgu had not grasped that the strength, and above all the solidarity of the network that had propelled his rise could equally well bring about his downfall. Grigore Plitos asked for the help of his patron, Prince Mihail Sturdza, who was to remind Iorgu who lay behind his social ascent: 'Let us separate her from such a tyrant, who after he has made his position, now comes with insolence, after all the torments he has caused her, to abandon her

38 For Moldavia, there are a considerable number of such ledgers. See, in this connection, Mihai Mîrza, 'Averea lui beizadea Ioniţă Cantemir după un catastif din 1755', in *Analele Institutului de Istorie Xenopol*, t. XLIX (2012), 409–437; Mihai Mîrza, 'Cheltuielile casei marelui vistiernic Toader Palade, după o seamă din anul 1752', in *Analele Ştiinţifice ale Universităţii Alexandru Ioan Cuza, Iaşi, Secţia*. Istorie, LIX (2013), 333–408; SJAN, Iaşi, Colecţia Documente P. 1023/2: Sama lui Şerban logofăt pentru cheltuiala casii dumisale Ioan Canta biv vel vistier pe anul acesta, precum arată anume înăuntru, leat 1777 ghenuar 1, f. 52. For Wallachia, these registers come later. See Constanţa Vintilă-Ghiţulescu, '"Condica de toate pricinile şi trebuinţele casii mele" de pitarul Dumitrache Piersiceanu de la Fundata (1804–1839)', in Dan Dumitru Iacob (ed.), *Avere, prestigiu şi cultură materială în surse patrimoniale. Inventare de averi din secolele XVI–XIX* (Iaşi: 2015), 523–553.

39 While he administered the estate and outside business, Elena kept records of the houses and servants in a ledger. SJAN, Iaşi, Colecţia Gh. Ghibănescu, MS 164, f. 20v.

40 Mihai-Răzvan Ungureanu, *Marea Arhondologie a boierilor Moldovei (1835–1856)* (Iaşi: 2014), 109; Gh. Platon, Al.-F. Platon, *Boierimea*, 117.

too! I will take his wealth and give it to her, for it is hers, and let him remain as he was [before], because it was for her sake that I gave him so much help and assistance with money.'[41]

This threat from his prince and protector Sturdza forced Iorgu to think again about his decision and he resumed his duty as a husband. His extra-marital affairs continued under his wife's tolerant gaze, but the economic benefits of the social network (which he could easily have lost) and the solidarity built around Elena determined him to be cautious and gradually to return to the conjugal bed.

Iorgu Hartulari pursued his business interests in a small community held together by various bonds of family or friendship. Elena's memoirs reflect very well this community, whose members prospered together, developing economic activities and celebrating their victories with parties and balls. An examination of Iorgu's network allows us to observe that it was made up of family members (his brothers, brothers-in-law, and nephews), friends belonging to the second rank of the boyar class, clients, and business partners, with whom he associated only in his financial and property 'speculations' (the Jewish bankers and merchants in the community, Turkish merchants).

The 'speculations' to which Elena alludes involved leasing estates: Iorgu would offer the owner a fixed sum to be paid twice a year, while he took charge of the harvest and strove to obtain as great a profit as he could by exploiting the peasants' labour.[42] He embarked on such speculations particularly with the hegumens of monasteries, who granted him the use of their lands. The experience was useful and helped him to take a step forward. Iorgu's leasing of land dedicated to monasteries led to him becoming the right-hand man of the prince of Moldavia, Mihail Sturdza, which brought him renown and authority, but also a reputation as someone greedy for wealth and lacking any moral

41 SJAN, Iaşi, Colecţia Gh. Ghibănescu, MS 164, f. 15r–16r.

42 He held a lease on the estate of Borca in Neamţ county, for which he paid the Metropolitan Diocese a fixed sum on the days of Saint George and Saint Demetrius; any additional revenue belonged to him. See the record of 21 April 1841, when he paid the Saint George's day instalment of 15,000 lei (SJAN, Iaşi, Colecţia Documente, 428/206). The Metropolitan Diocese considered that the income from the estate was much greater, so on 26 April 1841, it signed a new contract with Iorgu Hartulari, leasing the estate of Borca to him for the sum of 48,005 lei (SJAN, Colecţia Documente, 428/209). In addition to Borca, he also held a lease on the estate of Murgii, belonging to the Monastery of Neamţ (SJAN, Colecţia Documente, 427/250, 256).427/250, 256), and other estates in Moldavia, as may be seen from his carefully preserved contracts and receipts. See SJAN, Iaşi, Colecţia Documente, 427/ 259, 29 April 1849; 427/ 288, 27 December 1847.

principles.[43] An incident reported by Elena Hartulari shows how her husband was perceived in the community: on their daughter Maria's wedding day, the city was full of 'satires' (broadside pamphlets) ironically lamenting the fate of the new son-in-law, Şerban Cănănău, who had such a 'tyrannical' father-in-law. Written in a bitter tone and describing the abuses committed by Hartulari, the broadsides succeeded in scaring him, as he feared that Șerban would break off the agreement.[44] However, the immense dowry—'12,000 gold pieces in money and 3,000 gold pieces in silverware and jewellery and the best bed linen and clothes and two furnished rooms, plus a carriage worth 180 gold pieces'—was more important to him than his father-in-law's reputation.[45]

In addition to leasing estates, Iorgu was also involved in the timber trade. In this, he worked in association with Ottoman merchants, Jewish and Greek merchants who were active in the same line of business.[46] He also produced and sold spirits, which brought a substantial and steady income.[47] The money he made, he then invested in buying estates and other financial speculations. Moreover, he knew how to get a good price for his protection and for the influence that he managed to have in the community. This is abundantly clear from his dealings with the guild of Jewish merchants in Fălticeni, Austrian subjects, who on one occasion requested his help and protection.[48]

---

43 He took leases on estates belonging to monasteries dedicated to the Holy Sepulchre in Jerusalem. These were administered by the Board of Guardians of the Wealth of the Holy Sepulchre (*Epitropia Averilor Sfântului Mormânt*). In the age of print, the Board had standard contracts and issued printed receipts on which only the sum had to be entered by hand. See the contract of 23 April 1845 (SJAN, Iaşi, Colecţia Documente, 433/272) and the receipt of 26 October 1846 (SJAN, Iaşi, Colecţia Documente, 426/211). Other receipts are preserved in SJAN, Iaşi, Colecţia Documente 426/226, 227; 427/ 259; 427/288, 27.

44 SJAN, Iaşi, Colecţia Gh. Ghibănescu, MS 164, f. 31v–32r.

45 SJAN, Iaşi, Colecţia Gh. Ghibănescu, MS 164, f. 32v.

46 Contracts are preserved from a number of years. To give only a few examples: Contract of 1 June 1836, SJAN, Iaşi, Colecţia Documente, 428/160. The contract signed on 1 June 1840, renewed on 9 November 1841, with the Turkish merchant Abdul Ramiz (?) for delivery of timber. On 28 July 1842, Abdul Ramiz still owed Iorgu Hartulari money. The contract is written in Cyrillic, but signed by Abdul in Ottoman Turkish. The document recording the payment of the debt is written in Ottoman Turkish and Cyrillic, and signed by Abdul in Ottoman Turkish. SJAN, Iaşi, Colecţia Documente, 427/ 252, 255, 261, 262.

47 SJAN, Iaşi, Colecţia Documente, 427/ 253.

48 Iorgu Hartulari had a special relationship with Ştrul Focşăneanu, a leading figure among the Jews of Fălticeni, from whom he borrowed money to launch his business ventures (SJAN, Iaşi, Colecţia Gh. Ghibănescu, MS 164, f. 31v-32r). When Iorgu rose to be a notable of the town, known for his influence with Prince Mihail Sturdza, the Jewish community appealed for his help to resolve conflicts with the local boyars. See Artur Gorovei, *Folticenii. Cercetări istorice asupra oraşului* (Folticeni: 1938), 69–71, 73–74.

'Exact' in his business affairs during his lifetime, and keeping all his accounts with precision, Iorgu Hartulari made preparations for his posterity in good time. After the inconstancy of his youthful behaviour, he returned to his wife in the last years of his life, insisting at every opportunity on her role in building his immense fortune, and preparing her to take charge of his business affairs. In his testament, he named his wife as heir to his entire wealth, with the right to dispose of it as she wished, given that she had been its source.[49] Moreover, he took steps to ensure the transfer of authority, visiting estate after estate and summoning the peasants to get their goodwill by distributing gifts and invoking his decent treatment of them. They were advised to be obedient and to listen to the new mistress just as they had to him.[50] On his death, he left a considerable fortune, which he had succeeded in managing so that it brought in considerable income. However, it was not in the palpable form of money or goods, but was invested in his volatile 'speculations'. Elena may have been the source of this wealth, but she did not have the economic knowledge necessary to keep control of these financial speculations, which required practice and agency to make them work. The patrimony thus fell victim to the demands of creditors and the extravagance of the Hartulari children.

Consumption and Sociability

The first half of the nineteenth century saw a remodelling of the role played by women both in the promotion of a type of consumption and in the construction of a form of sociability. Leora Auslander observes that: 'The focus for women's consumption was the making of the family and the class.'[51] The 'evolution of consumption', which began somewhere in eighteenth-century England, as Jan de Vries has shown,[52] manifested itself much later in southeastern Europe. The wars of the late eighteenth and early nineteenth centuries, involving frequent military occupations, contributed to the promotion of a certain mode, a certain type of civility. Moldavia joined the European trend of consumption, through urbanization and the numeric growth of a population segment able to invest in consumption, and it underwent a series of institutional

49 SJAN, Iaşi, Colecţia Gh. Ghibănescu, MS 164, f. 45v.

50 SJAN, Iaşi, Colecţia Gh. Ghibănescu, MS 164, f. 42v–43v.

51 Leora Auslander, 'The Gendering of Consumer Practices in Nineteenth-Century France' in Victoria De Grazia, Ellen Furlough (eds.), *The Sex of the Things: Gender and Consumption in Historical Perspective* (California: 1996), 79.

52 Jan De Vries, *The Industrious Revolution: Consumer Demand and the Household Economy, 1650 to the Present* (Cambridge: 2008).

changes aimed at the construction of a modern state. Manolache Drăghici, writing the history of Moldavia in these years, attributed capital importance to the reforms introduced by the Organic Regulation and the Kiselyov administration in the transition to a new stage of society:

> The administration of Count Kiselyov was blessed by all classes of the Romanian people, for as long as he governed and long after, as an age in which, with his wise measures, he made our lands cleanse themselves of all the barbarous rust and oppressive customs that had remained in them from the Turks and from the Tatars through the subjection of the locals and the adoption of many Asiatic ways.[53]

Together with the institutions of modernity, the principality saw an explosion of 'institutions and discourses', to use Leora Auslander's words, centred around consumption.[54] Merchants travelled up and down Moldavia with their goods, while shops, more and more specialized in character, were opened in Iaşi, Bârlad, Focşani, Galaţi, Fălticeni, and Tecuci.[55] Moldavian consumption had its particularities, however: many goods continued to be brought from the Ottoman Empire, via Istanbul, Bursa, Sibiu, and Iaşi; the 'French' model was adopted through the intermediary of the Russian army of occupation; the local market was connected to the Viennese and German market, via Leipzig; and the boyar household itself produced a considerable part of the foodstuffs and textiles necessary for everyday life.

How did the local elites become informed about new fashions and tastes? Magazines devoted to fashion, interior decoration, garden layout, pavilions, etc. began to arrive from Leipzig and Vienna. Starting in the 1830s, a domestic press developed, with whole pages dedicated to consumption: advertisements for clothes and shoes, alimentary delicacies, outfits for balls and soirées, porcelain and silverware, announcements regarding the employment of qualified staff (teachers, engineers, designers, valets, maids, cooks, painters, gardeners, doctors, tailors, etc). May we, as Leora Auslander argues, speak of a directed consumption, with French society as its model?[56]

As her husband, Iorgu accumulated a sizeable capital, so little by little, Elena Hartulari entered into the logic of consumption. When their income

53 Postelnicul Manolachi Drăghici, *Istoria Moldovei pe timp de 500 de ani pînă în zilele noastre*, ed. Andrei Pippidi (Bucharest: 2017), 251.

54 Auslander, 'The Gendering of Consumer Practices', 81.

55 The presence of these travelling merchants, who wandered all over Moldavia, greatly frightened the authorities, who tried to limit their movement by means of various orders. See *Manualul Administrativ al Principatului Moldovei* (Iaşi: 1856), 404.

56 Auslander, 'The Gendering of Consumer Practices', 81.

rose and Iorgu attained important administrative positions, part of that capital was used to sustain their new social acquisitions. Elena invested in the fitting out of their residence in Fălticeni to match their new status, attending to furniture and interior decoration, clothes, and objects necessary for sociability.[57] The residence could accommodate the Hartulari couple with their children, numerous servants, guests, and sometimes occasional visitors.

Fălticeni was a small town on the road from Iaşi to Suceava. From a social point of view, the town was headed by a local second-rank boyar class, engaged in competition for offices in the local administration and holding properties in the surrounding villages.[58] The economic life of the town was maintained by a fairly large number of merchants, many of them Jews from neighbouring Bukovina and Galicia, who conducted trade with Vienna, Leipzig, and Istanbul.[59] Indeed, the town was known for the great fair organized on the day of the Holy Prophet Elijah (*Sfântul Ilie*), which brought together all Moldavia. Its fame had spread far and wide, and drew all sorts of people to the town every summer. Situated as it was near the border between Moldavia and Austrian Bukovina, Fălticeni was a place of migration both for Jewish merchants and for German craftsmen who had set up their workshops on the Moldavian side of the border. In accordance with the provisions of the Organic Regulation, a town council (*eforie*) was set up in 1832. It was charged with making the town more beautiful and salubrious. All the same, Fălticeni was 'modernized' with great difficulty, and only began to lose its rural appearance—with houses and shops crowded together and unsurfaced lanes, full of mud in the winter and dust in the summer—towards the end of the nineteenth century. As for health and hygiene, it was 1842 before the town had its first doctor, in the person of Ignatz Diaconovici. As we shall see from Elena Hartulari's memoirs, however, the medical profession was rapidly acquiring an important status in society, and he was soon joined by others. The following year, there were eleven doctors in Fălticeni, many of them Habsburg Jews and Germans.[60] The intellectual

57 New studies regarding the relation between material culture and gender identities highlight the roles and influence of women in the construction of sociability and of social networks. See Amanda Vickery, *Behind Closed Doors: At Home in Georgian England* (New Haven, CT – London: 2009); Amanda Vickery, *The Gentlemen's Daughter: Women's Lives in Georgian England* (New Haven, CT – London: 1998).

58 The *Catagrafia* of 1851 lists twenty-five boyars with property and sixty boyars without property in Suceava county, to which Fălticeni belonged (Gorovei, *Folticenii*, 125–126).

59 In 1851, there were 230 Jewish families living in the town (Gorovei, *Folticenii*, 125).

60 Gorovei, *Folticenii*, 171.

life of the town remained weak, however, and centred on the activities of the four private schools.[61]

In a small town of this sort, where everybody knew everybody else, there was fierce competition for social status. The model to follow was, of course, the Moldavian capital, Iaşi. Being stuck in the past and failing to adapt to the latest currents in fashion earned censure on the part of the community, in the form of the social exclusion of members who were considered behind the times and too set in their ways. And members of the elite needed one another, especially in a community where there were offspring to be married.

Provincial society was relatively slow to change. In the first half of the nineteenth century it took significant steps in the direction of adopting a 'European model'. However, the process was prolonged and foreign observers detected a mixture of old and new, European manners and oriental furnishings, adoption of the French language combined with ignorance of individual freedom and the continued owning of Gypsy slaves.[62] Gustav Adolf Ramsay, an officer in the Russian army, visited Iaşi in 1829 and expressed surprise at the 'mosaic' of costumes and languages: 'One hears the French language and sees French clothes, but equally [...] one sees Orientals smoking tobacco reclining on sofas, and ragged Gypsies busy about the house.'[63] And if this is how things looked in the capital of Moldavia, they were even 'worse' in provincial towns, where a few families of local boyars controlled the whole political game, holding positions in the administrative apparatus and using their influence to modify any measure coming from the central authorities

The consumption that developed around sociability helps us to understand the relations that individuals developed with goods and the space in which they were to be found, and to observe practices and behaviours adopted in order to highlight membership of a social group, to mark a social identity. Elena Hartulari's home must have been similar to other provincial boyar residences.[64] For the purposes of this paper, let us consider only the spaces dedicated to sociability: the salon, dining room, and cabinet. The salon was the principal room in a boyar residence, and had multiple functions, connected especially with sociability. The word *salon* itself entered the language

---

61 In 1839, 54 pupils attended these four schools (Gorovei, *Folticenii*, 218).

62 Bogdan Mateescu, *Familia în timpul robiei. O perspectivă demografică. Studii şi liste de populaţie din arhive* (Iaşi: 2015); Bogdan Mateescu, *Căsătoria robilor între alegerea cuplului şi voinţa stăpânului. Studiu şi documente din arhivă despre căsătoria robilor în Tara românească după 1830* (Braşov: 2014).

63 *Călători străini*, II, 389.

64 In this connection, see Dan Dumitru Iacob, *Elitele din Principatele Române în prima jumătate a secolului al XIX-lea. Sociabilitate şi divertisment* (Iaşi: 2015), 41–104.

as architecture adapted to the new forms of sociability: hitherto it had simply been called the 'big room' (*odaia mare*).[65] This big room could at any time be adapted, re-arranged to meet the requirements of a social event. It was in the salon that friends, acquaintances, and neighbours met to savour coffee and fruit conserves, to draw on pipes or narghiles, and to play cards or other society games. Social events were organized all through the year: visits and receiving hours, celebrations of religious festivals with family and friends, or events to mark special occasions. Among these were balls and consecration ceremonies of newly founded churches. The furniture of the salon would have been a mix between the new 'European' tendencies and oriental fashion. Richard Kunisch found the use of the word *salon* pretentious, and described the room dedicated to sociability by the boyars he visited in 1857 as follows:

> This expression is somewhat pretentious for a room whose flooring was of bricks and whose walls, like the shapeless stove, were whitewashed. An icon representing the Mother of God or Saint Nicholas constituted the only ornament in the homes of the richest and most noble persons. Around the walls, benches without upholstery were fixed, covered with coarse fabric. A large sofa, referred to as a bed, so high that to sit on it you had to climb two steps, occupied half of the room. A table in the corner, covered like the benches with coarse fabric, completed the furniture.[66]

If at first the salon was lined with sofas covered with coloured rugs, woven in the house or brought from Edirne or Constantinople, later we may presume that Elena progressed to the new trend and brought 'European' furniture from Iași or Czernowitz, consisting of armchairs, stools, and special tables for card games, while the walls were hung with tapestries and decorated with mirrors.[67]

Indeed, the shift from oriental to 'French' costume necessitated some adaptation of interior arrangements. Commenting ironically on this unsynchronized transition, Costache Negruzzi writes the following in a satirical piece in the newspaper *Albina Românească* (The Romanian bee):

> You have beds and straw mattresses in your salon and you consider that you will entice me to come and see you? But how shall I sit down on them without tearing all the laces and buttons that fasten me? Without the under-straps of my

65 The term used by Alecu Russo, *Scrieri alese* (Bucharest: 1970), 60. See also Iacob, *Elitele*, 62.

66 Richard Kunisch, *Bucureşti şi Stambul. Schiţe din Ungaria, România şi Turcia* (Bucharest: 2014), 108.

67 This was the furniture in the *agă* Scarlat Donici's salon on his estate in Vaslui county. See Corina Cimpoeşu, *Artă, modă, cultură europeană în Moldova, între 1830 şi 1860. Elemente ale procesului de modernizare culturală* (Iaşi: 2013), 170–171.

> trousers bursting? How can I put my noble *bonjour* jacket, so masterfully tailored by Orgie, with your bed made by an Armenian mattress-maker?'[68]

Elena Hartulari's salon would have been fitted out with pieces of furniture necessary for sociability: coffee table, chaises longues, couch (indispensable for social chat), and reading table. It was here that she spent many moments in the company of her friends, her confessor—Archimandrite Neonil of Neamț Monastery—, her brothers-in-law and sisters-in-law, drinking coffee, playing cards, and talking about this and that. It was here too that Iorgu Hartulari organized numerous card-playing sessions, bringing together his friends, neighbours, and other acquaintances.

This is perhaps the place to introduce the term 'semi-luxury' (*demi-luxe*) proposed by Jean-Claude Daumas to mark the transition from aristocratic luxury to the luxury of comfort. Semi-luxury products began to appear and to impose their presence in the 1840s, with the development of 'artistic industries incorporating bronzes, goldwork, clockmaking, and furniture.'[69] Due to ever rising demands and the growth of a middle class interested in comfort, a market in semi-luxury goods developed as a separate field, actively promoting itself by means of a press specially conceived to sustain and educate tastes in the interests of consumption.[70]

The Hartulari residence must have been furnished with semi-luxury items: pieces of furniture that could easily be moved aside when big events such as balls were organized. The Hartulari family ranked among the wealthy boyar families who organized social events that brought the community together, because their social definition depended on the recognition of others. As Oliver Schmitt has noted, social rituals have a huge potential in marking the belonging of a member to a given community.[71] As I have already shown, Iorgu Hartulari had become an important member of the Fălticeni community, where he exercised his authority, displayed his wealth, and maintained his reputation. Social practices bind a community together and offer its members the necessary instruments with which to affirm their social identity. The first grand social event recorded by Elena Hartulari was the consecration of a

68 Carlu Nervil [Costache Negruzzi], 'Magaziile Iaşilor. Veacul merge sporind', *Albina Românească*, n. 10, 3 Feburary 1846, 39.

69 Jean-Claude Daumas, *La revolution matérielle. Une histoire de la consummation, France XIX*e*–XXI*e *siècle* (Paris: 2018), 27.

70 Daumas, *La revolution matérielle*, 32.

71 Oliver Schmitt, 'Addressing Community in Late Medieval Dalmatia', in Eirik Hovden, Christina Lutter, Walter Pohl (eds.), *Meanings of Community across Medieval Eurasia. Comparative Approaches* (Leiden: 2016), 126.

church. On their estate at Huşi, the Hartulari family had erected from its foundations a church that was to become a sort of funerary chapel for the family. The good work of founding places of worship was a very common one among Moldavian and Wallachian boyars. It enhanced their social prestige in the eyes of the community, and at the same time formed part of an unwritten pact with the Divinity in preparation for the Last Judgement. The festivities dedicated to the event lasted three days and brought together 'all the foreigners and boyars of Fălticeni,'[72] Archimandrite Neonil, three priests, and two deacons. The presence of a large number of guests implies a very large consumption of both material and human resources. In the first place, Elena Hartulari had to prepare the house for some thirty guests. Some of them came accompanied by servants, arriving in carriages or droshkies, with coachmen in the driving seat. Food for people and animals was procured, to a large extent, from the Hartulari family estates. Elena describes herself as being talented at making fruit conserves, pickles, smoked meats, vodkas, sherbets, and rose water—in short, 'how to keep and to manage the house.'[73] Servants were brought in from the other Hartulari estates and the Gypsy slaves were dressed in livery in order to help out.

As hostess, Elena attended to the guests, but her authority was much diminished. Her husband participated in this event of great importance, both from a social and a religious point of view, which he himself had initiated, accompanied by his mistress: 'My husband and his mistress (*metresă*) took charge of everything, coming only occasionally to me to order whatever was required, restricting me to merely staying with the guests.' Elena Hartulari expresses with pain the offence, and above all the dishonour of such a situation: 'How improperly he treated me with his mistress in front of all those gathered, who all stayed for three days.' The word that best sums up the social status claimed by Elena Hartulari is *respectability*. She presents herself to others as a respectable, worthy woman, who deserves the pity of others without diminishing in any way the dignity and respect she demands. She attends to the guests, converses with them and maintains sociability; she takes care that there is food, coffee, and drink for everyone; she expresses piety, in view of the religious event that is being celebrated.

Things were very different when Iorgu Hartulari, having reached the apogee of his career, decided to organize a ball, bringing together local boyars, business associates, relatives, and friends. The fashion for such *loisirs* came with the Russian army and took hold rapidly, so that in almost every small market

72 SJAN, Iaşi, Colecţia Gh. Ghibănescu, MS 164, f. 18v–19v.

73 Jon Stobart, Mark Rothery (eds.), *Consumption and the Country House* (Oxford: 2016).

town dance parties were organized periodically for the local elite and foreigners (teachers, doctors, officers, prosperous merchants, etc.).

For this ball, Elena Hartulari was preoccupied with toilette (*toaletă*) and socialization through dance. 'I make myself a toilette more splendid than ever, appearing before everyone happy and contented,' she writes in her journal.[74] Elegant and expensive dresses, precious and pretentious jewellery, strong and fine *bottines* could be bought from shops in the city, and by 1840 the newspapers of the day were already advertising them. For example, Madame Neli Lenfant, probably a Frenchwoman, advertised the goods in her shop by means of the paper *Vestitorul Românesc* (The Romanian Herald). In 1845, her shop on Podul Caliţei in Bucharest offered ballgowns, cloaks, scarves, fancy shawls, fine linen and handkerchiefs, lace and feathers; all 'beautiful' and capable of satisfying the taste of the most demanding ladies. And should any of her clients not be satisfied with what they found in the shop, Madame Neli 'undertakes that in within twenty-four hours she can have ready a suit of clothes of the most elegant.'[75]

Men too could buy suitable clothes after reading advertisements in the gazettes. Monsieur K.M. Frank, Tailor of Vienna, for example, with a shop in Curtea Veche, Bucharest, promised 'the most elegant and inexpensive novelties in matters of men's clothing, brought from Paris itself: jackets, tailed coats, Codrington coats, trousers and waistcoats of various materials.' Should one be attending a fancy-dress ball, Mr Varembergh's shop on Podul Mogoșoaiei, Bucharest, stocked special items for such an occasion: 'silk domino cloaks in all colours, national costumes, characteristic and fancy', together with a variety of masks; in addition he offered in twelve hours to make any costume at a 'decent' price.[76]

The great attraction of such balls was the dances. Moldavia kept up-to-date with balls in Europe, not only learning the dance steps, but adopting the specified music for them. About this particular ball, Elena Hartulari writes: 'The polonaise began with me according to custom. Then the quadrille began, again with me; third I began to waltz with a couple of cavaliers.'[77] The exhibition of the richly adorned body, the exhibition of one's qualities as a dancer, the display of the most expensive ballroom decorations, the preparation of the tastiest dishes—these constituted the core of such a dancing event. Full attention

74 SJAN, Iaşi, Colecţia Gh. Ghibănescu, MS 164, f. 26r.
75 *Vestitorul Românesc*, Tuesday, January 9, no. 3, 1845.
76 *Vestitorul Românesc*, Saturday, April 28, no. 33, 1845.
77 SJAN, Iaşi, Colecţia Gh. Ghibănescu, MS 164, f. 25v–26r.

had to be given to the slightest detail, lest the next day the community sanction with gossip any deviation from what a 'successful' ball should be.

Social events were used by Elena to draw attention to the disagreeable situation in which she found herself: respectability was the order of the day for the urban elite. Family and honour were closely bound together, and unwritten social norms weighed heavily in the acceptance and validation of one's belonging to the community. Immediately after the events, friends and relations sanctioned Iorgu's behaviour and explicitly demanded that he control his conduct in public.[78]

Consumption and Knowledge

Maxine Berg has argued that 'new wealth had to be educated, and the choice, display, and use of the variety of goods had to be cultivated.'[79] This hypothesis is borne out by the experiences of the Hartulari family, who educated their tastes to the extent that their wealth permitted the accumulation of various goods, objects, and services. A luxury item bought or received as a present is not just a mere product; it generates emotion, stimulates thought, and offers pleasure.[80] For example, Elena Hartulari receives from her husband a 'brooch with brilliants' after his successful conclusion of a timber deal in Constantinople in 1836. Twenty-three years later, the brooch with brilliants prompts the widow Hartulari to recall with affection her late husband's journey. Through Elena's eyes, we discover her fascination with the Orient in general and Istanbul in particular. As she writes her memoirs in 1856, she still has a vivid memory of Iorgu Hartulari's reception by Mehmet Pasha, the head of the Ottoman naval department, known as 'pasha of the Tersane [arsenal]'. Shortly before his interview, Iorgu sent 'two large mirrors to put on the wall and a large clock with music to put on the table' as gifts to the pasha. There followed the usual reception ritual that was accorded to any princely envoy,[81] but which took on great significance in the imagination of Elena, eager to set down on paper the

78 SJAN, Iaşi, Colecţia Gh. Ghibănescu, MS 164, f. 2vr. See also Anne Martin-Fugier, *La Bourgeoise* (Paris: 1983); Adeline Daumard, *Les bourgeois et la bourgeoisie en France depuis 1815* (Paris: 1991).

79 Maxine Berg, *Luxury and Pleasure in Eighteenth-Century Britain* (Oxford: 2007), 41.

80 Maxine Berg, 'In pursuit of Luxury: Global History and British Consumer Goods in the Eighteenth Century', *Past and Present*, 182 (2004), 96.

81 Iorgu Hartulari had letters of recommendation from prince Mihail Sturdza to the bey of Samos, Stephanos Vogorides, who was Sturdza's father-in-law, and to the patriarch of Constantinople.

triumphs of her 'braggard' husband. 'Braggard' (*fanfaron*) is her characterization of Iorgu, who, once he had grown rich, was eager to boast of his wealth, making a show of his money and influence—but to return to our story:

> After my husband went in to the pasha, he made an obeisance, went into the middle of the room, made another obeisance, the pasha being on the bed, sitting Greek-style, holding a jasmine chibouk a fathom long, with a mouthpiece on the chibouk of the best amber and full of brilliants and a bowl the size of a *filcan*, which cost some 70 gold pieces. The pasha got up on his knees, my husband making an obeisance down to the ground, and he said to him: '*oturu boiar*', that is, 'sit down.' He sat down on a very luxurious armchair, beside the pasha. Immediately two dark-skinned Turks came up, one with a chibouk more expensive than the pasha's and the other with a *filcan* of coffee, but without the pasha speaking to him until the coffee was finished. My husband when he gave back the *filcan* put five *icosar*s down on the silver tray. In came another chibouk, five *icosar*s to him too. The Turks, both of them, made obeisances to him, thanking him for the tips he had given. After this ceremony the pasha began to speak in the Greek language, asking him first about the ruler of Moldavia, if he was healthy, and about the land, in what condition it was. They continued this conversation about half an hour, and then entered into the question of trade.[82]

Iorgu Hartulari ended his visit with the gesture of a parvenu grown rich overnight. Happy that he had sealed the timber deal, when he left the pasha's presence he threw *icosars*[83] to left and to right, thus offering a tip to the sentinels who guarded the palace.[84] The Turks encountered by Iorgu Hartulari in Istanbul were very different from the Turks of Elena's childhood, when they had invaded Iași and burned and looted the houses of the Christians: these Turks were friendly and impressed by the actions of the 'Moldavian merchant'.[85] Elena's thoughts follow his footsteps though 'the most important places' in Istanbul, through the markets where he bought many and varied things, presents for Prince Mihail Sturdza, for relatives, friends, and acquaintances. She writes that Iorgu made these visits 'for his memory'.[86] Through her husband's tales, Elena Hartulari sees the miraculous Orient, enjoys Hagia Sophia, Galata, and Pera, travels on the steamer, where she tastes champagne for the first time, throws *icosar*s to left and to right, shares out presents, is thrilled by the bittersweet taste of oranges, feels the sea breeze as she walks proudly on the deck

82 SJAN, Iaşi, Colecţia Gh. Ghibănescu, MS 164, f. 12r–14v.
83 Turkish coins.
84 SJAN, Iaşi, Colecţia Gh. Ghibănescu, MS 164, f. 12r–14v.
85 Ibid.
86 Ibid.

of the returning ship.[87] A brooch with brilliants stimulates the imagination, awakening emotion, generating knowledge.

Elena Hartulari often went to Czernowitz, where she sent her daughter Maria to boarding school. Capital of the Habsburg province of Bukovina, Czernowitz was a reference point for the local Moldavian elite.[88] It was there that the local boyars and the urban elite sent their children to complete their education, and there that they went to shop, or for cures and medical treatment. If Elena had been raised to be a 'good housewife' and a 'faithful wife', the same cannot be said about her daughter. Maria Hartulari was sent to *pensionnats* from the age of ten. She spent the first two years in Iaşi, first at a private school run by 'Madame Colen', and then at another run by 'Madame Gore' (probably Garet[89]). When she took ill, Elena brought her home for a while, and then moved her to Czernowitz, where she was enrolled in the *pensionnat* run by 'Madame Domenzil' (probably Dumézil).[90] Czernowitz was not a random choice: in addition to being an important educational centre, it was also a medical one. Maria learned French, German, and piano, and her health could be closely supervised by a doctor.[91] The German town offered Elena another sort of knowledge, more connected to the practicalities of life.[92] At Madame Dumézil's urging, Elena agreed to be consulted and tested by Doctor Zalheri (in fact her daughter's regular doctor), by three other doctors, and by a midwife. First the doctors prescribed her a diet:

> I was consulted three days in a row and the result was for me to have baths in whey for three summers, and medicines in the winter, and a very great diet. First to be barred from sorrows, which could not be, second, not to eat bitter or salted food, wine, or oranges for these three years, which I followed. No coffee with

87 On the steamship journey, see Constantin Ardeleanu, 'From Vienna to Constantinopol on Board the Vessels of the Austrian Danube Steam-Navigation Company (1834–1842)', in *Historical Yearbook*, VI, 2009, 187–202.

88 On Czernowitz under Habsburg rule, see Kurt Scharr, 'Czernowitz-Cernăuţi-Çernovcÿ (Tscherniwzi). Genese einer städtischen Kulturlandschaft in einem wechselnden politischen Ambiente', in Sergej W. Piwowarow (ed.), *Die Bukowina. Historische und ethnokulturelle Studien* (Tscherniwzi: 2007), 16–45.

89 At the time, the *pensionnat* founded and run by François and Isabelle Garet in Iaşi was one of the best in Moldavia. See Iacob, 'Copii de boieri', 151.

90 I have not yet managed to identify any 'Madame Domenzil' or similar running a *pensionnat* in Czernowitz in the 1830s and 1840s.

91 SJAN, Iaşi, Colecţia Gh. Ghibănescu, MS 164, f. 33r.

92 On the relation between women, consumption, and travel, see Evguenia Davidova, 'Women Travellers as Consumers: Adoption of Modern Ideas and Practices in 19th-Century Southeast Europe', in Constanţa Vintilă-Ghiţulescu (ed.), *Women, Consumption and the Circulation of Ideas in South-Eastern Europe, 17th–19th Century* (Leiden: 2018), 200–227.

> milk either, or black coffee, where I had a weakness for black coffee, every hour I would drink a cup, having a weakness for coffee, it came to me from sorrow.[93]

Then the doctors compiled a full-scale 'medical report', which they sent—via Elena—to her regular doctor in Fălticeni. At the time, to have a regular doctor was the habit of a very restricted elite. Doctors began to acquire importance only with the construction of the modern Romanian state. A large proportion of the doctors in Moldavia were foreign, and worked at the princely court or in the houses of great boyars and in the main cities. Doctors had to face not only the distrust of the population, however, but also the poor esteem in which their profession was held by the elite. Elena Hartulari's journal transmits important information about medical practice: the cures, diets, and spa visits that were already fashionable in Europe and were now taking shape in Moldavia too. Experiences of this sort were then reported to friends and relations, encouraging them to join this medical consumption, to the detriment of traditional empirical practices.

With Maria, Elena launched her struggle for the education of her children. Her two sons, Nicolae and Matei, were also enrolled in private schools. Nicolae was sent to Lemberg (L'viv) and Matei to Potsdam.[94] Their German education should be seen in relation to the education that the family's protector, Mihail Sturdza, offered his sons, whom he sent first of all to Luneville and Paris, and then to Berlin. When her patron sent his sons to Paris, Elena was quick to do the same. Through her French acquaintance Charles Malgouverné, who taught French at the Academy in Iaşi, she was able to send the two boys to study in Paris.[95] As Maria's marriage broke down after two years, and to give some direction to the young woman's unruly energies, her parents hastened to send her to Paris too, under the supervision of the same Charles Malgouverné and his wife.[96] This time, Maria went on a sort of educational trip, for the purpose of 'making noble acquaintances' and 'travelling'. Her companion was 'Madame Luba', who had been the governess of Mihail Sturdza's wife.[97]

It is very interesting to observe how the Hartulari family took the princely family as its model and tried to imitate it in everything. The interactions

---

93 SJAN, Iaşi, Colecţia Gh. Ghibănescu, MS 164, f. 33r.

94 SJAN, Iaşi, Colecţia Gh. Ghibănescu, MS 164, f. 33r. See also Andrei Pippidi, *Părinţi şi copii în Geneva lui Töpffer* in Nicoleta Roman (ed.), *Copilăria românească între familie şi societate (secolele XVII–XX)* (Bucharest: 2015), 343–360.

95 Urechia, *Istoria românilor*, vol. 4, 417.

96 For the divorce of Maria Hartulari and Şerban Cănănău, see SJAN, Iaşi, Colecţia Documente, 428/197.

97 SJAN, Iaşi, Colecţia Gh. Ghibănescu, MS 164, f. 33v.

between the two families were numerous, but never went beyond the relation between patron and client, master and servant. As a faithful and submissive client, Iorgu Hartulari took advantage of his master's trust in him to amass a considerable fortune. As for Elena, she was affectively bound to her spiritual patron, and ran to him every time she felt threatened or needed assistance. In a way, Iorgu Hartulari was a little 'master', dominating the local community and copying the behaviour of his patron. Of course Mihail Sturdza was clearly his superior when it came to education, but Iorgu strove to make up for this by investing in the education of his children. This is probably why he did not mix with the local boyar class where education was concerned. Elena writes that her husband had become very rich in a very short time.[98] With wealth came pride, boastfulness, and the desire to be recognized and appreciated as one of the foremost boyars of Moldavia. '[My sense of] honour is great' (*Filotimia îi mare*) was Iorgu's excuse when he refused a very good offer for the sale of an estate.[99] In other words, his honour and his ambition to be considered the foremost among the leading boyars in the community had to be reflected in any action. The same can be seen in the education of his children, in his display of luxury, in his behaviour. Of course this regard for honour was not his invention. The Hartulari family was imitating a model to which every thousand gold pieces it amassed brought it closer, a model that was present in society and that inspired many other families.

*

Elena Hartulari's interactions with various objects, goods, and places determined her to imitate and to adapt ideas, manners, tastes, and behaviours that would contribute to the promotion of a new lifestyle, a new way of seeing traditional society. The widow Elena Hartulari is the quintessence of these accumulations of knowledge. After Iorgu's death in 1850, and the fall of her patron Mihail Sturdza in 1849, Elena found herself faced with fierce family conflicts. Her two sons, her daughter, and her son-in-law joined together in the attempt to break away as much as possible of the wealth and power delegated to their mother / mother-in-law by her late husband. Now, in the middle of the nineteenth century, the world had changed and the networks of power had taken new paths, which determined Elena to go to war against everyone: her children, the prince, the metropolitan. Writing petitions and demanding audiences with the new prince, Grigore Alexandru Ghica (1849–1853, 1853–1856) and the new

98 SJAN, Iaşi, Colecţia Gh. Ghibănescu, MS 164, f. 12r.
99 SJAN, Iaşi, Colecţia Gh. Ghibănescu, MS 164, f. 36r.

metropolitan, Sofronie Miclescu (1851–1856), she fought to keep her position as mistress of the patrimony.[100] However her struggle brought to the foreground adversaries that were unfamiliar to her: the new institutions of the modern state with their bureaucracies, new networks with their various interests, new people in important positions of power. Her revolt became open when the new circles of power ignored her petitions and complaints. For example, in 1851, when her son Nicolae wanted to get married without her agreement, Elena sought the help of the metropolitan, just as she had always done before, convinced that she still held sufficient power to be listened to and could stop the marriage being celebrated by the Church. But the metropolitan gave Nicolae his agreement, to the distress of Elena, who burst into the Metropolitan Palace and shouted out her discontent:

> I go and enter at the metropolitan's [office], where there were also three archpriests, and I present myself that I am the *postelnic*'s wife Elena Hartulari! I have come to thank you for the help you have given me for my orphan Nicu, that you have taken all rights to yourself and you have married him without my consent! Cursing him to his face, that for any wrongdoing of his he will have to give account to the all-powerful Judge![101]

Elena Hartulari's journal offers a remarkable insight into the changes taking place in Moldavian society in the first half of the nineteenth century, giving a detailed analysis of everything from language to gender relations, from institutions to bureaucracy, from consumption to social status, from the perspective of a woman caught between tradition and modernity.

Reading Elena's memoirs, and then the numerous Hartulari family documents that have been preserved, covering a long period of time (1810–1880), the researcher is struck by the discrepancy between the calculated and avaricious Iorgu Hartulari and his sons, spendthrift and incapable of administering an estate. Unfortunately, we do not know what they studied in Paris, or whether they attended specific schools or simply polished their education with the help of private teachers and through participation in routine socializing. What is certain is that when their father died in 1850, Nicolae and Matei Hartulari did not have the necessary abilities to take over the immense property of the family. Matei remained in Paris for a time, in 1851–1852, but when he fell in love and threatened that he was going to marry a lady (*damă*) without fortune or position, Elena stopped his allowance and forced him to return home.[102] Caught

100 SJAN, Iaşi, Colecţia Gh. Ghibănescu, MS 164, f. 52v.
101 SJAN, Iaşi, Colecţia Gh. Ghibănescu, MS 164, f. 54v.
102 SJAN, Iaşi, Colecţia Gh. Ghibănescu, MS 164, f. 54v.

between the two worlds, the young Hartularis did not know how to put their French education to good use, but nor did they have the necessary levers for integration in Moldavian power networks. Although they married 'for love', following their mother's example, their marriages proved failures, both from the sentimental and the financial point of view.[103]

The discrepancies are also evident between Elena and her daughter Maria. Elena had been raised to be 'a good housewife and a faithful wife'. Her mother had repeated this obligation at every opportunity, and Elena would fulfil it conscientiously and down to the smallest detail. She had served her apprenticeship beside her mother, learning how to keep the house clean, how to prepare the larder for winter, how to impose her authority over the servants. In other words, Elena had followed a model that was current in the period. She had wanted something more for her daughter: French, German, piano, salon conversation. However it was a superficial education, and did not help Maria to spot the dangers of a society in which not only aristocrats but also various charlatans were trying their luck. Away from home from the age of ten and spending more time in the company of others than with her family, Maria quickly came to believe that she deserved more than a banal provincial life. Arriving in Paris aged eighteen, free and given to fanciful aspirations picked up from Romantic literature and instilled in her by her French governess,[104] she fell in love in 1849 with a Spanish Count Alba, who turned out to be nothing but an impostor. Maria Hartulari's youth was a continuous vaudeville, as she compromised her honour and squandered her dowry.[105] The model of the 'respectable bourgeoise' that was in fashion in the 1850s did not inspire her.[106] Her second marriage, made in haste and against the wishes of her parents in 1850, brought a dowry-hunter into the family, the lawyer Dimitrie Cracti.[107] Sought as a husband and sensing the weaknesses of the Hartulari family, Cracti took full advantage of the disagreements between mother and children, and managed step by step to transfer the profits of the estates and of the dowry to himself. When he had taken over all that he could from his mother-in-law, his wife, and brothers-in law, he played the divorce card very successfully. In the

---

103 SJAN, Iaşi, Colecţia Gh. Ghibănescu, MS 164, f. 54r–57r.

104 Maria continued her education at home, assisted, for a time, by a governess of French origin. SJAN, Iaşi, Colecţia Gh. Ghibănescu, MS 164, f. 30v. For female education and governesses, see Nicoleta Roman, 'Foreign Governesses in Wallachia in the First Half of the Nineteenth Century', *Aspasia*, 14 (2020), 37–56.

105 SJAN, Iaşi, Colecţia Gh. Ghibănescu, MS 164, f. 34r–v, 38v–40v.

106 Ionela Băluţă, *La Bourgeoise respectable. Réflexion sur la construction d'une nouvelle identité féminine dans la seconde moitié du XIXe siècle roumain* (Bruxelles: 2010).

107 SJAN, Iaşi, Colecţia Gh. Ghibănescu, MS 164, f. 41v.

1860s, we find Maria Hartulari writing petitions and letters in French seeking help against Dimitrie Cracti.[108]

The spectacular rise and resounding fall of the Hartulari family are part of Moldavian society's age of transition. 'Greek crossed with Moldavian,' as Constantin Sion described him, Dimitrie Cracti was the prototype of the new man who adapted quickly to the demands of the modern state.[109] He put little weight on obtaining titles, but carved out his path by making use of his knowledge, serving the modern state and serving himself.[110] A bureaucratic functionary, Cracti stepped easily into the new modern state, in which Moldavia and Wallachia were now joined as the United Principalities. He was the embodiment of the 'middle class', ready to carve out a place for himself and to make his way on the political stage.

108 SJAN, Iaşi, Colecţia Documente, 434/254.

109 Sion, *Arhondologia Moldovei.*, 160.

110 In 1853, Dimitrie was accorded the rank of 'spătar' as payment 'for services'. Vezi Ungureanu, *Marea Arhondologie*, 67.

Epilogue

In 1837, Niccolò Livaditti captured in vivid colours Moldavian society at what was in many respects a turning point. Of all the portraits he painted, that of the Alecsandri family is the most well-known, and the one most analysed by researchers due to the contrast it illustrates between the old and the new, between Ottoman and European material culture. The Alecsandris belonged to the middle layer of the boyar class, holding posts in the second rank of the Phanariot and post-Phanariot administration. Assembled under the painter's gaze, they pose for posterity in their best clothes. The father, the *vornic* Vasile Alecsandri, has dressed in his orange silk *anteri*, with a shawl of striped cashmere around his waist. Over the *anteri* he wears a *cüppe* of blue atlas, trimmed with mink, and on his chest he has hung his two decorations, generously awarded by the Russian Empire (the crosses of Saint Anne and Saint Stanislas). His wife Elena (née Cozoni, with Greek family roots) and their daughter Catinca are dressed in the latest fashion. Their dresses are low-cut in the Biedermeier manner, leaving their shoulders bare, they are decked with gold and precious stones, and their hair is carefully styled, with ringlets caressing their cheeks. Catinca seems to have interrupted the melody she is playing on the piano to look towards the painter; her fingers still touch the keys. Her mother holds a letter from their elder son, also Vasile, a student in Paris. His younger brother Iancu poses in the uniform of the local militia. The uniform and the sword are the new attributes of Romantic masculinity and the dream of families with any degree of prosperity.[1]

In a second portrait, also by Livaditti, painted in 1845, we find that Iancu has followed a military career and is now a major and a princely adjutant. Vasile Alecsandri the elder has remained faithful to the hierarchy of ranks and kept his Ottoman garb, while Vasile the younger, back from his studies, poses in the black frock coat fashionable in Paris, thus expressing his adoption of ideas of change and revolution.[2]

The two portraits provide us with information about nineteenth-century Moldavian society, but also about the destiny of the painter Livaditti himself. Born in Trieste around 1802, Niccolò came from a relatively well-off merchant family. His parents, Diamandi and Vasiliki Livaditti belonged to the Greek

1 See Sorin Iftimi, 'Societatea moldovenească de la jumătatea secolului al XIX-lea în portretistica lui Niccolo Livaditi', in Sorin Iftimi, Corina Cimpoeşu, Marcelina Brînduşa Munteanu (eds.), *Niccolo Livaditi şi epoca sa (1832–1858. Artă şi Istorie* (Iaşi: 2012), 47–52.

2 Ibid., 74–75.

Fig. 10
Niccolò Livaditti – The Alecsandri Family: *Vornic* Vasile Alecsandri, his wife Elena, his son Iancu, and his daughter Catinca, 1837, National Museum of Art, Bucharest

Fig. 11
Niccolò Livaditti – The Alecsandri Family: *Vornic* Vasile Alecsandri and his sons Iancu and Vasile, 1845, Art Museum, Iaşi.

diaspora in Trieste, and were actively involved in charitable works centred around the Orthodox parish of San Nicolò.[3] On his death in 1809, Diamandi left a considerable fortune to his wife, Vasiliki, and their six children (Cristoforo, Constantino, Evguenia, Alessandro, Niccolò, and Caterina): 40,000 florins, two houses, and a number of shops. Niccolò grew up in a world that was multi-confessional, multilingual, and diverse from a regional and social point of view, in which tolerance was an important factor in the acceptance of the other: 'a haven for men and commerce'.[4] It has been said that Niccolò's marriage to Carlotta Cianchi was not well received by her family, as Carlotta's mother, Medina Celli, a Catholic of Spanish origin, did not wish to see an Orthodox brought into the family, and that this led the couple to leave for the Orient. However, it is unclear how much truth there is in this story, particularly given that such mixed marriages were not uncommon in Trieste society.[5] The reason for Niccolò's departure seems to have been quite different. Starting from the 1830s, political and ideological tensions sparked nationalist debates, leading the members of this mixed community to position themselves on one side or the other.[6] Having aligned himself with Giuseppe Mazzini and the ideas of the Carbonari, Niccolò had to go into exile to save himself from the reprisals of the Austrian authorities. So he went for a short period to Istanbul, the exotic mirage of Romantic artists. From there he arrived in 1832 in Iași, where he settled for the rest of his life.[7] As the painter of the urban elite of Iași, Niccolò gradually became integrated in the Moldavian community, helped by his Orthodox faith, but also by the interest shown in his knowledge by a public more and more attracted by artistic and cultural manifestations. Sharing the same values as many of the young Moldavians recently returned from studies abroad and other foreigners who, like him, had found a refuge in Moldavia, Livaditti found a propitious environment in which to raise and educate his children, to build a house, and to ensure a future for himself. His paintings may be seen as a great

3 It seems that Diamandi Livaditti together with another two brothers came from the Morea around 1772. See David Do Paço, 'La creation de la communauté grecque orientale de Trieste par Giuseppe Maria Mainati (1719–1818)', in Valérie Assan, Bernard Heyberger and Jakob Vogel (eds.), *Minorités en Méditerranée au XIXe siècles. Identités, identifications, circulations* (Rennes: 2019), 31.

4 Reill, *Nationalists who Feared the Nation*, 81.

5 Jeana Gheorghiu, 'Un pictor moldovean din secolul trecut: Nicolò Livaditi', *Viaţa Românească*, 31, 8 (1939): 50–57.

6 On the effervescence of these intellectual currents around nations and nationalism in the first part of the nineteenth century see Isabella Maurizio and Konstantina Zanou (eds), *Mediterranean Diasporas: Politics and Ideas in the Long 19th Century* (London: 2015); Zanou, *Stammering the Nation*; Reill, *Nationalists who Feared the Nation*.

7 Iftimi, *Niccolo Livaditi—viaţa şi oprera (1802–1859)*, 19–20.

stage, on which Moldavian society presents itself, with its people, costumes, landscapes, ideas, and complex trajectories in a time of considerable social, cultural, and political challenges.

Through the prism of multiple biographies, this book has shown how people coped with historical changes, succeeding (or not) in constructing a home, in fashioning a way of belonging to a community, to a set of values, in finding a homeland. As I have shown, Dimitrie Foti Merișescu, born in Bucharest but of 'Greek' parents, was a part of these cohorts of mobile people caught on the road by the new ideological movements that were to construct the nationalisms of the nineteenth century. Learning Romanian in his neighbourhood school, 'stammering' some Bulgarian picked up from his Bulgarian classmates, speaking Greek at home, he would reinvent himself in the context of the national movements of the years 1840–1848 to seek a place in Moldavian intellectual circles, offering them the narrative of his life. Only that, as Konstantina Zanou has observed, cleavages were deepening and formerly fluid borders were starting to become rigid, institutionalizing forms of belonging, languages, and confessions.[8] Thus Merișescu appears in the administrative classification now as a Bulgarian, now as a Greek, even though he bought ranks and places in social and political networks, rising to the position of member (*cilen*) of the law-court in Piatra-Neamţ.

Many of the characters of this book were direct witnesses of war and revolution events, particularly in 1821, and later in 1848. I draw attention to just two of the episodes that profoundly marked south-east European society, contributing to the crystallization of liberal ideologies and the birth of national states. However very little reflection of these events is to be found in their writings. For Elena Hartulari, Filiki Hetaireia and Tudor Vladimirescu's movement in Wallachia meant exile and extreme poverty. The entry of the Ottoman army, summoned to re-establish order, led the Hartulari family to take refuge 'in the German land' (Suceava, in Habsburg Bukovina), leaving their house and goods in Iași prey to looting and fire.[9] Nor did the revolt of the Greeks, the Wallachians, or the Serbs arouse any emotional reverberation or display of patriotic enthusiasm in Cernea Popovici. On the contrary, he reaffirmed his Ottoman allegiance and did what he could to keep his life and his personal belongings safe. Moving on to 1848, Dimitrie Merişescu's manor became a refuge for the younger members of the family when liberal ideas took hold in Moldavia, but he was far too closely connected by affection, friendship, and obligations to the old elite and the old political structure to let himself be

8 Zanou, *Stammering the Nation*, 209–214.

9 SJAN, Iaşi, Colecţia Gh. Ghibănescu, MS 164, f. 52v.

carried away by the liberal movement of the young forty-eighters. As for Iorgu Hartulari, in spite of his mobility, his multilingualism, and his intelligence, he remained firmly bound to the authoritarian prince Mihail Sturdza and far from ideas that, indeed, did not represent him. Displaying 'a certain indifference',[10] my characters adapted to the new times, stepping back into the shadows of history, while others, interconnected by education, language, and social status, liberal in spirit and animated, to a large extent, by admiration for French civilization, prepared to take centre stage.

The army, and the numerous foreigners brought in to put military reforms into application contributed to the reorganization of societies and the establishment of 'new orders'.[11] Between 1830 and 1878, the world of southeastern Europe underwent profound changes. The revolt of the Serbs led in the end to the formation and recognition of a Serbian state; the Greek revolutionaries carved out a country for themselves; and the Principalities and Bulgaria passed through the Crimean War and then, with the Russian–Ottoman War of 1877–1878, gained their independence.[12] Throughout the period, old-regime hierarchies allowed liberal ideas to shape the 'new order'. Of course, all these transformations took place at different paces and involved different members of society.[13] They must also be seen in an international social and political context, taking into account the changes and political developments going on not just in the Ottoman Empire but also in France, Russia, Austria, and Britain.

In the Principalities, the Organic Regulations created the premises for social advancement through education. As all over southeastern Europe, there was a pressing need for professionals, and the princes of the Organic Regulation period were eager to send boyars' children abroad for study and training. Vasile

10 Mathieu Grenet shows that Philhellenism did not 'take hold of' everyone and characterizes the lack of reaction of the Greek diaspora in Venice as 'une certaine indifférence'. Grenet, *La fabrique communautaire*, 339.

11 Ali Yaycioğlu, 'Janissaries, Engineers and Preachers. How Did Military Engineering and Islamic Activism Change the Ottoman Order?' *Revue d'Histoire du XIXe Siècle*, 53, 2 (2016), 19–37; Ali Yaycioğlu, 'Guarding Traditions and Laws-Disciplining Bodies and Souls: Tradition, Science, and Religion in the Age of Ottoman Reform', *Modern Asian Studies* 52, 5 (2018), 1542–1603.

12 On the 'Eastern Question' see Lawrence P. Meriage, 'The First Serbian Uprising (1804–1813) and the Nineteenth-Century Origins of the Eastern Question', *Slavic Review*, 37, 3 (1978), 421–439; Dimitris Stamatopulos, *The Eastern Question or Balkan Nationalism(s). Balkan History Reconsidered* (Vienna: 2018); Mark Mazower, *The Balkans: A Short History* (New York: 2000); Barbara Jelevich, *History of the Balkans* (Cambridge-New York: 1983).

13 Marie-Janine Calic, *The Great Cauldron. A History of Southeastern Europe* (London: 2019), 196–251; Frederick F. Anscombe, 'The Balkan Revolutionary Age', *Journal of Modern History*, 84 (2012), 576–606.

Alecsandri was one such student. He arrived in Paris together with other young men, with the mission of studying in order to be of use to the 'homeland'. The princes' initiative was paralleled by many private initiatives, as boyars and prosperous merchants rushed to enrol their sons in prestigious schools in Paris, Vienna, Berlin, or Geneva. Just a decade earlier, such a move had not been well regarded, either by princes or by the Porte. For example, in 1825, when the grand *postelnic* Filip Lenș decided to send his three sons to study in France, he needed the agreement of Prince Grigore Ghica of Wallachia and the support of the French consul in Bucharest, Hugot. The consul wrote that the boyar 'Philippe Linchou' (Filip Lenș was the grandson of Thomas-François Linchou) had managed to amass a considerable fortune and to acquire an enviable position in society due to his direct relations with the Ottoman Empire. His choice of Paris and of the institution run by M. Lemoine was not at random, as international political circumstances enabled him to take advantage of his French roots and invest in a French education for his heirs.[14] As Hugot would also observe, Lenș's example was quickly followed by other boyars. Education abroad offered young men a different sort of knowledge, both through the use of a new language, French or German, and through having access to another kind of sociability. Gradually, they would come to question the institutions, hierarchies, and social conditions of their homeland.

'C'est le mérite qui est la vraie distinction,' writes the young Mihail Kogălniceanu, sent to study in Berlin by Prince Mihail Sturdza together with the prince's own sons. He came from a family in the second rank of the boyar class, which had risen through holding offices in the state administration. 'La naissance n'est rien; c'est un don qui est très mauvais dans certaines circonstances,' he continues, addressing his sisters and reflecting on the collapse of the old symbols of social distinction. 'Toutes ces distinctions, toutes ces chimères, toutes ces aristocraties ont disparu,' is the verdict of this young student in the frozen Berlin of 26 November/8 December 1835.[15] Mihail Kogălniceanu was somewhat hasty in his judgments regarding the end of an era, however. The boyar class was reorganized by princely decrees of 10 March 1835 for Moldavia and 12 May 1837 for Wallachia. Social status still counted for advancement in the state administration, despite the introduction of the principle of meritocracy.[16] Theoretically, any young man with education might obtain a post in

---

14 Hurmuzaki, *Documente*, XVI, 17–18, 25 May 1825, Bucharest.

15 Mihail Kogălniceanu, *Scrisori către surorile sale*, ed. Petre V. Haneş (Bucharest: 1934), 62–63.

16 Paul Negulescu, George Alexianu (eds.), *Regulamentele Organice ale Valahiei şi Moldovei* (Bucharest: 1944), 139–147.

the bureaucratic apparatus, but in practice, employment depended on social origins, on one's place in the hierarchy of ranks, and on inclusion in a network. Another Moldavian, who belonged to the same second level of the boyar class, but had not been fortunate enough to study abroad, saw things differently. For Gheorghe Sion, Moldavian society operated according to well-established mechanisms, in which social hierarchy and networks were still dominant in 1844:

> At that time, indeed not much knowledge, ability, or learning was required for someone to reach the high positions. He had to have either the prince's protection, or the resonant name of an aristocratic family to acquire posts or ranks.[17]

The road towards the new order involved many backward steps, reversals, and reformulations of the old. Southeastern Europe was going through a complicated process of separation from an Ottoman political system towards a reformulated system that could achieve as broad a participation in politics as possible.[18] Seeking to put aside the old order and bring in the new, Sion joined young Alecsandri and Kogălniceanu in the revolution of 1848. In the shadow of the Organic Regulations, a circle of intellectuals (mainly sons of boyars or of prosperous merchants) had taken shape that promoted liberal ideas and national ideologies, as had happened elsewhere.[19] The revolutionaries of 1848 burned the *Arhondologia* (the book of boyar ranks) and the Organic Regulations, the symbols of a society based on privilege, and hastened to proclaim 'justice, equality, fraternity'. However, to succeed, they needed more than passion and a new vocabulary. There had to be as large as possible a mass of educated people who could understand the new rights and participate in upholding the new institutions. Education was indeed beginning to play an important role in society. The greater and greater number of young people sent abroad to study, the opening of *pensionnats* everywhere, and most importantly, the growing number of foreign professionals called to contribute to the construction of the modern state provide incontestable evidence of this. All the same, the level of literacy remained low for a long time, and this did not favour reform or modernization.[20]

---

17 Gheorghe Sion, *Proză. Suvenire contimpurane* (Bucharest: 1956), 418.

18 Diana Mishkova, *Balkan Liberalisms: Historical Routes of a Modern Ideology*, in Roumen Daskalov and Diana Mishkova (eds.), *Entangled Histories of the Balkans*. vol. 2: *Transfers of Political Ideologies and Institutions* (Leiden: 2014), 99–198.

19 Calic, *The Great Cauldron*, 259–265.

20 On education in other regions see Calic, *The Great Cauldron*, 260; Ružica Popovitch, 'The Education of Women in 19th-Century Serbia', *Serbian Studies: Journal of the North American Society for Serbian Studies*, 29, 1–2 (2018), 137–150.

Foreigners of various origins had played their part in the modernization of the southeast European states, but in return for their help they demanded the right to be part of the community. Legislation adapted to this situation, in an attempt to create the necessary framework for their social absorption. The law codes of Ioan Caragea (1812–1818) in Wallachia and Scarlat Callimachi (1812–1818) in Moldavia took little notice of the status of foreigners: there were certain provisions for their naturalization, but we do not yet know to what extent these were applied in the everyday practice of justice.[21] As the Principalities began to construct a national identity and to seek elements useful for political legitimation, the need was felt for legislation on the status of foreigners. All through the eighteenth century and the early nineteenth, there were no letters of naturalization. A foreigner who came to Wallachia or Moldavia would become 'naturalized' gradually by going through a series of stages: settlement in a local community, practising a trade, marriage to a local spouse, establishment of fiscal residence. Assimilation and integration into the social fabric constituted a further stage; it might take several generations for this new belonging to become imprinted in the memory of the community, but it generally happened without the need to produce letters or certificates. The Phanariots were always interested in increasing the number of tax-payers and ensuring a stable population that could be easily counted in fiscal conscriptions. For both demographic and fiscal reasons, they thus encouraged the settlement of foreigners, and they had no interest in creating a complicated juridical framework that would make it harder for foreigners to become established members of the host community.

The Organic Regulations provided for two paths to naturalization: one fast, but without political rights, and the other more difficult, but giving access to political life. Enrolment in a corporation and the payment of taxes were sufficient for a foreigner to be included in the ranks of the 'locals' (*pământeni*). This measure was no more than a continuation of the Phanariot policy of increasing the number of tax-payers and knowing who they were by means of registration. A foreigner wanting to enjoy 'political rights' (*drepturi politice*), however, would have to make an application to the National Assembly (*Adunarea Obștească*),[22] providing information about his 'capital', 'other

21 Constantin Iordachi, 'From Imperial Entanglements to National Disentanglement: The "Greek Question" in Moldavia and Wallachia, 1611–1863', in Roumen Dontchev Daskalov and Tchavdar Marinov (eds.), *Entangled Histories of the Balkans*. vol. 1: *National Ideologies and Language Policies* (Leiden: 2013), 116.

22 The National Assemblies were created under the provisions of the Organic Regulations. They consisted of forty-two members in Wallachia and thirty-five members in Moldavia (including members by right—the metropolitan and bishops—and members elected

wealth', 'occupation', and 'proof that he is useful to the state'. It should be added that the foreigner had to be Christian and to have lived in the Principalities for ten years. The law then provided that, after investigation by the Assembly, the application be directed to the prince, who would decide whether or not to grant naturalization (variously termed *naturalizaţie* or *împământenire* at the time). Marriage to 'a local noblewoman' (*o pământeancă nobilă*) was no longer considered sufficient grounds for obtaining citizenship. It brought a reduction of the required period of residence from ten years to seven, but the other elements were still needed for acceptance among the 'locals' with political rights.[23] Once the law was passed, naturalization files started to appear on the agenda of the National Assembly.[24] However the number of foreigners who applied for official naturalization was not very large. An examination of the meetings of the Assemblies (of Moldavia and Wallachia) over a period of ten years has brought to light only a few dozen files. The procedure was a difficult and costly one, requiring not only knowledge of the information necessary for compiling a file, but also time and money. The candidate had to go to Iași or Bucharest to hand over the documents necessary for their economic and social identification, together with letters and 'attestations' on the part of the local community regarding their behaviour and 'useful acts'.[25] How many out of all the foreigners in the Principalities formally became 'locals' in this way is not known. Many found a home in these new states that had broken away from the Ottoman Empire, and naturalization by way of daily life was by far the more accessible method of acquiring the right of residence in Moldavia and Wallachia. This seems have been the route taken by Niccolò Livaditti, as I have so far found no formal naturalization application or letter in his name. In 1858, when the painter died in Iași and a succession file was compiled, there is no mention of the matter. His heirs were already part of the community: his wife, Carolotta Livaditti, a descendant of the Florentine Cianchi family, had converted to Orthodoxy and was known as Maria, while their children—Aglae,

---

from among the boyars). They amended and voted on legislative projects sent to them by the respective princes and drew the princes' attention to problems of public interest by means of reports. *Regulamentele Organice*, Chapter II, 9–12, 180–184.

23 *Regulamentele Organice*, 131, article 379, chapters 1–5.

24 Naturalization files were not on the agenda in every session. For example, for the session 1831–1832, I have found a single such file, and none for the following session, 1832–1833. The numbers increased as information spread, and the procedure became better known. *Analele Parlamentare ale României* (Bucharest: 1892–1903), VII/1, 28, 34, 36, 39, 44, 40; VIII/1, 335–338, IX/2, 23, 25, 26, 28, 39, 57, 60, 63; X/1, 358, 362, 372, 373, 375, 377–379, 381.

25 See the documents presented by Serghei Şuşanopulo in the session of 20 December 1831. *Analele Parlamentare*, II, (Bucharest: 1892), 15, 390–392.

Alexandru, and Achille—were prominent in Moldavian artistic life in the second half of the nineteenth century.[26]

The status of subject of a foreign power offered significant advantages in a period in which France, Britain, Prussia, Russia, and Austria were struggling to impose their influence in an Ottoman Empire that was also undergoing profound transformations.[27] It was in this context that Filip Lenş rediscovered and re-evaluated his French ancestry. As a great boyar of the first rank, according to the Organic Regulation classification in Wallachia,[28] he constructed a detailed genealogy of the noble Linchou family, including French and Spanish aristocrats. On this basis, he became a candidate for the Wallachian throne, on which occasion he was reminded that for all his impressive French roots, he had been 'Romanian' for too short a time for him to dare to aspire to such an honour.[29] A genealogy became an important instrument in the process of social identification, required even by the Organic Regulations in their provisions for the drawing up of registers of boyars (*arhondologii*), which called for 'documents and charters' (*documente și urice*) from those who were not among 'the families of ancient nobility' (*familiile cu învechită evghenie*).[30] The genealogical thrill went through the whole of society, as people hastened to collect and put together, as if in a jigsaw puzzle, documents (sometimes invented), diplomas, coats of arms, family trees, and ancestral portraits, copied from the votive murals in the narthexes of churches to adorn the walls of salons and cabinets.[31] All this playing with the past was inspired by European Romanticism and was part of the construction of a national ideology[32].

26 Iftimi, *Niccolo Livaditi*, 28–29.

27 Ariel Salzmann, 'Citizens in Search of a State: The limits of Political Participation in the Late Ottoman Empire', in Michael Hanagan and Charles Tilly (eds.), *Extending Citizenship, Reconfiguring States* (Lanham, Boulder, New York, Oxford: 1999), 37–66.

28 *Analele Parlamentare*, II, 171, Assembly of all boyars of the first rank, in the session of 8 November 1831.

29 Ibid., XII/1, 7. 'The late father of Filip Lenj being of French stock, he lived in this country as a Frenchman, until the end of his life; consequently, this son, that is the *vistier* Filip is born *French* and only begins to be *Romanian* from the time when he himself recognized his subjecthood to the ruler of this country, married a local noblewoman, and settled in this country, where he also took public posts.' Session of 26 November 1842.

30 Mihai-Răzvan Ungureanu, 'Genealogia ca expresie a definitiei sociale a boierimii moldoveneşti în epoca regulamentară', *Arhiva Genealogică*, III (VIII), 3–4 (1996), 107–136.

31 See in this connection the extraordinary genealogy constructed by the Sturza (Sturdza) family and read in the session of the National Assembly on 5 March 1842. *Analele Parlamentare*, XII/2, 1066–1069.

32 Joep Leerssen (ed.), *Encyclopedia of Romantic Nationalism in Europe*, 2 vols. (Amsterdam, 2018).

After the removal of the Phanariots, the 'Greeks' were no longer considered a danger, and they were left to get on with their lives. Furthermore, with the establishment of the Greek state, Greek migration slowed down and changed its direction. Many of the Phanariots who had settled in Moldavia or Wallachia were at the forefront of public life, holding important posts on the political stage. They had constituted the principal threat, as expressed in various ways for a century in the complaints of the boyars.[33] Now, however, it would have been hard to push them aside, as through active matrimonial strategies they had become mixed with the very boyars who had formerly contested them. Just as Merișescu, Hartulari, and Văcărescu had roots somewhere in the region of Epirus, Thessaly, or Macedonia, so did nineteenth-century nation-builders such as Alecsandri, Kogălniceanu, and Sion. At the same time, foreign subjects continued to pose a challenge: the problems raised by their status and the attempts to find juridical solutions contributed to the debate around naturalization and citizenship. The new 'danger' identified by the modern state was the Jews. It was around them, and under international pressure, that legislation on citizenship and naturalization would take shape in the United Principalities.[34]

Inevitably, the process of modernization in southeastern Europe also involved the status of women. They took advantage of the visibility offered by the new forms of sociability to take their place in the public space of cultural debates. Contacts and material and cultural exchanges with western Europe accelerated towards the end of the eighteenth century, and even more in the nineteenth. Elite women proved to be important agents in the spread of 'European' tastes in fashion, gastronomy, education, social behaviour, and knowledge. Through travel and education, women gradually emerged from the domestic space to take an interest in their representation in society. The differences between Elena Hartulari and her daughter Maria are vast. Elena was content to remain in the background of social representation, navigating in the shadow of her husband, whom she served faithfully, supporting him materially, emotionally, and socially in all his actions. Even her memoirs are about Iorgu Hartulari, and she never tires of praising the economic, linguistic, and social abilities that enabled him to build up an extensive property portfolio. When she became the mistress of this portfolio, Elena was lost. Together with the patrimony, she had also taken charge of business ventures that spread and

33 Georgescu, *Istoria ideilor politice româneşti*, 220.

34 Silvia Marton, '"Aici e vorba să dăm ceea ce avem mai bun: naţionalitatea". Naturalizare, cetăţenie şi românitate în parlamentul României (a doua parte a veacului al XIX-lea)', *Annals of the University of Bucharest / Political science series*, *8*, 35–51. https://nbn-resolving.org/urn:nbn:de:0168–ssoar-387397 [27.01.2021].

supported one another like tentacles anchored in networks and informal institutions. Elena was unable to acquire the symbolic capital that Iorgu had held within these networks and institutions. She did not know how to work with people and institutions. Her daughter, Maria Hartulari (formerly Cănănău, formerly Cracti) could adapt quickly to any context, manipulating people and institutions to attain her goals and defend her rights.

Writing about women and their roles in the Wallachian society of the Organic Regulation period, Ion Heliade Rădulescu attributed to them a major role in the raising of the 'good citizen': 'Woman is our first teacher, woman is the first occupation of our youth, woman alone is capable of making all the joy and misery of our manhood.' All the same, the road to the emancipation of women and their assumption of public roles would be a long and tortuous one, and it would take not just activism on the part of women but also a consensus in society. The Hartulari women laid a stone in the foundations of the reconstruction of women's roles in society; education and perseverance would add the rest. But not overnight, as Rădulescu remarks: 'It is madness for someone to imagine that he will set the world right with his shoulder; however this should not stop him from doing his duty.'[35]

35 Ion Heliade Rădulescu, 'Femeile sau cugetul acestei foi', *Curier de ambe sexe*, 2 (1837), 43–48.

References

Unpublished Archival Sources

ANIC: Arhivelor Naţionale, Istorice, Centrale, Bucharest [National and Historical Romanian Archives, Bucharest].
Fonds: Achiziţii Noi, Administrative Vechi, Departamentul Spătărie, Documente Munteneşti, Manuscrise, Microfilme, Mitropolia Ţării Româneşti, Vornicia Treburilor Dinlăuntru.

AN.AE: Archives Nationales, Paris.
Fonds: Consulats. Mémoires et Documents. Affaires Etrangères, Correspondance Consulaire. Constantinople.

AAE: Archives Des Affaires Etrangères, Paris.
Fonds: Correspondence Politique, Turquie; Correspondance Politique, Pologne.

BAR: Biblioteca Academiei Române [Library of Romanian Academy].
Fonds: Manuscrise, Documente istorice.

BNF: Bibliothèque Nationale de France, Paris.
Fond: Roumain 6. Documents généalogiques et administratifs relatifs aux familles de Linche et Carpinişanu (1570–1855).

HHStA: Österreichisches Staatsarchiv, Haus-, Hof-, und Staatsarchiv, Staatenabteilung.
Fonds: Moldau-Walachei I/26/, Brancovan (1767–1777); Vaccaresculi (1772–1773), Türkei.

SJAN: Serviciul Judeţean al Arhivelor Naţionale, Buzău [Departemental Service of National Archives].
Fonds: Subocârmuirea Plaiului despre Buzău.

SJAN: Serviciul Judeţean al Arhivelor Naţionale, Iaşi [Departemental Service of National Archives].
Fonds: Colecţia Gh. Ghibănescu, Manuscrise, Documente, Documente Moldoveneşti,

SJAN: Serviciul Judeţean al Arhivelor Naţionale, Vâlcea [Departemental Service of National Archives].
Fonds: Prefectura Judeţului Vâlcea.

Published Sources

1. *Collections of Documents*

Analele Parlamentare ale României, 12 vols. Bucharest: 1892–1903.

Caproşu, Ioan (ed.). *Documente privitoare la istoria oraşului Iaşi*, vols. 4–8. (Iaşi: 2001–2005).

Caproşu, Ioan, Ungureanu, Mihai-Răzvan (eds.). *Documente statistice privitoare la oraşul Iaşi*, 2 vols. Iaşi, 1997.

Carataşu, Mihai (ed.). *Documentele Văcăreştilor*. Bucharest, 1975.

Codul Calimah (1817). Bucharest, 1958.

Condica lui Mavrocordat. ed. Cornel Istrate. 3 vols., Iaşi, 2008.

Filitti, Ioan C. 'Arhondologia Munteniei de la 1822–1828', *Revista Arhivelor*, II, 4–5 (1927–1929): 19–49.

Gáldi, Ladislas. *Les mots d'origine néo-grecque en roumain à l'époque phanariote*. Budapest, 1939.

Gălăşescu, Alexandru G., *Eforia Spitalelor civile din Bucuresci, 1832–1932*, 2 vols. Bucharest, 1900.

Georgescu, Valentin Al., Popescu Emanuela (ed.). *Legislaţia urbană a Ţării Româneşti, 1765–1782*. Bucharest, 1975.

Giurescu, Constantin, Dobrescu, Nicolae (eds.). *Documente şi regeste privitoare la Constantin Brâncoveanu*. Bucharest, 1907.

Hartulari, Elena. "Istoria vieţii mele de la anul 1801", ed. by Gheorghe Ghibănescu, *Convorbiri Literare* 5–8 (1926), 729–745; 9–10 (1926), 841–855; 11–12 (1926), 915–926; 9–11 (1927): 291–312; 3–4 (1928): 69–78; 5–8 (1928), 301–308.

Greceanu, Ştefan. *Genealogiile documentate ale familiilor boiereşti*, 3 vols. Bucharest, 1911.

Hurmuzaki, Eudoxiu de (ed.). *Documente privitoare la istoria românilor*, 19 vols. Bucharest, 1884–1917.

Filitti, Ioan C. (ed.). *Lettres et extraits concernant les relations des Principautés roumaines avec la France (1728–1810)*. Bucharest, 1915.

Manualul Administrativ al Principatului Moldovei. Iaşi, 1856.

Iorga, Nicolae. "Les diplômes impériaux de Constantin Brâncoveanu, prince de Valachie", *Revue historique du sud-est européen*, XIV, 7–9 (1937): 177–186.

Iorga, Nicolae. 'Un cugetător politic moldovean de la jumătatea secolului al XIX-lea: Ştefan Scarlat Dăscălescu', *Analele Academiei Române. Memoriile Secţiunii Istorice*, 3d ser., XIII (1932): 1–56.

Iorga, Nicolae (ed.). 'Scrisori inedite ale lui Tudor Vladimirescu din anii 1814–1815', *Analele Academiei Române. Memoriile Secţiunii Istorice*, 2d ser., XXXVII (1914): 121–160.

Iorga, Nicolae (ed.). *Scrisori de boieri şi negustori olteni şi munteni către casa de negoţ sibiiană Hagi Pop*. Bucharest, 1906.

Iorga, Nicolae. 'Plângerea lui Ioan Sandu Sturza Vodă împotriva sudiţilor din Moldova', *Analele Academiei Române. Memoriile Secţiunii Istorice*, 2d ser., XXXV (1912–1913): 1–13.

Iorga, Nicolae (ed.). *Documente privitoare la familia Callimachi*, 2 vols. Bucharest, 1902.

Iorga, Nicolae (ed.). *Studii și documente cu privire la istoria românilor*. Bucharest, 1901, vol. III (1901); (1906), vol. XIV; (1907), vol. XVI (1907).

Iorga, Nicolae (ed.). *Acte şi fragmente cu privire la istoria românilor adunate din depozitele de manuscrise ale Apusului*, 2 vols. Bucharest, 1896.

Îndreptarea legii (*1652*) Bucharest, 1962.

Kogălniceanu, Mihail. *Scrisori către surorile sale*, ed. Petre V. Haneş. Bucharest, 1934.

Lazăr, Gheorghe (ed.). *Catastife de negustori din Ţara Românească* (*secolele XVIII–XIX*). Iaşi, 2016.

Mehmet, Mustafa A. (ed.). *Documente turceşti privind istoria României*, 3 vols. Bucharest, 1976–1986.

Negulescu, Paul, Alexianu, George (eds.). *Regulamentele Organice ale Valahiei şi Moldovei*. Bucharest, 1944.

Potra, George (ed.). *Documente privitoare la istoria oraşului Bucureşti* (*1594–1821*). Bucharest, 1961.

Potra, George (ed.). *Documente privitoare la istoria oraşului Bucureşti* (*1634–1800*). Bucharest, 1982.

Potra, George (ed.). *Documente privitoare la istoria oraşului Bucureşti* (*1821–1848*). Bucharest, 1975.

Pravilniceasca Condică (*1780*). Bucharest, 1957.

Racoviţă-Cehan, Mihai. *Familia Racoviţă-Cehan. Fişe nominale şi fotografii* (Bucharest: 1942).

Ungureanu, Mihai-Răzvan (ed.). *Marea Arhondologie a boierilor Moldovei* (*1835–1856*), Iaşi, 1997.

Urechia V.A. *Istoria românilor. Curs făcut la Facultatea de litere din Bucureşti*, 13 vols., 1891–1901.

Urechia, V.A. *Istoria şcólelor de la 1800 la 1864*, 4 vols. Bucharest, 1892–1901.

Veliman, Valeriu (ed.). *Relaţiile româno-otomane, 1711–1821. Documente turceşti*. Bucharest, 1984.

2. *Narrative Sources*

Antim Ivireanul. *Opere. Didahii*. Ed. Gabriel Ştrempel. Bucharest, 1996.

(de) Boyer, d'Argens, Jean-Baptiste. *Memoires du marquis d'Argens, Chambellan de Frédéric-le-Grand, roi de Prusse et directeur de l'Académie royale de Berlin; continent le récit des aventures de sa jeunesse, des anecdotes et des observations sur plusieurs événements du règne de Louis XV, et des personnes de ce temps*. Paris, 1807.

Boscovich, Ruggiero Giuseppe, *Giornale di un viaggio da Costantinopoli in Polonia dell'Abate Ruggiero Giuseppe Boscovich, con una sua relazione delle Rovine di Troja*. Bassano, 1784.

Brad-Chisacof, Lia (ed. and trans.). *Antologie de literatură greacă din Principatele Române*. Bucharest. 2003.

Bracewell, Wendy (ed.). *Orientations. An Anthology of East European Travel Writing, ca. 1550–2000*. Budapest, 2009.

Cantacuzino, Mihai. *Genealogia Cantacuzinilor*. Ed. by Nicolae Iorga. Bucharest, 1902.

Cantemir, Dimitrie. *Opere fundamentale*, vol. I (*Divanul. Istoria ieroglifică. Hronicul vechimei a romano-moldo vlahilor*). Bucharest, 2003.

Cantemir Dimitrie. *Descrierea Moldovei*, trans. Petre Pandrea. Bucharest, 1973.

Caracaş, Constantin. *Topografia Valahiei*. Ed. by Pompei Samarian, *O veche monografie a Munteniei de dr. Constantin Caracaş (1800–1828)*. Bucharest, 1937.

Cochelet, Adrien Louis. "Itinéraire des Principautés de Valachie et de Moldavie. Extraits d'un journal de voyage fait en 1834 et 1835 par M. Cochelet, ancient agent et consul general de France, en Valachie et en Moldavie, pour servir à l'itinéraire de ces principautés", *Bulletin de la Société Géographique* t. XIX (1835): 249–274.

Călătoria împăratului Iosif al II-lea în Transilvania la 1773. ed. Ileana Bozac and Teodor Pavel. Cluj, 2017.

Călători străini despre ţările române, eds. Maria Holban and Maria Magdalena, Alexandrescu-Dersca Bulgaru and Paul Cernovodeanu, 10 vols. Bucharest, 1973–2000.

Călători străini despre ţările române în secolul al XIX-lea, eds. Paul Cernovodeanu and Daniela Buşă, 6 vols. Bucharest, 2004–2007.

Colson, Felix, *De l'état présent et de l'avenir des principautés de la Moldavie et de la Valachie*. Paris, 1839.

Cronica Ghiculeştilor. Istoria Moldovei între anii 1695–1754. ed. Nestor Camariano and Ariadna Camariano-Cioran. Bucharest, 1965.

Del Chiaro, Anton Maria. *Istoria delle moderne rivoluzioni della Valachia*. Venice, 1718.

Depasta, Petru. 'Constantin-vodă sau scrisoarea faptelor vrednice de pomenire întâmplate în Dacia sub Constantin Mavrocordat', in: Constantin Erbiceanu, *Cronicari greci care au scris despre români în epoca fanariotă*. Bucharest, 2003, 295–335.

D'Hauterive, Alexandre. *Mémoire sur l'état ancien et actuel de la Moldavie (1787)*. Bucharest, 1902.

D'Hauterive, André Borel. 'Notice Historique et Genealogique sur la Maison de Linche', *Revue Historique de la Noblesse* tom II (1841): 365–373.

Didot, Ambroise Firmin. *Notes d'un voyage fait dans le Levant en 1816 et 1817*. Paris, 1821.

Dionisie Eclisarhul. *Scrieri alese. Hronograf, Predoslovii.* ed. Natalia Trandafirescu. Bucharest, 2004.

Drăghici, Postelnicul Manolachi. *Istoria Moldovei pe timp de 500 de ani pînă în zilele noastre.* ed. Andrei Pippidi. Bucharest, 2017.

Dobrescu, Ioan. 'Cronica meşteşugarului Ioan Dobrescu (1802–1830)'. ed. Ilie Corfus, *Studii si articole de istorie* VIII, (1966): 309–403.

Dumitrache Stolnic. 'Istoria evenimentelor din Orient cu referinţă la principatele Moldova şi Valahia din anii 1769–1774 de biv-vel stolnicul Dumitrache'. ed. Urechia V. A, *Analele Academiei Române. Memoriile Secţiei Istorice* 10 (1887–1888): 398–417.

Dyâb, Hanna. *D'Alep à Paris: Les pérégrinations d'un jeune Syrien au temps de Louis XIV. Ed. and* trans. Paule Fahmé, Bernard Heyberger, and Jérôme Lentin, Arles: 2015.

Emerigon, Balthazard-Marie. *Traité des assurances et des contrats à la gross.* Marseille, 1784.

Fotino, Dionisie. *Istoria Generală a Daciei sau a Transilvaniei şi a Moldovei* (first edition: *Historia tes palai Dakias ta nyn Transylvanyas, Wallachias, kai Moldavias ek diaphoron palaion kai neon syngrapheon syneranistheisa para Dionysios Photeinou.* Vienna, 1818–1819. Trans. and ed. George Sion. Bucureşci, 1859.

Golescu, Dinicu. *Însemnare a călătoriii mele, Costandin Radovici din Goleşti făcută în anul 1824, 1825, 182.* Bucharest, 1977.

Golescu, Iordache. *Scrieri alese.* ed. Mihai Moraru. Bucharest. 1990.

Greceanu, Radu. *Istoria domniei lui Constantin Basarab Brâncoveanu Voievod (1688–1714)*, ed. Autora Ilieş. Bucharest, 1970.

Istoria Ţării Româneşti de la octombrie 1688 până la 1717. Cronica Anonimă. ed. Constantin Grecescu. Bucharest, 1959.

Katsaitis, Markos Antonios. 'Călătorie de la Constantinopol la Iaşi şi de la Iaşi la Bucharest în anul 1742', trans. and ed. Dumitru Limona, in: Dumitru Limona. *Negustorii "greci" şi arhivele lor comerciale.* ed. Loredana Dascăl, Iaşi, 2016, 391–494.

Kogălniceanu, Mihail. *Cronicele României sau Letopiseţele Moldaviei şi Valahiei*, vol. 2. Bucharest, 1872.

Kogălniceanu, Pseudo-Enache. *Letopiseţul Ţării Moldovei de la domnia întâi şi până la a patra domnie a lui Constandin Mavrocordat voievod (1733–1774).* ed. Aurora Ilieş and Ioana Zmeu. Bucharest, 1987.

Kostaridou, Maria and Alex Drace-Francis (trans.). 'Marco Antonio Cazzaiti, 1742. A Venetian Greek in the Ottoman Balkans', in: Wendy Bracewell. *Orientations. An Anthology of East European Travel Writing, ca. 1550–2000, Budapest.* New York, 2009, 49–50.

Kunisch, Richard. *Bucureşti şi Stambul. Schiţe din Ungaria, România şi Turcia*, trans. Viorica Nişcov. Bucharest, 2014.

Lagarde, le comte de [Auguste-Louis-Charles de Messence, comte de Lagarde-Chambonas]. *Voyage de Moscou à Vienne par Kiow, Odessa, Constantinople, Bucharest et Hermanstadt, ou lettres adressées à Jules Griffith.* Paris. 1824.

[Lăcusteanu, Grigore]. *Amintirile colonelului Lăcusteanu.* ed. Radu Crutzescu. Bucharest, 1935.

Neculce, Ion. *Opere. Letopiseţul Ţării Moldovei şi O seamă de cuvinte,* ed. Gabriel Ştrempel. Bucharest, 1982.

Merişescu, Dimitrie Foti. *Tinereţile unui ciocoiaş. Viaţa lui Dimitrie Foti Merişescu de la Colentina scrisă de el însuşi la 1817.* Edited by Vintilă-Ghiţulescu, Constanţa. Bucharest, 2019.

Negruzzi, Costache. *Păcatele tinereţelor* [1857]. Bucharest, 1982.

Osman, Aga. *Prisonnier des infidèles: Un soldat ottoman dans l'Empire des Habsbourg,* ed. and trans. Frédérick Hitzel. Arles, 1998.

Peyssonnel, Claude-Charles de. *Traité sur le commerce de la Mer Noire.* Paris, 1787.

Popescu, Radu. *Istoria domnilor Ţării Rumâneşti.* ed. Mihail Gregorian. Bucharest, 1984.

Porter, James. *Observations on the Religion, Law, Governement and Manners of the Turks.* Dublin. 1768.

Poteca, Eufrosin. *Scrieri filosofice.* ed. Adrian Michiduţă. Craiova, 2008.

Raicevich, Stefan Ignatius. *Osservazioni Storiche, naturali e politiche intorno la Valachia et la Moldavia.* Naples, 1788.

Recordon, François. *Lettres sur la Valachie ou observations sur cette province et ses habitants écrites de 1815 à 1821 avec la rélation des dernièrs événements qui y ont eu lieu.* Paris, 1821.

Rosetti, Radu. *Amintiri. Ce am auzit de la alţii. Din copilărie. Din prima tinereţe.* Bucharest, 2013.

Rosetti, Radu. *Familia Rosetti. I. Coborâtorii moldoveni ai lui Lascaris Rousaitos.* Bucharest, 1938.

Russo, Alecu. *Cântarea României* [1850]. Bucharest, 1980.

Saumery, Pierre Lambert de. *Mémoires et avantures secrètes et curieuses d'un voyage du Levant,* vol. 2. Liège, 1732.

Sestini, Domenico. *Lettres de monsieur l'abbé Dominique Sestini, écrites á ses amis en Toscane, pendant le cours de ses voyages en Italie, en Sicile et en Turquie,* trans. Jean-Claude Pingeron. Vol. 3. Paris, 1789.

Sion, Constantin. *Arhondologia Moldovei. Amintiri şi note contimporane. Boierii Moldovei.* Bucharest, 1973.

Sion, Gheorghe. *Proză. Suvenire contimpurane* [1888]. Bucharest, 1956.

Solomon, Ioan. *Amintirile colonelului Ioan Solomon* [1862]. Vălenii de Munte, 1910.

Sulzer, Franz Joseph. *Geschichte des transalpinischen Daciens, das ist der Walachey, Moldau und Bessarabiens. Im Zusammenhange mit der Geschichte des übrigen Daciens als ein Versuch einer allgemeinen dacischen Geschichte mit kritischer Freyheit entworfen,* 3 vols. Vienna, 1781.

Soutzo, Nicolas. *Mémoires du Prince Nicolas Soutzo, grand-logothète de Moldavie, 1798–1871.* ed. Panaïoti Rizos. Vienne, 1899.

Urechia, V.A. *Din tainele vieţei. Amintiri contimporane (1840–1882)*. ed. Leonidas Rados. Iaşi, 2014.

Vaillant, Jean-Alexandre. *La Roumanie, ou Histoire, langue, littérature, orographie, statistique des peuples de la langue d'or, Ardialiens, Vallaques et Moldaves, résumés sur le nom de Romans*, 3 vols. Paris, 1844.

Văcărescu, Ianache. *Istoria Othomanicească*. ed. Gabriel Ştrempel. Bucharest, 2001.

Vârnav, Teodor. *Istoria vieţii mele. Autobiografie din 1845*. Iaşi, 2016.

Vârtosu, Emil. *Corespondenţa literară între Nicolae şi Iancu Văcărescu, 1814–1817*. Bucharest, 1938.

Wilkinson, William. *An Account of the Principalities of Wallachia and Moldavia: With Various Political Observations Relating to Them*. London, 1820.

Secondary Sources

Adanir, Fikret. 'Tradition and Rural Change in Southeastern Europe During Ottoman Rule', in: Daniel Chirot (ed.). *The Origins of Backwardness in Eastern Europe*. Berkeley–Los Angeles, 1989, 131–176.

Aksan, Virginia H. *Ottoman Wars, 1700–1870. An Empire Besieged*. London, 2007.

Aksan, Virginia. 'Whose territory and whose peasants? Ottoman boundaries on the Danube in the 1760s', in: Frederick F. Anscombe (ed.), *The Ottoman Balkans 1750–1830*. Princenton, 2006, 61–86.

Aksan, Virginia. 'Feeding the Ottoman Troops on the Danube, 1768–1774'. *War & Society* 13.1 (1995): 1–14.

Aksan, Virginia. *An Ottoman Statesman in War and Peace: Ahmed Resmi Efendi, 1700–1783*. Leiden, 1995.

Aksan, Virginia H. and Şimşek Veysel. 'Introduction: Living in the Ottoman House', *Journal of Ottoman Studies* 44 (2014): 1–8.

Amăriuţei, Mihai-Cristian, Cotovanu Lidia and Olar Ovidiu-Victor. 'Phanariot Donations to the Mega Spileon Monastery (18th Century)', *Annales Universitatis Apulensis. Series Historica* XVIII/1 (2014): 219–250.

Anastassiadou, Meropi, Heyberger Bernard (eds.). *Figures anonymes, figures d'élite. Pour une anatomie de l'Homo ottomanicus*. Istanbul, 1999.

Anastasopoulos, Antonis (ed.). *Provincial Elites in the Ottoman Empire*. Rethymno, 2005.

Andreozzi, Daniele. 'Croissance et économie licite, illicit et informelle à Trieste au XVIIIe siècle', in: Marguerite Figeac-Monthus and Christophe Lastécouères (eds.), *Territoires de l'illicite et identités portuaires et insulaires. Du XVIe siècle au XXe siècle*. Paris, 2012. 173–188.

Andreescu, Ştefan. 'Familia boierilor Băleni', in: Mihai Dimitrie Sturdza (ed.). *Familiile boiereşti din Moldova şi Ţara Românească. Enciclopedie istorică, genealogică şi biografică.* Bucharest, 2004, I, 224–230.

Anscombe, Frederick F. 'The Balkan Revolutionary Age', *Journal of Modern History* 84 (2012): 576–606.

Ardeleanu, Constantin. *The European Commission of the Danube, 1856–1948. An Experiment in International Administration.* Leiden, 2020.

Ardeleanu, Constantin. 'The Opening and Development of the Black Sea for International Trade and Shipping (1774–1853)', *Euxeinos* 14 (2014): 30–52.

Ardeleanu, Constantin. 'A British Meat Cannery in Moldavia (1844–1852)', *Slavonic and East European Review* 90.4 (2012): 671–704.

Ardeleanu, Constantin. 'From Vienna to Constantinople on Board the Vessels of the Austrian Danube Steam-Navigation Company (1834–1842)', *Historical Yearbook* VI (2009): 187–202.

Arnaud, Bartolomei, Guillaume Calafat, Mathieu Grenet and Jörg Ulbert (eds.). *De l'utilité commerciale des consuls. L'institution consulaire et les marchands dans le monde méditerranéen (XVIIe–XXe siècle).* Rome–Madrid, 2017.

Atanasiu, Mihai-Bogdan. 'Bucuroşi Muscalilor şi Greşiţi Prealuminatei Porţi. Oamenii Măriei Sale Dumitraşcu Vodă Cantemir, Pribegi la Harkov', in: Cristian Ploscaru, Mihai-Bogdan Atanasiu (eds.). *Elitele Puterii–Puterea Elitelor în spaţiul Românesc (secolele XV–XX).* Iaşi, 2018, 243–256.

Atanasiu, Mihai-Bogdan. *Din lumea cronicarului Ion Neculce. Studiu prosopografic.* Iaşi, 2015.

Auslander, Leora, 'Culture matérielle, histoire du genre et des sexualités', *Clio. Histoire des femmes* 40 (2014): 171–195.

Auslander, Leora, *The Gendering of Consumer Practices in Nineteenth Century France,* in: Victoria DeGrazia, Ellen Furlough (eds.). *The Sex of the Things: Gender and Consumption in Historical Perspective.* California 1996.

Baltacı, Cahit. 'The Importance of Kadı Registers for the Islamic World', *Studies on Turkish–Arab Relations* 2 (1987): 165–170.

Barbu, Violeta, *De la comunitatea patrimonială la comunitatea de destin: Zestrea în Ţara Românească în secolul al XVII-lea,* in: *De la comunitate la societate. Studii de istoria familiei din Ţara Românească sub Vechiul Regim.* Bucharest, 2007, 19–93.

Başaran, Betül. *Selim III, Social Control and Policing in Istanbul at the End of the Eighteenth Century. Between Crisis and Order.* Leiden, 2014.

Băluţă, Ionela. *La Bourgeoise respectable. Réflexion sur la construction d'une nouvelle identité féminine dans la seconde moitié du XIXe siècle roumain.* Bruxelles, 2010.

Bănescu, Nicolae. 'Entre Roumains et Grecs: Ce que nous apprend le passé', *Νέα Πολιτικά* 2.9 (1937): 1049–55.

Bedreag, Elena. 'Church Endowments and Family Inheritance in 18th-Century Moldavia', *Romanian Journal of Population Studies* 14.1 (2020): 5–18.

Bedreag Elena. 'Alianţele şi solidarităţile boierilor Ruseteşti în Tara Românească', *Studii şi Materiale de Istorie Medie* 35 (2017): 255–282.

Bedreag, Elena. 'Descendenţa şi averea marelui vornic Iordache Ruset', in: Dan Dumitru Iacob (ed.). *Avere, prestigiu şi cultură materială în surse patrimoniale. Inventare de averi din secolele XVI–XIX*. Iaşi, 2015, 157–203.

Bedreag, Elena. '"La vrerea me este să-i dau au ba dintr-ale mele lucruri". Diata marelui vornic Iordache Ruset', in: Mircea Ciubotaru and Lucian-Valeriu Lefter (eds.). *Mihai Dim. Sturdza la 80 de ani. Omagiu*. Iaşi, 2014, 571–586.

Bellavitis, Anna and Zucca Micheletto Beatrice (eds.). *Gender, Law and Economic Well-Being in Europe from the Fifteenth to the Nineteenth Century. North Versus South?* Abingdon, 2018.

Berg, Maxine. 'Sea Otters and Iron: A Global Microhistory of Value and Exchange at Nootka Sound, 1774–1792', *Past and Present*, 242 (2019): 50–82.

Berg, Maxine. *Luxury and Pleasure in Eighteenth-Century Britain*. Oxford, 2007.

Berg, Maxine. 'In Pursuit of Luxury: Global History and British Consumer Goods in the Eighteenth Century', *Past and Present* 182 (2004): 85–142.

Berindei, Dan. 'Urmaşii lui Constantin Brâncoveanu şi locul lor în societatea românească. Genealogie şi istorie', in: Paul Cernovodeanu, Florin Constantiniu (eds.), *Constantin Brâncoveanu*. Bucharest, 1989, 275–285.

Berindei, Dan and Irina Gavrilă. 'Analyse de la composition de l'ensemble des familles de grands dignitaires de la Valachie au XVIIIe siècle', in: *Comunicaciones al XV Congreso Internacional de las Ciencias Genealógica y Heráldica*. Madrid. 1983.

Bevilacqua, Alexander and Helen Pfeifer 'Turquerie: Culture in Motion, 1650–1750', *Past and Present* 221 (2013): 75–118.

Blancard, Théodore. *Les Mavroyéni. Essai d'étude additionnelle à l'histoire moderne de la Grèce, de la Turquie et de la Roumanie*. Paris, 1893.

Blanning, Timothy C.W. *Joseph II*. London, 2013.

van den Boogert, Maurits H. 'Resurrecting *Homo Ottomanicus*: The Constants and Variables of Ottoman Identity', *Journal of Ottoman Studies*, 44 (2014): 9–20.

van den Boogert, Maurits H. 'Intermediaries par excellence? Ottoman Dragomans in the Eighteenth Century', in: Bernard Heyberger and Chantal Verdeil (ed.). *Hommes de l'entre-deux. Parcours individuals et portraits de groupe sur la frontière de la Méditerranée (XVIe–XXe siècle)*. Paris, 2009, 95–114.

van den Boogert, Maurits H.. *The Capitulations and the Ottoman Legal System: Qadis, Consuls and Beratlis in the 18th Century*. Leiden, 2005.

Börekçi, Günhan. *On the Power, Political Career, and the Patronage Networks of the Ottoman Royal Favourites (late Sixteenth and Early Seventeenth Centuries)* https://www.academia.edu/38073778/On_the_Power_Political_Career_and_Patronage_

Networks_of_the_Ottoman_Royal_Favourites_Late_Sixteenth_and_Early_Seventeenth_Centuries [accessed 25.07.2020].

Bracewell, Wendy. 'Arguing from Experience: Travelees versus Travellers in Early Modern Exchanges', *Renaissance Studies* 33.4 (2019): 548–567.

Bracewell, Wendy and Alex Drace-Francis (eds.), *Balkan Departures. Travel Writing from Southeastern Europe*. New York, 2009.

Bracewell, Wendy and Alex Drace-Francis (eds.). *Under Eastern eyes. A Comparative Introduction to East European Travel Writing on Europe*. Budapest, 2008.

Braude, Benjamin and Bernard Lewis (eds.). *Christians and Jews in the Ottoman Empire. The Functioning of a Plural Society*. New York and London, 1982.

Brătianu, Gheorghe. 'Două veacuri de la reforma lui Constantin Mavrocordat, 1746–1946', *Analele Academiei Române Memoriile Secţiunii Istorice*, 3d ser., XXIX (1946): 395–461.

Brubaker, Rogers and Frederick Cooper. 'Beyond' identity', *Theory and Society* 29 (2000): 1–47.

Brubaker, Rogers. 'Au-delà de l'"identité"', *Actes de la Recherche en Sciences Sociales*, 139.4 (2001): 66–85.

Brummett, Palmira. 'You Say 'Classical', I Say 'Imperial', Let's Call the Whole Thing Off: Empire, Individual, and Encounter in Travel Narratives of the Ottoman Empire', *Journal of Ottoman Studies* 44 (2014): 21–44.

Brummett, Palmira. 'Placing the Ottoman in the Mediterranean World: The Question of Notables and Households', *Journal of Ottoman Studies*, XXXVI (2010): 75–91.

Brummett, Palmira. 'A Kiss is Just a Kiss: Rituals of Submission along the East–West Divide', in: Matthew Birchwood and Matthew Dimmock (eds.), *Cultural Encounters between East and West, 1453–1699*. Cambridge, 2005, 107–131.

Bucur, Maria. 'To have and to hold: Gender Regimes and Property Rights in the Romanian Principalities before World War I', *European History Quarterly* 48.4 (2018): 601–628.

Burke, Peter. *Exiles and Expatriates in the History of Knowledge, 1500–2000*. Waltham, 2017.

Calafat, Guillaume. 'Jurisdictional Pluralism in a Litigious Sea (1590–1630): Hard Cases, Multi-Sited Trials and Legal Enforcement between North Africa and Italy', *Past and Present*, 242 (2019): 142–178.

Calic, Marie-Janine. *The Great Cauldron. A History of Southeastern Europe*, trans. Elizabeth Janik. London, 2019.

Camariano-Cioran Ariadna, *Academiile Domneşti din Bucureşti şi Iaşi* (Bucharest: 1971).

Castiglione, Frank. 'Levantine' Dragomans in the Nineteenth Century Istanbul: The Pisanis, the British, and Issues of Subjecthood', *Journal of Ottoman Studies* XLIV (2014): 169–195.

Cazacu, Matei. *Des Femmes sur les routes de l'Orient. Le voyage à Constantinople au XVIIIe–XIXe siècles*. Genève, 1999.

Câlţia, Simion. *Aşezări urbane sau rurale? Oraşele din Ţara Românească de la sfârşitul secoului al 17-lea la începutul secolului al 19-lea*. Bucharest, 2011.

Cârstoiu, Cornel. *Ianache Văcărescu: Viaţa şi opera*. Bucharest, 1974.

Cernovodeanu, Paul. 'Strategii matrimoniale ruse în societatea românească din perioada regulamentară', *Arhiva Genealogică* IV (IX), 3–4 (1997): 243–252.

Cernovodeanu, Paul. 'Coordonatele politicii externe a lui Constantin Brâncoveanu. Vedere de ansamblu' in: Paul Cernovodeanu, Florin Constantiniu (eds.), *Constantin Brâncoveanu*. Bucharest, 1989, 123–138.

Cernovodeanu, Paul. 'Mobility and Traditionalism: The Evolution of the Boyar Class in the Romanian Principalities in the 18th Century', *Revue des Etudes Sud-est Européennes,* 24.3 (1986): 249–257.

Cernovodeanu, Paul. 'Înfiinţarea consulatului englez în Ţările Române (1803) şi activitatea sa până la 1807', *Revista română de studii internaţionale* V.1 (1971): 139–162.

Cerutti, Simona. *Étrangers. Étude d'une condition d'incertitude dans une société d'Ancien Régime*. Paris, 2012.

Cerasi, Maurice. 'The Formation of Ottoman House Type: A Comparative Study in Interaction with Neighboring Culture', *Muqarnas* 15 (1998): 116–156.

Chartier, Roger. *Lecturi şi cititori în Franţa Vechiului Regim*. Trans. Maria Carpov. Bucharest, 1997.

Cimpoeşu. Corina. *Artă, modă, cultură europeană în Moldova, între 1830 şi 1860. Elemente ale procesului de modernizare culturală*. Iaşi, 2013.

Ciucă, Marcel-Dumitru. 'Logofeţia Pricinilor Străine din Ţara Românească', *Revista Arhivelor,* LXVIII.3 (1991): 367–379.

Coller, Ian. 'East of Enlightenment: Regulating Cosmopolitanism between Istanbul and Paris in the Eighteenth Century', *Journal of World History* 21.3 (2010): 447–70.

Coman, Marian. *Putere şi teritoriu. Ţara Românească medievală (sec. XIV–XVI)*. Iaşi, 2016.

Coman, Marian. 'François-Thomas Linchou (1720–1760)', in: *Călători străini despre ţările române*. Supliment II. Bucharest, 2016, 253–258.

Condurachi, Jean D. *Câteva cuvinte asupra condiţiei juridice a străinilor în Moldova şi Ţara Românească până la Regulamentul Organic*. Bucharest, 1918.

Cornea, Paul. *Originile romantismului românesc. Spiritul public, mişcarea ideilor şi literatura între 1780–1840*. Iaşi, 2008.

Costache, Ştefania. 'From Ruscuk to Bessarabia: Manuk Bey and the Career of an Ottoman–Russian Middleman at the Beginning of the 19th Century', *Cihannüma,* III.1 (2017): 23–43.

Costache, Ştefania. 'The Ottoman–Russian–Habsburg Information Networks and the Negotiation of Ottoman Affairs on the Danube (1800–1820s)', *Revista Istorică* XXVI. 3–4 (2015): 249–280.

Costache, Ştefania. *At the End of Empire: Imperial Governance, Inter-Imperial Rivalry and "Autonomy" in Wallachia and Moldavia (1780s–1850s)*. PhD, University of Illinois, Urbana–Champaign, 2013.

Costache, Ştefania. 'Loyalty and Polical Legitimacy in the Phanariots'. Historical Writing in the Eighteenth Century', *Südost-Forschungen*, 69.70 (2010/2011): 25–50.

Cotoi, Călin. *Inventing the Social in Romania, 1848–1914. Networks and Laboratories of Knowledge*. Leiden, 2020.

Cotovanu, Lidia. *'Chasing Away the Greeks': The Prince-State and the Undesired Foreigners (Wallachia and Moldavia between the 16th and 18th Centuries)*, in: Olga Katsiardi-Hering and Maria A. Stassinopoulou (eds.). *Across the Danube. Southeastern Europeans and Their Travelling Identities (17th–19th C.)*. Leiden, 2017, 215–253.

Cotovanu, Lidia. *"Qu'on prie pour moi là-bas et ici". Donation religieuse et patriotism local dans le monde othodoxe (XVIe–XVIIe siècles)*, in: Radu G. Păun (ed.), *Histoire, mémoire et devotion. Regards croisés sur la construction des identities dans le monde orthodoxe aux époques byzantine et post-byzantyne*, Seyssel, 2016, 207–255.

Cotovanu, Lidia. 'L'émigration sud-danubienne vers la Valachie et la Moldavie et sa géographie (XVe–XVIIe siècles): La potentialité heuristique d'un sujet peu connu', *Cahiers balkaniques* 42 (2014): 2–19.

Cotovanu, Lidia. *Migrations et mutations identitaires dans l'Europe du Sud-Est (vue de Valachie et de Moldavie, XIVe–XVIIe siècles)*. PhD, EHESS, Paris, 2014.

Cristea, Ovidiu. 'Ştirea – «Marfă de lux». Mărturii veneţiene din primele decenii ale secolului al XVI-lea', *Revista Istorică* XIV. 3–4 (2003): 195–209.

Dankoff, Robert. *An Ottoman Mentality: The World of Evliya Çelebi*. Leiden, 2006.

Daumard, Adeline. *Les bourgeois et la bourgeoisie en France depuis 1815*, Paris, 1991.

Daumas, Jean-Claude. *La revolution matérielle. Une histoire de la consommation, France XIXe–XXIe siècle*. Paris, 2018.

Davidova, Evguenia. *Balkan Transitions to Modernity and Nation-States Through the Eyes of Three Generations of Merchants (1780–1890s)*. Leiden, 2012.

Davidova, Evguenia. 'Women Travellers as Consumers: Adoption of Modern Ideas and Practices in 19th-century Southeast Europe', in: Constanţa Vintilă-Ghiţulescu (ed.). *Women, Consumption and the Circulation of Ideas in South-Eastern Europe, 17th–19th Century*. Leiden, 2018, 200–227.

Davies, Brian L. *The Russo-Turkish War, 1768–1774. Catherine II and the Ottoman Empire*. London: 2016.

Davis, Natalie Zemon. *Fiction in the Archives. Pardon Tales and Their Tellers in Sixteenth Century France*. Stanford, CA, 1987.

Davison, Roderic H. '"Russian Skill and Turkish Imbecility": The Treaty of Kuchuk Kainardji reconsidered', *Slavic Review* 35.3 (1976): 463–483.

Dima, Eugenia. *Poemul Erotocrit a lui Vincenzo Cornaro în cultura română. Versiunea lui Alecu Văcărescu*. Iaşi, 2014.

De Vries, Jan. *The Industrious Revolution: Consumer Demand and the Household Economy, 1650 to the Present*. Cambridge, 2008.

Dobre, Anca. 'Points de vue de l'histoire nationale grecque et roumaine sur la question des Phanariotes', in: Paschalis Kitromilides and Anna Tabaki (eds.). *Relations gréco–roumaines. Interculturalité et identité nationale*. Athenes, 2004, 189–94.

Do Paço, David. 'Women in Diplomacy in Late Eighteenth-Century Istanbul', *Historical Journal* 64, 3 (2021): 1–23, DOI: 10.1017/S0018246X21000479.

Do Paço, David. 'A case of urban integration: Vienna's port area and the Ottoman merchants in the eighteenth century', *Urban History*, 48, 3 (2020): 1–19.

Do Paço, David. 'The Political Agents of Muslim Rulers in Central Europe in the 18th century', in: David Thomas and John Chesworth (eds.). *Christian–Muslim Relations. A Bibliographical History*, vol. 14 Central and Eastern Europe, 1700–1800. Leiden, 2020, 39–55.

Do Paço, David. 'Une collaboration économique et sociale: consuls et protecteurs des marchands ottomans à Vienne et à Trieste au XVIIIe siècle', *Cahiers de la Méditerranée* 98 (2019): 57–74.

Do Paço, David. 'La creation de la communauté grecque orientale de Trieste par Giuseppe Maria Mainati (1719–1818)', in: Valérie Assan, Bernard Heyberger and Jakob Vogel (eds.), *Minorités en Méditerranée au XIXe siècle. Identités, identifications, circulations*. Rennes, 2019, 25–44.

Do Paço, David. 'Trans-Imperial Familiarity: Ottoman Ambassadors in Eighteenth-century Vienna', in: Tracey A. Sowerby and Jan Hennings (eds.). *Practices of Diplomacy in the Early Modern World, c. 1410–1800*. London, 2017, 166–184.

Do Paço David. 'Extranéité et lien social: l'intégration des marchands ottomans à Vienne au XVIIIe siècle', *Revue d'histoire moderne et contemporaine*, 61, 1 (2014): 123–146.

Do Paço, David. *L'Orient à Vienne au dix-huitième siècle*. Oxford, 2015.

Do Paço, David. 'Comment le café devient viennois. Métissage et cosmopolitisme urbain dans l'Europe du XVIIIe siècle,' *Hypothèses 2011: Travaux de l'École doctorale d'histoire*. Paris, 2012, 343–353.

Doxiadis, Evdoxios. *The Shackles of Modernity: Women, Property, and the transition from the Ottoman Empire to the Greek State*. Cambridge – London, 2011.

Doxiadis, Evdoxios. 'Women, Wealth, and the State in Greece (1750–1860)', in: Evguenia Davidova (ed.). *Wealth in the Ottoman and Post-Ottoman Balkans. A Socio-Economic History*. London, 2016, 9–29.

Drace-Francis, Alex. '"Like a member of a free nation, he spoke without shame": foreign travellers as a trope in Romanian cultural tradition', in: Corinne Fowler, Charles Forsdick and Ludmila Kostova (eds.). *Travel and ethics: theory and practice.* New York, 2021, 183–203.

Drace-Francis, Alex. *The traditions of invention. Romanian ethnic and social stereotypes in historical context*. Leiden, 2013.

Drace-Francis, Alex. 'Towards a Natural History of East European Travel Writing', in Wendy Bracewell and Alex Drace-Francis (ed.). *Under Eastern eyes. A Comparative Introduction to East European Travel Writing on Europe*. Budapest, 2008, 1–26.

Drace-Francis, Alex. *The Making of Modern Romanian Culture. Literacy and the Development of National Identity*. London, 2006.

Drace-Francis, Alex. 'A Provincial Imperialist and a Curious Account of Wallachia: Ignaz von Born', *European History Quarterly* 36.1 (2006): 61–89.

Duindam, Jeroen. *Versailles, Vienna, and Beyond: Changing Views of Household and Government in Early Modern Europe*. Jeroen Duindam, Tülay Artan, Metin Kunt (eds.). *Royal Courts in Dynastic States and Empires. A Global Perspective*. Leiden, 2011, 401–432.

Duindam, Jeroen. *Vienna and Versailles: The Courts of Europe's Dynastic Rivals, 1550–1780*. Cambridge, 2003.

Dumas, Juliette. '*Müste'min* Dealing with the Ottoman Justice: Role and Strategy of the Ambassador', *Oriente Moderno* 93 (2013): 477–484.

Durães, Margarida, Fauve-Chamoux Antoinette, Ferrer Llorenç, Kok Jan (eds.). *The Transmission of Well-Being. Gendered Marriage Strategies and Inheritance Systems in Europe (17th–20th Centuries)*. Bern–Berlin–Bruxelles–Frankfurt am Main–New York–Oxford–Vienna, 2009.

Dursteler, Eric. 'Identity and Coexistence in the Eastern Mediterranean, ca. 1600', *New Perspectives on Turkey*, 18 (1998): 113–130.

Dursteler, Eric R. V*enetians in Constantinople: Nation, Identity, and Coexistence in the Early Modern Mediterranean*. Baltimore, 2006.

Eldem, Edhem. 'The French Nation of Constantinople in the Eighteenth Century as Reflected in the Saints Peter and Paul Parish Records, 1740–1800', in: Patricia M.E. Lorcin and Todd Shepard (eds.). *French Mediterraneans: Transnational and Imperial Histories*. Lincoln, NE – London, 2016, 131–159.

Eldem, Edhem. '(A Quest for) the Bourgeoisie of Istanbul. Identities, roles and conflicts', in: Ulrike Freitag, Nora Lafi (eds.). *Urban Governance Under the Ottomans: Between Cosmopolitism and Conflict*. London, New York, 2014, 159–186.

Eldem, Edhem. 'Un bourgeois d'Istanbul au milieu du XIXe siècle: Le livre de raison de Mehmed Cemal Bey, 1855–1864', in: Nathalie Clayer, Erdal Kaynar (eds.). *Penser, agir et vivre dans l'Empire ottoman et en Turquie: Etudes réunies pour François Georgeon*. Paris – Leuven, 2013, 372–406.

Eldem, Edhem. 'Greece and the Greeks in Ottoman History and Turkish Historiography', *Historical Review* 6 (2009): 27–40.

Eldem, Edhem. 'Foreigners on the Threshold of Felicity: The Reception of Foreigners in Ottoman Istanbul', in: Donatella Calabi and Stephan Christensen (eds.). *Cultural*

Exchange in Early Modern Europe, II. Cities and Cultural Exchange in Europe, 1400–1700. Cambridge, 2007, 114–131.

Eldem, Edhem. 'Capitulations and Western Trade. Western Trade in the Ottoman Empire: Questions, Issues and Sources', in: Suraiya Faroqhi (ed.). *The Cambridge History of Turkey*, vol. 3, *The Later Ottoman Empire, 1603–1839*. Cambridge, 2006, 283–335.

Eldem, Edhem. 'French Trade and Commercial Policy in the Levant in the Eighteenth-Century', *Oriento Moderno* 18.79. 1 (1999): 27–47.

Eldem, Edhem. *French Trade in Istanbul in the Eighteenth Century*. Leiden, 1999.

Elias, Norbert. *La civilisation des mœurs*. Trans. by Pierre Kamnizer. Paris, 1973.

Elias, Norbert. *La société de cour*. Trans. by Pierre Kamnizer. Paris, 1985.

Elliot, Matthew. 'Dress Codes in the Ottoman Empire: The Case of the Franks', in: Suraiya Faroqhi and Christoph K. Neumann (eds.). *Ottoman Costumes: From Textile to Identity*, Istanbul, 2005, 103–123.

Esmer, Tolga U. 'Notes on a Scandal: Transregional Networks of Violence, Gossip, and Imperial Sovereignty in the Late Eighteenth-Century Ottoman Empire', *Comparative Studies in Society and History* 58.1 (2016): 99–128.

Evans, Robert John Weston. *Austria, Hungary, and the Habsburgs. Central Europe c. 1683–1867*. Oxford, 2006.

Exertzoglou, Haris. 'The Cultural Uses of Consumption: Negotiating Class, Gender, and Nation in the Ottoman Urban Centers during the 19th Century', *International Journal of Middle East Studies* 35 (2003): 77–101.

Falierou, Anastasia. 'Urban Transformation of the Mytilenian Bourgeoisie: The Case of the Kourtzis Family', *Revista Istorică* XXIX.1–2 (2018): 141–161.

Falierou, Anastasia. 'European Fashion, Consumption Patterns, and Intercommunal Relations in 19th-Century Ottoman Istanbul', in: Constanţa Vintilă-Ghiţulescu (ed.). *Women, Consumption, and the Circulation of Ideas in South-Eastern Europe, 17th–19th Centuries*. Leiden, 2017, 150–168.

Faroqhi, Suraiya. 'The Material Culture of Global Connections: A Report on Current Research', *Turcica* 41 (2009): 403–431.

Faroqhi, Suraiya (ed.) *The Cambridge History of Turkey*, vol. 3. *The Later Ottoman Empire, 1603–1839*. Cambridge, 2006.

Faroqhi, Suraiya. *Subjects of the Sultan: Culture and Daily Life in the Ottoman Empire*. London, 2005.

Faroqhi, Suraiya. *Artisans of Empire. Crafts and Craftspeople Under the Ottomans*, London, 2009.

Faroqhi, Suraiya and Deguilhem Randi (eds.). *Crafts and Craftsmen of the Middle East. Fashioning the Individual in the Muslim Mediterranean*. London, 2005.

Faroqhi, Suraiya. 'Moving Goods Around, and Ottomanists too: Surveying Research on the Transfer of Material Goods in the Ottoman Empire', *Turcica* 32 (2000): 435–466.

Feci, Simona. 'Mobilité, droits et citoyenneté des femmes dans l'Italie medievale et moderne', *Clio. Histoire des Femmes* 43 (2016): 47–72.

Filitti, Ioan C. 'România faţă de capitulaţiile Turciei', *Analele Academiei Române. Memoriile Secţiunii Istorice*, 2d ser., t. XXXVIII (1915–1916): 128–135.

Fischer, Wladimir. 'Dositej Obradović and the Ambivalence of Enlightement', in: Harald Heppner and Eva Posch (eds.). *Encounters in Europe's Southeast. The Habsburg Empire and the Orthodox World in the Eighteenth and Nineteenth Centuries*. Bochum, 2012, 217–230.

Fischer, Wladimir. 'Creating a National Hero. The Changing Symbolics of Dositej Obradović (1811–1911)', in: Susan Ingram, Markus Reisenleitner and Cornelia Szabo-Knotik (eds.). *Cultural Practices and the Formation of Imagined Communities around 1900*. Vienna, 2001, 101–121.

Findley, Carter Vaughn. 'Ebu Bekir Ratib's Vienna Embassy Narrative: Discovering Austria or Propagandizing for Reform in Istanbul?', *Wiener Zeitschrift für die Kunde des Morgenlandes* 85 (1995): 41–80.

Findley, Carter Vaughn. 'Political culture and the great households', in: Suraiya Faroqhi (ed.). *The Cambridge History of Turkey*, vol. 3. Cambridge, 2006, 65–80.

Findley, Carter Vaughn. 'The Legacy of Tradition to Reform: The Origins of the Ottoman Forreign Ministry', *International Journal of Middle East Studies* 1 (1970): 224–357.

Florescu, George D. *Din vechiul Bucureşti. Biserici, curţi boereşti şi hanuri între anii 1790–1791 după două planuri inedite*. Bucharest, 1935.

Fotić, Aleksander. 'Tracing the Origin of a New Meaning of the Term Re'āyā in the Eighteenth-Century Ottoman Balkans', *Balcanica* XLVIII (2017): 55–66.

Frangakis-Syrett, Elena. 'Networks of Friendship, Networks of Kinship: Eighteenth-Century Levant Merchants', *Eurasian Studies* 1.2 (2002): 184–205.

Gavriş, Simion-Alexandru. *Viaţa şi opiniile prinţului Grigore Mihail Sturdza, 1821–1901*. Iaşi, 2015.

Georgescu, Valentin Al. *Bizanţul şi instituţiile româneşti până la mijlocul secolului al XVIII-lea*. Bucharest, 1980.

Georgescu, Vlad. *Istoria ideilor politice româneşti*. Munich, 1987.

Ginzburg Carlo. *The Cheese and the Worms: The Cosmos of a Sixteenth-Century Miller*. Trans. John Tedeschi and Anne C. Tedeschi. Harmondsworth, 1992.

Ginzburg, Carlo and Poni Carlo, 'La micro-histoire', *Le débat* 10, 17 (1981): 133–136.

Gjorgjiev, Vančo and Sarakinski Vojislav. 'The Many Nationalities of Hristofor Žefarović', *Analele Universităţii Ovidius, Constanţa, Seria Istorie* 16 (2019): 5–17.

Ghobrial, John-Paul A. 'Introduction: Seeing the World like a Microhistorian', *Past and Present*, 242 (2019): 1–22.

Ghobrial, John-Paul A. 'The Secret Life of Elias of Babylon and the Use of Global Microhistory', *Past and Present*, 222 (2014): 51–93.

Ghobrial, John-Paul A. 'Moving Stories and What They Tell Us: Early Modern Mobility Between Microhistory and Global History', *Past and Present* 242 (2019, 243–289.

Göçek, Fatma Müge. *Rise of the Bourgeoisie, Demise of Empire: Ottoman Westernization and Social Change*. Oxford, New York, 1996).

Göçek, Fatma Müge. *East Encounters West: France and the Ottoman Empire in the Eighteenth Century*. New York, 1987.

Goffman Erving. *L'arrangamnet des sexes*. Trans. by Henri Maury. Paris, 2002.

Gonţa, Alexandru. 'Femeia şi drepturile ei de moştenire în Moldova după obiceiul pământului', *Anuarul Institutului de Istorie şi Arheologie "A.D. Xenopol" Iaşi* XVII (1980): 597–602.

Gorovei, Artur. *Folticenii. Cercetări istorice asupra oraşului*. Folticeni, 1938.

Gradeva, Rossitsa. *'On 'Frenk' Objects in Everyday Life in Ottoman Balkans: the case of Sofia, Mid-17th–mid-18th Centuries'*, in: Siomnetta Cavaciocchi (ed.). *Europe's Economic Relations with the Islamic World 13th–18th Centuries*. Florence, 2007, 769–799.

Gradeva, Rossitsa. 'On Zimmis and their Church Buildings: Four Cases from Rumeli', in: Eugenia Kermeli and Oktay Özel (eds.). *The Ottoman Empire: Myths, Realities and "Black Holes". Contributions in Honour of Colin Imber*. Istanbul, 2006, 203–237.

Gradeva, Rossitsa. 'Osman Pazvantoğlu of Vidin: Between Old and New', *Interdisciplinary Journal of Middle Eastern Studies* (2005): 115–161.

Gradeva, Rossitsa. 'The Ottoman Balkans – a Zone of Fractures or a Zone of Contacts?', in: Almut Bues (ed.). *Zones of Fracture in Modern Europe: the Baltic Countries, the Balkans, and Northern Italy*. Wiesbaden, 2005, 61–75.

Gradeva, Rossitsa. 'War and Peace Along the Danube: Vidin at the End of the Seventeenth Century', *Oriente Moderno* 20.81 (2001): 149–175.

Gradeva, Rossitsa. 'Orthodox Christians in the Kadı Courts: The Practice of the Sofia Sheriat Court, Seventeenth Century', *Islamic Law and Society* 4.1 (1997): 37–69.

Greenblatt, Stephen J. *Renaissance Self-Fashioning: From More to Shakespeare*. Chicago, 1980.

Greene, Molly. *A Shared World: Christian and Muslims in the Early Modern Mediterranean*. Princeton, NJ, 2000.

Grenet, Mathieu. *La fabrique communautaire. Les Grecs à Venise, Livourne et Marseille, 1770–1840*. Rome, Athènes, 2016. https://books.openedition.org/efa/9120.

Grenet, Mathieu. 'Consuls et "nations" étrangères: état des lieux et perspectives de recherche', *Cahiers de la Méditerranée* 93 (2016): 25–35.

Grenet, Mathieu. '"Grecs de nation", sujets ottomans: experience diasporique et etre-deux identitaires, v. 1770–v. 1830', in: Jocelyne Dakhlia, Wolfgang Kaiser (eds.). *Les musulmans dans l'histoire de l'Europe*, t.II, *Passages et contacts en Méditerranée*. Paris, 2013, 311–344.

Grigoruţă, Sorin. 'Aspecte din viaţa şi activitatea unui doctor de la curtea lui Grigore al III-lea Ghica. Docotorul Fotache', *Anuarul Institutului de Istorie "A.D. Xenopol"* LI (2014): 81–91.

Grigoruţă, Sorin. *Boli, epidemii şi asistenţă medicală în Moldova (1700–1831)*. Iaşi, 2017.

Grigoruţă, Sorin. 'Aspecte din viaţa şi activitatea unui doctor de la curtea lui Grigore al III-lea Ghica. Doctorul Fotache', *Anuarul Institutului de Istorie "A.D. Xenopol"* LI (2014): 81–91.

Grigoruţă, Sorin. 'Un doctor ieşean din a doua jumătate a veacului XVIII: Dracache Depasta', *Anuarul Institutului de Istorie "A.D. Xenopol"* XLVII (2010): 33–47.

Groebner, Valentin. *Who Are You? Identification, Deception, and Surveillance in Early Modern Europe*. New York, 2007.

Günay, Nilüfer Alkan. 'A Study of Social Network Analysis: The Âyan of Bursa in the Late 18th Century', *Gazi Akademik Bakış/Journal of Gazi Academic* 5.10 (2012): 30–49.

Hanley, Will. 'What Ottoman Nationality Was and Was Not', *Journal of the Ottoman and Turkish Studies Association* 3.2 (2016), 277–298.

Harrison, Carol E. *The Bourgeois Citizen in Nineteenth-Century France. Gender, Sociability, and the Uses of Emulation*. Oxford, 1999.

Hathaway, Jane. *The Politics of Households in Ottoman Egypt: The Rise of the Qazdağlis*. Cambridge, 1997.

Iacob, Dan Dumitru. 'Copii de boieri la pension. Educaţia în familia postelnicului Iancu Costache-Negel (1838–1861)', in: Cătălina Mihalache, Leonidas Rados (eds.). *Educaţia publică şi condiţionările sale (secolele XIX–XX)*. Iaşi, 2015, 145–196.

Iacob, Dan Dumitru. *Elitele din Principatele Române în prima jumătate a secolului al XIX-lea. Sociabilitate şi divertisment*. Iaşi, 2015.

Iacob, Dan Dumitru (ed.). *Avere, prestigiu şi cultură materială în surse patrimoniale. Inventare de averi din secolele XVI–XIX*. Iaşi, 2015.

Iancu, Andreea-Roxana. 'Adopter ou nourrir un enfant en Valachie, XVIIIe–XIXe siècles: norme et pratique. Etude de cas', *Méditerranées* 37 (2004): 237–277.

Iftimi, Sorin, Corina Cimpoeşu, and Marcelina Brînduşa Munteanu (eds.), *Niccolo Livaditi şi epoca sa (1832–1858). Artă şi Istorie*. Iaşi, 2012.

Iftimi, Sorin, 'Societatea moldovenească de la jumătatea secolului al XIX-lea în portretistica lui Niccolo Livaditi', in: Sorin Iftimi, Corina Cimpoeşu, Marcelina Brînduşa Munteanu (eds.). *Niccolo Livaditi şi epoca sa (1832–1858. Artă şi Istorie*. Iaşi, 2012, 47–52.

İnalcik, Halil. 'The Emergence of Big Farms, Çiftliks: State, Landlords and Tenants', in: Jean-Louis Bacqué-Grammont, Paul Dumont (eds.). *Contributions à l'histoire économique et sociale de l'Empire ottoman*, Louvain, 1983, 105–126.

Instituţii feudale din Ţările Române. Dicţionar, eds. Ovid Sachelarie and Nicolae Stoicescu. Bucharest, 1988.

Ion, Christina. 'The Present Creates the Past: The 'Phanariots' in the Romanian Text Books during the Second Half of the 19th Century', *Revue d'Etudes sud-est européennes* 33.1–2 (1995): 41–47.

Iordachi, Constantin. *Liberalism, Constitutionalism, Nationalism, and Minorities. The Making of Romanian Citizenship, c. 1750–1918*. Leiden, 2019.

Iordachi, Constantin. 'From Imperial Entanglements to National Disentanglement: The "Greek Question" in Moldavia and Wallachia, 1611–1863', in: Roumen Daskalov, Tchavdar Marinov (eds.). *Entangled Histories of the Balkans*, vol. I: *National Ideologies and Language Policies*, Leiden, 2013, 67–148.

Isabella, Maurizio and Konstantina Zanou (eds). *Mediterranean Diasporas: Politics and Ideas in the Long 19th Century*. London, 2015.

Ivanova, Dzeni. 'Ottoman Subjects, Habsburg Allies. The Reaya of the Chiprovtsi Region (Northwestern Bulgaria) on the Front Line, 1688–1690', in: Colin Heywood, Ivan Parvev (eds.). *The Treaties of Karlowitz (1699). Antecedents, Course and Consequences*. Leiden, 2019, 110–130.

Jelavich, Barbara. *History of the Balkans*, 2 vols. Cambridge–New York, 1983.

Jianu, Angela. 'Dora d'Istria: un dar făcut Europei', in: Violeta Barbu, Maria-Magdalena Székely, Kinga S. Tüdős, Angela Jianu. *Grădina Rozelor. Femei din Moldova, Ţara Românească şi Transilvania (sec. XVII–XIX)*. Bucharest, 2015, 331–339.

Jianu, Angela. 'Women, Dowries and Patrimonial Law in Old Regime Romania, c. 1750–1830', *Journal of Family History* 34.2 (2009): 189–205.

Jianu, Angela. 'Elena Hartulari's Story: The Presentation of the Emotional Self,' in: Faruk Bilici, Ionel Cândea, and Anca Popescu (eds). *Enjeux politiques, économiques et militaires en Mer Noire, XIVe–XXIe siecles – Etudes à la mémoire de Mihail Guboglu*. Brăila, 2007, 429–449.

Judson, Pieter M. *The Habsburg Empire: A New History*, Cambridge, MA, 2016.

Kaczka, Mariusz Wieław. 'The Gentry of the Polish–Ottoman Borderlands: The case of the Moldavian-Polish Family of Turkuł/Turculeţ', *Acta Poloniae Historica* 104 (2011): 133–150.

Kafadar, Cemal. *Between Two Worlds. The Construction of the Ottoman State*. Berkeley, CA, 1995.

Kaiser, Wolfgang. 'Extranéités urbaines à l'époque moderne', in: Pilar González-Bernaldo, Manuela Martini and Marie-Louis Pelus-Kaplan (eds.), *Etrangers et sociétés. Représentations, coexistences, interactions dans la longue durée*. Rennes, 2008, 77–86.

Kaiser, Daniel H. 'Gender, Property, and Testamentary Behavior: Eighteenth-Century Moscow Wills', *Harvard Ukrainian Studies* 28.1–4 (2006): 161–170.

Katsiardi-Hering, Olga, Madouvalos Ikaros. 'The Tolerant Policy of the Habsburg Authorities Towards the Orthodox People from South-Eastern Europe and the

Formation of National Identities (18th–early 19th Century)', *Balkan Studies* 49 (2014): 6–34.

Katsiardi-Hering, Olga. 'Christian and Jewish Ottomans Subjects: Family, Inheritance and Comercial Networks between East and West (17th–18th C.)', in: Simonetta Cavaciocchi (ed.). *The Economic Role of the Family in the European Economy from the 13th to the 18th Centuries*, Florence, 2009, 409–440.

Keller, Katrin. *Hofdamen. Amtsträgerinnen im Wiener Hofstaat des 17. Jahrhunderts*. Vienna, Böhlau, 2005.

Keller, Katrin. 'Ladies-in-Waiting at the Imperial Court of Vienna from 1550 to 1700: Structures, Responsibilities and Carrier Patterns', in: Nadine Akkerman, Birgit Houben (eds.). *The Politics of Female Households: Ladies-in-waiting across Early Modern Europe*, Leiden, 2013, 73–97.

Kermeli, Eugenia. 'Marriage and Divorce of Christians and New Muslims in Early Modern Ottoman Empire: Crete 1645–1670', *Oriente Moderno* 93 (2013): 527–546.

Kettering, Sharon. 'Patronage in Early Modern France', *French Historical Studies*, 17. 4 (1992): 839–862.

Kettering, Sharon. 'Patronage and Kinship in Early Modern France', *French Historical Studies* 16.2 (1989): 408–435.

Kettering, Sharon. 'Gift-Giving and Patronage in Early Modern France', *French History* 2 (1988): 131–51.

Kitromilides, Paschalis M. *The Enlightenment as Social Criticism: Iosipos Moisiodax and Greek Culture in the Eighteenth Century*. Princeton, 1992.

Kivelson, Valerie A. 'Muscovite 'Citizenship': Rights without Freedom', *Journal of Modern History* 74 (2002): 465–489.

Kivelson, Valerie A. 'The Effects of Partible Inheritance: Gentry Families and the State in Muscovy', *Russian Review* 53.2 (1994): 197–212.

Klein, Denise (ed.). *The Crimean Khanate between East and West (15th–18th Centuries)*. Wiesbaden, 2012.

Klein, Denis. 'The Sultan's Envoys Speak: The Ego in 18th Century Ottoman Sefâretnâmes on Russia', in: Ralf Elger and Yavuz Köse (eds.). *Many Ways of Speaking About Self: Middle Eastern Ego-Documents in Arabic, Persian and Turkish (14th–20th Century)*. Wiesbaden, 2010, 89–103.

Knopper, Françoise. 'Le cosmopolitisme viennois', *Dix-Huitième Siècle* 25 (1993): 129–151.

Kołodziejczyk, Dariusz. *The Crimean Khanate and Poland-Lithuania. International Diplomacy on the European Periphery (15th–18th Century). A Study of Peace Treaties Followed by an Annotated Edition of Relevant Documents*. Leiden, 2011.

Kołodziejczyk, Dariusz. 'The "Turkish Yoke" Revisited: The Ottoman Non-Muslim Subjects between Loyalty, Alienation and Riot', *Acta Poloniae Historica* 93 (2006): 177–195.

Kołodziejczyk, Dariusz: 'Semiotics of Behavior in Early Modern Diplomacy: Polish Embassies in Istanbul and Bahçesaray', *Journal of Early Modern History* 7.3–4 (2003): 245–256.

Korchmina, Elena. 'The Practice of Personal Finance and the Problem of Debt among the Noble Elite in Eighteenth-Century Russia', in: Andreas Schönle, Andrei Zorin, and Alexei Evstratov (eds.). *The Europeanized Elite in Russia, 1762–1825. Public Role and Subjective Self.* Illinois, 2016, 116–135.

Kollmann, Nancy Shields. *The Russian Empire, 1450–1801.* Oxford, 2017.

Kostantaras, Dean J. 'Christian Elites of the Peloponnese and the Ottoman State, 1715–1821', *European History Quarterly* 43.4 (2013): 628–656.

Kovács, Nándor Erik, 'The Legal Status of the Danubian Principalities in the 17th Century as Reflected in the Şikayet Defteris', *Güney-Doğu Avrupa Araştırmaları Dergisi* 1 (2014): 1–23.

Kubiska-Scharl, Irene and Pölzl Michael, *Die Karrieren des Wiener Hofpersonals, 1711–1765, eine Darstellung anhan der Hofkalender und Hofparteienprotokolle*, Vienna, 2013.

Kunt, Metin Ibrahim, 'Ethnic Regional (*Cins*) Solidarity in the Seventeenth-Century Ottoman Establishment', *International Journal of Middle East Studies* 5.3 (1974): 233–239.

Laiou, Sophia. 'Between Pious Generosity and Faithful Service to the Ottoman State: The *Vakıf* of Nikolaos Mavroghenis, End of the Eighteenth Century', *Turkish Historical Review* 6 (2015): 151–174.

Laiou, Sophia. 'Entre les insurgés reaya et les indisciplinés ayan: la révolution grecque et la réaction de l'Etat ottoman', in: Marios Hadjianastasis (ed.). *Frontiers of the Ottoman Imagination. Studies in Honour of Rhoads Murphey*, Leiden, 2015, 213–228.

Laiou, Sophia. 'Patronage Networks in the Aegean Sea, End of the 18th – Beginning of the 19th Century', in: Marinos Sariyannis (ed.). *New Trends in Ottoman Studies*, Rethymno, 2014, 413–423.

Laiou, Sophia. 'The Ottoman Greek "Merchants of Europa" at the beginning of the 19th century', in: Evangelina Balta, Georgios Salakidis, Theoharis Stavrides (eds.). *Festschrift in Honor of Ioannis P. Theocharides. Studies on the Ottoman Empire and Turkey*. Istanbul, 2014, 313–331.

Laiou, Sophia. 'Christian Women in an Ottoman World: Interpersonal and Family Cases Brought Before the Shari'a Courts During the Seventeenth and Eighteenth Centuries. (Cases Involving the Greek Community)'. in: Amila Buturović and Irvin Schick (ed.), *Women in the Ottoman Balkans. Gender, Culture and History*, London, 2007, 243–271.

Lamarche, Marrese Michelle. '"The Poetics of Everyday Behavior" Revisited. Lotman, Gender, and the Evolution of Russian Noble Identity', *Kritika: Explorations in Russian and Eurasian History* 11.4 (2010): 701–739.

Landais, Benjamin. 'Être français dans le Banat du XVIIIe siècle', *Etudes Vauclusiennes* 84 (2019): 45–58.

Landais, Benjamin. 'Enregistrer l'ethnicité au XVIIIe siècle: L'identification des migrants ottomans à la frontière habsbourgeoise', *Revue d'histoire moderne et contemporaine* 66.4 (2019): 89–120.

Lazăr, Gheorghe. 'De la Râmnic la Veneţia şi Sfântul Mormânt. Catastiful negustorului Constantin Malache (secolul al XVIII-lea)', in: Laurenţiu Rădvan (ed.). *Oraşe vechi, oraşe noi în spaţiul românesc. Societate, economie şi civilizaţie urbană în prag de modernitate (sec. XVI–jumătatea sec. XIX)*. Iaşi, 2014, 79–89.

Lazăr, Gheorghe. 'Les logothètes de la chancellerie princières de la Valachie (XVIIe siècle). Considérations préliminaires pour une recherché prosopographique', *Istros* XX (2014): 601–619.

Lazăr, Gheorghe. 'Un testament şi o poveste de viaţă: cazul negustorului Cernea Popovici', in: Cristian Luca, Claudiu Neagoe, Marius Păduraru (eds). *Miscellanea Historica: in honorem Professoris Marcel-Dumitru Ciucă septuagenarii*, Brăila–Piteşti, 2013, 597–624.

Lazăr, Gheorghe. 'In umbra puterii. Negustori "prieteni ai domniei" şi destinul lor (Ţara Românească, secolul al XVII-lea)', in: Ovidiu Cristea, Gheorghe Lazăr (eds.). *Vocaţia istoriei. Prinos Profesorului Şerban Papacostea*. Brăila, 2008, 605–634.

Lazăr, Gheorghe. 'Marchands Ottomans en Valachie (XVIIe–XVIIIe siècles)', in: Faruk Bilici, Ionel Cândea, Anca Popescu (eds.), *Enjeux Politiques, Economiques et Militaires en Mer Noire (XIVe–XIXe siècles). Etudes à la Mémoire de Mihai Guboglu*. Brăila, 2007, 291–314.

Lazăr, Gheorghe. *Les marchands en Valachie, XVIIe–XVIIIe siècles*. Bucharest, 2006.

Lazăr, Mariana. 'Spre lumea 'de dincolo', trecând împreună prin lumea pământeană. Marele vornic Iordache Creţulescu şi soţia sa, domniţa Safta Brâncoveanu', in: Mircea Ciubotaru, Lucian-Valeriu Lefter (eds.). *Mihai Dim. Sturdza la 80 de ani. Omagiu*. Iaşi, 2014, 799–822.

LeDonne, John P. *Absolutism and Ruling Class. The Formation of the Russian Political Order, 1700–1825*. Oxford, 1991.

Leerssen, Joep (ed.). *Encyclopedia of Romantic Nationalism in Europe*, 2 vols. Amsterdam, 2018.

Lejeune, Philippe. *Le Pacte autobiographique*. Paris, 1975.

Lemny, Ştefan. *Cantemireştii. Aventura europeană a unei familii princiare din secolul al XVIII-lea*. Trans. Magda Jeanrenaud. Iaşi, 2013.

Lemny, Ştefan. *Jean-Louis Carra (1742–1793). Parcours d'un révolutionnaire*. Paris, 2000.

Lemny, Ştefan. 'La critique du régime phanariote: clichés mentaux et perspectives historiographiques', in: Alexandru Zub (ed.), *Culture and Society: Structures, Interferences, Analogies in the Modern Romanian History*. Iaşi, 1985, 17–30.

Limona, Dumitru. *Negustorii "greci" şi arhivele lor comerciale*. ed. Loredana Dascăl. Iaşi, 2016.

Livanios, Dimitris. 'The Quest for Hellenism: Religion, Nationalism and Collective Identities in Greece, 1453–1913', *The Historical Review/La Revue Historique* III (2006): 33–70.

Lloyd, Martin. *The Passport: The history of Man's Most Travelled Document*. Kent, 2008.

Lowenthal, Cynthia. *Lady Mary Wortley Montagu and the Eighteenth-Century Familiar Letter*. Athens, GA and London, 2010.

Luca, Cristian. 'Il raguseo Stefano Ignatz Raicevich, diplomatico dell'impero e promotore del progetto di espansione asburgica alla foce del Danubio', *Annuario dell'Istituto Romeno di Cultura e Ricerca Umanistica di Venezia, XII–XIII, 2010–2011* (2015): 157–169.

Lyberatos, Andreas. 'From Stratum Culture to National Culture: Integration Processes and National Resignification in 19th century Plovdiv', *Balkanologie. Revue d'études pluridisciplinaires* XIII.1–2 (2011): 1–24.

Lyberatos, Andreas. 'Men of the Sultan: The Beglik Sheep tax Collection System and the Rise of Bulgarian National Bourgeoisie in Nineteenth-Century Plovdiv', *Turkish Historical Review* 1 (2010): 55–85.

Mackridge, Peter. 'Enlightenment or Entertainment? The Intolerable Lightness of Phanariot Literature, 1750–1800', *Revue des Etudes Sud-Est Europeennes*, LVIII.1–4 (2020): 119–138.

Mackridge, Peter. 'Some Greek Literary Representations of Greek Life and Language in the Late Eighteenth Century', *Revista de Istorie şi Teorie Literară* X.1–4 (2016): 171–195.

Mackridge, Peter. *Language and National Identity in Greece, 1766–1976*. Oxford, 2009.

Mackridge, Peter. 'Aspects of Language and Identity in the Greek Peninsula Since the Eighteenth Century', *The Newsletter of the Society Farsarotul* XXI&XXII. 1–2 (2007–2008): 1–18.

Marinescu, Florin. *Etude généalogique sur la famille Moruzi*. Athens, 1987.

Marinov, Tchavdar. 'The "Balkan House": Interpretations and Symbolic Appropriations of the Ottoman-Era Vernacular Arhitecture in the Balkans', in: Roumen Daskalov, Tchavdar Marinov, Diana Mishkova and Alexander Vezenkov (eds.). *Entangled Histories of the Balkans*, vol. 4. *Concepts, Approaches and (Self-)Representations*. Leiden, 2017, 440–593.

Martin-Fugier, Anne. *La Bourgeoise*. Paris, 1983.

Marton, Silvia. '"Aici e vorba să dăm ceea ce avem mai bun: naţionalitatea". Naturalizare, cetăţenie şi românitate în parlamentul României (a doua parte a veacului al XIX-lea)', *Annals of the University of Bucharest / Political science series* 8 (2006): 35–51.

Mason, Paul. *Histoire du commerce français dans le Levant au XVIIIe siècle*. Paris, 1911.

Masters, Bruce. 'Christians in a changing world' in: Suraiya N. Faroqhi (ed.). *The Cambridge History of Turkey*, vol. 3. *The Later Ottoman Empire, 1603–1839*. Cambridge, 2006, 272–279.

Mat'a, Petr. 'The false Orsini from over the Alps: Negotiating aristocratic identity in late medieval and early modern Europe', *Römische historische Mitteilungen*, 55 (2013): 155–218.

Mateescu, Bogdan. *Familia în timpul robiei. O perspectivă demografică. Studii şi liste de populaţie din arhive*. Iaşi, 2015.

Mateescu, Bogdan. *Căsătoria robilor între alegerea cuplului şi voinţa stăpânului. Studiu şi documente din arhivă despre căsătoria robilor în Tara românească după 1830*. Braşov, 2014.

Mazower, Mark. *The Balkans: A Short History*, New York, 2000.

Mărieş, Stela. *Supuşii străini din Moldova în perioada 1781–1862*. Iaşi, 1985.

Mărieş, Stela. 'Activitatea lui Ignaţiu Ştefan Raicevich, primul consul al Austriei în Ţările Române (1782–1786)', *Cercetări Istorice* VI (1975): 123–140.

McLean, Paul D. *The Art of the Network. Strategic Interaction and Patronage in Renaissance Florence*, London 2007.

Meriage, Lawrence P. 'The First Serbian Uprising (1804–1813) and the Nineteenth-Century Origins of the Eastern Question', *Slavic Review* 37.3 (1978): 421–439.

Meteş, Ştefan. *Moşiile domnilor şi boierilor din ţările române în Ardeal şi Ungaria*. Arad, 1925.

Mihordea, Vasile. 'Un agent politic al ţărilor noastre: Daniel Fonseca', *Revista Istorică* XXIX. 1–6 (1943): 93–132.

Mihordea, Vasile. 'Biblioteca domnească a Mavrocordaţilor', *Analele Academiei Române. Memoriile Secţiunii Istorice*, 3d ser., XXXII.16 (1940): 359–371.

Mihordea, Vasile. *Politica orientală franceză şi ţările române în secolul al XVIII-lea (1749–1760)*. Bucharest, 1937.

Mihordea, Vasile. 'Giuseppe-Antonio Pisani, medicul lui Constantin Racoviţă', *Revista Istorică*, 22.7–9 (1936): 235–250.

Mihordea Vasile. 'De Hauterive, secretar domnesc în Moldova (1785)', *Revista Istorică*, 21.1–3 (1935): 33–41.

Mishkova, Diana. *Beyond Balkanism: The Scholarly Politics of Region Making*. London, 2018.

Mishkova, Diana. 'Balkan Liberalisms: Historical Routes of a Modern Ideology', in: Roumen Daskalov and Diana Mishkova (eds.). *Entangled Histories of the Balkans*. vol. 2: *Transfers of Political Ideologies and Institutions*. Leiden, 2014, 99–198.

Mîrza, Mihai. 'Revolta boierilor moldoveni din vara anului 1750: Reconstituire factologică, ipoteze, semnificaţii', in: Cristian Ploscaru, and Mihai-Bogdan Atanasiu (eds.), *Elitele puterii, puterile elitelor în spaţiul românesc (secolele XV–XX)*. Iaşi, 2018, 257–289.

Mîrza, Mihai. 'Cheltuielile casei marelui vistiernic Toader Palade, după o seamă din anul 1752', *Analele Ştiinţifice ale Universităţii Alexandru Ioan Cuza, Iaşi, Secţia Istorie* LIX (2013): 333–408.

Mîrza, Mihai. 'Socotelile vistiernicului Toader Palade cu diecii de vistierie, după un catastif de la mijlocul secolului al XVIII-lea', *Ioan Neculce. Buletinul Muzeului de istorie a Moldovei* XVI–XVIII (2012): 115–135.

Mîrza, Mihai. 'Averea lui beizadea Ioniţă Cantemir după un catastif din 1755', *Anuarul Institutului de Istorie Xenopol* XLIX (2012): 409–437.

Mousnier, Roland. 'Les concepts d' "ordres" d' "états", de "fidélité" et de "monarchie absolue" en France de la fin du XVe siècle à la fin du XVIIIe', *Revue Historique*, t. 247, Fasc. 2, 502 (1972): 289–312.

Moureau, François. *La plume et le plomb. Espaces de l'imprimé et du manuscrit au siècle des Lumières*. Paris, 2006.

Munteanu, Luminiţa. 'Being Homo Balkanicus without Knowing it: The Case of Anton Pann', in: *Turkey and Romania. A History of Partnership and Collaboration in The Balkans*. Istanbul, 2016, 123–138.

Murgescu, Bogdan. '"Fanarioţi" şi "pământeni": religie şi etnicitate în definirea identităţilor în Ţările Române şi în Imperiul Otoman', in: Bogdan Murgescu, *Ţările Române între Imperiul Otoman şi Europa Creştină*. Iaşi, 2012.

Murgescu, Bogdan C. 'Balances of Trade and Payments between the Ottoman Empire and Central Europe (16th–18th centuries)', in: Simonetta Cavaciocchi (ed.). *Relazioni economiche tra Europa e mondo islamico secc. XIII–XVIII*. Florence, 2007, 961–980.

Murphy, Orville T. *Charles Gravier, Comte De Vergennes: French Diplomacy in the Age of Revolution, 1719–1787*. New York, 2009.

Odobescu, Alexandru. *Opere*, vol. 2. Bucharest, 1967.

Olar, Ovidiu-Victor. 'Dimitrie Cantemir', in: David Thomas and John Chesworth (eds.). *Christian–Muslim Relations. A Bibliographical History*, vol. 14. *Central and Easter Europe (1700–1800)*. Leiden, 2020, 304–322.

Olar, Ovidiu. 'Logofătul de taină. Viaţa, aventurile şi traducerile lui Vlad Boţulescu de Mălăieşti', in: Emanuela Timotin, Ovidiu Olar (eds.). *Vlad Boţulescu de Mălăieşti, Scrieri*. Bucharest, 2013, 13–37.

Osipian, Alexandr. 'Trans-Cultural Trade in the Black Sea Region, 1250–1700: Integration of the Armenian Trading Diaspora in the Moldavian Principality', *New Europe College. Black Sea Link Program Yearbook 2012–2013* (2013): 111–156.

Oţetea, Andrei. *Tudor Vladimirescu şi mişcarea eteristă în ţările româneşti, 1821–1822*. Bucharest, 1945.

Oţetea, Andrei. *Tudor Vladimirescu şi revoluţia de la 1821*. Bucharest, 1971.

Pakucs, Mária. '"This is their profession". Greek merchants in Transylvania and their Networks at the End of the 17th century', *Cromohs: Cyber Review of Modern Historiography* 21 (2017–2018): 36–54.

Pakucs, Mária. 'Between "'Faithful Subjects"' and "'Pernicious Nation"': Greek Merchants in the Principality of Transylvania in the Seventeenth Century', *Hungarian Historical Review* 6.1 (2017): 111–137.

Pakucs-Willcocks, Mária. *Sibiu-Hermannstadt. Oriental Trade in Sixteenth Century Transylvania*. Köln–Weimar–Vienna, 2007.

Pál, Judit. 'Armenian Society in 18th Century Transylvania', in: Gyöngy Kovács Kiss (ed.). *Studies in the History of Early Modern Transylvania*. Highland Lakes, NJ, 2011, 151–178.

Panaite, Viorel. 'Power Relationships in the Ottoman Empire. Sultans and the Tribute Paying Princes of Walachia and Moldavia (16th–18th Centuries)', *Revue d'Etudes sud-est européennes*, 33.1–2 (1999–2000): 47–78.

Panaite, Viorel. 'Wallachia and Moldavia according to the Ottoman Juridical and Political View, 1774–1829', in: Antonis Anastasopoulos and Elias Kolovos (eds.). *Ottoman Rule and The Balkans, 1760–1858. Conflict, Transformation, Adaptation*. Rethymno, 2007, 21–44.

Panaite, Viorel. 'The Re'ayas of the Tributary Protected Principalities: The Sixteenth Through the Eighteenth Centuries', *International Journal of Turkish Studies* 9.1 (2003): 79–104.

Panaite, Viorel. 'Being a Western Merchant in the Ottoman Mediterranean', in: Deyfi Kenan (ed.). *Isam Papers. Ottoman Thought, Ethics, Law, Philosophy-Kalam*. Istanbul, 2013, 91–136.

Panaitescu, Damian. 'The Ottoman Empire and the Preservation of Wallachia's Fiscal Potential (1730–1774)', *Revista Economică* 66.6 (2014): 56–76.

Panzac, Daniel. 'Politique sanitaire et fixation des frontières. L'exemple ottoman (XVIIIe–XIXe siècles)', *Turcica* 31 (1999): 87–108.

Panzac, Daniel. *La peste dans l'Empire ottoman, 1700–1859*. Louvain, 1985.

Papacostea, Şerban. *Oltenia sub stăpânirea austriacă (1718–1739)*. Bucharest, 1998.

Papacostea, Şerban. 'La grande charte de Constantin Mavrocordato (1741) et les réformes en Valachie et en Moldavie', in: *Symposium. L'Epoque phanariote*. Thessaloniki, 1974, 365–367.

Papacostea-Danielopolu, Cornelia. 'L'organisation de la Compagnie grecque de Braşov (1777–1850)', *Balkan Studies* 14 (1973): 312–323.

Papacostea-Danielopolu, Cornelia. 'La Companie grecque de Braşov. La lutte pour la conservation des privileges (1777–1850)', *Revue des études sud-est européennes* 12 (1974): 59–78.

Papastamatiou, Demetrios, 'The Right of Appeal to State Intervention as a Means of Political Mobilization of the Reaya in the Ottoman Provinces: Some Preliminary Remarks on the Eighteenth-Century Morea (Peloponnese)', in: Antonis Anastasopoulos (ed.). *Political Initiatives 'from the Bottom Up' in the Ottoman Empire*. Rethymno, 2012, 165–190.

Păun, Radu G. 'Ianache Văcărescu', in: David Thomas şi John Chesworth (eds.). *Christian–Muslim Relations. A Bibliographical History*, vol. 14. Central and Eastern Europe (1700–1800). Leiden, 2020, 364–381.

Păun, Radu G. 'Some Remarks about the Historical Origins of the "Phanariot Phenomenon" Moldavia and Wallachia (16th–19th centuries)', in: Gelina Harlaftis, Radu Păun (eds.). *Greeks in Romania in the Nineteenth Century*. Athens, 2013, 47–94.

Păun, Radu G. 'Réseaux de livres et réseaux de pouvoirs dans le sud-est de l' Europe: le monde des dragomans (XVIIe–XVIIIe siècles)', in: Frédéric Barbier, István Monok (eds.). *Contribution à l'histoire intellectuelle de l' Europe: réseaux du livre, réseaux des lectures*. Budapest, 2008, 63–107.

Păun, Radu G. 'Les grands officiers d'origine gréco-levantine en Moldavie au XVIIe siècle. Offices, carriers et stratégies de pouvoir', *Revue des études sud-est européennes* XLV.1–4 (2007): 153–195.

Păun, Radu G. 'Les Gréco-Levantins dans les Pays Roumains: voies de penetration, étapes et strategies de maintien', *Studia Balcanica* 25 (2006): 304–316.

Păun, Radu G. *Pouvoirs, offices et patronage dans la Principauté de Moldavie au XIXe siècle: l'aristocratie roumaine et la pénétration gréco-levantine*. PhD diss., EHESS, Paris, 2003.

Peirce, Leslie. 'Beyond Harem Walls: Ottoman Royal Women and the Exercise of Power', in: Dorothy O. Helly and Susan M. Reverby (eds.). *Gendered Domains. Rethinking Public and Private in Women's History*. Ithaca, NJ – London, 1992.

Peretz, M.I. *Privilegiul masculinităţii în Pravilniceasca Condică Ipsilanti şi în Legiuirea Caragea*. Bucharest, 1905.

Petrovsky, Konrad, '"Those Violating the Good, Old Customs of Our Lands": Forms and Functions of Graecophobia in the Danubian Principalities, 16th–18th Centuries', in: Hakan T. Karateke, H. Erdem Çipa and Helga Anetshofer (eds.). *Disliking Others: Loathing Hostility, and Distrust in Premodern Ottoman Lands*. Brighton, 2018, 187–218.

Petrovszky, Konrad. 'Marginal Notes in South Slavic Written Culture. Between Practising Memory and Accounting for the Self', *Cahiers du monde russe* 58 (2017): 483–502.

Philliou, *Christine. Biography of an Empire: Governing Ottomans in an Age of Revolution*, Berkeley, 2011.

Pippidi, Andrei. *Documente privind locul românilor în Sud-estul Europei*. Bucharest, 2018.

Pippidi, Andrei. 'Părinți și copii în Geneva lui Töpffer' in: Nicoleta Roman (ed.). *Copilăria românească între familie și societate (secolele XVII–XX)*. Bucharest, 2015, 343–360.

Pippidi, Andrei. *Byzantins, Ottomans, Roumains. Le Sud-Est Européen entre l'héritage impérial et les influences occidentales*. Paris, 2006.

Pippidi, Andrei. *Tradiţia politică bizantină în Ţările Române în secolele XVI–XVIII*. Bucharest, 2001.

Pippidi, Andrei. 'Originele familiei Rosetti şi confirmarea unei mărturii a lui Neculce', *Anuarul Institutului de Istorie şi Arheologie "A.D. Xenopol"* XX (1983): 275–180.
Pippidi, Andrei. 'Rapports de Raguse avec les pays roumains', in: idem, *Hommes et idées du Sud-Est européen à l'aube de l'âge modern*. Paris, Bucharest, 1980, 65–124.
Pippidi, Andrei. 'Mysticisme et rationalism au Phanar: le cas de Daniel de Fonseca', in: idem, *Hommes et idées du Sud-Est européen à l'aube de l'âge moderne*. Paris, Bucharest, 1980, 237–252.
Pippidi, Andrei. 'Notules Phanariotes. I: Panagiodoros', *O Eranistis* 15.1 (1979): 101–114.
Pippidi, Andrei. 'Aux origines du regime phanariote en Valachie et Moldavie', *Revue des études sud-est européennes* XI.2 (1973): 353–355.
Pippidi, Andrei. 'Phanar, Phanariotes, Phanariotisme', *Revue des études sud-est européennes* XIII.2 (1975): 231–239.
Pippidi, Andrei. 'Lecturile unui boier muntean, acum un veac: Ioan Manu', *Revista de Teorie Literară"* 20.1 (1971): 105–119.
Pippidi, Andrei. 'Date noi despre Roseteşti şi pământurile lor la sfârşitul secolului al XVIII-lea', *Carpica* IV (1971): 331–341.
Platon, Alexandru Florin. *Geneza burgheziei în Principatele Române (a doua jumătate a secolului al XVIII-lea – prima jumătate a secolului al XIX-lea). Preliminariile unei istorii*. Iaşi, 1997.
Platon, Gheorghe, Platon Alexandru-Florin. *Boierimea din Moldova în secolul al XIX-lea. Context european, evoluţie socială şi politică (Date statistice şi observaţii istorice)*. Bucharest, 1995.
Poboran, George. *Istoria oraşului Slatina*. Slatina, 1908.
Popovitch, Ružica. 'The Education of Women in 19th-Century Serbia', *Serbian Studies: Journal of the North American Society for Serbian Studies* 29.1–2 (2018): 137–150.
Pośpiech, Andrzej. 'Majątek osobisty szlachcica w świetle wielkopolskich pośmiertnych inwentarzy ruchomości z XVII w.', *Kwartalnik Historii Kultury Materialnej* 29.4 (1981): 463–482.
Pratt, Mary Louise. *Imperial Eyes: Travel Writing and Transculturation*. New York, 1992.
Pylia, Martha. 'Conflits Politiques et Comportements des Primats Chrétiens en Morées, avant la Guerre de l'independence', in: Antonis Anastasopoulos and Elias Kolovos (eds.). *Ottoman Rule and The Balkans, 1760–1858. Conflict, Transformation, Adaptation*. Rethymno, 2007, 137–148.
Quataert, Donald (ed.). *Consumption Studies and the History of the Ottoman Empire 1550–1922*, New York, 2000.
Quataert, Donald. 'Clothing Laws, the State and Society in the Ottoman Empire, 1720–1829', *International Journal of Middle Eastern Studies* 29.3 (1997): 403–425.
Raeff, Marc. 'The Bureaucratic Phenomena of Imperial Russia, 1700–1905', *American Historical Review* 84.2 (1979): 399–411.

Rauscher, Peter. 'Comparative Evolution of the Tax Systems in the Habsburg Monarchy, c. 1526–1740: The Austrian and the Bohemian Land', in: Simonetta Cavaciocchi (ed.). *La Fiscaltà nell'economia europea, secc. XIII–XVIII/ Fiscal Systems in the European Economy from the 13th to the 18th Centuries*. Florence, 2008, 291–320.

Rădulescu, Ion Heliade. 'Femeile sau cugetul acestei foi', *Curier de ambe sexe* 2 (1837): 43–48.

Rădulescu, Theodora. *Sfatul domnesc şi alţi mari dregători ai Ţării Româneşti din secolul al XVIII-lea. Liste cronologice şi cursus honorum*. Bucharest, 1972.

Rădvan, Laurenţiu (ed.). *Oraşe vechi, oraşe noi în spaţiul românesc. Societate, economie şi civilizaţie urbană în prag de modernitate (sec. XVI–prima jumătate a secolului al XIX-lea)*. Iaşi, 2014.

Rădvan, Laurenţiu. 'Foreign Merchants in Iaşi (17th–18th centuries)', *Istros* 18 (2012): 453–480.

Reill, Kirchner Dominique. *Nationalists Who Feared the Nation: Adriatic Multi-Nationalism in Habsburg Dalmatia, Trieste, and Venice*. Stanford, 2012.

Reill, Kirchner Dominique. 'Away or Homeward Bound? The Slippery Case of Mediterranean Place in the Era before Nation-States', in: Isabella Maurizio and Konstantina Zanou (eds). *Mediterranean Diasporas: Politics and Ideas in the Long 19th Century*. London, 2015, 136–152.

Reindl-Kiel, Hedda. *The Must-Haves of a Grand Vizier: Merzifonlu Kara Mustafa Pasha's Luxury Assets, Wiener Zeitschrift für die Kunde des Morgenlandes*. 106 (2016): 179–221.

Reindl-Kiel, Hedda. 'Luxury, Power Strategies and the Question of Corruption: Gifting in the Ottoman Elite (16th–18th Centuries)', in: Yavuz Köse (ed.). *Şehrâyîn. Die Welt der Osmanen, die Osmanen in der Welt, Wahrnehmungen, Begegnungen und Abgrenzungen: Festschrift Hans Georg Majer*. Wiesbaden, 2012, 107–120.

Rétat, Pierre (ed.). *La Gazette d'Amsterdam, miroir de l'Europe au XVIIIe siècle*. Oxford, 2001.

Rizo-Rangabé, Eugène. *Livre d'or de la noblesse phanariote en Grèce, en Roumanie, en Russie et en Turquie, par un phanariote*. Athènes, 1892.

Robarts, Andrew. 'Imperial confrontation or regional cooperation?: Bulgarian migration and Ottoman–Russian relations in the Black Sea region, 1768–1830s', *Turkish Historical Review* 3.2 (2012): 149–167.

Rohdewald, Stefan, Stephan Conermann, Albrecht Fuess (eds.). *Transottomanica. Osteuropäisch–osmanisch–persische Mobilitätsdynamiken. Perspektiven und Forschungsstand*. Göttingen, 2019.

Roman, Nicoleta. 'Starting a married life: Women and goods in the mid-nineteenth-century Romanian towns of Pitești and Câmpulung', in: Annette Caroline Cremer (ed.). *Gender, Law and Material Culture. Immobile Property and Mobile Goods in Early Modern Europe*, London, 2020, 239–263.

Roman, Nicoleta. 'Foreign Governesses in Wallachia in the First Half of the Nineteenth Century', *Aspasia* 14 (2020): 37–56.

Roman, Nicoleta. 'Dowry Constracts, Women's Objects and the Circulation of Goods in Mid-Nineteenth Century Romanina Families. The Case of Oltenia', *Revista Istorică* XXIX.1–2 (2018): 105–139.

Roman, Nicoleta. 'Women in Merchant Families, Women in Trade in Mid-19th Century Romanian Countries' in: Constanţa Vintilă-Ghiţulescu (ed.). *Women, Consumption, and the Circulation of Ideas in South-Eastern Europe, 17th–19th Centuries.* Leiden, 2017, 169–199.

Rothman, E. Natalie. *The Dragoman Renaissance. Diplomatic Interpreters and the Routes of Orientalism.* Ithaca, NY, 2021.

Rothman, E. Natalie. *Brokering Empire: Trans-Imperial Subjects between Venice and Istanbul.* Ithaca, NY. 2012.

Rothman, Natalie E. 'Becoming Venetian: Conversion and Transformation in the Seventeenth-Century Mediterranean', *Mediterranean Historical Review* 21 (2006): 39–75.

Roudometof, Victor. 'From *Rum Millet* to Greek Nation: Enlightenment, Secularization, and National Identity in Ottoman Balkan Society, 1453–1821', *Journal of Modern Greek Studies* 16 (1998): 11–48.

Sadat, Deena. 'Rumeli Ayanlari: The Eighteenth Century', *Journal of Modern History* 44.3 (1972): 346–363.

Sahlins, Peter. *Unnaturally French: Foreign Citizens in the Old Regime and After.* Ithaca, NY, 2004.

Sahlins, Peter. 'Citizenship and the Droit d'Aubaine in France: A Response to Simona Cerutti', *Annales: Histoire, Sciences Sociales* 63.2 (2008): 385–398.

Sajdi, Dana. *The Barber of Damascus: Nouveau Literacy in the Eighteenth-Century Ottoman Levant.* Stanford, CA, 2013.

Sajdi, Dana. 'A Room of His Own: The "History" of the Barber of Damascus (fl. 1762)', *The MIT Electronic Journal of Middle East Studies, Crossing Boundaries: New Perspectives on the Middle East* 3 (2003): 19–35.

Salzmann, Ariel. *Citizens in Search of the State: The Limits of Political Participation in the Late Ottoman Empire*, in: Michael Hanagan and Charles Tilly (eds.). *Extending Citizenship, Reconfiguring States.* New York, 1999, 37–66.

Scharr, Kurt. 'Czernowitz-Cernăuţi-Çernovcÿ (Tscherniwzi). Genese einer städtischen Kulturlandschaft in einem wechselnden politischen Ambiente', in: Sergej W. Piwowarow (ed.), *Die Bukowina. Historische und ethnokulturelle Studien* (Tscherniwzi: 2007), 16–45.

Schmitt, Oliver Jens. *Les Levantins. Cadres de vie et identities d'un groupe ethno-confessionnel de l'Empire Ottoman au "long" 19e siècle.* Istanbul, 2007.

Schmitt, Oliver Jens. 'Addressing Community in Late Medieval Dalmatia', in: Eirik Hovden, Christina Lutter, Walter Pohl (eds.). *Meanings of Community across Medieval Eurasia. Comparative Approaches*. Leiden, 2016, 125–148.

Schönle, Andreas, Andrei Zorin, and Alexei Evstratov (eds.). *The Europeanized Elite in Russia, 1762–1825. Public Role and Subjective Self.* DeKallb, 2016.

Seng, Yvonne J. 'The Şer'iye Sicilleri of the Istanbul Müftülüğü as a Source for the Study of Everyday Life', *Turkish Studies Association Bulletin* 15.2 (1991): 305–325.

Shafir, Nir. 'Phanariot Tongues: The Mavrocordatos Family and the Power of the Turkish Language in the Eighteenth-Century Ottoman Empire'. *Oriente Moderno*, 101 (2021): 181–220.

Smentek, Kristel. 'Looking East. Jean-Etienne Liotard, the Turkish Painter', *Ars Orientalis* 39 (2010): 84–113.

Smiley, Will. *From Slaves to Prisoners of War. The Ottoman Empire, Russia and International Law*. Oxford, 2018.

Smyrnelis, Marie-Carmen. *Une société hors de soi: Identités et relations sociales à Smyrne aux XVIIIe et XIXe siècles*. Paris, 2006.

Sowerby, Tracey A. and Jan Hennings, (eds.), *Practices of Diplomacy in the Early Modern World c. 1410–1800*. London and New York, 2017.

Stamatopoulou-Vasilakou, Chrysothemis. 'Greek Theater in Southeastern Europe and the Eastern Mediterranean from 1810 to 1961', *Journal of Modern Greek Studies* 25 (2007): 267–284.

Stamatopulos, Dimitris. *The Eastern Question or Balkan Nationalism(s). Balkan History Reconsidered*. Vienna, 2018.

Stobart, Jon, Rothery Mark (eds.). *Consumption and the Country House*. Oxford, 2016.

Stoicescu, Nicolae. *Dicţionar al marilor dregători din Ţara Românească şi Moldova*. Bucharest, 1971.

Stoianovich, Traian. 'The Conquering Balkan Orthodox Merchant', *Journal of Economic History* 20 (1960): 234–313.

Stollberg-Rilinger, Barbara. 'Maria Theresa and the Love of Her Subjects', *Austrian History Yearbook* 51 (2020): 7–9.

Stollberg-Rilinger, Barbara. *Maria Theresia. Die Kaiserin in ihrer Zeit. Eine Biographie*. Munich, 2017.

Stollberg-Rilinger, Barbara. *Zur moralischen Ökonomie des Schenkens bei Hof* (*17.–18. Jahrhundert*), in: Werner Paravicini (ed). *Luxus und Integration: Materielle Hofkultur Westeuropas vom 12. bis zum 18. Jahrhundert*. Munich, 2010, 187–202.

Stollberg-Rilinger Barbara, *Les vieux habits de l'empereur. Une histoire culturelle des institutions du Saint-Empire à l'époque moderne*. Trans by Christophe Duhamelle. Paris, 2008.

Sturdza, Mihai Dimitrie. *Familiile boiereşti din Moldova şi Ţara Românească. Enciclopedie istorică, genealogică şi biografică*, 2 vols. Bucharest, 2004.

Sturdza, Mihai Dimitrie. *Grandes Familles de Grèce, d'Albanie et de Constantinople. Dictionnaire Historique*. Paris, 1983.

Subrahmanyam, Sanjay. *Three Ways to Be Alien: Travails and Encounters in the Early Modern World*. Waltham, MA, 2011.

Subrahmanyam, Sanjay. *Courtly Encounters: Translating Courtliness and Violence în Early Modern Eurasia*. Cambridge, 2012.

Szabo, Franz A. *Kaunitz and Enlightened Absolutism 1753–1780*. Cambridge, 1994.

Székely, Maria Magdalena. 'Structuri de familie în societatea medievală moldovenească', *Arhiva Genealogică*, IV (IX).1–2 (1997): 59–117.

Taki, Victor. *Limits of Protection: Russia and the Orthodox Coreligionists in the Ottoman Empire*. Pittsburgh, 2015.

Tappe, E.D. 'Bentham in Wallachia and Moldavia', *Slavonic and East European Review* 29.27 (1950): 66–76.

Tezcan, Baki. *The Second Ottoman Empire. Political and Social Transformation in the Early Modern World*. Cambridge, 2010.

Torpey, John. *The Invention of the Passport. Surveillance, Citizenship and the State*. Cambridge, 2000.

Tietze, Andreas. 'The Balkans and Ottoman Sources – Ottoman Sources and the Balkans', in: Henrik Birnbaum, Speros Vryonis jr. (eds.). *Aspects of the Balkans. Continuity and Change*. (The Hague–Paris: 1972), 285–297.

Todorova, Maria. *Imagining the Balkans*. Oxford – New York, 2009.

Todorova, Maria. *Balkan Family Structure and the European Pattern. Demographic Developments in Ottoman Bulgaria*. Budapest – New York, 2006.

Trivellato, Francesca. 'Microstoria/Microhistoire/Microhistory', *French Politics, Culture&Society*, 33, 1 (2015): 122–134.

Trivellato, Francesca. 'Is There a Future for Italian Microhistory in the Age of Global History?' *California Italian Studies*, II, 1 (2011), https://escholarship.org/uc/item/0z94n9hq [accessed 11.08.2021].

Trivellato, Francesca. *The Familiarity of Strangers: the Sephardic Diaspora, Livorno, and Cross-Culture Trade in the Early Modern Period*. New Haven, CT, 2009.

Tuchelt, Klaus (ed.). *Türkische Gewänder und osmanische Gesellschaft im achtzehnten Jahrhundert: Facsimile-Ausgabe des Codex "Les portraits des differens habillemens qui sont en usage à Constantinople et dans tout la Turquie" aus dem Besitz des Deutschen Archäologischen Institutes in Istanbul*. Graz, 1966.

Ţighiliu, Iolanda. 'Domeniul lui Constantin Brâncoveanu'. Paul Cernovodeanu, Florin Constantiniu (eds.). *Constantin Brâncoveanu*. Bucharest, 1989, 123–138.

Ungureanu, Mihai-Răzvan. *Convertire şi integrare religioasă în Moldova la începutul epocii moderne*. Iaşi, 2004.

Ungureanu, Mihai-Răzvan. 'Genealogia ca expresie a definitiei sociale a boierimii moldoveneşti în epoca regulamentară', *Arhiva Genealogică*, III (VIII). 3–4 (1996): 107–136.

Ungureanu, Mihai-Răzvan and Petronel Zahariuc. 'Documente privitoare la începuturile coloniei protestante din Moldova', in: Ovidiu Cristea, Petronel Zahariuc and Gheorghe Lazăr (eds.). *Aut viam inveniam aut faciam. In honorem Ştefan Andreescu.* Iaşi, 2012, 451–466.

Vasiliu, Mihai. *Istoria teatrului românesc*. Bucharest, 1971.

Văcaru, Silviu. *Diecii Ţării Moldovei în prima jumătate a secolului al XVII-lea*. Iaşi, 2006.

Vârtosu, Emil. *Mărturii noi din viaţa lui Tudor Vladimirescu*. Bucharest, 1941.

Velichi, Constantin N. *La contribution de l'émigration bulgare de la Valachie à la renaissance politique et culturelle du people bulgare (1762–1850)*. Bucharest, 1970.

Veinstein, Gilles. 'Les tatars de Crimée et la seconde election de Stanislas Leszczynski', *Cahiers du monde russe et sovietique*, 11.1 (1970): 24–92.

Veinstein, Gilles. 'On the Çiftlik Debate', in: Çağlar Keyder, Faruk Tabak (eds.). *Landholding and Commercial Agriculture in the Middle East*. Albany, NY, 1991, 35–53.

Vickery, Amanda. *Behind Closed Doors: At Home in Georgian England*. Yale, 2010.

Vickery, Amanda. *The Gentlemen's Daughter: Women's Lives in Georgian England*. Yale, 1998.

Vintilă-Ghiţulescu, Constanţa. 'Legal Process and the Meanings of Justice (dreptate) in Eighteenth Century Romania', *Crime, Histoire & Sociétés/ Crime, History & Societies*, 23.2 (2019): 5–27.

Vintilă-Ghiţulescu, Constanţa. 'Marié à un étranger, marié à l'étranger. Mobilité et statut social dans l'Europe du Sud-Est (1780–1830)', *Bulletin de correspondance hellénique moderne et contemporaine*, 1 (2019), https://journals.openedition.org/bchmc/296.

Vintilă-Ghiţulescu, Constanţa. 'Shawls and Sable Furs: How to be a Boyar under the Phanariot Regime (1710–1821)', *European Historical Yearbook*, 20 (2019): 137–158.

Vintilă-Ghiţulescu, Constanţa, '"Curls and Forelocks": Romanian Women's Emancipation in Consumption and Fashion, 1780–1850', in Constanţa Vintilă-Ghiţulescu (ed.). *Women, Consumption, and the Circulation of Ideas in South-Eastern Europe, 17th–19th Centuries*. (Leiden: 2017), 124–150.

Vintilă-Ghiţulescu, Constanţa. '"Condica de toate pricinile şi trebuinţele casii mele" de pitarul Dumitrache Piersiceanu de la Fundata (1804–1839)', in: Dan Dumitru Iacob (ed.). *Avere, prestigiu şi cultură materială în surse patrimoniale. Inventare de averi din secolele XVI–XIX*, Iaşi, 2015, 523–553.

Vintilă-Ghiţulescu, Constanţa. *Patimă şi desfătare. Despre lucrurile mărunte ale vieţii cotidiene în societatea românească, 1750–1860*. Bucharest, 2015.

Vintilă-Ghiţulescu, Constanţa. *Evgheniţi, ciocoi, mojici. Despre obrazele primei modernităţi româneşti (1750–1860)*. Bucharest, 2013.

Vintilă-Ghiţulescu, Constanţa. 'Usage des corps/ usage des mots au tribunal. Conflits et réconciliations dans la société roumaine (1750–1830)', in: Claude Gauvard, Alessandro Stella (eds.), *Couples en justice, IVe–XIXe siècle*. Paris, 2013, 197–213.

Vintilă-Ghiţulescu, Constanţa. *În şalvari şi cu işlic. Biserică, sexualitate, căsătorie şi divorţ în Ţara Românească a secolului al XVIII-lea*. Bucharest, 2011.

Vintilă-Ghiţulescu, Constanţa. 'Autour du divorce: disputes et réconciliations au tribunal (Valachie, 1750–1830)', *Annales de Démographie Historique* 2 (2009): 77–99.

Vivo, Filippo de.'Microhistoris of Long-Distance Information: Space, Movement and Agency in the Early Modern News', *Past and Present*, 242 (2019): 179–214.

Vivo, Filippo de. 'Public Sphere or Communication Triangle? Information and Politics in Early Modern Europe', in: Massimo Raspocher (ed.). *Beyond the Public Sphere. Opinions, Publics, Spaces in Early Modern Europe*. Bologna and Berlin, 2012, 115–136.

Vogel, Christine. 'Diplomatic Writing as Aristocratic Self-Fashioning: French Ambassadors in Constantinople', in: Tracey A. Sowerby, Joanna Craigwood (eds.). *Cultures of Diplomacy and Literary Writing in the Early Modern Word*. Oxford, 2019, 190–203.

Vogel, Christine. 'The Caftan and the Sword. Dress and Diplomacy in Ottoman–French Relations Around 1700', in: Claudia Ulbrich and Richard Wittmann (eds.). *Fashioning the Self in Transcultural Settings: The Uses and Significance of Dress in Self-Narratives*, Würzburg, 2015, 25–45.

Wasiucionek, Michał. *The Ottomans and Eastern Europe. Borders and Political Patronage in the Early Modern World*. London–New York, 2019.

Wasiucionek, Michał. 'Greek as Ottoman? Language, Identity and Mediation of Ottoman Culture in the Early Modern Period', *Cromohs: Cyber Review of Modern Historiography*, 21 (2017–2018): 70–89.

Wasiucionek, Michał. 'Conceptualizing Moldavian Ottomanness: Elite Culture and Ottomanization of the Seventeenth-Century Moldavian Boyars', *Medieval and Early Modern Studies for Central and Eastern Europe* 8 (2016): 39–78.

Wasiucionek, Michał. 'Ethnic Solidarity in the Wider Ottoman Empire Revisited: Cins and Local Political Elites in 17th-Century Moldavia and Wallachia', in: Marinos Sariyannis (ed.), *New Trends in Ottoman Studies*. Rethymno, 2014, 232–245.

Weber, Max. 'Bureaucracy', in: Malcolm Watters (ed.). *Modernity. Critical Concepts in Sociology*, vol. III, *Modern System*. London, New York, 1999.

Weber, Max. *Economy and Society: An Outline of Interpretive Sociology*. Trans. Guenther Roth and Claus Wittich. Berkeley, 1978.

Wolff, Larry. *Inventing Eastern Europe: The Map of Civilization on the Mind of the Enlightenment* (Stanford: 1994).

Xourias, Yannis. 'L'européanisation fictive des Phanariotes', *Cahiers balkaniques*, Hors-série (2015) [accessed 19 March 2020].

Yaycioğlu, Ali. 'Guarding Traditions and Laws–Disciplining Bodies and Souls: Tradition, Science, and Religion in the Age of Ottoman Reform', *Modern Asian Studies* 52.5 (2018): 1542–1603.

Yaycioğlu, Ali. 'Janissaries, Engineers and Preachers. How Did Military Engineering and Islamic Activism Change the Ottoman Order?' *Revue d'Histoire du XIX*[e] *Siècle* 53.2 (2016): 19–37.

Yaycioğlu, Ali. *Partners of the Empire: The Crisis of the Ottoman Order in the Age of Revolutions*. Stanford, CA, 2016.

Yaycioğlu, Ali. 'Provincial Power-Holders and the Empire in the Late Ottoman. Conflict or Partnership?', in: Christine Woodhead (ed.). *The Ottoman World*. London and New York. 2012, 436–452.

Yeşil, Fatih. 'How to Be(come) an Ottoman at the End of the Eighteenth Century', *Journal of Ottoman Studies* 44 (2014), 123–139.

Yıldıx, Aysel. Kokdaş, İrfan, 'Peasantry in a Well-protected Domain: Wallachian Peasantry and Muslim Çiftlik/Kışlaks under the Ottoman Rule', *Journal of Balkan and Near Eastern Studies* 22.1 (2018): 175–190.

Zachariadou, Elizabeth A. 'Co-Existence and Religion', *Archivum Ottomanicum* 15 (1997): 119–129.

Zahariuc, Petronel. 'Despre o casă de pe Uliţa Mare şi despre o poveste cu drepturile femeii din Moldova (prima jumătate a secolului al XVIII-lea)', *Ioan Neculce. Buletinul Muzeului Municipal "Regina Maria"* I (2019): 29–50.

Zahariuc, Petronel. '"Au milieu de l'étranger". Deux documents de donation pour le monastère de Lipnic de Bulgarie', in: Snezhana Rakova, Gheorghe Lazăr (eds), *Au Nord et au Sud du Danube. Dynamiques politiques, sociales et religieuses dans le passé*. Brăila, 2018, 153–166.

Zahariuc, Petronel, 'Bacşişuri, mătăsuri şi argintării. Călătoria boierilor moldoveni la Constantinopol în 1822', in: Dan Dumitru Iacob (ed.). *Inventare de avere în secolele XVII–XIX*. Iaşi, 2015, 311–369.

Zahariuc, Petronel. 'Sugestii genealogice pentru o cercetare a începuturilor burgheziei române', *Revista de Istorie Socială* IV–VII (2005): 26–36.

Zanou, Konstantina. *Transnational Patriotism in the Mediterranean, 1800–1850: Stammering the Nation*. Oxford, 2018.

Zarinebaf, Fariba. *Mediterranean Encounters. Trade and Pluralism in Early Modern Galata*. California, 2018.

Zarinebaf, Fariba. *Crime and Punishment in Istanbul 1700–1800*. Berkeley, 2010.

Zarinebaf, Fariba. 'From mahalle (neighborhood) to the market and the courts: women, credit, and property in eighteenth-century Istanbul', in: Jutta Gisela Sperling and Shona Kelly Wray (eds.). *Gender, property, and law in Jewish, Christian, and Muslim communities in the wider Mediterranean, 1300–1800*. London and New York, 2009, 224–237.

Zaugg, Roberto. 'Entre diplomatie et pratique judiciaries: la condition des étrangers sous l'Ancien Régime napolitain', *Revue d'histoire maritime*, 17 (2014): 322–323.

Zaugg, Roberto. *Stranieri di antico regime. Mercanti, giudici e consoli nella Napoli del Settecento*, Rome, 2011.

Zeletin, Ştefan. *Burghezia română. Originea şi rolul ei istoric* [1925]. Bucharest, 1997.

Index